Foreign Language Teaching and the Environment: Theory, Curricula, Institutional Structures

Foreign Language Teaching and the Environment

Theory, Curricula, Institutional Structures

Edited by
Charlotte Ann Melin

THE MODERN LANGUAGE ASSOCIATION OF AMERICA
New York   2019

© 2019 by The Modern Language Association of America
All rights reserved
Printed in the United States of America

MLA and the MODERN LANGUAGE ASSOCIATION are trademarks owned by the Modern Language Association of America. For information about obtaining permission to reprint material from MLA book publications, send your request by mail (see address below) or e-mail (permissions@mla.org).

Library of Congress Cataloging-in-Publication Data

Names: Melin, Charlotte, editor.
Title: Foreign language teaching and the environment : theory, curricula, institutional structures / edited by Charlotte Ann Melin.
Description: New York, NY : The Modern Language Association of America, 2019.
  | Series: Teaching languages, literatures, and cultures, ISSN 1092-3225 ; 6
  | Includes bibliographical references and index.
Identifiers: LCCN 2019011179 (print) | LCCN 2019011999 (ebook) | ISBN 9781603293952 (EPUB) | ISBN 9781603293969 (Kindle) | ISBN 9781603293945 (pbk.) | ISBN 9781603294676 (cloth)
Subjects: LCSH: Ecolinguistics—Study and teaching. | Second language acquisition—Study and teaching. | Human ecology—Study and teaching.
Classification: LCC P39.5 (ebook) | LCC P39.5 .F67 2019 (print) | DDC 418.0071—dc23
LC record available at https://lccn.loc.gov/2019011179

Teaching Languages, Literatures, and Cultures 6
ISSN 1092-3225

Cover illustration of the paperback and electronic editions:
Linda Lomahaftewa, *Untitled (Geometric and Wave Designs, 1965–1975)*, H-461, gift of the artist, 2016. Courtesy of the IAIA Museum of Contemporary Native Arts, Santa Fe, NM.

Published by The Modern Language Association of America
85 Broad Street, suite 500, New York, New York 10004-2434
www.mla.org

CONTENTS

Introduction: Environmental Thinking through Language

Charlotte Ann Melin

Foreign language programs today find themselves at the center of discussions about change in higher education at the very moment when the emergence of the environmental humanities and sustainability studies is creating new opportunities for curricular innovation. There are many reasons to welcome this development as crucial to redefining how we teach language, literature, and culture in the twenty-first century, as this collection, *Foreign Language Teaching and the Environment: Theory, Curricula, Institutional Structures*, is designed to do. Language is fundamental to our ability to interpret the world, and our attitudes about nature express the deep cultural interconnectedness of environment, economy, and society. Such knowledge depends on translingual and transcultural competence, as does ultimately our ability to address global challenges like climate change (see MLA Ad Hoc Committee; Eppelsheimer et al.). "Earth needs the humanities," Stephanie LeMenager and Stephanie Foote observe in laying out the case for the sustainable humanities (575), and that need resonates profoundly with teaching and learning across our disciplines.

Environmental concerns surround us, whether in a beginning language course, where a lesson focuses on shopping for local food at an open-air market, or in an advanced literature seminar, in which canonical texts raise complex questions about the cultural values expressed when we try to define nature. In the real world, spontaneous experiences as basic as everyday recycling constantly direct our attention toward environmental relations with the world. For language learners, particularly at the early stages, encounters with such external matters through rich curricular content, well-designed tasks, and multifaceted learning experiences contribute to the progressive development of complex language skills. By cultivating connections with other disciplines where this content is found, foreign language programs can construct their identities anew. Indeed, the more interdisciplinary our partnerships become, the more they build bridges between the humanities and the sciences. Such reciprocal collaborations strengthen the position of foreign languages within higher education while the presence of environmental concerns in all areas of knowledge invites discovery of the dynamic interdependence of language, culture, and our surrounding world.

With interdisciplinarity, however, many challenges arise, ranging from the limitations in expertise encountered by nonspecialists moving into unfamiliar subject areas to the logistical complexity of arranging for experiential learning opportunities and collaborative teaching. The purpose of this volume is to provide models for teaching environmental and sustainability topics, with the aim of stimulating more such work through small initiatives that can ultimately have system-wide implications. Beyond providing examples of interest to language-teaching specialists and scholars in literature, culture, and language programs, the collection explores factors key to successful implementation of cross-curricular initiatives in language programs. It examines theoretical issues pertinent to combining sustainability studies with foreign languages, curricular models transferrable to a range of instructional contexts, and program structures supportive of teaching cultures and languages across the curriculum.

Environment and Sustainability: A Definition of Terms

Whereas environmental humanities and sustainability studies initiatives are becoming more common in the higher education landscape, language programs (whether the nomenclature describing them is *foreign, modern, second,* or *heritage languages*) have a long tradition within the academy shaped by rarely questioned assumptions about what we teach. This volume hopes to productively restructure this work by encouraging dialogue with new knowledge areas. The terms *environment* and *sustainability* are themselves capacious, yet represent only the starting points for diverse intellectual projects and teaching praxis that are equally, though quite differently, productive. *Foreign Language Teaching and the Environment* takes both perspectives into account by presenting projects that draw on their complementary strengths.

With the term *environment*, emphasis is placed on the cultural dimensions of how we live in the world and how the project of the environmental humanities is invoked. Frequently discussed in terms of scholarly practices like literary ecocriticism, the environmental humanities takes an interdisciplinary approach to analyzing issues like ecological crisis and notions of the Anthropocene in terms of their underlying aesthetic, historical, and philosophical implications. Here we encounter the critical and interpretive work of Lawrence Buell, Ursula K. Heise ("Globality" and "Hitchhiker's Guide"), Timothy Morton (*Ecology*), Dipesh Chakrabarty, Rob Nixon, and others. These impulses motivated the Modern Language Association (MLA) volume edited by Frederick O. Waage, *Teaching Environmental Literature: Materials, Methods, Resources*, and the subsequent collection edited by Laird Christensen, Mark C. Long, and Waage, *Teaching North American Environmental Literature* (Christensen et al.). Professional organizations like the Association for the Study of Literature and the Environment (ASLE), founded in 1992, and a growing number of international organizations support the work of environmental humanities scholars.

Sustainability, meanwhile, points us in the direction of scientific reflection about our relation with the world we inhabit. As the Brundtland report states in its salient definition of the term, *sustainability* means the wise use of resources for "development that meets the needs of the present without compromising the ability of future generations to meet their own needs" (Brundtland et al. 43). On higher education campuses in the United States, sustainability studies have grown through the teaching and research interests of faculty members in the sciences and humanities alike. Frequently these initiatives connect with the priorities of administrators interested in finding efficient ways to manage campus infrastructures. The Association for the Advancement of Sustainability in Higher Education (AASHE), founded in 2005, supports such professional work, including in ways that help leverage the mission of scholarly organizations like ASLE.

With attention to both these issues on campuses comes a realization that, as James J. Farrell explains, "College is a place where students [can] think twice about American culture and ecosystems" (xii). To their own surprise, faculty members (including some who have felt marginalized by institutional prioritization of so-called grand challenges) have found renewal through environmental humanities and sustainability studies initiatives. Mobilized by a sense of purpose, they have helped create positive synergy between the humanities and sciences. In the process, faculty networking has produced ways to bridge the "two cultures" divide famously described by C. P. Snow. That we now speak about program sustainability or ecology signals the development of affinities among many disciplines (LeMenager and Foote; Walther). Rather than limiting themselves to a single agenda, colleagues participating in these efforts have found that a big-tent model welcoming all interested parties leads to rapid evolution.

Toward Models for Teaching
Language and Environment

Envisioned as a collection that explores the intersection of ecocriticism theory, second language acquisition (SLA) research, and disciplinary fields, *Foreign Language Teaching and the Environment* strives to represent ways in which progressive language departments are being reconceived as programs of relevant and viable cross-disciplinary studies. It seeks to confront monolingualism, which Heise called "one of ecocriticism's most serious intellectual limitations" ("Hitchhiker's Guide" 513), a point emphatically underscored in her essay "Globality, Difference, and the International Turn in Ecocriticism." One of the benefits of tackling this topic through a cross-language approach is that it allows focus on core principles of curriculum design—use of authentic content (materials created for native speakers), structure of meaningful tasks, and organization by means of backward planning that proceeds from strategic objectives. The field of environmental humanities has a well-established commitment to pedagogy visible in publications like David W. Orr's *Earth in Mind*; Christopher Uhl's *Developing Ecological Consciousness*; the essay collection *Teaching Environmental Literacy: Across Campus and across the Curriculum*, describing system-wide initiatives at Indiana University (Reynolds et al.); Sidney I. Dobrin and Christian Weisser's *Natural Discourse: Toward Ecocomposition*; and Sasha Matthewman's *Teaching Secondary English As If the Planet Matters*. These models can be repurposed to serve as inspiration for teachers of courses in the foreign languages. The present volume provides an introduction to teaching sustainability and environmental humanities topics in language, literature, and culture courses, with an emphasis on *post-communicative* approaches—those that advocate attention to multifaceted work on literacy instead of concentrating on speaking skills.

In this way, *Foreign Language Teaching and the Environment* seeks to encourage foreign language programs to reshape courses, pedagogies, and curricular tracks using current best practices. Modeling ways in which the integration of environmental dimensions can become an intentional vehicle for the teaching of cultural perspectives at every level, this book presents signature projects. It advocates a central role for foreign languages within the educational landscape through the teaching of linguistically and conceptually challenging material that offers learners significant content. Exploring the implications of collaborative interdisciplinary work, the essays suggest how pilot initiatives can stimulate curricular innovation. Many of these considerations resonate with the recommendations of the 2007 Modern Language Association (MLA) report "Foreign Languages and Higher Education: New Structures for a Changed World," which stressed the indelible connection between functional language ability and larger "critical language awareness, interpretation and translation, historical and political consciousness, social sensibility and aesthetic perception" (MLA Ad Hoc Committee 237–38). Rather than viewing environmental matters as a mere subfield, the essays make us aware that the scale and interconnection of challenges like climate change, food security, and community resilience necessarily mean that quotidian cultural practices, cultural heritage, and metacultural values are inextricably linked and ontologically equivalent. Such a view expands the boundaries of knowledge and challenges hierarchical divisions.

The Context of Post-Communicative Foreign Language Teaching

Foreign Language Teaching and the Environment follows in the footsteps of previous publications in the MLA Teaching Languages, Literatures, and Cultures series, notably *Learning Foreign and Second Languages*, edited by Heidi Byrnes, and *Remapping the Foreign Language Curriculum*, coauthored by Janet Swaffar and Katherine Arens. In diverse ways, the individual essays in this volume are indebted to them and the authors of the MLA report (especially Claire Kramsch), as well as to the work of other second language acquisition specialists who have refined our understanding of the nature and scope of language teaching and learning in recent decades (see also Paesani and Allen). Collectively these efforts have directed attention to the symbolic dimensions of language and subjective aspects of language learning (Kramsch), the importance of task design (Byrnes et al., "Taking"), the role played by multiple literacies and genre concepts (Kern; Swaffar and Arens), and the need for curricular articulation directed toward the development of advanced language abilities (Byrnes, "Constructing"; Byrnes et al., *Realizing*). Their contributions are frequently referenced by the authors in the present volume. This work reminds foreign language departments and programs of their unique intellectual identity and role in higher education. Reaffirming the value of intentional language teaching practice embodied in the American Council on the Teaching of Foreign Languages's *ACTFL Proficiency Guidelines* and the National Standards in Foreign Language Education Project's (NSFLEP) *Standards for Foreign Language Learning*, this book insistently questions the persistent division between language and content courses.

The value of bridging this two-tiered divide is well known, yet it is increasingly clear that the future vitality of foreign language programs depends on overcoming this separation. The intellectual disconnect between general liberal education learning outcomes and classes focused on skills is symptomatic of awkward alignment (see Mills and Norris). Thus, curricular innovation to promote environmental literacy as a desired competency can become a starting point for broader transformation and curricular coherence. The redesign of individual courses can catalyze change by sparking reflection on how we teach the five Cs of Communication, Culture, Connections, Comparisons, and Communities (see NSFLEP) in terms of environmental literacy objectives (Melin 188). The success of such efforts depends on local, institutional, and even chance factors: the interests of students, salient models, faculty energies, administrative support, community contacts, and spontaneous opportunities.

Whereas a number of the described projects began with the modest redesign of instructional modules or traditional courses, most generated further impact and change. In some essays, the focus is on environmental topics in the context of language learning for special purposes—in courses for international business, health care, social work, or STEM fields (see Byrnes, "German" 1). In others, the inclusion of cultural narratives about the environment gives voice to the experiences of heritage language learners. For indigenous communities, environmental awareness is inseparable from linguistic survival and raises important issues concerning cultural sustainability, as confirmed in ecolinguistics research and United Nations policy documents (Fill and Müllhäusler; Skutnabb-Kangas et al.). Several of the essays furthermore map connections between study abroad experiences and place-based environmental learning that have implications for reaching wider student audiences.

Common to the essays is the case they make for the use of authentic multimedia materials and real-world curricular enhancements accessible on the Internet. Visual images, blogs, and personal electronic devices offer a powerful means to awaken awareness of cultural perspectives and cultivate sensitivity toward environmental attitudes (see Barnes-Karol and Broner; Ter Horst and Pearce). Target language materials intended for native speaker audiences and readily available through educational, government, and public domain Web sites provide a rich source of authentic materials that can be repurposed for language teaching. As pioneering efforts make clear (Eppelsheimer; Braunbeck; Arnett and Levine), these materials push instructors to work with unfamiliar subject matter in new ways. As more sophisticated engagement with diverse text types, textual thinking, and vocabulary becomes necessary, our language teaching and learning contexts are reshaped. Dynamic content challenges us to devise a process for curriculum design and delivery that can be responsive to an ever-changing knowledge and materials base.

Impetus for curricular development of this kind comes in part from the theoretical and methodological discussions of content-based instruction (CBI) and content and language integrated learning (CLIL), which are points of reference in several of the essays. Both CBI and CLIL (the nomenclature of the Council of Europe) have proven productive in the teaching of English as a second language and in elementary, secondary, and immersion education settings (Stryker and Leaver; Brinton et al.). For educators incorporating environmental and sustainability content into courses, the notion of the "counterbalanced approach" proposed by Roy Lyster offers a means to conceptualize the relation between content and language. Mindful of the importance of portable and deep language skills emphasized in the *Common European Framework of Reference for Languages* (Council of Europe), Do Coyle, Philip Hood, and David Marsh similarly recommend an approach that integrates culture and content with language learning (Coyle et al.). The procedures CBI and CLIL offer for identifying authentic materials assets, mining vocabulary, designing tasks, and establishing outcomes assessments can be profitably applied for the development of courses about the environment and sustainability, or, indeed, productively transferred to other content as well.

Organization of the Essays

The curricular innovation *Foreign Language Teaching and the Environment* seeks to encourage hinges on our ability to translate theory into curricular practice. For this reason, the collection is divided into three sections: "Theory," "Curricula," and "Institutional Structures." Because the intended audience includes nonspecialists, teachers in a variety of educational settings, and diverse stakeholders in areas related to foreign language education, the volume strives to present transferrable models and information about a wide range of resources. The essay authors are experienced teacher-scholars active at all levels who represent a wide variety of institutions and instructional contexts (colleges and universities, study abroad, and experiential learning). Although each essay exemplifies work in a specific language, the curricular models are adaptable beyond those fields.

In "Theory," three essays map distinct approaches to conceptualizing the teaching of environmental humanities and sustainability studies topics in the foreign languages. Recognizing the close links between critical thinking, language acquisition, and "glocal" citizenship values, Patricia Anne Simpson and Marc James Mueller locate theoretical grounding for teaching environmentalism in a metacultural narrative about the greenness of German culture, which raises for consideration the perspectives of systems thinking and holistic ethics. Drawing on the work of the environmental educator David W. Orr, Annette Sampon-Nicolas describes how the teaching of literature can shift to an interdisciplinary approach that allows learners to combine the study of literary, nonfiction, and cinematic texts with investigation of the complex role nature plays in these works. To address the need for new educational paradigms at a time when student interests are prompting foreign language programs to move beyond traditional offerings in linguistics, culture, and literature courses, Maggie A. Broner proposes a design thinking model as a strategy for encouraging creativity and intensive language use on the part of learners.

The essays in "Curricula" represent a broad spectrum of languages and initiatives, clustered into groups that reflect three thematic strands: emphasis on literature teaching, focus on language learning (especially at the advanced level), and strategies for experiential or place-based learning. Francophone literature is central to the first essay, where Abbey Carrico takes theoretical impetus from the work of Gaston Bachelard for the redesign of a French studies course on literature and culture; Carrico discusses how such content can prompt students to consider how our global interaction with water has changed throughout history and to reflect on water's meaning for them in the present. In an essay provocatively titled "Can Literature Save the Planet? Lessons from Latin America," Odile Cisneros argues that Latin America, with its mix of European and indigenous roots and history of land conquest and exploitation, as well as its many recent environmental poet-activists, presents fertile ground for the development of a Spanish and Portuguese literature course focusing on ecocritical interpretation. Attending to the special value of poetry as an object of study, Defne Erdem Mete analyzes how the concept of the intercultural speaker can challenge us to reflect on the place of nature in our thinking, in this case the national memory of Turkey and Turkish cultural values.

The cluster of four essays that appear next offer insights into SLA perspectives on the teaching and learning of languages at the upper-division level, using specific curricular treatments. María J. de la Fuente describes how, with institutional support, a third-year Spanish conversation class was redesigned as an advanced oral communication course on environmental and social sustainability in Latin America. Nobuko Chikamatsu describes a multifaceted language course designed for advanced Japanese-language students in the United States that employs lectures by bilingual area studies specialists to investigate the themes of the earthquake, tsunami, and environmental catastrophe in Fukushima, Japan. Haidan Wang turns attention to how the inclusion of a thematic unit on sustainability and environmental protection in an advanced business-language course for professionals learning Chinese has been shaped using a "post-communicative" inductive learning framework as a model. Olesya Kisselev and William Comer describe the development of an advanced Russian course on the environment offered in the context of a flagship program.

Their contribution connects with the final two essays in this section, which are also devoted to less commonly taught languages (LCTLs) that tend to receive less attention on campuses in the United States. These accounts, however, are keenly attuned to the untapped potential roles experiential and place-based learning have in the curriculum. Describing a multifaceted educational experience that includes on campus and study abroad components cotaught by biological sciences and Russian-language faculty members, Thomas P. Hodge offers a model for extended learning. Finally, Margaret Ann Noodin's essay details how educational work at and beyond coastal educational institutions along the shores of Lake Superior and Lake Michigan has exposed native and non-native students to the science, philosophy, and stories of *Gichigaming* as they gain proficiency in Anishinaabemowin.

The closing section, "Institutional Structures," presents three models for building capacity for foreign language teaching related to the environmental humanities and sustainability studies. These perspectives demonstrate the power of collaborative work across languages and with diverse constituencies. Laura Barbas-Rhoden, Beate Brunow, and Britton W. Newman describe how a modern languages department at a small liberal arts institution (Wofford College, in South Carolina) integrated environmental topics into the curriculum. Through grassroots interest on the part of students and faculty members, this process linked modest first efforts to learning outcomes for global learning literacy that have become an institutional priority. Patricia W. Cummins explains how the development of an international relations seminar at Virginia Commonwealth University, related to environmental perspectives and global health issues, led to success in securing external grants that benefited the sciences, foreign languages, and partners in French West Africa. The concluding essay by Vialla Hartfield-Méndez, Karen Stolley, and Hong Li shows how the large-scale Piedmont Project at Emory University (a multidisciplinary faculty-development and curricular-innovation program begun in 2001), which promotes sustainability studies across the curriculum, has profoundly affected foreign language departments. The coda points to common themes in the volume as a whole. Recognizing the potential that sustainability and environmental humanities initiatives have for transforming foreign language programs, it recommends processes of curricular change that can be started with small pilot initiatives and nurtured over time to strengthen curricular coherence.

Climate change is the greatest challenge we face globally in the twenty-first century. For faculty members who ask themselves what the humanities have to "contribute to the creation of a more sustainable world," as Daniel J.

Philippon encourages us to do (163), the answer is clearly quite a lot—particularly in the foreign languages. This collection shows deep commitment on the part of educators to the value of the humanities, as well as to the environmental future of the planet. The discussions here about linguistic competencies and learning outcomes represent the best that language teaching has to offer today. Exploration of environmental topics leads to larger questions related to social justice, philosophical inquiry, and human imagination. The collection makes clear that language programs can set in motion the process of rethinking the relation between literary and social discourses and reflect on the creation of new ways of thinking that prepare us to meet the challenges of the twenty-first century. The themes that surface in *Foreign Language Teaching and the Environment*—discovery, innovation, collaboration, reflection, and interdisciplinarity, all in relation to communities—underscore the vital importance of ongoing curricular reform and continually innovative thinking.

Readers are encouraged to visit the Foreign Language Teaching and the Environment group on *Humanities Commons*, where contributors have deposited to the *Commons Open Repository Exchange* (*CORE*) additional pedagogical materials associated with the topics in this volume.

WORKS CITED

ACTFL Proficiency Guidelines 2012. American Council on the Teaching of Foreign Languages (ACTFL), 2012, www.actfl.org/sites/default/files/pdfs/public/ACTFL ProficiencyGuidelines2012_FINAL.pdf. Accessed 6 Jan. 2015.

Arnett, Carlee, and Glenn S. Levine. "From the Editors." *Die Unterrichtspraxis / Teaching German*, vol. 46, no. 2, 2013, pp. iii–iv.

Barnes-Karol, Gwendolyn, and Maggie A. Broner. "Using Images as Springboards to Teach Cultural Perspectives in Light of the Ideals of the MLA Report." *Foreign Language Annals*, vol. 43, no. 3, 2010, pp. 422–45.

Braunbeck, Helga G. "Competition, Connection, and Collaboration in Smaller German Programs." *Die Unterrichtspraxis / Teaching German*, vol. 44, no. 2, 2011, pp. 146–53.

Brinton, Donna, et al. *Content-Based Second Language Instruction.* U of Michigan P, 2003.

Brundtland, Gro Harlem, et al. *Our Common Future: World Commission on Environment and Development.* Oxford UP, 1987.

Buell, Lawrence. *The Environmental Imagination: Thoreau, Nature Writing, and the Formation of American Culture.* Harvard UP, 1995.

Byrnes, Heidi. "Constructing Curricula in Collegiate Foreign Language Departments." Byrnes, *Learning*, pp. 262–95.

———. "German for Specific Purposes." *The Encyclopedia of Applied Linguistics*, edited by Carol A. Chapelle, Wiley-Blackwell, 2013, pp. 1–8.

———, editor. *Learning Foreign and Second Languages: Perspectives in Research and Scholarship*. Modern Language Association of America, 1998.

Byrnes, Heidi, et al. *Realizing Advanced Foreign Language Writing Development in Collegiate Education: Curricular Design, Pedagogy, Assessment*. Special issue of *The Modern Language Journal*, vol. 94, no. s1, 2010.

Byrnes, Heidi, et al. "Taking Text to Task: Issues and Choices in Curriculum Construction." *ITL—International Journal of Applied Linguistics*, vol. 152, 2006, pp. 85–110.

Chakrabarty, Dipesh. "The Climate of History: Four Theses." *Critical Inquiry*, vol. 35, no. 2, 2009, pp. 197–222.

Christensen, Laird, et al., editors. *Teaching North American Environmental Literature*. Modern Language Association of America, 2008.

Council of Europe. *Common European Framework of Reference for Languages: Learning, Teaching, Assessment*. Cambridge UP, 2001.

Coyle, Do, et al. *CLIL: Content and Language Integrated Learning*. Cambridge UP, 2010.

Dobrin, Sidney I., and Christian Weisser. *Natural Discourse: Toward Ecocomposition*. State U of New York P, 2002.

Eppelsheimer, Natalie. "Food for Thought: 'Exolitsches und Hausmannskost' Zum Interkulturellen Lernen." *Die Unterrichtspraxis / Teaching German*, vol. 45, no. 1, 2012, pp. 5–19.

Eppelsheimer, Natalie, et al. "Claiming the Language Ecotone: Translinguality, Resilience, and the Environmental Humanities." *Resilience*, vol. 1, no. 3, Fall 2014. *JSTOR*, www.jstor.org/stable/10.5250/resilience.1.3.005. Accessed 25 Aug. 2016.

Farrell, James J. *The Nature of College*. Milkweed, 2010.

Fill, Alwin, and Peter Müllhäusler, editors. *The Ecolinguistics Reader: Language, Ecology and Environment*. Continuum, 2001.

Heise, Ursula K. "Globality, Difference, and the International Turn in Ecocriticism." *PMLA*, vol. 123, no. 3, 2013, pp. 636–43.

———. "The Hitchhiker's Guide to Ecocriticism." *PMLA*, vol. 121, no. 2, 2006, pp. 503–16.

Kern, Richard. *Literacy and Language Teaching*. Oxford UP, 2000.

Kramsch, Claire. *The Multilingual Subject*. Oxford UP, 2009.

LeMenager, Stephanie, and Stephanie Foote. "The Sustainable Humanities." *PMLA*, vol. 127, no. 3, 2012, pp. 572–78.

Lyster, Roy. *Learning and Teaching Languages through Content: A Counterbalanced Approach*. John Benjamins Publishing, 2007.

Matthewman, Sasha. *Teaching Secondary English As If the Planet Matters*. Routledge, 2011.

Melin, Charlotte. "Climate Change: A 'Green' Approach to Teaching Contemporary Germany." *Die Unterrichtspraxis / Teaching German*, vol. 46, no. 2, 2013, pp. 185–99.

Mills, Nicole, and John Norris, editors. *AAUSC 2014 Volume: Issues in Language Program Direction: Innovation and Accountability in Language Program Evaluation*. Cengage Learning, 2015.

MLA Ad Hoc Committee on Foreign Languages. "Foreign Languages and Higher Education: New Structures for a Changed World." *Profession*, 2007, pp. 234–45.

Morton, Timothy. *Ecology without Nature*. Harvard UP, 2009.

Nixon, Rob. *Slow Violence and the Environmentalism of the Poor*. Harvard UP, 2011.

NSFLEP (National Standards in Foreign Language Education Project). *Standards for Foreign Language Learning: Preparing for the Twenty-First Century*. Allen Press, 1996.

Orr, David W. *Earth in Mind: On Education, Environment, and the Human Project.* Island Press, 2004.

Paesani, Kate, and Heather Willis Allen. "Beyond the Language-Content Divide: Research on Advanced Foreign Language Instruction at the Postsecondary Level." *Foreign Language Annals*, vol. 45, no. s1, 2012, pp. s54–s75.

Philippon, Daniel J. "Sustainability and the Humanities: An Extensive Pleasure." *American Literary History*, vol. 24, no. 1, 2012, pp. 163–79.

Reynolds, Heather L., et al., editors. *Teaching Environmental Literacy: Across Campus and across the Curriculum.* Indiana UP, 2010.

Skutnabb-Kangas, Tove, et al. "Sharing a World of Difference: The Earth's Linguistic, Cultural and Biological Diversity." UNESCO Publishing, 2003.

Snow, C. P. *The Two Cultures.* Cambridge UP, 1998.

Stryker, Stephen B., and Betty Lou Leaver, editors. *Content-Based Instruction in Foreign Language Education: Models and Methods.* Georgetown UP, 1997.

Swaffar, Janet, and Katherine Arens. *Remapping the Foreign Language Curriculum.* Modern Language Association of America, 2005.

Ter Horst, Eleanor E., and Joshua M. Pearce. "Foreign Languages and Sustainability: Addressing the Connections, Communities, and Comparisons Standards in Higher Education." *Foreign Language Annals*, vol. 43, no. 3, Fall 2010, pp. 365–83.

Uhl, Christopher. *Developing Ecological Consciousness.* Rowman & Littlefield, 2004.

Waage, Frederick O., editor. *Teaching Environmental Literature: Materials, Methods, Resources.* Modern Language Association of America, 1985.

Walther, Ingeborg. "Ecological Perspectives on Language and Literacy: Implications for Foreign Language Instruction at the Collegiate Level." *ADFL Bulletin*, vol. 38, no. 1, 2007, pp. 6–14.

PART ONE | *Theory*

German Is the New Green? Language, Environmentalism, and Cultural Competence

Patricia Anne Simpson
and Marc James Mueller

schwarzwald, wurzelleichte	black forest, rootlightness
1 augenblickspoem im frühjahr	1 poem of a springmoment
nicht greifbar, sage ich	not to grasp, I say
die architektur aus wald & schwarz & sog ins	the architecture out of forest & black & vortex into
innere – als sei die dunkle farbgewähr die	the inside – as the dark colorpromise the
insgeheime weite & flügelschlag der sprache	expanse underneath & wingbeat of language
: 1 alphabet der hölzer . . .	: 1 alphabet of wood . . .

—José F. A. Oliver, *Fahrtenschreiber* ("Worldometer"; trans. Marc James Mueller)[1]

At a time when many foreign language departments are under pressure to redefine their educational mission, attention to the growing importance of ecological knowledge in higher education in the United States can be a means to attract new learners and retain students throughout a degree program. Such a change has far-ranging implications, because it asserts a vital intersection between the humanities and STEM disciplines. German environmentalism figures large in political, economic, and technological arenas. In German studies, the teaching of language and literature can be productively expanded by incorporating attention to the cultural roots and historical dimensions of environmentalism, as well as to its present.

Acknowledging the interrelatedness of language acquisition, critical thinking, and "glocal" citizenship, this essay argues that an innovative approach to teaching environmentalism encompasses not only the cognitive tools of systems thinking and holistic ethics but also linguistic and interpretive skills grounded in ecopoetics.

In the translated excerpt from the contemporary Spanish-German poet José F. A. Oliver quoted above, language bridges the common divide between culture and nature; between perceptions of the human and non-human world; between an interior cognitive landscape and the *Umwelt* ("environment"; literally, "the world around us"). Oliver's use of multiple languages and dialects transcends national and linguistic borders, enabling the expression of a transcultural identity and worldview. Similarly, poetic language can productively blur the boundaries between cultural and natural spheres, thereby acknowledging language and literature's "generative potential and transformative function within the larger discursive system of cultural knowledge and semiotic practices" (Zapf 19). In the classroom, literary texts inhabit the intersection of holistic ethics, environmental literacy, cultural literacy, language proficiency, and transcultural sensitivity. Thus the philosophical dimensions to the curricular transformation we envision enable the integration of the history, cultures, and activism of German environmentalism into all levels of the undergraduate language and culture curriculum.

In higher education settings, outcomes involving environmental thinking and global perspectives depend on a pedagogy that can convey a profound and encompassing identity between citizenship and stewardship. Yet, whereas environmental education warrants a transnational, transhistorical, and even planetary perspective, the category of the *national* remains relevant not only in the contemporary academy but also in ecological politics. In the foreign language classroom, however, we face the challenges of advocating global thinking while teaching a nonlocal national language. The Federal Republic of Germany and German-speaking Europe's spatial identity is socially constructed by a specific cultural history that unfolds within an equally specific relation to the natural world that proposes a responsibility of human stewardship that transcends the Faustian notion of ceaseless striving at the expense of nature and voices an ethics of vigilant respect—at least as projected to the outside world. Canonical texts, such as Goethe's *Faust*, leave legacies. Environmental patriotism derived from being green has become fundamental to national identity (Uekötter 2).[2] In the foreign language classroom in the United States, the uniqueness of Germany's role in global environmental history can ground a holistic curriculum. When we underscore the relevance of environmental knowledge in the foreign language classroom, we move away from an anthropocentric worldview toward biocentrism, understood as an ethical commitment to the interconnectedness of human and nonhuman life in the universe. This reconfiguring of the foreign language curriculum insists on environmental literacy as a significant learning outcome alongside proficiency in the target language; it adds environmental literacy to more conventionally conceived cultural competence.

Political activism and cultural history have shaped environmentalism in Germany; teaching that model can inspire learners who engage with these cultural investments to comprehend connections between the foreign language classroom and citizenship. To corroborate this claim, we first highlight vital connections between the sociopolitical context of contemporary Germany and its deep historical and cultural roots. These connections clarify the unique circumstances in twentieth- and twenty-first-century German environmentalism. Germany, we claim, invented what we think of as constituting nature, which both underlies and transcends a Cartesian, rational, capitalist repository of knowledge. In taking a critical approach, we conclude that the resulting ecological knowledge is predicated not only on a motivated relation between a landscape or natural environment and a self, or even a proprietary relation between a culturally constructed nature and nation, but also on fraught and fractured history. Through an ecopoetic approach to the acquisition of cultural knowledge, a curriculum focused on environmental literacy can bridge conceptual gaps between the human and nonhuman world. Ecopoetics conventionally derives from the study of nature poetry, a focus on the environment in literary texts, and attention to ecologies; it also accommodates an extraliterary "sense of place" that incorporates cultural memory (Goodbody, "Sense" 55). Although much scholarship on ecocriticism has argued persuasively for the privileged place of literature (Goodbody and Rigby 4)—and we do not disagree with this approach—what we propose is a greater integration of ecological knowledge using multiple points of entry into a discourse about environmental epistemologies. Those points of entry involve German-speaking Europe's history, politics, and contemporary commitment to personal and state-sponsored practices that are predicated on environmental protection. The resulting pedagogical discourse mediates between theory and practice in our curricular design and delivery, with the goal of greening the curriculum.

From History to Environmental Literacy

Rather than isolating environmental courses in the curriculum, we argue for a more integrated, systems-thinking process that proceeds from history to environmental literacy. Germany and a German-language legacy are positioned, we claim, to contribute significantly to the development of environmental engagement and activism due to three important factors. First, Germany has a cultural history of responding to episodes of catastrophic destruction of nature. Second, the environment led to critical thinking in the context of East-West issues of political activism and environmental degradation. These historical case studies can illuminate the interrelations among individual responsibility, environmental ethics, and collective action. Finally, Germany today demonstrates a historically derived awareness that environmental issues are always global, which contributes to the current enthusiasm for everything "green." Working within this history, we overcome nationalizing categories of knowledge. Such cultural ecology aims for a greater unity of knowledge—and languages, too, play a role. Hubert Zapf writes, "Language as a cultural ecosystem is especially important here as a shaping factor in the process of cultural evolution" (80). Without claiming any special status for one language, we must integrate language acquisition with literature as cultural ecology and promote ethical outcomes by greening the curriculum.

Contemporary German environmental activism emerged from a place of vulnerability and traumatic memory that was a constitutive element in contemporary, postwar, post–Berlin Wall identities. But the present has a past. In his discussion of Aleida Assmann's work, Axel Goodbody determines that "places associated with traumatic events such as military defeat and the Holocaust have played an equally important role in fixing and mediating individuals' identification with the nation in recent times" (*Nature* 59). Traumatically inscribed spaces, for this reason, factor into the construction of a green German identity. From the national traumas of war, defeat, and division, movements emerged around a German relation to the environment that expanded political activism across authority structures and state systems. At the core of our pedagogical conception, we find ourselves revisiting Immanuel Kant's imperative that connects the natural and ethical worlds. In the frequently quoted conclusion to his *Critique of Practical Reason*, Kant writes, "Two things fill the mind with ever new and increasing admiration and reverence, the more often and more steadily one reflects on them: the starry heavens above me and the moral law within me" (133; 5.161). Contemporary disciplines, often suffused with skepticism about such ethical exuberance, raise obstacles to thinking about the starry skies and moral laws. Beyond the most quoted passage, Kant continues with a deliberation on intimacy between the external world and the "invisible self," mediated by cognition: "and I cognize that my connection with that world (and thereby with all those visible worlds as well) is not merely contingent, as in the first case, but universal and necessary" (133; 5.161). Kant's insight into the homology between the external world and the inner self undergirds holistic curricular design, which attempts to overcome the perceived division by historicizing nature beyond theories of space as socially constructed and illuminating the "invisible self" as an environmentally literate individual.

German literary history, from an environmentally literate perspective, has invented nature by forging connections between human subjectivity and the environment. This consciousness emerges when catastrophe threatens to cross borders. In one example, the widespread public protests in Germany against nuclear technology in the aftermath of the Fukushima disaster in 2011 were not, as many claim, an irrational reaction but rather, for most Germans, based on firsthand experience: the worst nuclear accident in history occurred in April 1986 when a reactor exploded in the Ukrainian city of Chernobyl (then part of the USSR), exposing large expanses of central Europe to radioactive fallout. This event is still deeply engraved in the national memory and thus must be an integral component of the environmentally literate foreign language curriculum.

Environments of Cold War Germanys

Ecological knowledge, then, becomes one framework for literature study, but as something that is much more than one theme among others. Beyond the idyllic or pastoral, poetry and literature speak to the history of a relation between a national and topographical identity informed by a scarred and scorched earth engraved into collective consciousness. Contributing factors to this identity include an understanding of history, place-based identity, recognition of the role of individual responsibility, collective political activism, and staking a claim for social change. From the perspective of the literary canon, German Romanticism in particular, those spaces signify the imperative of beauty, the landscape of repose, and the promise of human subjective rejuvenation. There is a disjunction between historical space and a presumably ahistorical natural world. This tension informs not only German national identity but also the way we teach German in the foreign language classroom. For this reason, we introduce the positive features of green German culture without sanitizing the trauma of its historical context; it is necessary to teach the controversies of environmentalism alongside analysis of environmental practices and texts.

The history of controversy over the environment exemplifies the types of ethical decision-making and systems-thinking convictions that we believe belong in the classroom where language instruction coexists with environmental history. In the West, Petra Kelly helped found the first Green Party in 1979. Catastrophes can lead to environmental activism within a nation and its cultural expressions (Uekötter 103–07; Gerstenberger and Nusser 1–9), but a divided Germany in the twentieth century experienced an upsurge in the politicization of the environment that had global repercussions. Across the political divide, an epiphany in East German environmental thought occurred after the meltdown of Chernobyl in 1986. These events, after the juggernaut of unification (1990) erased traces of East German political agency, are important for an understanding of the relation between environmental awareness and political positions. Environmental trajectories intersected and connected critical politics in both East and West. Of the democratic groups that debated at the Roundtable Talks in 1989–90, some members became Bündnis 90 ("Alliance 90") and ultimately joined forces in 1993 to form the post-Wall political party Bündnis 90 / Die Grünen ("Alliance 90 / The Greens"). On a national scale, activist politics are represented in the incorporation of environmental protections into the German constitution. East German environmental activism constitutes its own chapter of global environmental history (Uekötter 134–38).

Literary works emerging from the confluence of ecological devastation and the creative process provide our students with access to distant events in a systems-thinking approach. Here we establish connections among place, memory, and collective identity toward developing a new sense of "ecological sustainability" even from the cultures of state socialism (Good-body, *Nature* 62). In our curriculum, we turn, for example, to fiction about Chernobyl and the experience of censorship in the German Democratic Republic (GDR) that engages confrontationally with the dire consequences on human health from environmental catastrophe (see appendixes 1 and 2). These works, among others, demonstrate the generative relation between language and literature, informed by environmental ethics and political history, that shapes our curriculum. Students inevitably question contemporary contexts when confronted with historical constructs.

In order to elaborate on the issue of how green Germany really is, more than twenty-five years after the fall of the Wall, we integrate the range of answers to this question into all levels of language instruction; it is important to use current, authentic materials that address these issues directly. That can mean radical change in how we update courses and maintain some logic in the learning outcomes of our entire curriculum. Germany's *Energiewende* ("energy transition"; literally, "energy turn") in the early twenty-first century represents a prime example of environmental politics that foreground a commitment to sustainability. This environmental investment has such resonance that, as Frank Uekötter notes, *The New York Times* adopted it as a foreign borrowing (1). The *Energiewende* signifies a nationwide project to convert a twentieth-century economy that was heavily dependent on electricity from conventional sources into a system based on renewable energy while moving toward independence from nuclear power. Significantly, the *Energiewende* is not a top-down project: the pursuit of greater sustainability and of more environmentally responsible decisions in the production sector, as in consumers' daily lives, is grounded on a strong societal consensus. Even though the country takes the environment and environmentalism seriously, however, it does not necessarily follow that Germans can claim true environmental citizenship. Their green collective consciousness is selective; many are prepared to make environmental exceptions in favor of economic interests. These inconsistencies become teachable moments in the classroom.

At the level of introductory German, the happy spin on German environmentalism present in many textbooks proves insufficient to represent adequately a complex reality. Despite demonstrable achievements, Germans are ultimately unable to bridge the nature-culture divide with ideological consistency. In our view, we need citizens to acknowledge the effects of humanity on the planet: to own a deeper and more critical understanding of daily practice and planetary consequences of their behavior, including an awareness of the unsettling contradictions that trouble environmental debates, because we live in the Anthropocene. This Anthropocene era exists "because humankind has caused mass extinctions of plant and animal species, polluted the oceans and altered the atmosphere, among other lasting impacts" (Stromberg). In the light of this new reality, the ecological humanities plays a role, not only in finding purchase for the STEM disciplines but for leveraging individual responsibility into environmental citizenship.

Theoretical and Practical Perspectives

The sense of urgency in public debates on the environment and the wide societal support for ecological measures in Germany resonate with a commensurate sense of urgency about environmentalisms in our classrooms and curriculum. Yet, as Daniel J. Philippon observes in "Sustainability and the Humanities: An Extensive Pleasure," academic institutions have a history of neutralizing any sense of urgency (164). His eloquent advocacy of the humanities' contribution to the definition of sustainability, meaning, and perspective refers to the work of others who identify human behavior as the cause of so many environmental problems: "if the problem is human behavior, then how can the humanities *not* play a crucial role . . . ?" (164). The humanities in general and language learning in particular provide different tools for decision-making processes that embrace an imperative to redefine the relations among globalization, national identity, and ethical world citizenship. This paradigm shift casts new light on cultural traditions that define the German literary landscape. The subjective and literary responses to nature shape the German national imaginary much in the way the rhetoric of the frontier and the ideology of Western expansion defined identities and politics in the United States for more than a century. German literature and philosophy constantly reinvent the relation between human subjectivity and nature: German medieval poetry, Faustian projects, and Romanticism attest to the literary, cultural, and philosophical constructions of the natural world that preface texts about human alienation, concomitant with the growth of urban centers throughout the nineteenth century and subsequent catastrophes caused by human activity. In this environmental paradigm shift, modernity, urbanization, and German-specific history in the twentieth and twenty-first centuries can be read as extensions of a long-term cultural inheritance regarding the construction of nature as a sacred, national space. In the foreign language curriculum, cultural artifacts provide the opportunity to bridge a gap between literary and cultural studies and the topic-based study of contemporary sociopolitical questions by structuring preparatory courses to provide a foundation in environmental literacy both within and beyond the project of reading national literatures. Ecological issues like deforestation, nuclear power and catastrophe, loss of biodiversity, the effect of industry on landscapes, urbanization and corporate agriculture, and the dystopian processes of technology can be taught through canonical texts and contexts that convey pedagogically an environmental unconscious that, we believe, must become explicit.

Within the larger environmental paradigm shift, environmental humanities can inform the pedagogical aspirations of our discipline at all levels of the curriculum. With ever-increasing emphasis on STEM disciplines in higher education, holistic curricular design aimed at achieving larger literacy goals should be a top priority for programs because humanistic knowledge and international literacy have value. German curriculum design, where efforts are underway to connect environmental education and thinking, thus enables foreign language departments to implement changes that facilitate the integration of language, culture, and "the field's intellectual content" (Swaffar and Arens 15). The goals of attaining linguistic proficiency, cultural literacy, and intercultural competence constitute the contribution foreign language departments make to the humanities. Janet Swaffar and Katherine Arens formulate this critical skill and explore its implications for contemporary citizenship:

> Literacy describes what empowers individuals to enter societies; to derive, generate, communicate, and validate knowledge and experience; to exercise expressive capacities to engage others in shared cognitive, social, and moral projects; and to exercise such agency with an identity that is recognized by others in the community. (2)

The integrated curriculum these authors elaborate has the potential to bridge multiple gaps: for example, those between formal language instruction and cultural studies; lower- and upper-division courses; plural pedagogical strategies and learning outcomes; and second language acquisition as a constitutive and practical skill ensconced in the humanities and the social sciences. Long-term commitment to incorporating environmental literacy can bridge another gap, communicative in nature, experienced by individuals on a human scale. This can be accomplished by examining global phenomena of such a vast scale that human agency becomes overshadowed. In the 2007 Modern Language Association (MLA) report on foreign languages, the authors write: "Language is a complex multifunctional phenomenon that links an individual to other individuals, to communities, and to national cultures" (MLA Ad Hoc Committee). A holistic curriculum, geared toward systems thinking and intercultural literacy, can overcome the divisions implied in national defense toward the greater goal of sustainability.

While these critical comments point out one of the challenges for foreign language programs, they obscure the significant fact that students often enroll in particular language courses precisely because they not only desire but demand skills with practical application. Students admittedly want to gain proficiency in languages that they believe will enhance their economic competitiveness, emphasized on campuses in the United States variously as readiness, experiential learning, service learning, or career pathways, among others. The various articulations of the "gospel of efficiency" (Alaimo 560; qtd. in Zapf 19; see also Hays) have in common a deleterious effect on the humanities and on humanities epistemologies. With reference to Claire Kramsch's groundbreaking work on the place of foreign language instruction, Bartell M. Berg observes that "language learning and education policy in the United States are often driven by two large concerns: economic competitiveness and national defense" (216). Yet the most challenging threat to national security is posed by climate change. Environmental degradation plays a leading role in mass migration, armed conflict, forced displacement, and border crises. Foreign language study that is articulated with ecological literacy and sustainability or with environmental studies has crucial importance, situated as it is at the nexus of global competency, holistic—or at least expanded—approaches to defining and solving problems, and international education and the STEM disciplines (Downey et al.). The addition of environmental awareness to the repertoire of the university curriculum thus bridges the notorious gap between languages and economic and strategic competitiveness.

Focus on contributions of German-language culture to ecology and environmentalism has the potential, we argue, not only to bridge a gap, but also to foster an integrated, holistic context for mutually beneficial cooperation among the humanities and the STEM disciplines through knowledge of texts about environmental ethics, civic virtue, and systems thinking. Although much work has occurred to share best practices for teaching "'green' approaches to German language and culture" (Arnett and Levine iii), including innovative syllabi and assessment tools, few voices speak to the metapolitics of environmental literacy for the foreign languages. Little has been done to overcome the contradiction inherent in the project of teaching a specific national language with the goal of attaining environmental literacy informed by the imperative to understand ecology without borders. The foreign language classroom itself must become the site where the profound contradiction at the core of the pedagogical project is explored.

One way we have found to address this contradiction productively is to approach it not from an individual but a societal perspective, using systems thinking. Systems thinking invites learners to see beyond their immediate needs, surroundings, even life spans and to situate human subjectivity in an amplified perspective that emphasizes connections rather than divisions. German environmental consciousness provides an example amenable to systems-thinking analysis that can be converted into learning outcomes in the foreign language classroom without any pretension to teaching particular ethical, moral, or political positions. The growing appreciation for Alexander von Humboldt's "invention of nature," the title of a widely read book by Andrea Wulf, has popularized systems thinking in relation to the environment. We as educators can take this example and locate it in the national context of a foreign language classroom. Thus, using the historical distance of literary and cultural texts, we can ask questions about cultural values and make space for difficult moral, ethical, and political debates. Creating this space, we believe, is the purpose of education—and literature: we attempt to create a sense of common ground. By teaching environmental literacy, we contribute to global citizenship in the real world. Teaching environmental literacy, here through German-language curricula, helps faculty members theorize and realize the goals of foreign language departments on both idealistic and practical levels. These pressures include the need to be economically and ethically aware and practical at the same time. The shifted epistemologies of environmental knowledge demonstrate a connection between ethics and everyday life: "This reflects our belief that citizens and their everyday life choices, rooted as they are in local communities and local ecological webs, but with connections that ripple out over the globe and to the future, are the foundations of a sustainable society" (Reynolds et al. 17–18). Realizing a sustainable society is not an attainable learning outcome, but approaching language and culture instruction in a way that encompasses both natural and cultural sites has positive outcomes. This approach replaces the narrowly national as an epistemological category and incorporates historical and moral narratives that should be central in the quest for relevance.

Environmental Humanities and German Culture

The environmental humanities comprises "a diverse and emergent field of cross-disciplinary research that seeks to analyze and investigate the complex interrelationships between human activity (cultural, economic, and political) and the environment, understood in its broadest sense" (TORCH). In our field, the centrality of literature and science of the nineteenth century emphasizes the confluence of the disciplines. Turning to the five-volume work *Kosmos* (1845–62) of Alexander von Humboldt, the Prussian naturalist, geographer, and explorer who traveled through Amazonia during the late 1700s, we and our students discover Humboldt defined nature as a "planetary interactive causal network operating across multiple scale levels, temporal and spatial" (Walls ix). Recognizing connections between "deforestation, environmental change, and depopulation" (Walls ix), Humboldt became one of the first scholars to alert his contemporaries to ecological issues from a global, even planetary, perspective. Environmental historians credit Humboldt with the origin of the intellectual movement, grounded in the spirit and times of Rousseau, Sturm und Drang ("storm and stress"), and Romanticism (Radkau 12), exemplifying the integration of science, language, literature, and relevance in a holistic curriculum. Acknowledging the need for systems thinking via the German scientific tradition of Humboldt, we bring the larger goals of environmental humanities into the classroom through specific German cultural examples. Our seminars situate the philosophical and scientific models in a linguistic and historical context that shows the turn to language and landscape through a discourse congruent with emerging nationalism.

In the classroom, reference to Humboldt can bridge conceptual gaps for contemporary students who are steeped in the political oppositional thought characteristic of the United States. In the introduction to *Teaching Secondary*

English As If the Planet Matters, Sasha Matthewman provides a template for teaching ecocritical thought through the discipline of teaching English to design and deliver a curriculum that accounts for the "planetary emergency": "English is the subject that encourages and develops reflection, debate and emotional and aesthetic responses to cultural issues and texts" (1). Matthewman's comments obtain in the study of English, yet invite our attempt to adapt the insights into the instruction of German and other languages as one goal of the environmental humanities, which is to overcome the perceived binary between the human and nonhuman worlds that accords humans a position outside nature (Rose et al. 3), thus allowing them to assume, presumably, complete control—of their own destiny, as of the environment. Such an approach necessarily resonates transnationally, highlighting the need for the historicizing of national cultures and comparative reflection.

In a holistic curriculum, a human anthropocentric perspective would be replaced with a *"biocentrism"*; humanity would be an inseparable *part* of the environment (Clark, *Cambridge Introduction* 2; our emphasis). The natural world can only assume the value that humans assign to it; hence, it will necessarily lack intrinsic meaning (Rose et al. 3), or at least any meaning that might be ethically binding for humankind. In contrast, a holistic view of nature, such as the one we also encounter in the "deep ecology" concept by the Norwegian scholar Arne Naess (95–96), understands the whole world, in every dimension, as a "contact zone" in which human and nonhuman entities, social and natural processes are part of one and the same interdependent system (Rose et al. 2; Lidström and Garrard 36). Deep ecology signifies a radical and engaged philosophy of nature that recognizes the interdependence of all forms, regardless of their use value for humanity.

Conventionally, the natural sciences and humanities generate knowledge differently: the former perceive, describe, empirically test, theorize, and form paradigms to understand the natural world, whereas the latter forms of cognition are presumed to be unsystematic. Knowledge, however, is neither closed nor reducible to its fundamental parts; it is rather a holistic matrix that interconnects every being—human and nonhuman—on planet Earth. Here the environmental humanities can be instrumental in a rejection of reductionism and accounts of "self-contained, rational decision-making subjects" (Rose et al. 2). Such a worldview implies far-reaching ethical consequences for autonomous human actions: humanity would forfeit a sense of ownership of nature that allowed the use, abuse, and exploitation of the environment to meet unlimited human demands; instead, our actions would be guided by the principle of what is good for the biosphere as a whole (Clark, *Cambridge Introduction* 2), as we see in José F. A. Oliver's poems about the Black Forest.

When we turn to literature, and especially the genre of poetry, we give students access to emotional, sensory, and ethical dimensions of human experience through works that engage with universal issues. In particular, contemporary intercultural verse, such as Oliver's, negotiates often conflicting linguistic and cultural positions, revealing unsettling boundaries and static systems of knowledge and meaning. Often informed by "non-unitary, nomadic or rhizomatic views" (Braidotti 5), such poetry thus promotes an alternative, relational, and process-oriented subjectivity that lends itself not only to issues of difference and otherness but also to holistic sustainability or the universal interconnectedness of a postanthropocentric thinking. Once contextualized with holistic theories and practices, such as "deep ecology," such poetic texts gain even more value and relevance in the classroom; they allow students to connect with the materials in an individual as well as universal way. The acquisition of language in this manner thus includes the ability to understand texts holistically as a "cultural ecosystem" (Zapf 80); these insights into sustainability can function within regimes of knowledge shaped both by Humboldt's invention of nature and contemporary literary practice.

The goal of bridging the divide between man and nature remains unachieved, even in the face of the most pressing environmental issue of our time: global climate change. Climate change hovers on the periphery of consciousness as an abstract notion, its consequences deferred either in time (to the future) or located remotely in place (always somewhere else). Data and information do not adequately represent its human dimensions; rather, humanity urgently needs the dualism of imaginative internal landscapes (produced by consciousness, modern society, and culture) and external landscapes (our *Umwelt*, or the natural environment), which traditional paradigms of thought have only passively acknowledged (Lidström and Garrard 43). Zapf writes, "Language thus decisively contributes to the emergence of internal worlds of consciousness and culture that are characteristic of the cultural evolution" (80). In the foreign language classroom, language and literature mediate between these internal and external landscapes.

They enable us to forge strong connections between speaking and thinking, to extend learning outcomes to everyday practices beyond the classroom.

Within the ecological humanities, Deborah Bird Rose and Libby Robin argue, we work "across the great binaries of western thought." For this work, nature poetry becomes more than a topic of literary historical periods. It activates the imagination and emotion of students. It bridges the nature-culture, human-nonhuman divides that have dominated consciousness and Cartesian cognitive models for centuries. It moves us from compartmentalizing environmental issues as individual choice to comprehending that only societies, indeed an imagined global community, can address them. Moreover, the foreign language classroom, where the scope of topics ranges from daily practices to global perspectives, lends itself to this process. In beginning- and intermediate-level language courses we engage students in discussions about personal behavior and make comparisons with Germany when treating topics of recycling, individual consumption, energy sources, transportation issues, and ultimately geopolitical issues. We can analyze the dominance of individualism that exists at the core of consumer culture (Clark, "Some Climate Change Ironies") while interrogating the construction of German green society. We can use encounters with contemporary German art and literature as an entry point to discussing ecological discourses that propose models for a strong and credible *"trans-individual"* ethos (Lidström and Garrard 49), a dimension that transcends the realm of isolated and immediate needs of the individual and moves toward universal concerns and goals. Such work can contribute to the development of socially oriented attitudes while students engage actively in learning about language and cultural history and themselves inhabit the world with a "trans-individual" ethos.

As humanists and German studies scholars, we do not take a position on the science. Instead, we analyze and interpret responses from a particular historical, cultural, and linguistic context in the service of greening the curriculum. Much of the available literature on teaching environmental literacy focuses on curricula specific to individual institutions and/or programs or to national traditions and languages (for English, see Matthewman; for German, see Arnett and Levine; for North American literature, see Christensen et al.). This work provides a crucial foundation for rethinking the twenty-first-century curriculum. The holistic ethics that inform the design of the program outlined above appeal to a wide range of postsecondary learners who expect theoretical challenges and practical skills from their undergraduate education. Beyond the important work of incorporating textbook chapters and ancillaries on the environment (Becker et al. 149–51), it is important that we also contribute our own experiences in the introductory language classroom to lay a foundation for developing the necessary linguistic skills to progress in all categories of competence throughout the program. An environmental literacy focus motivates engaged learning that results in cumulative skills at the advanced level, where we emphasize cultural literacy through the teaching of contemporary issues, such as immigration, integration, social justice, and environmentalism.

While we do not claim to have created the ideal curriculum, we have learned that designing our offerings with the goal of attaining environmental literacy helps students understand that language acquisition, cultural knowledge, and ecological ethics are interconnected; they reinforce biocentric values that ultimately influence everyday life and citizenship beyond the classroom. We coordinate in planning our curricular offerings to ensure that we have the skill level to interchange courses. Our courses do sometimes revert to a thematic environmental approach by necessity. Although we agree on environmental literacy as an optimal learning outcome, ultimately, we cannot evaluate students on their openness to a particular political viewpoint or assess them on their environmental ethics; instead we integrate relevant material about the history of German literature, culture, and technological innovations and its relation to the natural world; we cover the history of ecological activism, and the economic and environmental controversies that benefit from systems thinking and holistic approaches to knowledge. Ecocriticism and environmental ethics have the goal of integrating all levels of language instruction with cultural and intercultural literacy. The program culminates in the capstone seminar and project on "Green Germany" (see appendix 2). In the midst of wide-ranging and raging discussions about the Anthropocene era, the environmentally aware foreign language classroom can create a different type of pedagogical space in which the *Umwelt* ("environment") can mediate a discussion about the place of the individual in an interconnected world.

Cultural and literary studies in the environmental humanities can question and even destabilize traditional closed knowledge systems while sensitizing the students to an alternative, more holistic, and thus planetary worldview that integrates human and nonhuman spheres on equal terms. If we begin from a planetary premise, we can accommodate national cultures and world languages into that paradigm through systems thinking. In practice, the individual can gain a different sense of connectedness and responsibility for the environment—and consequently, a new form of environmental agency that transcends the normative passive and consuming attitude towards nature. In order to go beyond the individual level, toward the "trans-individual," however, German cultural and literary studies can offer its students additional knowledge that exceeds classroom learning outcomes: the environmental consciousness of contemporary Germany's citizens and many of its political and economic actors, thus providing a real-world context for ecological criticism, ecopoetic texts, or any other form of green art. We hope to educate students who can understand the "wingbeat of language" and learn the "alphabet of wood," forging connections across cognitive skills and activism, bridging the nature-culture divide. The facts remain: any notion of the environment, global studies, and planetary history exceeds national and regional boundaries, languages, and economies. Ultimately, students will be reminded that individuals will not be able to save the world, only ecocosmopolitical citizens who engage in communities, societies, and beyond.

NOTES

1. Reproduced with the kind permission of Suhrkamp Verlag.
2. Many literary and cultural scholars have changed the way we read and teach canonical texts including and beyond Goethe's *Faust* (see Schaumann and Sullivan).

APPENDIX 1: ACTFL LEVELS*
IN RELATION TO ACTIVITIES, CONTENT, AND TEXTS

Level	Activities	Content and texts
Novice Low	The color green; vocabulary words pertaining to the natural world	*Natur, Wasser, Luft, See* (nature, water, air, lake/sea)
Novice Mid	Recycling vocabulary	Images, questions, objects, emphasis on cognates
Novice High	Sentence building around recycling, leisure time, self in environment	Exercises around human interaction with nature
Intermediate Low	Short poems, focus on nature and subjectivity	J. W. von Goethe, "Mailied" (1771; "May Song"); Eduard Mörike, "Im Frühling" (1828/32; "In Spring")
Intermediate Mid	Urban versus rural	Ludwig Fels, "City-Poem" (1975); Andra Schwarz, "Dorfgedichte" (2015; "Village poems")
Intermediate High	Cold wars and green politics; background, biographies, and contexts	Green initiatives in West and East; short bio of Petra Kelly; independent documentary (filmed illegally) about environmental degradation and the GDR chemical industry: "Bitteres aus Bitterfeld" (1988; "Bitter Things from Bitterfeld")
Advanced Low	Focus on one element and associated cultural concepts	Water across myth and history: Friedrich de la Motte Fouqué, *Undine* (1811); and essay from Axel Goodbody and Berbell Wanning, eds., *Wasser – Kultur – Ökologie: Konstanten und Wandel in der sozialen und kulturellen Bedeutung des flüssigen Elements* (2008; "Water—Culture—Ecology: Constants and Change in the Social and Cultural Meaning of the Fluid Element")
Advanced Mid	Visual arts, focus on identification with nature	Paintings by Caspar David Friedrich and discussion
Advanced High	Visual cultures, focus on national spaces and natural destruction	Nations and natures in the twentieth century: Paintings by Anselm Kiefer, for example, traumatic history "inscribed" on the landscape
Superior	Project-based work	Undergraduate/graduate seminar: Natur, Umwelt, und Kultur im Anthropozän (Nature, Environment, and Culture in the Anthropocene; see appendix 2)

ACTFL Proficiency Guidelines 2012. American Council on the Teaching of Foreign Languages (ACTFL), 2012, www.actfl.org/sites/default/files/pdfs/public/ACTFLProficiencyGuidelines2012_FINAL.pdf.

APPENDIX 2: SAMPLE SYLLABUS FOR
NATUR, UMWELT, UND KULTUR IM ANTHROPOZÄN
(NATURE, ENVIRONMENT, AND CULTURE IN THE ANTHROPOCENE)

MODUL 1:* Einführung in die Literatur und Kultur des anthropozänischen Zeitalters (Introduction to the Literature and Culture of the Anthropocene)

Überblick über die Evolution vom Begriff "Natur" (Overview of the Evolution of "Nature" as a Concept)

Einführung in die Theorien des menschlichen Zeitalters (Introduction to Theories of the Human Age)

Assign theoretical and critical readings, both in German and English, to introduce the topic.

MODUL 2: Nationalismus und Natur: Die Problematik der Natur im Dritten Reich (Naturalism and Nature: The Problematic of Nature in the Third Reich)

Assign readings and images that establish and interrogate a relationship between post-Romantic projections of nature; the appropriation of landscape as nation; the naturalizing of a bond between forests, rivers, mountains, annexed territories; and pathological articulations of German nationalism.

MODUL 3: Die verfremdete Natur in der Nachkriegszeit (Alienated Nature in the Postwar Period)

Wolfgang Borchert, *Draussen vor der Tür* (1946; *The Man Outside* [1952])

The radio play illustrates the consequences of war and historical trauma on human subjectivity, represented by the destruction of the natural world as the foundation of meaning.

MODUL 4: Exil, Gedächtnis, und räumliche Existenz (Exile, Memory, and Spatial Existence)

Anna Seghers, "Der Ausflug der toten Mädchen" (1946; "The Excursion of the Dead Girls" [2017]); "Post ins Gelobte Land" (1946; "Mail to the Promised Land")

Seghers explores the relationships among war, displacement, and memory.

MODUL 5: Lyrik ohne Natur: Aschen und Schornsteine (Poetry without Nature: Ashes and Chimneys)

Gedichte von Paul Celan und Nelly Sachs (selected poems by Paul Celan and Nelly Sachs)

The poetry can be read as well in the context of the authors' epistolary exchange and, if appropriate, can precede a discusson of Anselm Kiefer's paintings inspired by Celan's poetry.

MODUL 6: Sprache als Geographie der Identitäten (Language as Geography of Identities)

Geschichten von Emine Sevgi Özdamar (stories by Emine Sevgi Özdamar)

Geschichten und Kommentar von Yoko Tawada (stories and commentary by Yoko Tawada)

The stories selected situate human subjectivity in a perceived "German" natural and national environment.

MODUL 7: Katastrophen I (Catastrophes, part 1)

Monika Maron, *Flugasche* (1981; *Flight of Ashes* [1986])

To varying degrees, this and the subsequent module focus on accounts of environmental catastrophe in the GDR, demonstrating a socialist, as well as capitalist, failure of stewardship.

MODUL 8: Katastrophen II (Catastrophes, part 2)

Christa Wolf, *Störfall: Nachrichten eines Tages* (1987; *Accident: A Day's News* [1989])

MODUL 9: Die Entdeckung der Natur in der Moderne (The Discovery of Nature in Modernity)

Daniel Kehlmann, *Die Vermessung der Welt* (2004; *Measuring the World* [2007])

The literature of exploration connects with the scientific enterprise in this novel about Alexander von Humboldt and Carl Friedrich Gauss.

MODUL 10: Neue Natursubjektivität: Lyrik (New Nature Subjectivity: Poetry)

Gedichte von José F. A. Oliver, Durs Grünbein u.a. (Poetry by Oliver and Grünbein, among others)

Contemporary poetry explores the relations between human subjectivity and the generative capacity of language.

MODUL 11: Die Umwelt und Protestkultur (The Environment and Protest Culture)

Nicol Ljubic, *Ein Mensch brennt* (2017; "A Human Is Burning")

This novel is based on the life and death of Hartmut Gründler (1930–77), whose self-immolation protested the Federal Republic's misinformation about atomic energy.

* Modules generally correspond to weeks in an academic semester, with flexibility to include assignments, presentations, cocurricular activities, and additional theoretical readings.

WORKS CITED

Alaimo, Stacy. "Conserving This, Conserving That." *PMLA*, vol. 127, no. 3 (May 2012), pp. 558–64.

Arnett, Carlee, and Glenn S. Levine, editors. *Die Unterrichtspraxis / Teaching German*, vol. 46, no. 2, 2013. Special issue on teaching environmental topics.

Becker, Angelika, et al. "Greening the German Classroom: Starting Points for a Cultural Lesson." Arnett and Levine, pp. 149–62.

Berg, Bartell M. "Perspectives on the German *Energiewende*: Culture and Ecology in German Instruction." Arnett and Levine, pp. 215–29.

Braidotti, Rosi. *Transposition: On Nomadic Ethics*. Polity, 2006.

Christensen, Laird, et al., editors. *Teaching North American Environmental Literature*. Modern Language Association of America, 2008.

Clark, Timothy, editor. *The Cambridge Introduction to Literature and the Environment*. Cambridge UP, 2011.

———. "Some Climate Change Ironies: Deconstruction, Environmental Politics and the Closure of Ecocriticism." *The Oxford Literary Review*, vol. 32, 2010, pp. 131–49.

Downey, Gary Lee, et al. "The Globally Competent Engineer: Working Effectively with People Who Define Problems Differently." *Journal of Engineering Education*, vol. 95, no. 2, Apr. 2006, pp. 107–22.

Gerstenberger, Katharina, and Tanja Nusser, editors. *Catastrophe and Catharsis: Perspectives on Disaster and Redemption in German Culture and Beyond*. Camden House, 2015.

Goodbody, Axel. *Nature, Technology, and Cultural Change in Twentieth-Century German Literature: The Challenge of Ecocriticism*. Palgrave Macmillan, 2007.

———. "Sense of Place and *Lieu de Mémoire*: A Cultural Memory Approach to Environmental Texts." Goodbody and Rigby, pp. 55–67.

Goodbody, Axel, and Kate Rigby, editors. *Ecocritical Theory: New European Approaches*. U of Virginia P, 2011.

Hays, Samuel P. *Conservation and the Gospel of Efficiency: The Progressive Conservation Movement, 1890–1920*. U of Pittsburgh P, 1999.

Kant, Immanuel. *Critique of Practical Reason*. Edited and translated by Mary Gregor, introduction by Andrews Reath, Cambridge UP, 1997. Cambridge Texts in the History of Philosophy.

Lidström, Susanna, and Greg Garrard. "'Images Adequate to Our Predicament': Ecology, Environment and Ecopoetics." *Environmental Humanities*, vol. 5, 2014, pp. 35–53.

Matthewman, Sasha. *Teaching Secondary English As If the Planet Matters*. Routledge, 2011.

MLA Ad Hoc Committee on Foreign Languages. "Foreign Languages and Higher Education: New Structures for a Changed World." *Profession*, 2007, www.mla.org/Resources/Research/Surveys-Reports-and-Other-Documents/Teaching-Enrollments-and-Programs/Foreign-Languages-and-Higher-Education-New-Structures-for-a-Changed-World.

Naess, Arne. "The Shallow and the Deep, Long-Range Ecology Movement: A Summary." *Inquiry*, vol. 16, no. 1, 1973, pp. 95–100.

Oliver, José F. A. *Fahrtenschreiber* ["Worldometer"]. Suhrkamp, 2010.

Philippon, Daniel J. "Sustainability and the Humanities: An Extensive Pleasure." *American Literary History*, vol. 24, no. 1, Spring 2012, pp. 163–79.

Radkau, Joachim. *The Age of Ecology: A Global History*. Translated by Patrick Camiller, Polity, 2014.

Reynolds, Heather L., et al., editors. *Teaching Environmental Literacy: Across Campus and across the Curriculum*. Indiana UP, 2010.

Rose, Deborah Bird, et al. "Thinking through the Environment, Unsettling the Humanities." *Environmental Humanities*, vol. 1, 2012, pp. 1–5.

Rose, Deborah Bird, and Libby Robin. "The Ecological Humanities in Action: An Invitation." *Australian Humanities Review*, vols. 31–32, Apr. 2004, www.Austra lianhumanitiesreview.org/archive/Issue-April- 2004/rose.html.

Schaumann, Caroline, and Heather Sullivan, editors. *German Ecocriticism in the Anthropocene*. Palgrave Macmillan, 2017.

Stromberg, Joseph. "What Is the Anthropocene and Are We in It?" *Smithsonian Magazine*, Jan. 2013, www.smithsonianmag.com/science-nature/what-is-the-anthro pocene-and-are-we-in-it-164801414/. Accessed 28 June 2018.

Swaffar, Janet, and Katherine Arens. *Remapping the Foreign Language Curriculum*. Modern Language Association of America, 2005.

TORCH (Oxford Research Centre in the Humanities). "Environmental Humanities." www.torch.ox.ac.uk/envirohum. Accessed 30 June 2015.

Uekötter, Frank. *The Greenest Nation? A New History of German Environmentalism*. MIT Press, 2014.

Walls, Laura Dassow. *The Passage to Cosmos: Alexander von Humboldt and the Shaping of America*. U of Chicago P, 2009.

Wulf, Andrea. *The Invention of Nature: Alexander von Humboldt's New World*. Knopf, 2015.

Zapf, Hubert. *Literature as Cultural Ecology*. Bloomsbury, 2016.

Sustainability Literacy in French Literature and Film: From Solitary Reveries to Treks across Deserts

Annette
Sampon-Nicolas

While we marvel at technological advances as our global society moves forward in the twenty-first century, we mourn the environmental and socioeconomic problems that continue to plague the Earth. Given that the well-being of our planet is at stake, foreign language teachers might ask whether it is their responsibility to educate for sustainability literacy. In *Remapping the Foreign Language Curriculum*, Janet K. Swaffar and Katherine Arens argue that foreign languages foster multiple literacies that empower "individuals to enter societies; to derive, generate, communicate and validate knowledge and experience; to exercise expressive capacities to engage others in shared cognitive, social, and moral projects; and to exercise such agency with an identity that is recognized in the community" (2). Accordingly, as the humanities refocus on the role of literacy and social context, so too must foreign languages.

This essay explores the imperative to embrace a new model of education that will engage students in learning about the interconnectedness of our multispecies world, sustainability, and global solidarity—the belief "that unity of humankind can be established on the basis of some basic or core human values" (Korab-Karpowicz 305). Foreign language courses—in particular advanced-level offerings that address literacy, critical thinking, and cultural comparisons—are ideal settings for educating for sustainability literacy. Such literacy is essential to our collective twenty-first-century global identity, but it requires transformative educational practices. As we design foreign language courses, we should strive to employ a greater variety of teaching methods and keep in mind the necessity of more comprehensive goals, which include making students more aware of principles that reach beyond forming citizens who will participate in the economic world. Specifically, as twenty-first-century educators, we should strive to imbue our students with a sense of global citizenship to instill personal responsibility that will translate into their making more sustainable choices. When we sensitize students to issues that affect them, and indeed all humankind on our planet, we prepare them to become global citizens, leaders, and stewards of the global commons (Bennett et al.).

This essay explores theoretical frameworks for teaching sustainability literacy and introduces a model for teaching an advanced French language course that applies those frameworks to classical literary texts, contemporary world literature, and film. This model advocates teaching new literacies through activities that foster critical thinking, problem solving, communication, collaboration, and experiential learning. To accomplish these larger learning outcomes, students need to study worldwide problems and reflect on what they have learned in a final project. This culminating project requires them to examine their place and responsibilities in their local environment and community while considering global concerns and addressing the complexity of perspectives on these issues.

Reorienting Education in the United States: Models for Sustainability Literacy and Global Awareness

According to the prominent environmental educator David W. Orr, the failure of education is not simply a lack of skills in specific subjects. Rather, "it is a failure to educate people to think broadly, to perceive systems and patterns, and to live as whole persons" (2). Orr sees the pressing need for profound educational reform as stemming from "the rapid decline in the habitability of the earth" (2). To address this issue, he proposes the redesign of both education and educator preparation, so that teachers might nurture young people to help heal industrial damage, redress environmental injustices, and become responsible global citizens who act in solidarity with the earth and its people (3). These are challenging goals to be sure; nevertheless, they are possible if sustainability literacy becomes a primary goal of education.

Multiple definitions of environmental and sustainable education exist. In this essay, *environmental education* refers to the process of examining ecological issues and working to improve our surroundings, whereas *sustainability education* involves a more profound examination of how human activity affects the environment. When we speak of *sustainability literacy*, we thus refer to the ability to exercise "the skills, attitudes, competencies, dispositions and values that are necessary for surviving and thriving in the declining conditions of the world in ways which slow down that decline as far as possible" (Stibbe 10). Knowledge is about learning and gaining information; literacy is about being able to use what we learn and turn it into positive action. For twenty-first-century citizens, both environmental and sustainability education are necessary. Furthermore, as Andrés R. Edwards argues, "We must shift from merely sustaining to *thriving*. The transformation from sustainability to *thriveability* challenges us to expand our imaginations and create the future we want for ourselves and for future generations" (4). As educators, our role is to help students develop their full potential and become responsible citizens. These goals are not limited by language but rather deeply connected to our ability to use language. Our objectives as foreign language practitioners must accordingly embrace the study of the interconnected relationships between cultural, socioeconomic, and environmental conditions that lead to sustainability literacy.

Globally, debates about failure in educational systems, along with recommended standards and reforms, have been at the forefront of the news for decades. The dissimilarities between the goals expressed by educational programs in other countries and those in the United States are, however, striking. Programs in Canada and in many countries in the European Union require the study of world geography and at least one foreign language, in addition to math and sciences. In the United States, despite much debate, the Common Core State Standards stress English language and mathematics. Thus, despite public discussion about globalization, foreign languages are not considered essential to living in a global society. Meanwhile, Denmark, Scotland, and France have already implemented environmental and sustainable education programs for kindergarten through high school.[1] These developed countries, which have strong historical traditions of respecting the environment in both urban centers and natural spaces, recognize that sustainability literacy is crucial to society in the twenty-first century. Their environmental education programs accordingly reflect the interrelation of disciplines, the development of analytical skills, civic engagement, and global solidarity.

Whereas nationally the United States lags behind in sustainability education, state governments acknowledge the importance of environmental literacy, because its value relates to an identifiable purpose of preparing students for their economic future.[2] Such mandated environmental and sustainable education serves a greater mission—that of instilling new behaviors and educating global citizens. Indeed, environmental education has been part of the European Union agenda since the late 1980s (Binstock 13). Although not every country in the European Union addresses environmental education to the same extent, it is considered "as important to European environmental policy as environmental protection legislation and market based instruments in efforts to gear human behavior toward more environmentally sustainable patterns" (Nicolae, qtd. in Binstock 13).

With no nationally mandated environmental education in the United States, some states and nonprofit organizations have implemented programs at the state level. In 1990, Congress found that increasing threats to human health and the global environment warranted environmental education and consequently passed the National Environmental Education Act (NEEA) to fund programs. This legislation proposes the integration of environmental education across the K–12 curriculum, linking this effort to educational reform for environmental literacy. According to NEEA, "An environmentally literate person is someone who, both individually and together with others, makes informed decisions concerning the environment; is willing to act on these decisions to improve the wellbeing of other individuals, societies, and global environment; and participates in civic life." This imperative to educate broadly should be taken as an invitation to design curricula that encourage students to become proficient in multiple literacies, most crucially sustainability literacy. Turning now to the question of how to design such a foreign language course, let us examine a model that integrates interdisciplinary sustainability lessons, analytical skills, and experiential activities and that contributes to redefining foreign language education. Foreign language teachers are trained to teach language, culture, and literature; few are prepared, however, to embrace teaching sustainability through a global lens. In the United States, foreign language educators at the postsecondary level looking for guidance on integrating sustainability into their curriculum may turn to guidelines developed by the National Education Association (NEA) and the American Council on the Teaching of Foreign Languages (ACTFL). Another important resource, Partnership for Twenty-First-Century Learning (a coalition of educators and business leaders), has worked with NEA and with ACTFL in developing a list of skills, interdisciplinary themes, and academic content indispensable for training postsecondary school students to be successful workers and active citizens in the global community. This national coalition recommends development of world language skills, global awareness, and financial, economic, business, entrepreneurial, civic, health, and environmental literacies. Like the five Cs—Communication, Cultures, Connections, Comparisons, and Communities—of foreign language education articulated by ACTFL (*World-Readiness Standards*), the skills map for world languages (*Twenty-First-Century Skills Map*) illustrates how these skills and interdisciplinary themes can be woven into language classes. Its suggestions for developing creativity, critical thinking, problem solving, communication, collaboration, information, media, and technology skills do not include environmental literacy per se, but its aspiration of cultivating citizens knowledgeable about the interconnectedness of socioeconomic and global environmental problems underscores that foreign language educators play a vital role in educating for global awareness.

Given that our goals can no longer be limited to educating students to be workers in a monolingual economic community, global environmental and sustainability literacy must realistically become part of our mission as educators. We as a society want students to find gainful, meaningful employment. We also want them to commit to the global common good as arrived at through sustainable living. Foreign language educators already teach global awareness, as exemplified by ACTFL's world-readiness standards for learning languages (see Summary), and by current French, German, and Spanish Advanced Placement (AP) language and culture courses that focus on such topics as the environment, diversity, tolerance, economic issues, health, human rights, nutrition and food safety, and peace and war. Students preparing for the AP exams are advised to look at the origins and possible solutions to global environmental, political, and social challenges. To their credit, too, publishing companies have begun to integrate chapters on environmental and social issues in foreign language textbooks.[3] Clearly, cultural materials and experiential learning activities in combination with literary texts can raise students' preparedness for civic, environmental, and global challenges.

Nurturing Sustainability Literacy:
From Solitary Reveries to Treks across Deserts

As the Partnership for Twenty-First-Century Learning framework recommends, before citizens can take individual and collective action toward addressing environmental challenges, they must "demonstrate knowledge and understanding of the environment and the circumstances and conditions affecting it, particularly as relates to air, climate, land, food, energy, water and ecosystems" (*Framework*). These concepts are generally taught by science educators; outside an advanced immersion setting, scientific lessons will rarely be taught in a target language setting. What interdisciplinary literature and culture courses have to offer, on the other hand, is the opportunity to explore themes, such as food and water resources, through authentic materials that reflect culturally rich and diverse bioregions in relation to their respective cultural values and societal conditions.

In the advanced interdisciplinary course From Solitary Reveries to Treks across Deserts (see appendix), students explore the complex interrelations between human beings and the natural world through close textual and visual analysis, personal experiences, and experiential activities. Landscape and culture leave a permanent imprint on writers, filmmakers, and photographers, making their creations an effective springboard for introducing and examining environmental, socioeconomic, and cultural issues. Although the key objective in this course remains the learning and practice of a second language, the emphasis on developing analytical skills helps students understand the challenges faced by people from various cultures across the globe.

Matching my skill set and research expertise with content, as all instructors must do in designing such a course, I include Jean-Jacques Rousseau's *Les rêveries du promeneur solitaire* ("Reveries of the Solitary Walker"), an autobiographical text emphasizing the importance of nature in the eighteenth century, and Colette's *Sido*, which reveals her twentieth-century relationship to nature. Present-day francophone writers and filmmakers offer immersion into global natural settings and cultural traditions as well, while simultaneously revealing insights into sustainability issues. For instance, Chinese-born French academician François Cheng's novel, *Le dit de Tian-yi* ("The River Below"), and writer-filmmaker Dai Sijie's *Balzac et la Petite Tailleuse chinoise* ("Balzac and the Little Chinese Seamstress") were used to introduce students to lush Chinese landscapes, Buddhist and Daoist relationships to the natural world, and multifaceted issues such as the controversial construction of the hydroelectric Three Gorges Dam.[4] Additionally, Nobel laureate Jean-Marie Gustave Le Clézio's novel *Désert* ("Desert"), set in both the Sahara and France, presents geographical juxtapositions that foreground environmental, economic, political, and social issues that are intricately woven together and fosters reading and interpretation through an interdisciplinary and global lens. Similar textual and visual materials can be selected to nurture socioeconomic and global awareness, because they offer the opportunity to study environmental, cultural, and multispecies diversity. Moreover, many francophone writers and filmmakers share a profound relationship to place and a commitment to social and environmental justice that makes their work particularly suitable for such courses.

Redefining Foreign Language Education by Considering the Local and the Global

In order to examine the close relationship between a writer and the environment, let us begin with Rousseau, France's first ecologist, whose meditations describe his relation to the biologically diverse world before the industrial revolution. Rousseau defines his own sense of place by mapping his surroundings through words. Reading Rousseau encourages students to question their own relation to our nonhuman world and grapple with the importance of place in their own lives, especially when literary analysis is coupled with tasks that incorporate experiences close to home.

One such assignment is inspired by the "Sense of Place Map" designed by Mitchell Thomashow to focus attention on our personal relation to place and ecological identity (193). Students paint, draw, or make collages that reflect their emotional attachments to places they have lived. Thomashow explains that this nontraditional task requires students to delve deeply into their individual experiences with location: "This map becomes a form of storytelling, a document that explains a person's relationship to the earth" (195). Through this compelling project, students realize the complexity of their interactions with place, particularly if they have frequently moved or traveled. Students' descriptive presentations of their "Sense of Place Map" also yield surprises, however, for they reveal that definitions of "place" can include such varied locales as the inside of their own heads, the four walls of their room, or a cabin on a lake. These ideas about locale do not necessarily connect to nature, rural areas, or even urban spaces. Furthermore, not everyone can relate to the idea of an ecological identity, since the experience of nature is too frequently missing from our daily lives. Many students believe that being in nature requires visiting a state park or designated wilderness area. They often do not realize that simply walking across campus is certainly an experience in nature. Most of them have not spent their childhoods playing outside, so positive reactions to contact with dirt, sand, or insects are rare. Richard Louv developed the expression "nature-deficit disorder" to describe this "growing gap between children and nature" (3). Whereas psychologists and educators agree that spending more time in nature is vitally important for present and future generations whose daily lives are so intertwined with technology, for postsecondary students, college may be the last opportunity before they enter the workforce to cultivate this sense of place in a concentrated and analytical way and to engage with the natural environment both individually and collectively.

Tellingly, "Sense of Place Map" presentations develop a feeling of community that is often in direct opposition to students' developed sense of individualism. These collective, community-building discussions lead to questions of *ecological identity*, which, according to Thomashow, "includes a person's connection to the earth, perception of the ecosystem, and direct experience of nature" (3). He clarifies that to have a balanced ecological identity we need "both scientific awareness and reverence for the processes of life, both personal stories and the responsibility of a citizen" (xxi). Because of growing populations, pollution, and finite resources, we face environmental issues that result from problems in people's beliefs and actions, posits Richard Borden (26). He notes that childhood activities in nature, such as camping, hunting, or fishing, are formative experiences that help people become environmentally committed and feel responsible for the future (32).

Whereas foreign language educators cannot make up for students' lack of childhood experiences in the outdoors, they can create opportunities for positive experiences in nature that change both their conceptions of nature and sense of responsibility to the environment (Borden 34). Since many of our students seem to have had little exposure to the natural world, a focus on the environment emphasizes the connection between academic pursuits and the community of real-world ecosystems in which we all live. In *The Nature of College*, James J. Farrell's insightful analysis of what matters to college students and how they can learn to become strong advocates for sustainability, he argues that college is the ideal place for students to think about culture and ecosystems, examine habits, and learn new behaviors (xiii). Pairing the "Sense of Place Map" assignment, which helps students discover their personal ecological identity, with a French translation of our university's sustainability pledge allows students to assess their environmental footprint regarding recycling practices, energy use, food waste, water conservation, and transportation choices ("Hollins University").

Here, experiential learning beyond the four walls of a traditional classroom helps students develop vital skills. Since many millennial students appear to be inseparable from their technology, experiential learning has become a key method to connect them to the outdoor environment. Leslie K. Hickcox reasons that through a hands-on approach students can acquire new skills and interact with their teachers in a more personal manner (123). Indeed, close mentoring and engaging learning environments are vital for student success and often part of liberal arts colleges' mission statements. As Adrianna J. Kezar and Jillian Kinzie elucidate, "Quality undergraduate curriculum requires coherence in learning, synthesizing experiences, ongoing practice of learned skills, and integrating education with experience" (149). In contrast to assignments that require thinking about the natural environment in the abstract, experiential activities introduce students to the physical world, leading them to question their own relation to nature. Successful activities can include campus walks identifying plants, weeding a community garden, painting a recycling bin, and cooking and sharing a local and sustainable meal that includes vegetables from a community garden. Disconcerting though it may be to discover that some students are afraid of dirt, it is rewarding to guide them through the identification of edible plants by leaf shapes and fragrance, and to see their amazement as they discover that a beautiful flower will become an okra pod or a tomatillo. By integrating such activities, teachers can help students understand the interconnections within their community.

After discussions of personal ecological identity and sustainability practices, students turn to unfamiliar global cultures and landscapes. In order to appreciate the array of topographical regions around the globe, as well as to learn unfamiliar vocabulary, they view Yann Arthus-Bertrand's film *HOME* (available on *YouTube* with narrations in several languages). Shot almost entirely from above the earth, it shows the beauty and diversity of life on our planet and how we are threatening its ecological balance. *HOME* introduces themes that are studied throughout the course: water resources, renewable energies, forest exploitation, agriculture, food production, production and consumption of consumer goods, and human migrations. In general, students have a basic understanding of such environmental issues but need guidance in drawing connections between environmental conditions, population growth, economic growth, and social dimensions, including health, lodging, consumption, education, employment, culture, and social equity. Through its associations with fighting climate change and preserving biodiversity, ecosystems, and natural resources, sustainability literacy promotes social cohesion and solidarity across space and generations (*Green Evénements*). When interwoven throughout any course of this kind, these principles provide ground for discussions focused on the ACTFL standards, including comparisons of living, economic, and environmental conditions, and encourage students to demonstrate their understanding of cultures and their ability to make interdisciplinary connections.

The layering of multiple visual and written texts offers opportunities to appreciate the relation between humans and nature and develops sustainability knowledge through a process of mutual reinforcement. Although environmental issues are not always instantly noticeable, the more students analyze such texts, the more these ecological problems become apparent. With repeated exposure to materials that span the twentieth and twenty-first centuries, students have abundant opportunities to compare past conditions to the present and consider future implications. As they study global cultures, they reflect on how our access to material resources is affected by socioeconomic divisions and consider what changes might lead to greater social justice and equity. For all issues, I challenge students to question the goals, values, and needs that are at stake for people living in each of these various environments. Problems relating to the availability of energy, resources, food, and water are studied along with their effects on populations inhabiting specific regions.

A pivotal text for exploring these issues is Jean-Marie Le Clézio's novel *Désert*, which offers rich material for developing *environmental awareness*, an understanding of the fragility of our environment and the importance of its protection. *Désert* alternates between two narratives set in different time periods: the early 1900s, when nomadic tribes flee across the Moroccan desert to escape French troops, and the 1970s, when descendants of the nomads live in shacks outside an urban Moroccan city and eventually immigrate to Marseilles. In this early-twentieth-century narrative, nomads trek across the desert under conditions of extreme heat, thirst, starvation, and exhaustion only to find dried up streams and little food. Their experiences remind us just how dependent we are on healthy natural ecosystems for our survival (Edwards 7). Living in extreme climatic conditions, the nomads are constantly forced by natural and political conditions to be on the move. When students compare the psychological effects and physical consequences of violence and war depicted in *Désert* to current events, they notice similarities between the novel and the plight of millions of displaced people fleeing war-torn landscapes in the twenty-first century. Study of the novel encourages similar explorations of human migration, food security, the dispossessed, material possessions, and consumerism, which are all essential to the discussion of sustainability. Moreover, *Désert* introduces traditional ecological knowledge (TEK), which is "an understanding of ecosystems and their interrelationships," used by indigenous peoples (Edwards 7). The novel exemplifies TEK through descriptions of constellations and dune formations used by the nomads to cross deserts. This form of place-based knowledge contrasts sharply with today's education dominated by fact-based learning, memorizing, technological skills, and professional preparation. *Désert* describes the psychological effects of poverty, war, exile, immigration, and unemployment on health, food, water, education, living conditions, and the environment.

Although for skilled readers Le Clézio's vivid descriptions help them imagine the desert settings, for today's visually oriented students who are still developing interpretive skills, documentaries and short clips are valuable enhancements whose introduction often sparks discussions about how to "read" both images and texts. According to Eva Brumberger, although students are constantly exposed to visual material, they are not necessarily visually literate and need to learn both visual and verbal literacy (46). Frequent juxtapositions and comparisons between the textual and the visual and between past and present urban conditions prompt students to make comparisons with their own urban environments.

Because students often find rural or wilderness environments less accessible, we view *Women of the Sand*. Filmed at an oasis in the Mauritanian desert, this documentary shows the strength of nomadic women and the preservation of traditional cultural values. Stunning settings aside, desert life is far from idyllic. The film depicts the daily threat of desertification that women combat by building branch walls to hold back the sand in temporary efforts to protect fertile soil for planting vegetables during the rainy season. Seeing the quotidian struggle faced by people across the globe encourages students to draw connections with the living conditions of underprivileged people in rural and urban environments in their own countries of origin. This intercultural exposure reinforces students' development of critical thinking skills that require higher order thinking and ethical reasoning.

Living in a Material World

It is one thing to read a factual description about food and water scarcity but another to visualize how people live. In this class, analysis of global conditions is enhanced by close examination of images from Peter Menzel's *Hungry Planet: What the World Eats*. Photographs on this Web site depict what an average family eats in a week, which raises awareness about how different cultures, environments, and economic circumstances influence the cost of food when students are asked to work in small groups to describe and discuss the images. Gwendolyn Barnes-Karol and Maggie A. Broner, in their insightful essay on the use of images to teach cultural perspectives, encourage foreign language teachers to reach beyond the traditional description of food and cultural practices to address the significance of controversial food issues such as obesity, malnutrition, and mechanized agriculture in this globalized era (430). Such images help students understand the complex relations between culture, food, and social inequities.

Material examples of the problems associated with food security can also be examined using film, such as Agnès Varda's remarkable documentary *Les glaneurs et la glaneuse (The Gleaners and I)*, which investigates poverty, gleaning, recycling, consumerism, and wasteful throwaway societies. As Varda crosses the countryside, she discovers the beauty of heart-shaped potatoes discarded for their imperfections. She explores early morning Paris markets, meeting people of all ages picking up discarded herbs, fruits, and vegetables. Hence gleaning affords a perfect opportunity to discuss the billions of dollars of food wasted in the Western world and to share the ingenious advertising campaign "Inglorious Fruits and Vegetables." This campaign, started by Intermarché (the third-biggest grocer in France), encourages people to buy and consume imperfectly shaped fruits and vegetables ("Légumes moches"). Many of Western society's ideas and values are brought into question as students discuss Varda's film and Intermarché's campaign. By viewing other ways of living, students question their own beliefs and values, stretch abilities in tasks that exercise communicative competence, and demonstrate intercultural understanding and sustainability thinking.

Ultimately, the concept of cultural community must become the most fundamental aspect of sustainability literacy emphasized in such a class. Whereas some students quickly relate to poverty and social justice issues, others—raised in a culture devoted to individualism—more gradually discover the rewards of community engagement through participation in a microfinance activity. For this assignment, highlighting the interconnectedness of the global community, students view photographs and read stories on the Web site for Kiva, a nonprofit microfinance organization that helps alleviate poverty around the world through activism. As the initiator of the project, I ask that they weigh a number of factors before proposing a loan: geographic location, gender equality, economic sector, and green commitment. Reading Web sites in the target language that describe entrepreneurial groups, students put their language and intercultural skills to tangible use. In this way, the foreign language literature course centered on sustainability thinking becomes an opportunity to consider how what we consume as individuals and as a society affects the present and future of the global environment.

Teaching for living in a material world means that in a course where students read literary texts that give them a glimpse into historical events, they also come face-to-face with how present-day problems relate to personal choice. Discussion of personal choice brings sustainability issues closer to home, makes students aware of how other cultures confront similar issues, and contributes to developing more sustainable living models. As students inventory their multiple belongings (a linguistically manageable task recommended by Farrell), they can examine what it means to live sustainably, which requires more complex thinking. When they are challenged to think about cultural values, they reflect on their realistic needs to survive and thrive in an effort to contribute to slowing the decline of the world's resources, not only for themselves, but for future generations.

Knowledge about water resources, renewable energies, biodiversity, endangered species, desertification, deforestation, soil degradation, agriculture, food production, social justice, production and consumption of consumer goods, and human migrations effectively translates into sustainability thinking when students are given an opportunity to synthesize their learning through a final project. For this exercise, students choose a topic that has piqued their curiosity and, instead of writing a traditional research paper, transpose their research into a creative project that, according to

Tom Romano, "arises from research, experience, and imagination" (*Blending* x). This multigenre research project, which encourages divergent thinking, must contain an informational essay, a letter to the reader, and at least six other genres, including one visual element. Whether the student works on arctic biodiversity, tiny houses, green tourism, GMOs, environmental justice, the Great Pacific Garbage Patch, or roof gardens, the topic must be researched, analyzed, and presented with possible solutions for a global context that takes into account human beings and our physical planet. By connecting themes explored over the semester, the multigenre project stimulates new collective discussions that enhance the journey towards sustainability literacy.

Although one class alone cannot come close to educating for sustainability literacy, it can, as the model described here shows, be designed to broaden students' understanding of global perspectives and environmental awareness of cultures and bioregions. Through study and analysis of socioeconomic and ecological conditions across cultures, students become active learners who engage "with real life issues" (Stibbe 11). As we are faced with innumerable environmental and socioeconomic challenges, Edwards reminds us: "More significantly, *thriveability* embodies the innate qualities that define our humanity—our capacity for empathy, compassion, collaboration, playfulness, creativity, enthusiasm and love" (4; my emphasis). Environmental and sustainability education call for everyone to respect and preserve the natural world from further anthropogenic destruction (e.g., climate change, environmental destruction, species extinction). Because of our focus on global awareness, we as foreign-language educators must play a crucial role in nurturing the universal human qualities Edwards mentions, educating the citizens of tomorrow for sustainability literacy so that we can live to see the next generation thrive.

NOTES

1. The Danish Ministry of Education launched its educational strategy for sustainable development as part of the United Nations Decade of Education for Sustainable Development 2005–2014 (*Education for Sustainable Development: A Strategy*). In Scotland, there is a greater focus on an integrated and coherent approach to sustainable development (*Education for Sustainable Development [ESD]*). In France, a system of environmental education for sustainable development was introduced in all French schools K–12 (Ricard).
2. According to former Virginia Governor Terry McAuliffe: "Learning about our environment is a great way for children to understand important scientific concepts that will prepare them for the new [Virginia] economy" ("Governor").

3. Although prepackaged curricula that are revised every five years cannot keep up with our rapidly changing world, several intermediate French textbooks contain chapters on the environment, including *Quant à moi*, by Jeannette D. Bragger and Donald B. Rice, and *À votre tour!*, by Jean-Paul Valette and Rebecca M. Valette.
4. *A Journey in the History of Water: Struggles, Energy, Myths, Conflicts* is a multilingual tracked documentary.

APPENDIX: SAMPLE SYLLABUS FOR
FROM SOLITARY REVERIES TO TREKS ACROSS DESERTS:
THE LANDSCAPES OF FRANCOPHONE CULTURES

Summary

What do you think of when you hear the word *nature*? What is the Earth to people in Africa, the Caribbean, or Asia? How is nature imagined, and what is humanity's relation to it? Premised on these questions, this class invites students to explore the relation between humans and their environment through the study of literature, nonfiction, and films. Using an interdisciplinary and global lens, students examine interactions between human beings and the complex natural world. Because so many topics, such as art, philosophy, painting, writing, music, sculpture, gardens, agriculture, food, health, science, economics, and political science, are intrinsically linked to nature, a class focused on this theme can draw from a large variety of materials.

Readings and Films

Readings

Le dit de Tian-yi, by François Cheng; *Désert*, by Jean-Marie Gustave Le Clézio; *Pluie et vent sur Télumée Miracle*, by Simone Schwarz-Bart; *L'homme qui plantait les arbres*, by Jean Giono; *Les rêveries du promeneur solitaire*, by Jean-Jacques Rousseau.

Films

The Gleaners and I (Varda), *Food Beware: The French Organic Revolution* (Jaud), *The Last Trapper* (Vanier), *Women of the Sand* (Lobo), *Sugar Cane Alley* (Palcy), *HOME* (Arthus-Bertrand).

Assignments

"SENSE OF PLACE MAP." Students create an artistic portrayal of their relation to the world through locations in past, present, and future, considering both journeys and habitations. These maps invite students to explore how place helps construct identity and to investigate their personal relation to nature, landscapes, ecosystems and their inhabitants, and sacred spaces. For a detailed discussion of the "Sense of Place Map," see Thomashow (192–99).

REFLECTION JOURNAL. For each day's reading, film, or lecture, students write one page comprising questions for class discussion; a list of surprising or interesting things about the material; and a brief reflection on the interconnections between the reading, film, or talk and something from another class or setting. Students are encouraged to consider questions such as, What can we learn from the materials? Do they relate to sustainability? How might they change our thinking or worldview?

NATURE JOURNAL. Students use a recycled journal to write everything that comes to mind about nature. For ideas about keeping a nature journal, see Gisel.

MULTIGENRE RESEARCH PAPER. The multigenre research project is an interdisciplinary study of a particular aspect of nature and the global environment: philosophy, religion, ecofeminism, music, visual arts, food and agriculture, gardens and parks, and so on. For more information, see Romano (*Multigenre*); Langstraat.

FACILITATION OF CLASS DISCUSSIONS. When acting as facilitators, students study the readings thoroughly and prepare (1) a brief historical summary of the context and (2) a series of discussion questions or exercises to involve the group in exploring the material. They have the option to supplement the discussion with visual or oral materials to enhance understanding.

GROUP PRESENTATION. Students present a study of the geography and environmental conditions of a country related to the course materials.

LOCAL COMMUNITY AND PERSONAL RESPONSIBILITY. Students examine their carbon footprint using an online calculator ("Carbon Footprint Calculator"), take a sustainability pledge ("Hollins University") and read the Earth Charter ("Earth Charter"), design and paint a recycling bin, work five hours with volunteers in a local community garden, and participate in cooking a community dinner made with locally sourced vegetables.

WORKS CITED

Arthus-Bertrand, Yann, director. *HOME*. 2009. *YouTube*, uploaded by Singulibrium, 3 Dec. 2014, www.youtube.com/watch?v=ghkQoJoipbM. Accessed 29 Apr. 2016.

Barnes-Karol, Gwendolyn, and Maggie A. Broner. "Using Images as Springboards to Teach Cultural Perspectives in Light of the Ideals of the MLA Report." *Foreign Language Annals*, vol. 43, no. 3, 2010, pp. 422–45.

Bennett, Douglas C., et al. "An Education for the Twenty-First Century: Stewardship of the Global Commons." *Liberal Education*, vol. 98, no. 4, Fall 2012. Association of American Colleges & Universities (AAC&U), www.aacu.org/publications-research/periodicals/education-twenty-first-century-stewardship-global-commons. Accessed 3 June 2015.

Binstock, Matt. "A Survey of National Environmental Education for Sustainable Development: Laws and Policies: Lessons for Canada." Canadian Institute for Environmental Law and Policy, 2006, www.cielap.org/pdf/EE_ESDpolicy.pdf. Accessed 3 June 2015.

Borden, Richard. "Ecology and Identity." *Proceedings of the First International Ecosystems-Colloquy*, edited by Peter Borelli, Man and Space, 1986, pp. 25–41.

Bragger, Jeannette D., and Donald B. Rice. *Quant à moi: Témoignages des Français et des Francophones*. 5th ed., Heinle, 2013.

Brumberger, Eva. "Visual Literacy and the Digital Native: An Examination of the Millennial Learner." *Journal of Visual Literacy*, vol. 30, no. 1, 2011, pp. 19–46.

"Carbon Footprint Calculator." *The Nature Conservancy*, 2018, www.nature.org/greenliving/carboncalculator/. Accessed 2 June 2018.

Cheng, François. *Le dit de Tian-yi* [The River Below]. Livre de Poche, 2001.

Colette, Sidonie-Gabrielle. *Sido*. My Mother's House *and* Sido, Livre de Poche, 1990.

Dai Sijie. *Balzac et la Petite Tailleuse chinoise* [Balzac and the Little Chinese Seamstress]. Gallimard, 2001.

"The Earth Charter." *The Earth Charter Initiative*, www.earthcharter.org. Accessed 2 June 2018.

Education for Sustainable Development: A Strategy for the United Nations Decade 2005–2014. Danish Ministry of Education, Department of Higher Education and International Cooperation, 2009, www.planipolis.iiep.unesco.org/sites/planipolis/files/ressources/denmark_unsd_strategy.pdf. Accessed 4 June 2018.

Education for Sustainable Development (ESD) in the UK: Current Status, Best Practice and Opportunities for the Future. United Kingdom National Commission for UNESCO (United Nations Educational, Scientific, and Cultural Organization), Mar. 2013, www.unesco.org.uk/wp-content/uploads/2015/03/Brief-9-ESD-March-2013.pdf. Accessed 2 June 2018.

Edwards, Andrés R. *Thriving beyond Sustainability: Pathways to a Resilient Society*. New Society, 2010.

Farrell, James, J. *The Nature of College: How a New Understanding of Campus Life Can Change the World*. Milkweed Editions, 2010.

Framework for Twenty-First-Century Learning. Partnership for Twenty-First-Century Learning, 2016, www.p21.org/storage/documents/docs/P21_framework_0816.pdf. Accessed 4 June 2018.

Giono, Jean. *L'homme qui plantait les arbres* [The Man Who Planted Trees]. Reader's Digest, 1953.

Gisel, Bonnie Johanna. "Environmental Education: Keeping a Nature Journal." Sierra Club, 2002, www.vault.sierraclub.org/education/nature_journal.asp. Accessed 2 June 2018.

"Governor McAuliffe Signs Environmental Literacy Executive Order." *The Washington Sun*, www.thewashingtonsun.com/2015/04/governor-mcauliffe-signs-environmental-literacy-executive-order/. Accessed 2 June 2018.

Green Evénements, www.green-evenements.com/en. Accessed 2 June 2018.

Hickcox, Leslie K. "Personalizing Teaching through Experiential Learning." *College Teaching*, vol. 50, no. 4, 2002, pp. 123–28.

"Hollins University: Make Your Personal Sustainability Pledge." Environmental Advisory Board, hollins.qualtrics.com/jfe/form/SV_eKj8zqH7NhQi6eV. Accessed 2 June 2018.

Jaud, Jean Paul, director. *Food Beware: The French Organic Revolution*. First Run Features, 2009.

A Journey in the History of Water: Struggles, Energy, Myths, Conflicts. Directed by Terje Dale. Norwegian Broadcasting, 2001.

Kezar, Adrianna J., and Jillian Kinzie. "Examining the Ways Institutions Create Student Engagement: The Role of Mission." *Journal of College Student Development*, vol. 47, no. 2, 2006, pp. 149–72.

Korab-Karpowicz, W. Julian. "Inclusive Values and the Righteousness of Life: The Foundation of Global Solidarity." *Ethical Theory and Moral Practice*, vol. 13, no. 3, 2009, pp. 305–13.

Langstraat, Lisa. "Multigenre: An Introduction." *Writing@CSU / The Writing Studio*, Colorado State University, 1993–2018, www.writing.colostate.edu/gallery/multigenre/introduction.htm. Accessed 2 June 2018.

Le Clézio, Jean-Marie Gustave. *Désert*. Gallimard, 1985.

"Légumes moches: goûtés et approuvés!" *Intermarché*, www.intermarche.com/home/canal-intermarche/developpement-durable/legumes-moches--goutes-et-approu.html. Accessed 6 June 2015.

Lobo, Ricardo, director. *Women of the Sand*. Third World Newsreel, 2008.

Louv, Richard. *The Nature Principle: Human Restoration and the End of Nature-Deficit Disorder*. Algonquin Books of Chapel Hill, 2011.

Menzel, Peter. "Hungry Planet Family Food Portraits (Thirty-Six Images)." *Hungry Planet Family Food Portraits*, www.menzelphoto.photoshelter.com/gallery/Hungry -Planet-Family-Food-Portraits/G0000zmgWvU6SiKM/C0000k7JgEHhEq0w. Accessed 11 June 2015.

National Environmental Education Act (NEEA). Environmental Protection Agency (EPA), www.epa.gov/education/national-environmental-education-act. Accessed 18 June 2016.

Orr, David W. *Earth in Mind: On Education, Environment, and the Human Prospect.* Island Press, 1994.

Palcy, Euzhan, director. *Sugar Cane Alley.* New Yorker Video, 2004.

"Read the Standards." Common Core State Standards Initiative, www.corestandards. org/read-the-standards. Accessed 18 June 2016.

Ricard, Michel. *Education for Sustainable Development: A Strategy for the United Nations Decade 2005–2014: France: General Introduction into the School System of Environmental Education for Sustainable Development.* Comité national français de la Décennie des Nations Unies de l'Éducation pour le développement durable / Ministère de l'Écologie et du Développement durable, www. unesdoc.unesco.org/ images/0015/001533/153319.pdf. Accessed 2 June 2018.

Romano, Tom. *Blending Genre, Altering Style: Writing Multigenre Papers.* Boynton/Cook Publishers, 2000.

———. *Multigenre Research Paper Assignments.* 2006, www.users.miamioh.edu/ romanots/assignments.htm.

Rousseau, Jean-Jacques. *Les rêveries du promeneur solitaire* [Reveries of the Solitary Walker]. Gallimard, 1971.

Schwarz-Bart, Simone. *Pluie et vent sur Télumée Miracle* [The Bridge of Beyond]. Editions du Seuil, 1972.

Stibbe, Arran. *The Handbook of Sustainability Literacy: Skills for a Changing World.* Green Books, 2009.

Summary of *World-Readiness Standards for Learning Languages.* American Council on the Teaching of Foreign Languages (ACTFL), www.actfl.org/publications/ all/world-readiness-standards-learning-languages/standards-summary. Accessed 18 June 2016.

Swaffar, Janet K., and Katherine Arens. *Remapping the Foreign Language Curriculum: An Approach through Multiple Literacies.* Modern Language Association of America, 2005.

Thomashow, Mitchell. *Ecological Identity: Becoming a Reflective Environmentalist.* MIT P, 1995.

Twenty-First-Century Skills Map. American Council on the Teaching of Foreign Languages (ACTFL), www.actfl.org/sites/default/files/pdfs/21stCenturySkillsMap/ p21_worldlanguagesmap.pdf. Accessed 2 June 2018.

Valette, Jean-Paul, and Rebecca M. Valette. *À votre tour!* 2nd ed., Houghton Mifflin, 2007.

Vanier, Nicolas, director. *The Last Trapper.* Tf1 Video, 2004.

Varda, Agnès, director. *The Gleaners and I* [*Les glaneurs et la glaneuse*]. Zeitgeist Films, 2002.

World-Readiness Standards for Learning Languages. American Council on the Teaching of Foreign Languages (ACTFL), www.actfl.org/sites/default/files/publications/ standards/World-ReadinessStandardsforLearningLanguages.pdf. Accessed 4 June 2018.

Sustainability, Design Thinking, and Spanish: Unleashing Students' Agency, Empathy, and Innovation

Maggie A. Broner

How in a course about sustainability in Latin America did we end up with a rooftop garden at St. Olaf College in Minnesota? The story begins with students discovering unarticulated needs in their local community by empathizing with the reality of people living very far away. It shows how a methodology called design thinking can help students discover new knowledge, especially in foreign language programs. But, more important, it is a story about giving students agency in their own learning and encouraging them to unleash their innovative spirit by bringing their whole selves into the educational enterprise. Along the way, students learned a great deal about Latin America and their local communities and practiced Advanced and Superior Spanish functions. Together we grew a new curriculum from the realization that sustainability and foreign language should function as complementary subjects.

Sustainability is a global problem, and foreign language study promotes an understanding of global cultural narratives and cultures. We cannot solve sustainability challenges by concentrating on one culture; we have to be conversant in the narratives of multiple cultures and create dialogue among them. Students who have that intercultural competence are better positioned to be actors of change. In developing my course, I focused on Latin America as the context in which to study sustainability because of the complex interrelationships among its people, politics, and environment.

To frame the course, I drew on the methodology of design thinking for reasons of scope, pedagogical compatibility, student agency, interdisciplinarity, and creativity. Design thinking's process allows us to address so-called grand challenge questions like sustainability.

From Sustainability to Design Thinking in Foreign Languages

Environmental literacy is a key interdisciplinary subject that students should develop to succeed in work and life in the twenty-first century (*Framework* 2; MLA Teagle Foundation 2). Multiple authors have made a persuasive case for including sustainability as a topic of study through a foreign language (Eppelsheimer et al.; Melin; Ter Horst and Pearce; Prádanos). Because sustainability considers the complex interconnection of economic and environmental factors with social and cultural ones, it is a salient topic that can act as a bridge between the existing foreign language curriculum and other fields. The study of sustainability in foreign language contexts invites students to analyze cultural texts (literary and nonliterary) in connection with their other areas of specialization. This bridging is especially relevant given that most language majors tend to have a primary major in a discipline other than language (MLA Office of Research); bridging has positive effects on students' language proficiency and learning motivation (Ter Horst and Pearce 367).

In foreign language education, we extract cultural narratives from the voices and the stories we study through texts, interactions, and observations (MLA Teagle Foundation 4); thus, we are well positioned to include sustainability as part of our studies. In an increasingly globalized world, our field can help students uncover those narratives that reveal sustainable or unsustainable practices in given societies (MLA Ad Hoc Committee 4). Hence, foreign languages are in an ideal position to make a contribution to the study of sustainability beyond the confines of the language classroom.

In *The Nature of College* James Farrell reminds us of the centrality of culture in the sustainability debate: "Sustainability isn't a technical problem, it's a cultural problem, and we are that culture" (252). He notes that "we always experience nature through cultural frames, that the American eye is always connected to the American 'I,' and that Americans grow up learning certain ways of seeing nature. . . . But we've invented a 'culture of nature,' so once we're socialized, we always come to understand nature *through* culture" (4). Farrell goes on to identify some prevalent American cultural narratives and what they mean for the chance to "design" a more sustainable future based on "common sense" (256). For Farrell, sustainability should be about the "pursuit of happiness" and creating stories that lead to new narratives— a "new American dream" to help us "live happily ever after" (259–61).

Foreign language programs offer a new entry into this conversation. In a globalized world, we need to expand these new stories with narratives from other places. Foreign languages can be loci to have exactly these kinds of conversations, to unearth the cultural narratives that inform other societies and examine how they play into the creation of a wider culture of nature. Our students have been socialized to look at this culture of nature through the values of the United States. Foreign language study can widen that lens. Charlotte Melin furthermore observes that one way to "reshape" a curriculum based on sustainability is "around 'challenge questions' that organize 'problem-focused' programs of study" (116). To that end, I propose that design thinking is one framework that facilitates this curricular approach in the foreign language classroom in a particularly effective way.

Design thinking is a process-oriented methodology or set of principles used to design solutions for complex problems. For design thinkers "problems are just opportunities for design in disguise" (IDEO 16). Predicated on the belief that the future can be better (IDEO 16), design thinking approaches problems optimistically by aiming to unleash the innovator in all of us (Kelley and Kelley). This approach resonates with Farrell's assertion that sustainability is about hope and "[h]ope ends in action. Hope is not something to have, it's something to *do*" (255).

A methodology originated in the world of product design, design thinking has slowly entered the world of education. The design process typically starts with a challenge question and progresses through a series of overlapping phases: discovery, interpretation, ideation, experimentation, and evolution.[1] These phases are sequenced to advance stepwise from identifying the problem (or challenge question) to developing a solution.

When used as a framework for foreign language education, design thinking offers a principled, step-by-step, organic structure for class instruction that can foster the development of Advanced-level proficiency through a variety of modes of communication; promote student agency and engagement; advance "collaborative, team-based, cross-disciplinary" work (Curedale 13); and nurture "creative confidence" (Kelley and Kelley 1). Design thinking's phases—discovery, interpretation, ideation, experimentation, and evolution—move from divergent thinking (brainstorming) to convergent thinking (focusing on a limited set of ideas that merit further exploration) in a cycle that is recursive and thus compatible with second language acquisition best practices recommendations.

Phased instruction corresponds as well to what occurs at the Advanced and Superior proficiency levels of foreign language acquisition (*ACTFL Proficiency Guidelines* 5–6). Each design thinking phase requires a particular set of tasks that create natural contexts for each level's function. In carrying out the design challenge—which utilizes storytelling in various forms—students use, learn, and practice the language used for narration and description in different time frames, instead of using the artificial contexts that instructors are sometimes forced to create for particular language functions. Similarly, they use varied oral and written modes: from conducting interviews to presenting information, creating a *download*, participating in brainstorms, or delivering a *pitch*.[2] Because these functions and modes fit together neatly and naturally, students understand why we ask them to carry out the tasks. The undertakings require collaborative interdisciplinary work, and the interpretation phase additionally requires that students tap into the information they have gleaned from interviews during the discovery phase and multiple additional sources, including their other majors. Asking learners to be their whole selves in the foreign language classroom and to contribute their entire experience and knowledge gives students agency. This holistic integration of language modes and functions, combined with student agency, is a powerful argument for design thinking as a principled way to deploy current and experimental pedagogies of many kinds.

At its core, design thinking is about developing agency and empathy for people and their circumstances; thus, we can use it to construct a more human-centered curriculum. Its central tenet of empathy resonates with the values of foreign language education (Kramsch; MLA Ad Hoc Committee; MLA Teagle Foundation; Piccardo and Aden): "Design thinking combines empathy for people and their contexts with the tools to discover insight" (Curedale 13; see also Brown; Puccio and Cabra 162). In other words, it is predicated on "empathy as a way of knowing" (Farrell 11).

Foreign language curricula tend to be organized around texts (literary and nonliterary) as cultural objects of study that provide students with a window into the worldviews and mind-sets of other people. Typically, teachers select static texts, knowing what we want our students to learn from the outset. In other words, as teachers, we tend to control the content, the questions, and the answers. Design thinking offers a different paradigm: the cocreation of new knowledge. Instead of focusing on text-centered instruction, design thinking is human-centered because it requires that we deal with people and their stories to discover new knowledge. It begins with and prioritizes personal stories and their context as key evidence; all other texts become tributaries. Relying on real-time narratives means teachers must be willing to relinquish some control over the content, but that change allows us a principled way to enlarge the scope of our teaching to embrace new content as we unearth unarticulated or "unmet needs" (Brown 76), especially in the stories we gather from the people we interview.

When the focus becomes people and their stories, students are put at the helm of the learning process and gain agency as they discover, gather, and process evidence. Such agency is fundamental if we are to engage in a sustainability education that goes from understanding to action (Farrell 254–56). Teachers can still provide the topic, the initial challenge, the structure for the design thinking process, the methods of discovery, and the initial background texts, but they need to welcome changes to the syllabus as students start to gain new insights from other sources of inspiration.

Such interactive learning requires flexibility to align our expected learning outcomes with the discovery process. By following the design thinking process, students learn about a topic or issue that affects real people, but, more meaningfully, they propose possible solutions that can be carried out of the classroom and into environments they care about. Students become innovators who propose solutions in an incremental, nonlinear fashion that builds and evolves through testing along the way.[3] In the end, they design better solutions and experience more meaningful and engaged learning, all in Spanish. They are pushed to develop linguistic skills that go beyond those that are traditionally tied to the Advanced level, such as description, narration, compare and contrast (*ACTFL Proficiency Guidelines* 5). As we give students more incentive to use the language functions needed for real-life oral interactions, they learn to plan, negotiate, compromise, make comparisons, include others, build consensus, collaborate, persuade, and propose solutions, all in the target language.

Design Thinking in Action:
Putting It All Together

For the pilot class on sustainability in Spanish, I identified a topic that would bridge our current offerings and students' changing areas of interest, especially STEM (see appendix 1 for a summary of phases, activities, and texts). My work has long been interdisciplinary; thus I recognized in design thinking a framing structure and synthesis process that I had long been seeking to teach sustainability, promote collaborative work, design a course around challenge questions, unleash creativity and innovation, and ultimately challenge disciplinary silos. In the twenty-first century, when "narrow learning is not enough" (*College Learning* 15), design thinking guides wide learning. Additionally, I wanted to create a course that focused on Latin America and its complex relation with food systems, including an exploration of agricultural practices, land rights, labor relations, soil exploitation, unsustainable production practices, and national and international commerce. This intersectionality provides a rich cultural, political, and environmental context for studying food sustainability.

The course I created was for the four-week intensive January term at St. Olaf College, a small four-year liberal arts college. The class offers credit in oral communication (a requirement in the general education curriculum), in environmental studies, and as an elective for the Spanish major, where completion of a fifth-semester Spanish course is a prerequisite. Unlike traditional conversation courses that concentrate on speaking and privilege an instrumental focus, the course's dual emphasis is on intellectual development as well as Advanced language proficiency. It emphasizes both content and critical thinking by asking students to engage with contemporary issues through a variety of media (aural, visual, and written).

The instructional architecture was presented in the first elements students encountered: an introduction, followed by the design challenge or central question (IDEO 19) and formation of design teams. We launched this course with the design challenge: How might we enable more sustainable practices in food production in Latin America? Our starting point was to interview Latin Americans involved in food-production systems and to develop empathy for their unarticulated needs. As we immersed ourselves in the stories collected from our interviews and triangulated these with information from lectures and a variety of texts, we came face-to-face with the challenges of trying to tackle such a global question when the class desired a tangible, local result, so we modified our central question to the following: How might lessons from sustainable or unsustainable food practices in Latin America influence sustainability practices on campus?

For the duration of the course, students were organized into five four-person interdisciplinary teams, selected for their diverse perspectives. Design thinking emphasizes that the best teams are those with people who have deep knowledge in one or two areas as well as breadth of knowledge in additional areas, sometimes called "T-shaped" individuals (Brown 27; *College Learning* 15–16). To solve our challenge, we were going to have to think as psychologists, biologists, philosophers, chemists, mathematicians, artists, and Spanish learners developing the intercultural competence to access and interpret cultural information through the actual voices of people affected by the issues under study.

Before we launched into our design challenge, students needed to learn something about design thinking per se. We started with a quick-start workshop to familiarize students with the process of design thinking, that is, its phases and methods. There are several classic examples used to introduce the methodology, ranging from reinventing the gift-giving experience to redesigning a backpack to the question I chose, "How might we redesign the driving experience?" Using this exercise, we walked through the phases and methods of the innovation cycle in a short period of time. This activity familiarizes students with the design process itself. The workshop demonstrated to participants that in spite of the appearance of a messy process—ideas written on small pieces of paper taped to walls, the chaotic interactions of brainstorming sessions, detours in the lesson plan, and the like—design thinking in reality follows a well-defined plan. This initial workshop laid the foundation for later work, generated excitement for the task ahead, and served as an initial bonding experience for participants. Afterward we moved into the five phases of design thinking, referred to using the nomenclature of *Design Thinking for Educators* (IDEO 13): discovery, interpretation, ideation, experimentation, and evolution.

The discovery phase of the course, where students are encouraged to develop empathy for people and situations affected by a central question (called the design challenge), requires divergent thinking and asks students to adopt an expansive mind-set, rather than a forced solution (IDEO 15). On their way to exploring this challenge, students immersed themselves in multimodal sources, mostly in Spanish: interviews, cultural readings, newspaper texts, a movie, and a novel. Selected English sources were discussed in Spanish; these included interviews and readings on sustainability (see appendix 2). In addition, sustainability experts in chemistry, biology, and art history gave presentations, and we carried out two campus field trips: one visited food services and another did a sustainability tour of our institution.

To understand the current debates about food in society, we needed to develop a basic understanding of the Latin American historical context that underlies contemporary conversations. From a historic point of view, and to counteract the presentism prevalent in our field (Farrell 16; Kramsch 307; Melin 105),[4] it was important to understand the symbiotic relation that indigenous people had (and continue to have) with *la Pacha Mama* ("Mother Earth"). In particular, we focused on the repercussions of the Spanish conquest and other historical periods on the environment. We also explored *Sumak Kawsay*,[5] a notion often translated in Spanish as *el buen vivir* ("good living"; Gudynas 442; Huanacuni Mamani 2; Prádanos 339; Radcliffe 240), and how it could help us imagine a new way to look at sustainability in foreign language classes (see Prádanos).

Largely driven by student interests, our discussions touched on such matters as ethanol production (its influence on the price of corn, a food staple with ancestral cultural ties for millions of Latin Americans); the banana industry (its exploitive labor practices, as well as repercussions on environment, health, biological diversity, and political conflicts); the cultivation and export of coffee (its effects on soil, biodiversity, and the *cultivadores* ["coffee growers"]); beef production (its environmental footprint); and production of quinoa from the Andes. Although students came into the class with some background understanding of these topics, as they delved into them more deeply, they were most affected by the voices of the people they interviewed. For example, students were surprised about what they learned from interviewees regarding quinoa. One person, a vegan from the United States who promoted eating and buying local food, was willing to buy protein-rich imported quinoa due to a conviction that a vegan lifestyle was inherently more ethical and sustainable than other choices. Because my students shared the interviewee's cultural narrative, they did not question it during the discovery phase. During the interpretation phase, however, students compared this view with other voices (gathered from interviews and readings) and began to realize that the overharvesting of quinoa for export has a detrimental effect, not only on the environment but also on the communities that have lived on this grain for centuries—so much so that people in Andean communities are now eating rice instead because it is less expensive (Bazile et al. 454). This realization, which led to realignment of diverse real-time narratives, illustrates how the design process can produce complexity and critical thinking, especially when interviews are incorporated.

As a central feature of the discovery phase, indeed of the entire course curriculum, interviews as texts became an important means for students to "learn from experts and from users" (IDEO 34). To address sustainability meaningfully, we must consider how it affects *users*, that is, real people. By listening to people's stories, we empathize with them and their circumstances. Through stories we also discover unarticulated needs and overlooked problems; in other words, through narrative and language we realize the need for change.

For such interviews, it is important to include a variety of interviewees, from *extreme users* (experts or people directly affected) to complete novices who have no experience with the topic (Curedale 238; IDEO 29). This range encourages a diversity of viewpoints; our extreme users included a vegetarian student from Latin America, a vegan student from the United States, a professor of social science and agriculture in Latin America, a hog farmer from Mexico, and a community organizer from Latin America. Each interview was carried out by a pair of students: one to ask questions and the other to take notes. Some interviews were conducted face-to-face, whereas others took place on the phone or by *Skype*. Eleven of the interviews were carried out in Spanish, nine in English.

Once students finished their interviews, each team compiled interview data onto Post-it notes (one idea per note) and placed these on a poster board as part of the *download* step of the discovery phase, a process intended to highlight important information and memorable quotations from the interviews. In addition to memorable excerpts, posters included notes with a pseudonym for and basic information about the interviewee, important ideas, and translations (when required). The result was a display that told the story of each participant; each interview team then presented orally in

Spanish, transitioning us into the interpretation phase. As we moved from the discovery to the interpretation phase, all posters were presented on the same day in order to immerse course participants in the data. To explain who interviewees were, tell their stories, and convey empathy, students needed to narrate in all present and past time frames.

Storytelling is the heart of the interpretation phase, which is when we synthesize, discover meaning, and turn discoveries into a clear path for action (IDEO 39). Interpretation, in design thinking, is a physical activity. In small groups, students walked around the posters, now displayed in stations, and talked about the findings as they went. They looked for patterns that emerged from the data and picked up the relevant Post-it notes and regrouped them. Essentially, the original posters were deconstructed and remade into new ones. By the end of this activity, the whole class had discovered new patterns worthy of additional exploration or "areas of opportunity" (IDEO 19).

For example, as students circulated, they discovered the repercussions of the increased demand for quinoa on the Andean indigenous communities that have been growing quinoa for millennia and how this demand negatively affected the soil. These relationships had not been apparent in the readings or presentations up to that point. When Andean indigenous stories were processed alongside the story told by the vegan interviewee (a story students had previously accepted unquestioningly), they now could see that consumers who believe it is better to buy organic, vegan, and local food do not always understand the real cost of food. These seemingly benign choices made by food-conscious individuals seem to illustrate the behavior Farrell refers to as those "no big deal" decisions frequently encountered in college life that end up having a negative influence on the environment and the communities affected by our actions (30). Similarly, students were challenged in their assumptions about the desirability of organic, local, and exported products. These findings emerged as "areas of opportunity" that prompted us to delve deeper into the literature about the cultivation of quinoa. That is, we looped back into the discovery phase to pick up more contextual information about quinoa in a recursive process.

As students framed these emergent questions, making sense of the information pieces while discovering areas of opportunity and possible unmet needs, they started seeing themselves as *producers* of knowledge (exercising their agency in the process) and not just as *recipients*. At this point we moved into the ideation phase, using "How might we . . ." questions for brainstorming.

During brainstorming, I invited students to think creatively, because in this phase we are not interested in coming up with the so-called right idea. Rather, we want to generate lots of ideas using rules for brainstorming that encourage participation by all because "[if] you want a good idea, start with many" (Kelley and Kelley 78).[6] Since feasibility is not an issue in this phase of the design thinking process, "wild" ideas are encouraged (IDEO 51). Students worked in four-person teams, each with a designated moderator, and spent fifteen minutes developing questions like the following: How might we educate communities on the difference between sustainable and healthy? How might we increase awareness of the origin and the real cost of food? How might we promote sustainable individual eating habits? Students wrote down one idea on a Post-it note, read the idea out loud, and then stuck the note on the wall. All students participated in the exercise, since it is set up to give all students a chance to offer ideas. The session moved fast. Moderators kept students on task and reminded teammates of the brainstorming rules. The entire activity was carried out in Spanish.

From the over three hundred ideas generated, we selected ten to experiment with in the next phase. The value of this brainstorming process lies in students' discovery that an underlying issue is something that demands their own agency and empathy (e.g., for quinoa farmers and consumers). Once this happened, they owned the call to find ways to educate themselves and others about the real cost of food and, as one student said, they "were transformed by it." We were ready to begin the experimentation phase.

In the experimentation phase, participants choose an idea and bring it to life by transforming it into action (IDEO 57). The best method is to build a tangible model or prototype of the idea to learn more about the idea itself as well as its feasibility and potential for development (IDEO 57). In Tim Brown's words, in this phase we are "building to think and building to learn" (87). Prototyping is a key feature of the experimentation phase. Prototypes are not intended to be finished solutions; rather they are *low resolution* versions of ideas (such as a sketch, a mock-up built with clay, or a skit) that can be quickly made and shared with others in order to learn from feedback. Seeking feedback with low-resolution prototypes allows students to fail early and then modify, improve, or even discard solutions before spending too many resources or too much emotional energy on them

(Brown 17; Kelley and Kelley 23). This process can make our generally risk-averse students uncomfortable, but the exercise liberates them and gives them the useful life skills of resilience and adaptability.

Many ideas surfaced in the interpretation phase, when out of empathy for quinoa farmers and consumers students posed the question "How might we incorporate local food so that it is a viable and ethical option?" Then one team began building a prototype rooftop garden using cardboard as the roof and cupcake liners as the planters. This simple model allowed the team to present their idea to other class members, gather feedback, and build a second prototype. The second version incorporated feedback and transformed into an aromatic rooftop herb garden, as students realized they could not grow quinoa on the roofs of St. Olaf but could produce herbs for use by our food service and students. The second prototype was shown both to other students and to individuals who might eventually be in charge of implementing such a change. Given the time constraints of our January term, the students carried out only two prototypes for their ideas. Because part of our design challenge was to apply our findings from the discovery, interpretation, ideation, and experimentation phases to our campus, the prototypes reflected practical innovations to make our community more sustainable.

As we moved into the final evolution phase of the design thinking process, we pitched our idea to potential stakeholders, meaning that course participants had to determine their audience and what arguments would get traction for their ideas (IDEO 72). Because the class did not have time to make the rooftop garden idea actually happen, this phase was an exercise in imagination. Still, it allowed students to reflect on the process that led them to the design of the garden, as we imagined a future in which our idea solved a real sustainability problem that might positively affect our interviewees. Students critically evaluated their solution and conducted a needs analysis. To do so, they returned to the initial design challenge and considered how the solution they devised spoke to it. After completing this needs analysis, they then prepared a final *pitch*, or presentation, for a potential audience of stakeholders. For the pitch, course participants retold the story of the process and project. This cumulative final assignment reinforced their training in the design thinking method, because course participants had to walk the rest of the students through every phase—from the reasoning behind the idea, the evidence that came from the interviews and the secondary texts, and the lessons learned during experimentation to the pitch that looked at what it would take to implement the idea and what would constitute success. To conclude the course, then, we carried out a group reflection about the process and its fitness for learning about sustainability, especially the soft skills acquired and how these abilities could translate to life outside college.

Why Design Thinking in the Foreign Languages?

A number of process-oriented methodologies, such as STEM to STEAM (Bybee) and project-based learning (Markham), have been proposed and could be used to explore issues related to sustainability challenges. Design thinking, however, is uniquely attractive as a methodology because when we become *design thinkers* (Kelley and Kelley), we create or dream solutions to difficult questions by developing empathy for the problem and the people affected by it. We want to know the stories of these people in order to discover their unarticulated needs.

As students develop transcultural competence, crucial to the mission of foreign language learning, they "see the world through the eyes of others" (MLA Ad Hoc Committee 2) and learn to "to reflect on the world and themselves" (MLA Ad Hoc Committee 4). We recognize, as did the authors of the Teagle report, that "the global economy and our ethnically diverse society need citizens who understand the languages, traditions, and histories of other cultures as well as their own" (MLA Teagle Foundation 4). With its emphasis on the development of empathy, design thinking offers a sound framework for studying sustainability in a foreign language context.

Design thinking provides a feasible methodology that answers Melin's call for process-oriented approaches to studying sustainability in the foreign languages, aligns with the core of empathy that the MLA Ad Hoc Committee report asserts for foreign language education, and promotes Advanced-level language functions and communication modes. Considering the added bonuses of natural contexts in which to teach functions and modes and the high levels of student agency fostered, the design thinking framework is not only suitable but also ideal. Furthermore, the methodology provides a natural context for Advanced and Superior oral Spanish functions through tasks that require different communication modes (interpersonal, interpretive, and presentational), translation, and effective group and interdisciplinary work.

The course described in this essay allowed us, the participants, to explore sustainability from a global and local perspective. For Farrell, the only way we can hope for an "ecological revolution" is to "choose to *live* it where we are" (261). Design thinking afforded us an effective, principled way to pursue a challenge question and produce local solutions based on the knowledge acquired during the exploration and discovery phases from Latin America.

Ultimately, a particularly valuable outcome of the course was that students unearthed and problematized cultural assumptions that they would not have challenged otherwise. They also realized that as a result of their own agency, they felt the call to action envisioned by Farrell as "transforming environmentalism into their everyday lives, creating a sort of *in*vironmentalism as an integral element of who we are and what we do" (260). The cultural texts, insights from interviews, observations, lectures from outside experts, and structured activities used in the design thinking approach formed the basis for a deeper comprehension of the challenge. Although carried out in Spanish in this course, the principles are transferrable to other languages, other levels, and many other topic areas.

As we think about the future of the liberal arts education, such a class offers an experimental model that allows us to bring students together for interdisciplinary work, combined with a process that encourages teamwork, empathy, creativity, adaptability, and innovation—all skills demanded of our students as they enter the workplace. In this course foreign languages were a catalyst for educational change. Invited to learn content by taking ownership of texts and activities, students became actors in the creation of new sustainability stories (Stibbe 13). Awakening from a state of unconsciousness, they began to act conscientiously in their own community (Farrell 30). As Farrell wisely observed, education of this kind has a powerful effect on the future, because "[s]tudents always make history, but now they have the opportunity to make it by design" (Farrell 260).

NOTES

I'd like to thank my students for trusting that the process of design thinking with the topic of sustainability was a worthy adventure. I also deeply thank the late Jim Farrell and my colleagues in environmental studies for their willingness to share their expertise and help me become more conversant in the field. I am indebted to Bleco Rubinstein and Machu Araoz for introducing me to design thinking and to Irve Dell for teaching me how to use it. Thanks to Gwendolyn Barnes-Karol and our unending dialogue about pedagogical innovation in the foreign language classroom, and to Su Smallen and Wendy Allen, who provided helpful comments to earlier versions of this essay.

1. For ease of understanding, I use terms adapted from *Design Thinking for Educators* (IDEO). Brown uses "Inspiration, [interpretation,] Ideation, Action" (16).
2. I include descriptions for "download" and "pitch" later in this paper. See IDEO (51) for tips on brainstorming. For interviews, I suggest the following: Assign pairs of students to do two interviews (at least one in Spanish). Students find interview subjects and set up meetings. The instructor provides an e-mail introduction explaining the project assignment and requests interviewee participation. Ideally, all interviews could be lined up in advance. Learning how to ask good open-ended questions using standard anthropology interview techniques helps uncover people's underlying unarticulated needs; the instructor provides tips on how to carry out good interviews, and students develop some questions as a group. Before the interview, teams can take turns practicing interviewing techniques. Tips for good interviews include the following: identify topics; prepare opening remarks and a list of questions; develop open-ended questions (avoid leading questions and don't jump to conclusions); ask for the whole story and avoid yes-no questions; empathize and listen carefully; be on the lookout for good quotations (see IDEO 31).
3. See the d.school manifesto (dschool.stanford.edu/resources/george-kembels -dschool-operators-handbook).
4. To strike a balance and avoid the presentism common in foreign language courses (Melin 105 ; Kramsch 307; Farrell 16), I included readings on the culture and civilization of Latin America and a novel, in addition to contemporary expository sources.
5. This worldview, adopted by some Andean countries rooted on an indigenous world vision (*cosmovisión*), proposes development that is culture- and community-centric and environmentally balanced (Gudynas 442; Radcliffe 240).
6. See also the rules for brainstorming presented in *Design Thinking for Educators* (IDEO 51).

APPENDIX 1: DESIGN THINKING PHASES,
KEY ACTIVITIES, AND SAMPLE TEXTS

Design thinking phase	Key activities	Sample texts (full citations in appendix 2)
Introduction to design thinking	"Quick-start workshop" "Ready, set, design" (alternative introduction to method)	IDEO, *Design Thinking for Educators* Cooper-Hewitt, "Ready, Set, Design"
Formulate challenge question	Construct inspiration board on sustainability (before unveiling challenge question) Select interdisciplinary teams	Ask students to bring 4–5 examples of items that illustrate sustainability Have students fill out background and interest questionnaire before the first day of class to aid in selection of teams

(continued)

Design thinking phase	Key activities	Sample texts (full citations in appendix 2)
Discovery (because the process is recursive, texts will be introduced as students discover themes and areas of opportunities)	Read background texts on culture, civilization, and sustainability Learn from observations (e.g., field trips) Learn from experts Refine challenge question Carry out interviews (requires selection of users and setup of calls or face-to-face interviews) Take notes on interviews (look for good quotations) Take notes on presentations (look for good quotations) *Download* each interview on Post-it notes and create a poster for each user Tell the *story* of each *user* to the class (storytelling)	General readings on oral registers (Azevedo) Introduction of ACTFL proficiency levels General readings on culture and civilization of Latin America (Fox) Selected general readings on sustainability (e.g., Brundtland et al.; García Mira and Vega Marcote; Karl-Henrik et al.; Ortíz de Mendivil; Gallopín) *Sumak Kawsay* "Buen Vivir" (e.g., "República de Bolivia Constitución"; Grupo Fénix; Gudynas; Huanacuni Mamani; Hombres de Maíz; Radcliffe) Presentations from experts Field trips (e.g., campus, food services, community) Movie *También la lluvia* (directed by Icíar Bollaín)
Interpretation	Analyze data (look for patterns and interesting quotations from users and background work) Discover areas of opportunities Formulate "How might we" questions	Readings on food systems (Barruti; Camacho Zandoval; *MasAgro*; McNeill; Svampa) Readings on quinoa (Bazile et al; "Orígenes" [FAO]; Jacobsen) Selections from Galeano
Ideation	Brainstorm Select ideas (to move to experimentation phase)	Rules for brainstorming Novel *La loca de Gandoca* by Anacristina Rossi Selections from *The Nature of College* by James Farrell Selections from Carta Encíclica (Encyclical Letter) by Pope Francis
Experimentation	Build prototype Seek feedback Rebuild Do needs analysis (to help decide audience for the pitch)	This phase is hands-on. Students need access to materials to build their prototypes (e.g., cardboard, paper cups, clips, glue, foil, pipe cleaners, tape, color markers, construction paper, play dough, etc.)
Evolution	Make pitch (final project presentation)	Evidence from interviews, observations, prototypes, and texts to support pitch

APPENDIX 2: SUSTAINABILITY IN LATIN AMERICA

Course Description

Sustainability is one of the most pressing current issues facing the Spanish-speaking world. Defined as "development which meets the needs of current generations without compromising the ability of future generations to meet their own needs" (Brundtland et al.), this course explores how sustainability presents challenges and opportunities for Latin America in the twenty-first century. Through various cultural texts (literary and nonliterary) as well as through the voices of different stakeholders (users), this course aims to develop general sustainability literacy—the ability to unearth the cultural narratives embedded in the different discourses about sustainability—and develop empathy for people and places affected by societal practices and policies. In addition, the course uses a process-based approach (design thinking) to explore how lessons learned about sustainability (or lack thereof) from Latin America can help create change in students' own communities. This class is an immersion experience in Spanish. Students work in interdisciplinary teams.

Course Objectives

Students will

develop a current panoramic view of the culture and civilization of Latin America with particular emphasis on sustainability;

develop general sustainability literacy;

identify, analyze, and comment on the multiple perspectives and stories that emerge in diverse texts (literary and nonliterary) and from the voices of real people;

critically reflect on Latin American and American perspectives on issues related to sustainability;

use the appropriate oral language, register, and discursive conventions to comment on, analyze, and present a variety of literary and nonliterary texts;

be introduced to a process-based methodology known as design thinking in order to promote collaborative, creative, and interdisciplinary work through training in its tools and methods;

become agents of their own learning by changing the focus of the course content as they interact with real-time narratives and other texts, establish evidence, and learn from experimentation. In doing so, students will be invited to design novel solutions.

Texts and Data Sources

Interviews of people in Latin America and in the United States involved in food production, interested in food, or affected by food

Readings on culture and civilization to contextualize stories from the interviews and information from other texts

ACTFL proficiency guidelines

Readings about sustainability in general and about Latin America in particular

Articles on sustainability from current Latin American and Spanish newspapers and other media outlets

También la lluvia, film directed by Icíar Bollaín

La loca de Gandoca, novel by Anacristina Rossi

Presentations from experts in different fields (art, chemistry, economics, biology, etc.)

Key Assignments with Oral Components

Design challenge

Other oral communication assessment

"Sed de saber" ("Thirst for Knowledge") TED-style talk on sustainability connected to student interest (outside of Spanish) and Latin America

"Cuando me topo con la sostenibilidad" ("When I Bump into Sustainability") (photographic activity with "artist statement" and presentation; adapted from an activity designed by David Van Wyllen [personal communication with Van Wyllen])

Mural of *La loca de Gandoca* (visual representation of novel)

"Cumbre de la sostenibilidad" ("Sustainability Summit")

Key Course Texts

ACTFL Proficiency Guidelines 2012. American Council on the Teaching of Foreign Languages (ACTFL), 2012, www.actfl.org/sites/default/files/pdfs/public/ACTFLProficiencyGuidelines2012_FINAL.pdf.

Azevedo, Milton. "Variación contextual." *Introducción a la lingüística española*, 3rd ed., Wiley, 2009, pp. 316–45.

Barruti, Soledad. *Mal comidos: Cómo la industria alimentaria Argentina nos está matando*. Espejo de la Argentina Planeta, 2013.

Bazile, Didier, et al., editors. *Estado del arte de la quinua en el mundo en 2013*. Food and Agriculture Organization of the United Nations (FAO) / Centre de Coopération Internationale en Recherche Agronomique pour le Développement (CIRAD), 2014, www.fao.org/3/a-i4042s.pdf.

Brundtland, Gro, et al. *Report of the World Commission on Environment and Development: Our Common Future*. United Nations, 1987, www.un-documents.net/our-common-future.pdf. Accessed 19 May 2015.

Camacho Zandoval, Ana Cristina. "Café Sostenible, Bien Cotizado." *El Financiero*, 2011. Accessed 6 Jan. 2014.

Carta Encíclica *Laudato Si'* del Santo Padre Francisco sobre el cuidado de la casa común. La Santa Sede ["the Holy See"], www.fao.org/3/a-i5461b.pdf. Accessed 4 Aug. 2017.

Farrell, James. *The Nature of College: How a New Understanding of Campus Life Can Change the World*. Milkweed Editions, 2010.

Fox, Arturo. *Latinoamérica: Presente y pasado*. 4th ed., Pearson Education, 2011.

Galeano, Eduardo. *Úselo y tírelo: El mundo visto desde una ecología latinoamericana*. Grupo Editorial Planeta, 1994.

Gallopín, Gilberto. "La sostenibilidad ambiental del desarrollo en Argentina: tres futuros." *Medio ambiente y desarrollo*, vol. 91, Oct. 2004, archivo.cepal .org/pdfs/2004/S049721.pdf. Accessed 20 Dec. 2013.

García Mira, Ricardo, and Pedro Vega Marcote. *Sostenibilidad, valores y cultura ambiental*. Ediciones Pirámide, 2009.

Grupo Fénix. Grupo Fénix, www.grupofenix.org/grupo-fenix/. Accessed 7 July 2015.

Gudynas, Eduardo. "*Buen Vivir*: Today's Tomorrow." *Development*, vol. 54, no. 4, 2011, pp. 441–47. *Springer Link*, link.springer.com/article/10.1057/ dev.2011.86. Accessed 20 Jan. 2015.

Hombres de Maíz. 2014, hombresdemaiz.com.mx/. Accessed 7 June 2015.

Huanacuni Mamani, Fernando. *Vivir Bien / Buen Vivir: Filosofía, políticas, estrategias y experiencias regionals andinas*. Coordinadora Andina de Organizaciones Indígenas (CAOI), 2010. *Scribd*, www.scribd.com/ document/73331286/Huanacuni-Vivir-Bien. Accessed 15 Dec. 2014.

IDEO. *Design Thinking for Educators*. 2nd ed., Apr. 2013, designthinkingfor educators.com/toolkit/.

Jacobsen, Sven Erik. "La producción de quinua en el sur de Bolivia: Del éxito económico al desastre ambiental." *Agricultures*, Dec. 2012, www .agriculturesnetwork.org/magazines/latin-america/desertificacion/ la-produccion-de-quinua-en-el-sur-de-bolivia. Accessed Jan. 4, 2014.

Karl-Henrik, Robèrt, et al. *Manual de sostenibilidad: Planeando estratégicamente para la sostenibilidad*. El Instituto de Tecnología de Blekinge, 2012.

MasAgro: Modernización sustentable de la agricultura tradicional. Estados Unidos de México, Secretaría de Agricultura, Ganadería, Desarrollo Rural, Pesca y Alimentación, 2 Jan. 2014, masagro.mx/index.php/es/. Accessed 6 June 2015.

McNeill, William H. "How the Potato Changed the World's History." *Food: Nature and Culture*, vol. 66, no. 1, 1999, pp. 67–83.

"Orígenes e historia." *Quinua 2013 Año Internacional*, Food and Agriculture Organization of the United Nations (FAO), 2013, www.fao.org/quinoa -2013/what-is-quinoa/origin-and-history/es/. Accessed 5 Jan. 2014.

Ortíz de Mendivil, Enrique. *Educación ambiental para la sostenibilidad: El medio ambiente y su relación con la ecobionomía y la sostenibilidad*. Instituto Mediterráneo Publicaciones, 2013.

Radcliffe, Sarah A. "Development for a Postneoliberal Era? *Sumak Kawsay*, Living Well and the Limits to Decolonisation in Ecuador." *Geoforum*, vol. 43, 2012, pp. 240–49.

"Ready, Set, Design." Cooper-Hewitt, 2011, www.cooperhewitt.org/2011/09/ 09/ready-set-design/. Accessed 20 Dec. 2013.

"República de Bolivia Constitución política del estado." República de Bolivia, 2009, www.ftierra.org/index.php/component/attachments/download/6. Accessed 3 Aug. 2017.

Rossi, Anacristina. *La loca de Gandoca*. Legado, 2009.

Svampa, Maristella. "Consenso de los commodities y lenguajes de valoración en América Latina." *Nueva Sociedad*, vol. 244, Mar.-Apr. 2013, pp. 30–46.

También la lluvia. Directed by Icíar Bollaín, screenplay by Paul Laverty, performances by Luis Tosar, Gael García Bernal, Juan Carlos Aduviri, AXN et al., 2010.

WORKS CITED

ACTFL Proficiency Guidelines 2012. American Council on the Teaching of Foreign Languages (ACTFL), 2012, www.actfl.org/sites/default/files/pdfs/public/ACTFL ProficiencyGuidelines2012_FINAL.pdf. Accessed 20 July 2015.

Bazile, Didier, et al., editors. *Estado del arte de la quinua en el mundo en 2013*. Food and Agriculture Organization of the United Nations (FAO) / Centre de Coopération Internationale en Recherche Agronomique pour le Développement (CIRAD), 2014.

Brown, Tim. *Change by Design*. Harper Business, 2009.

Brundtland, Gro, et al. *Report of the World Commission on Environment and Development: Our Common Future*. American Association for the Advancement of Science (AAAS), 1987, www.un-documents.net/our-common-future.pdf. Accessed 19 May 2015.

Bybee, Rodger. "What is STEM Education?" *Science*, vol. 27, 2010, p. 996, science .sciencemag.org/content/sci/329/5995/996.full.pdf. Accessed 28 April 2015.

College Learning for the New Global Century. Association of American Colleges & Universities (AAC&U), 2007, www.aacu.org/sites/default/files/files/LEAP/Global Century_final.pdf. Accessed 5 May 2015.

Curedale, Robert. *Design Thinking: Process and Methods Manual*. Design Community College, 2013.

Eppelsheimer, Natalie, et al. "Claiming the Language Ecotone: Translinguality, Resilience, and the Environmental Humanities." *Resilience: A Journal of the Environmental Humanities*, vol. 1, no. 3, 2014, pp. 54–68. *JSTOR*, www.jstor.org/stable/10 .5250/resilience.1.3.005?&seq=1#page_scan_tab_contents. Accessed Nov. 2015.

Farrell, James. *The Nature of College: How a New Understanding of Campus Life Can Change the World*. Milkweed Editions, 2010.

Framework for Twenty-First-Century Learning. Partnership for Twenty-First-Century Learning, 2016, www.p21.org/our-work/p21-framework. Accessed 15 May 2015.

Gudynas, Eduardo. "*Buen Vivir*: Today's Tomorrow." *Development*, vol. 54, no. 4, 2011, pp. 441–47. *Springer Link*, link.springer.com/article/10.1057/dev.2011.86. Accessed 20 Jan. 2015.

Huanacuni Mamani, Fernando. *Vivir Bien / Buen Vivir: Filosofía, políticas, estrategias y experiencias regionals andinas*. Coordinadora Andina de Organizaciones Indígenas (CAOI), 2010. *Scribd*, www.scribd.com/doc/64246135/Buen-Vivir-Fernando -Hunacuni-Mamani. Accessed 15 Dec. 2014.

IDEO. *Design Thinking for Educators*. 2nd ed., Apr. 2013, designthinkingforeducators .com/toolkit/. Accessed 20 June 2013.

Kelley, Tom, and David Kelley. *Creative Confidence: Unleashing the Creative Potential within Us All*. Crown Business, 2013.

Kramsch, Claire. "Teaching Foreign Languages in an Era of Globalization: Introduction." *The Modern Language Journal*, vol. 98, no. 1, 2014, pp. 296–311.

Markham, Thom. "Project Based Learning." *Teacher Librarian*, vol. 39, no. 2, 2011, pp. 38–42.

Melin, Charlotte. "Program Sustainability through Interdisciplinary Networking: On Connecting Foreign Language Programs with Sustainability Studies and Other Fields." *Transforming Postsecondary Foreign Language Teaching in the United States,* edited by Janet Swaffar and Per Urlaub, Springer, 2014, pp. 103–22.

MLA Ad Hoc Committee on Foreign Languages. "Foreign Languages and Higher Education: New Structures for a Changed World." *Profession,* 2007, pp. 234–45. Modern Language Association of America, 2007, www.mla.org/Resources/ Research/Surveys-Reports-and-Other-Documents/Teaching-Enrollments-and -Programs/Foreign-Languages-and-Higher-Education-New-Structures-for-a -Changed-World. Accessed 25 May 2014.

MLA Office of Research. *Data on Second Majors in Language and Literature, 2001–2013.* Modern Language Association of America, Feb. 2015, www.mla.org/content/ download/31117/1320962/2ndmajors200113.pdf. Accessed 13 May 2015.

MLA Teagle Foundation Working Group. *Report to the Teagle Foundation on the Undergraduate Major in Language and Literature.* Modern Language Association of America, 2009, www.mla.org/pdf/2008_mla_whitepaper.pdf. Accessed 20 Mar. 2012.

Piccardo, Enrica, and Joëlle Aden. "Plurilingualism and Empathy: Beyond Instrumental Language Learning." *The Multilingual Turn in Languages Education: Opportunities and Challenges,* edited by Jean Conteh and Gabriela Meier, Kindle ed., Multilingual Matters, 2014, pp. 234–57.

Prádanos, Luis I. "La enseñanza del español en la era del antropoceno: Hacia la Integración de la sostenibilidad en las clases de español como lengua extranjera." *Hispania,* vol. 98, no. 2, 2015, pp. 333–45.

Puccio, Gerard J., and John F. Cabra. "Organizational Creativity: A Systems Approach." *The Cambridge Handbook of Creativity,* edited by James C. Kaufman and Robert J. Sternberg, Cambridge UP, 2010, pp. 145–73.

Radcliffe, Sarah A. "Development for a Postneoliberal Era? *Sumak Kawsay,* Living Well and the Limits to Decolonisation in Ecuador." *Geoforum,* vol. 43, 2012, pp. 240–49.

Stibbe, Arran. *Ecolinguistics.* Routledge, 2015.

Ter Horst, Eleanor E., and Joshua M. Pearce. "Foreign Languages and Sustainability: Addressing the Connections, Communities, and Comparisons Standards in Higher Education." *Foreign Language Annals,* vol. 43, no. 3, Fall 2010, pp. 365–83.

PART TWO | *Curricula*

Reflections on Water: Inspiring Environmental Consciousness through Engagement with French Texts

Abbey Carrico

In their natural environment of sand, sedimentary rock, or other gel medium, the intricate patterns of Liesegang rings are impressive in their regularity and stunning in their expansiveness, resembling banded agate stone. Despite much scientific interest over the years, these naturally occurring precipitates still lack an exact model for artificial replication. In a beginning chemistry class at Virginia Military Institute students were charged with investigating which chemical reactions (such as pH level) may lead to the creation of this phenomenon and presented their findings at an interdisciplinary undergraduate research forum. As an assistant professor of modern languages and cultures and as a presentation judge, my primary concern was not, however, to learn the specific composition hypothesized to form these rings. Instead, I was more interested in the students' thought processes motivating the experiment and the conclusions they could draw. I asked: Why does this matter? Why does or should this matter to me, a nonspecialist? To them, as nascent researchers? To the fields of geology and chemistry, and to the overall quest for knowledge? I sought what ecocritic Daniel J. Philippon succinctly but appropriately identifies as the humanities' contribution to sustainability efforts and to humanistic inquiry: meaning and perspective (164).

In response to my questions, some students hesitated: they had not thought beyond their particular focus and could not paint broader strokes about the significance, justifications, or implications of their work. Other students, however, engaged in the type of critical thinking that is regularly fostered in humanities classrooms but sometimes lacking in other domains, that of "questioning categories" and "questioning contexts" (Philippon 165–66). These students' answers suggested links between chemistry, economics, environmental preservation, and aesthetics and thus revealed how the environment can act as a bridge between various academic (and non-academic) categories and interests. As one student proposed, if landscapers knew how to replicate Liesegang rings, they could recreate them as part of their garden designs and therefore profit both financially and visually. Another deduced that if pH levels were indeed found to have an effect on the formation of this phenomenon, environmental scientists could work backward to identify which regions suffer, or will suffer, more from acid rain. And one student in particular was inspired by an appreciation of beauty, claiming that a scientist's goal is to explain beauty in the natural world.

The appreciation of beauty, along with the curiosity surrounding it, gives rise to much research in the fields of languages, cultures, literatures, and environmental studies. Discovering not only the beauty of a piece of literature but how the work itself intersects with other, and oftentimes not obvious, domains is at the core of my course L'eau: Réflexions du présent dans le passé ("Water: Reflections of the Present in the Past").[1] The current essay first situates this course within the field of ecocriticism, a growing area in French studies whose foundation fundamentally engages both the humanities and the sciences and whose theoretical model allows scholars to pursue multiple interpretative methods. The essay then details the course design and structure before finally offering applications for further curriculum design, all in an effort to model how the teaching of literature and culture can inspire ecological consciousness in students in meaningful and productive ways.

French Studies and Ecocriticism

The formalized yet diverse study of literature and the environment (ecocriticism) has been underway for some time in English departments, having emerged from what Ursula K. Heise calls the "rapidly diversifying matrix of literary and cultural studies in the 1990s" (503). And yet, in relation to other historical shifts in literary studies, ecocriticism's emergence was relatively late. As Heise explains, "most of the important social movements of the

1960s and 1970s left their marks on literary criticism long before environmentalism did" (505). She credits this delay to literary theory itself, which, from the 1960s to the 1990s, encouraged "a fundamentally skeptical perspective that emphasized the multiple disjunctures between forms of representation and the realities they purported to refer to" (505). In other words, in a time when environmental problems were gaining political and social ground and urgency, cultural and literary theorists were less concerned with taking pragmatic, activist roles and more with questioning theories of representation and critiquing historical discourse. As Heise points out, though, by the beginning of the 1990s, "the theoretical panorama in literary studies had changed" (505). American cultural studies, for instance, emerged and "styled itself antitheoretical as much as theoretical" (Heise 505). Relying essentially on both theoretical and practical approaches, ecocriticism was therefore able to take root in the methodological diversity that fields such as American cultural studies promoted.

Ecocriticism has since evolved into environmental humanities divisions at several institutions, reaching beyond cultural studies programs and English departments and encouraging multidisciplinary work. The environmental humanities program at the University of Washington, for example, is led in part by language and literature scholars and encourages its humanities and science students to look at how "views of the environment are shaped by culture through the lens of literature, cinema, and art" (Keene). As a field, though, ecocriticism has only recently started to be more fully and purposefully integrated into French and francophone programs.[2] Some of its later reception in these programs has been because environmental curricula and ecocriticism readers have traditionally included mostly American and British works classified as nature writing.[3] Concerned with how differences in cultures shape ecological perspectives, Stephanie Posthumus insists that "to diversify ecocriticism," avoid an overuniversalization of the field, and encourage its entry into more language and literature departments (and thus broaden the curricula), we must not simply "translate terms such as *nature writing* or *wilderness* in other languages" (86; my trans.). The goal of ecocriticism within different programs is to analyze the specificities of texts in their particular cultural and linguistic contexts, which will undoubtedly lead to more precise explorations of how writers navigate their place in the natural world and portray the environment in their works. At its core, ecocriticism allows for "cultural specificities" (Posthumus 87) while supporting cross-disciplinary and cross-specialty work. Its "triple allegiance to the scientific study of nature, the scholarly analysis of cultural representations, and the political struggle for more sustainable ways of inhabiting the natural world" (Heise 506) uniquely positions it as a bridge between subfields within the humanities and the larger divisions between the humanities and the sciences.

As Stephanie LeMenager and Stephanie Foote point out, however, humanities scholars as a whole have been criticized for not taking part in "discussions of what sustainability is and might be" (572), a practical component necessary for ecocriticism's success as a scholarly field and social movement. One method of taking part in such sustainability conversations from within the humanities is to develop courses demonstrating that "sustainability and the humanities have always been compatible projects" (LeMenager and Foote 572). As humanities and literature scholars, we have the unique training and perspective required to situate humans and their cultural representations within geographical, historical, and social spaces. We account for methodological and cultural differences while recognizing parallels across divisions. As Cheryll Glotfelty says, "[We] give books to students and say, Read these . . . [believing] that books can change and have changed the world" (qtd. in Balaev 613). It is from this point of view that my course on water and French texts emerged and can serve as a model for other instructors who believe ecological awareness and eventual action are motivated from engagement with literary and artistic creations.

Course Design: L'eau: Réflexions du présent dans le passé

In L'eau: Réflexions du présent dans le passé, students are asked to examine the claim that place and space, and in particular water, have an influence on writers, artists, and their creations. They are not given scientific apparatuses to work with, but instead literature, which models "new ways of collectively understanding the possible. At the level of language, genre, form, and style, . . . the process of narrative is a sustained effort in world making" (LeMenager and Foote 577). Students are encouraged to let their own questions and concerns about the environment surface as they engage in detailed readings and analyses of texts that treat the environment in a variety of ways, paying careful attention to how form and content intersect to create meaning and perspective.

As a constant source of creative inspiration, water has the ability to transcend time and place, allowing readers access to the works of writers and artists who may be unknown to them but whose interactions with the natural world offer connections to modern-day ecological concerns. In nineteenth-century France, writers and artists were inspired by water and explored its representation in diverse ways. At the beginning of the century, Romanticists relied on water's symbolism to express melancholy and nostalgia. Later, modernization and industrialization generated conflicted relations between humans and the environment that were readily portrayed in fin de siècle texts. The works that emerged from the changing human-nonhuman relations throughout the nineteenth century teach not only about the aquatic in its physical milieu but also about specific cultural practices of the time. Furthermore, water as metaphor, symbol, or other literary device teaches about textual production, technique, and style. As Gaston Bachelard writes, "[Water] appears to us as a total being: it has a body, a soul, a voice. Perhaps more than any other element, water is a complete poetic reality" (24; my trans.). As a "complete poetic reality," the aquatic element serves and has served artists as well as scholars in its unique position at the intersection of various domains in the humanities and sciences.

The course L'eau: Réflexions du présent dans le passé is designed to simultaneously expose students to a variety of genres (novels, poetry, paintings, etc.), each treating water in a different manner, and to encourage students' own critical, reflective thinking concerning human-nonhuman interactions. Rather than study works that have been canonized as nature writing or seen as activist at the time of their production, however, students analyze texts whose portrayal of the environment may at first seem minimal. On close examination of specific scenes and themes developed in these works, students discover (sometimes to their surprise) that ecological concerns are present in much literature depicting humans and their place in the world. As Loretta Johnson explains, "Ecocriticism, once the literary arm of environmentalism, has evolved into a multidisciplinary approach to all environmental literature, which, if ecocriticism does its work, will be all literature. Period" (12). The overall course goal is to open the field of ecocriticism to all literature that portrays the environment, whether figuratively or literally, in order to gain a more complete picture of the human-nonhuman relation and its evolution (or lack thereof) in French texts. Although students primarily read nineteenth-century literature, they explore the notion that the twentieth and twenty-first centuries are not unlike the nineteenth in that water still plays a dominant role in many literary and artistic creations. At the end of the course they are asked to consider how past representations of water intersect with modern-day problems and what can be done to preserve this ecological and creative resource in the future.

The class is designed as a special topics offering for students at the high-intermediate to low-advanced levels of college French. It can also serve as an introduction to literature and interpretive methods survey course, particularly if the students' proficiency levels are more intermediate than advanced, and if past exposure to French texts is limited. In addition to fostering discussion and reflection on the topic of water in French literature, the course has the practical goals of reinforcing language skills, deepening reading comprehension, and developing writing competency in the form of a sustained argument and literary analysis. Since the theme and ecocritical framework require a sophistication of thought often beyond the students' linguistic abilities in French, course objectives related to communicative skills are included, supporting the very real need for continued development across all skill sets in literature classes.[4] Students are asked to read texts, analyze details of form and content, and synthesize their own ideas, all in the target language. To account for varying levels, as well as highlight the most significant environmentally themed passages in the selected works, the course program includes excerpts rather than full texts (except in the case of shorter poetry and works of art). Limiting the reading assignments benefits the students by reducing learner anxiety, allowing for more nuanced and detailed interpretations, and focusing discussion on relevant themes. Instructors must be sensitive, therefore, to the learners' linguistic limitations, as well as to the difficulty of the texts, in order to facilitate meaningful dialogue and replace a pedagogy that separates language instruction from content-based instruction with "'a broader and more coherent curriculum in which language, culture, and literature are taught as a continuous whole'" (MLA Ad Hoc Committee, qtd. in Allen 369). If instructors do not pay attention to students' competency and any cognitive difficulties they face, the larger course goal of inspiring environmental consciousness through engagement with texts may not be met.

The overall course structure adapts strategies used to design content-based instruction units that focus on developing skills through content and context. The introduction to the course asks students to consider the definition and role of water and why it should be studied, serving as the "Setting the Stage" phase intended "to activate students' background knowledge, and to prepare students for the learning process," as recommended by Judith L. Shrum and Eileen W. Glisan (64). The three main sections of the course (see table 1) incorporate salient aspects of the "Providing Input / Engaging Learners," "Guided Participation," and "Extension" phases of the content-based instruction unit, specifically contextualizing the language,

Table 1. Course Program for
L'eau: Réflexions du présent dans le passé

Theme	Genre or movement	Text(s)
Introduction	Philosophy, sustainability	Gaston Bachelard, *L'eau et les rêves: Essai sur l'imagination de la matière* (1942; "Water and Dreams: An Essay on the Imagination of Matter")
PART 1: RIVERS AND LAKES: SOURCES OF LOVE AND LOSS		
Love	Poetry, lieder, Romanticism	Wilhelm Müller, "Die schöne Müllerin" / *La belle meunière* ("The Miller's Beautiful Daughter"; translated from German, 1820); Franz Schubert's lieder based on Müller's poems (1823)
Drowning	Novel, narrative memoirs, Romanticism	George Sand, *Lélia* (1833); Gustave Flaubert, *Les Mémoires d'un fou* (1838; "Memoirs of a Madman")
Mourning	Poetry, Romanticism	Victor Hugo, *Les Contemplations* (1856; "The Contemplations")
PART 2: THE OCEAN: SOURCE OF INSPIRATION AND FEAR		
Inspiration	Virtual art, film, modernism, oceanography	Bibliothèque Nationale de France, "La mer: Terreur et fascination" (2004; "The Unknown Sea"); Jacques-Yves Cousteau, *Le monde du silence* (1956; "The Silent World")
Fear	Science fiction	Jules Verne, *Vingt mille lieues sous les mers* (1869; *Twenty Thousand Leagues under the Sea*)
Contemplation	Painting, impressionism	Eugène Boudin, *La plage de Trouville* (1864; "The Beach at Trouville"); Pierre-Auguste Renoir, *Enfants au bord de la mer à Guernesey* (1883; "Children by the Sea in Guernsey"); Claude Monet, *Mer agitée à Étretat* (1883; "Stormy Sea in Etretat")
PART 3: FLOODS AND SPRINGS: SOCIAL USES OF WATER		
Flooding	Short story, naturalism	Émile Zola, *L'inondation* (1880; "The Flood")
Medicine and capitalism	Novel, realism	Guy de Maupassant, *Mont-Oriol* (1887; Mont Oriol, *or A Romance of Auvergne*)
Sustainability	Web series, flash forward	TV5.org, "Coup de pouce pour la planète" ("A Helping Hand for the Planet")

"helping the learner to solve a problem or perform a task," and having the student carry out "culminating activities that integrate multiple skills and standards" (Shrum and Glisan 64). Students encounter a variety of authentic materials (poems, short stories, films, etc.) and must actively and constantly engage on the level of comprehension and analysis. Throughout the course, they are asked to pay particular attention to language difficulties in the texts and to the greater theme of environmental representation, reflecting on what they are in the process of learning. For the final part of the course, the "Closure" stage (Shrum and Glisan 64), students synthesize what they have learned by bridging concepts and observations from nineteenth-century works with contemporary sustainability concerns. As a whole, the course moves from broad issues to analyses of culturally specific examples and back to broader principles. By its conclusion, students have had time to process information, form their own observations, and reflect on the course content and their own learning while gaining the competencies necessary to express their ideas in French.

The three main parts of the course move chronologically and contextually by work, sometimes veering off for purposes of discourse comparison related to style or genre. Dividing the course into sections allows for a slower rhythm within each part and thus helps develop students' communicative skills while also granting periodic summaries and transitions between texts and subject matter. Since each division is based on the type of water studied and the motif evoked in the selected works, instructors are able to help students develop textual or medial interpretation methods as they examine specific representations of the environment. As can be seen in table 1, each type of water is coupled with a genre or movement that represents water in a specific way and opens up student understanding of the time period. As medical advancements were made throughout the century, for example, so too were changes in the social uses of water, reflecting a struggle between artificial and natural resources. The works in the course program offer students a representative selection of well-known writers and artists whose representations of the environment have not traditionally been studied as a collective social and cultural discourse from an ecocritical perspective.

The first section explores the symbolic register of rivers and lakes in song and poetry (Müller, Schubert, Hugo), in memoir narratives (Flaubert), and in novels (Sand) while helping students develop the analytical reading skills necessary for literary interpretation. In these texts, students discover the stylistic personification of water; the struggle between humans and the natural world; and the varying ways in which poetry, song, and narrative can represent the same element from different perspectives, revealing paradoxes and raising questions such as, Is water a friend or foe? A source of love or loss? Does water imitate humans or do humans mimic water? How is the writer's imagination and text informed by the aquatic? These types of questions, focusing on both content and form, are asked in reading guides designed by the instructor to facilitate textual comprehension and engagement outside class, as well as during in-class discussions.[5] For example, students first study a French version of Müller's "Die schöne Müllerin" ("The Miller's Beautiful Daughter") before listening to Schubert's musical interpretation.[6] Marked equally by harmony and dissonance, both the poetic and musical compositions are inspired by a river's rhythmic flow, therefore evoking a succession of conflicting emotions. Students are asked to compare the visceral effects of both works before employing *explication de texte* ("close reading") methods, analyzing the aquatic content, both figurative and literal, alongside the poetic structure and literary devices.

In the second section of the course, students continue to investigate the paradoxes of water in its multiple roles and representations through an examination of the ocean as literary and artistic motif inspiring scientific discovery (Verne) and impressionist expression (Boudin, Renoir, Monet). They develop the learning skills of digital humanities by exploring media forms such as the virtual art exposition "La mer: Terreur et fascination" ("The Unknown Sea"). In this exhibit, students navigate pictorial histories of the sea; read excerpts ranging from classical texts to contemporary ecological essays; and watch interviews with experts from various disciplines, including the president of a group of marine writers and an oceanographer. Encouraged again to consider the interconnectedness of style and content, students study Jacques-Yves Cousteau's groundbreaking film *Le monde du silence* ("The Silent World"), in which Cousteau records his underwater adventures. As Noëlle Rouxel-Cubberly explains, with film "students are invited to go beyond the knowledge of facts and to engage in reflective thinking, tying together products, practices, and perspectives depicted in the films" (119).[7] For one scene of the film, for instance, students are asked to comment on the narrator's voice as it overlays and echoes the ocean's tone. As images and sounds of the ocean dominate the screen, students must consider how the auditory intersects with the visual and creates meaning for the viewer. The film is not simply about oceanic discovery, but about the ways in which this discovery is portrayed to the audience so as to highlight the ocean's dual ability to inspire fascination and fear. Furthermore, offering students the chance to study the themes of the course through several art forms accounts for diverse learning styles (auditory, visual, kinesthetic) as well as varied interest in artistic genre, involving more students in the learning process.

In the third section of the course, students investigate social uses of water and the changing dynamic between humans and the environment at the end of the nineteenth century. Here, they once again encounter different types of water: rivers used for cultivation (Zola) and natural springs used for financial profit and medical experimentation (Maupassant). In a side-by-side study of rhetorical devices, students compare two excerpts from Guy de Maupassant's *Mont-Oriol* (Mont Oriol, *or A Romance of Auvergne*), each illustrating the period's transforming relationship to water. Medical terms mark the first passage, relaying the aquatic's healing capacities, whereas financial vocabulary dominates the second, revealing humans' ability to manipulate natural resources for profit. Maupassant's text and Émile Zola's *L'inondation* ("The Flood") expose the conflicted relation between humans and nonhumans and the role this struggle plays in literature. Since sustainable efforts are still dominated by a conflicted and complicated relation between humans and nonhumans, these texts serve as a pertinent transition between past representations and present ecological issues.

In a synthesis project consisting of a reflection paper and an oral presentation, students investigate contemporary sustainability concerns and make comparisons with the themes and issues explored in the earlier works. They each choose a different report from TV5's "Coup de pouce pour la planète" ("A Helping Hand for the Planet"), a Web series on sustainable development, to inform them about a specific environmental problem facing the world. In a *flash forward* as well as circular move, students return to the point of departure for the course when they were asked to consider the role of water and the reasons why we should study it. Now, though, having further developed their linguistic abilities, cultural competencies, critical thinking, and interpretive techniques, they are better equipped to analyze these problematics from an inspired perspective and perhaps can even answer the question at the heart of humanities' inquiry: Why does this matter? Throughout the course, students' perceptions about water broaden as they consider its symbolic meaning in artistic creation, concrete influence on social systems, and applications in their lives.

Applications and Reflection

In L'eau: Réflexions du présent dans le passé, students study a carefully cho-sen selection of works that allows them to situate literary and artistic genres within a thematic and historical context. They explore evolving human-nonhuman interactions and representations and examine how nineteenth-century French perceptions of water are replicated or challenged today. Throughout the course it becomes clear that water significantly marked nineteenth-century French literature and thought, whether used to symbol-ize emotions, present new ideas, or portray conflicts between humans and the natural world. The course uniquely contributes to the rise of ecocriticism in French studies through its inclusion of works not readily associated with nature writing or environmental readers. By engaging texts that are not part of an activist agenda or whose usual inclusion in course programs is due to other textual problematics, students are able to see firsthand how texts serve multiple purposes and permit multiple interpretations. For example, George Sand's *Lélia* is traditionally included in French curricula to highlight a female author, demonstrate innovation in literary style, or contribute to discussions of gender or religion. In this course, though, *Lélia* is studied from an ecological perspective, as part of the unit on rivers and lakes as sources of love and loss. As students consider the aquatic space of the drowning scene, they discover that death by water is not simply about plot but also, perhaps more important, about the natural element itself. Water is the key organiz-ing thread to this course, permitting a common point of discussion between texts, genres, content, and form. Students come to the course with ideas about water and the environment and leave better equipped to discuss these ideas and expand on them in French.

Although this particular theme and selection of texts work well to ex-pand the scope of ecocritical literature in course curricula and foster im-portant discussions concerning the evolution of thought and creation in nineteenth-century French literature, this course offers just one example of how literature can be taught to inspire broader thinking and eventual action in students. The most successful part of the class rests in its overarching goal to unpack cultural specificities while exploring larger environmental con-cerns. To create a similar course, the theme, language, time period, and text selection could all change, but the structure should move logically and con-textually to help students situate changing thought and make comparisons between genres and representations.[8] Similar courses should, above all, allow time for learner reflection and include synthesis projects in which students compare and contrast contemporary concerns with past representations. The key is for educators in the environmental humanities to remember that, although inspiration cannot be forced and consciousness and activism cannot be ensured, discussions can be started and questions posed; this, after all, is one of the humanities' most significant contributions to sustainability.

NOTES

1. This course was initially piloted in spring 2012 at Florida State University. The current essay discusses the course program as taught at Virginia Military Institute in fall 2014 and spring 2017.
2. For more on the development of ecocriticism in French studies, see Blanc et al.; Finch-Race and Posthumus; Posthumus; and Suberchicot.
3. Posthumus points out that, although there do exist French nature writers such as Jean-Jacques Rousseau and Jean-Henri Fabre, the content of their works is specific to their own cultures and should not be collapsed into a homogeneous category with American and English nature writers (87).
4. See Connors et al.; Frantzen; Kern; Martin; and Scott for resources on the importance of employing second language acquisition research in the literature classroom.
5. As second language acquisition research has shown, teaching students how to read by providing practical, level-appropriate guidance is too often excluded from the advanced literature classroom, impeding student contribution and comprehension. Reading guides can be created by the instructor to reduce anxiety and facilitate confidence and better understanding in the learner. These guides may include prereading activities, such as vocabulary-building exercises or open-ended inquiries; content questions to inform the instructor of student comprehension difficulties; and analytical questions that help students notice literary devices at work in the texts. See Fecteau or Frantzen for more on developing effective reading strategies; see Dema and Moeller for inquiry-based teaching techniques; and see Kern for process-oriented writing advice.
6. Although most texts studied in this course come from a French canon, I selected Müller's poem in order to discuss pre-Romantic and Romantic portrayals of the environment, the German and French literary movements being closely related.
7. For more on multimedia instruction and developing cultural awareness in learners, see Herron et al.; Etienne and Vanbaelen.
8. This specific course could include selections from a wider range of French and francophone works, from the early modern to the postcolonial periods, to demonstrate a continued literary concern with place and space.

WORKS CITED

Allen, Heather Willis. "A Multiple Literacies Approach to the Advanced French Writing Course." *The French Review*, vol. 83, no. 2, Dec. 2009, pp. 368–85.

Bachelard, Gaston. *L'eau et les rêves: Essai sur l'imagination de la matière.* Librairie José Corti, 1942.

Balaev, Michelle. "The Formation of a Field: Ecocriticism in America—An Interview with Cheryll Glotfelty." *PMLA*, vol. 127, no. 3, May 2012, pp. 607–16.

Blanc, Nathalie, et al., editors. *Écologie et politique*, vol. 36, Syllepse, 2008.

Connors, Logan J., et al. "Three Strategies for Promoting Intellectual Engagement in Advanced Undergraduate Seminars." *The French Review*, vol. 87, no. 4, May 2014, pp. 111–26.

Dema, Oxana, and Aleidine J. Moeller. "Teaching Culture in the Twenty-First-Century Language Classroom." *Touch the World: Selected Papers from the 2012 Central States Conference on the Teaching of Foreign Languages*, edited by Tatiana Sildus, Crown Prints, 2012, pp. 75–91.

Etienne, Corinne, and Sylvie Vanbaelen. "Paving the Way to Literary Analysis through TV Commercials." *Foreign Language Annals*, vol. 39, no. 1, Spring 2006, pp. 87–98.

Fecteau, Monique L. "First- and Second-Language Reading Comprehension of Literary Texts." *The Modern Language Journal*, vol. 83, no. 4, Dec. 1999, pp. 475–93.

Finch-Race, Daniel A., and Stephanie Posthumus, editors. *French Ecocriticism: From the Early Modern Period to the Twenty-First Century*. Peter Lang, 2017.

Frantzen, Diana. "Rethinking Foreign Language Literature: Towards an Integration of Literature and Language at All Levels." *SLA and the Literature Classroom: Fostering Dialogues*, edited by Virginia M. Scott and Holly Tucker, Heinle & Heinle, 2002, pp. 109–30.

Heise, Ursula K. "The Hitchhiker's Guide to Ecocriticism." *PMLA*, vol. 121, no. 2, Mar. 2006, pp. 503–16.

Herron, Carol, et al. "A Classroom Investigation: Can Video Improve Intermediate-Level French Language Students' Ability to Learn About a Foreign Culture?" *The Modern Language Journal*, vol. 86, no. 1, Spring 2002, pp. 36–53.

Johnson, Loretta. "Greening the Library: The Fundamentals and Future of Ecocriticism." *Choice*, vol. 47, no. 4, Dec. 2009, pp. 1–13.

Keene, Jennifer M. "Art + Science = Environmental Humanities." *French and Italian Studies*, University of Washington, 25 Nov. 2013, frenchitalian.washington.edu/news/2013/11/25/art-science-environmental-humanities. Accessed 1 June 2015.

Kern, Richard. *Literacy and Language Teaching*. Oxford UP, 2000.

LeMenager, Stephanie, and Stephanie Foote. "The Sustainable Humanities." *PMLA*, vol. 127, no. 3, May 2012, pp. 572–78.

Martin, Laurey K. "Breaking the Sounds of Silence: Promoting Discussion of Literary Texts in Intermediate Courses." *The French Review*, vol. 66, no. 4, Mar. 1993, pp. 549–61.

MLA Ad Hoc Committee on Foreign Languages. "Foreign Languages and Higher Education: New Structures for a Changed World." *Profession*, 2007, pp. 234–45.

Philippon, Daniel J. "Sustainability and the Humanities: An Extensive Pleasure." *American Literary History*, vol. 24, no. 1, Spring 2012, pp. 163–79.

Posthumus, Stephanie. "Vers une écocritique française: Le contrat naturel de Michel Serres." *Mosaic: A Journal for the Interdisciplinary Study of Literature*, vol. 44, no. 2, June 2011, pp. 85–100.

Rouxel-Cubberly, Noëlle. "The Film Trailer Project: French Films as Textbooks." *The French Review*, vol. 88, no. 1, Oct. 2014, pp. 117–33.

Scott, Virginia M. "An Applied Linguist in the Literature Classroom." *The French Review*, vol. 74, no. 3, Feb. 2001, pp. 538–49.

Shrum, Judith L., and Eileen W. Glisan. *Teacher's Handbook: Contextualized Language Instruction*. 2nd ed., Heinle & Heinle, 2000.

Suberchicot, Alain. *Littérature et environnement: Pour une écocritique comparée*. Honoré Champion, 2012.

Can Literature Save the Planet? Lessons from Latin America

Odile Cisneros

Firmly rooted in North America and Europe, environmental approaches to literature only began gaining ground in the context of Latin America in the second decade of the twenty-first century. Not surprisingly, then, when it comes to comprehensive pedagogical discussions of the subject, the territory is virtually uncharted.[1] Still, Latin America, with its mix of European and indigenous roots, its history of land conquest and exploitation, and its distinguished environmental poet-activists, arguably stands as an ideal habitat for ecocriticism and ecopedagogy. That was my intuition when I designed Latin American Literature and the Environment, the first course with a green focus in the Department of Modern Languages and Cultural Studies at the University of Alberta. Originally taught in fall 2014, this third-year Spanish language and literature course successfully attracted a cohort of enthusiastic students. Based on that experience, the present essay proposes guidelines for curriculum design in the target language (Spanish, with some inclusion of Brazilian material taught in translation). I begin by describing some of the main theoretical and methodological difficulties involved in integrating and adapting the existing body of ecocritical theory to the context of Latin America, particularly, the local-global tensions as well as the appropriateness of ecocriticism to Latin American literature. I then turn to other pedagogical challenges raised by ecocriticism's interdisciplinary nature and how these relate to the learning outcomes for the course. The remainder of the essay is devoted to discussing the details of the course and suggestions for potential variants. My objective is to start a broad discussion on curriculum design possibilities that can bring ecocritical concerns to the teaching of Spanish and of Latin American literature. I see the integration of environmental approaches into second language acquisition and literature and culture courses in the target language as an effective way to renew our curriculum at a time of dwindling enrollments. More important, I hope to show how this pedagogy can have a long-lasting, transformative influence on our students in the face of current ecological challenges.

In such a course, perhaps the first and main issue is the difficulty of acknowledging the region's historical, literary, and ecological specificity while engaging the important debates in ecocriticism that have taken place in the Anglo-American context since the 1990s. This involves understanding and profiting from the way ecocriticism developed in Britain and North America[2] and simultaneously acknowledging Latin America's own *sense of place*, to use Ursula K. Heise's term. In *Sense of Place and Sense of Planet*, Heise pays attention to the "cultural and rhetorical traditions particular to the United States, where rootedness in place has long been valued as an ideal" (9). For Heise, this investment in a sense of place found in the American tradition is not necessarily present in other traditions, leading her to conclude that "assumptions that frame environmentalist and ecocritical thought in the United States cannot simply be presumed to shape ecological orientations elsewhere" (*Sense of Place* 9). Two questions emerge here: first, whether such an investment or rootedness in place exists in the Latin American tradition that may shape its ecocritical thought; and, second, what the particularities of such a Latin American sense of place might be. With no intention to fully answer them, I merely raise these questions as critical and pedagogical guiding thoughts. In a more recent article where she discusses the international turn in ecocriticism, Heise further explores such local-global tensions, arguing that "[p]lace in its varying material and symbolic significations figures centrally in comparative ecocriticism as a way of mapping relations between culture and nature" ("Globality" 639). What, then, is Latin America's ecocritical "place," in the sense of both its rootedness in a particular locale and its location within a larger (global) ecocritical map? How should it engage with theorizations that have emerged previously and in different contexts?

Laura Barbas-Rhoden, one of the first authors to write on ecocriticism and ecopedagogy in Latin America, finds that analyzing contemporary Latin American narratives through the lens of environmental justice is a "more logical place for Latin American ecocriticism to engage with ecocritical debates" (*Ecological Imaginations* 7). This approach corresponds to the development Lawrence Buell calls the "second wave" of ecocriticism (6–8). Yet the engagement of Latin American literature with nature predates the contemporary period and the emergence of the concept of environmental justice, so a more comprehensive approach is warranted. Scott M. DeVries, for instance, suggests that "for the articulation of a history of literary ecology in Spanish America, the starting point must go farther back" than the last forty years (3). These considerations raise several quandaries. How do we (as teachers and as scholars) engage with literature that vastly predates the development of ecocriticism? What do ecocritical approaches add to our ability to interpret and analyze literatures? How do we engage with larger questions of our ethical responsibility toward nature in our readings and pedagogy?

Beyond the broad theoretical and methodological questions of how Latin American literature engages with ecocritical debates from other periods and contexts, there are also more specific pedagogical challenges related to the interdisciplinary nature of ecocriticism. As a practice that studies, in Cheryll Glotfelty's famous definition, "the relationship between literature and the physical environment" (xviii), ecocriticism requires students to be exposed to basic vocabulary and issues in ecology prior to literary analysis. This methodology, William Rueckert suggests, may allow us to "develop an ecological poetics by applying ecological concepts to the . . . reading, teaching, and writing about literature" (107). The development of such an "ecological poetics" has implications that go beyond the specific linguistic and literary goals of our course. As Jonathan Bate argues, "works of art can themselves be imaginary states of nature, imaginary ideal ecosystems, and by reading them, by inhabiting them, we can start to imagine what it might be like to live differently upon the earth" (*Song* 250–51). In other words, the purpose of our activities as ecocritics and as teachers engaging in ecopedagogy is directly tied to imagining different ways of relating to nature. These ideas significantly shaped my thinking about the goals for the course, which involved a progression from mastering a number of definitions and basic vocabulary, to becoming familiar with a corpus of authors, to describing attitudes toward nature in literary texts, to the final goal of independently reading and analyzing literature from an ecocritical perspective. As specific course outcomes, I expected students to be able to define ecocriticism or green studies; discuss five themes or approaches in ecocriticism and develop appropriate vocabulary to explore them; list five major literary figures from Latin America who have engaged literature and environmental thinking; describe how literature can uniquely inform ecological thinking and environmental attitudes; and perform a reading of a short literary text from an ecocritical perspective.

Regarding the acquisition of the basic concepts and vocabulary related to ecology, my experience proved that resources in this area appeared to be more readily available in English, particularly when working out of North America. Some multilingual material may be obtained through international organizations such as the United Nations, the European Union, and Greenpeace. Likewise, the Government of Canada's online terminology and linguistic data bank *TERMIUM Plus* has recently expanded to also include Spanish and Portuguese. If the occasional recourse to materials in English becomes a practical necessity, their use can be balanced by providing students with target-language discussion questions and exercises aimed at consolidating the concepts and providing linguistic practice. Since many basic ecology terms have quite straightforward equivalents in Spanish (and Portuguese), students can quickly acquire the vocabulary needed while reflecting on linguistic differences. The term "carbon cycle," for example, prompted a discussion on the false English-Spanish cognates *carbon-carbón*, which translate respectively as *carbono* and *coal*. Likewise, the words *environment* and *environmentalism* (Spanish: *medio ambiente* and *ambientalismo*; Portuguese: *meio ambiente* and *ambientalismo*) triggered an interesting meditation. I point out to students that, despite their different etymologies, these expressions reveal similar human-centered assumptions. The English word *environment* comes from the French *environner* ("to surround") and Spanish and Portuguese *ambiente* derive from the Latin *ambĭens, -entis* ("that which encircles or surrounds"). In both cases, the spatial metaphor implies the point of view of the human: the environment is, literally, whatever surrounds *us*.

This kind of discussion exemplifies the intellectual leap this course aims to perform, where scientific knowledge and vocabulary are acquired for practical purposes but also become the target of critical interrogation. Useful for describing and analyzing literature, the concepts and terminology are also significant in terms of the attitudes toward nature they reveal when subjected to cultural analysis. For instance, *nature*, a concept that on the surface might seem straightforward, needs to be systematically prob-lematized. In the process, students begin to see our complex understandings of nature, culture, and related concepts. Many of these issues are widely debated in the theoretical sources mentioned earlier and may be presented by the instructor via lectures, yet the length and level of difficulty of such sources might not make them suitable for direct use in the second-language classroom. Instead, entries such as "Nature," "Culture," and "Ecology" from Raymond Williams's classic *Keywords* provide thought-provoking yet merci-fully short discussions of terms we employ in ecocritical debates and that we often take for granted. And though Williams studies the history of these words in the English domain, Spanish and Portuguese translations are avail-able and can yield useful comparisons, particularly of cross-cultural differ-ences (see Pons; and Vasconcelos, respectively).

Such attention to language helps uncover assumptions about human relations to nature, one of several aims in this course, alongside other learn-ing objectives. Overall, I tried to keep the general course outcomes modest, acknowledging that if learners are grappling with new content (ecocriti-cal concepts and approaches), linguistic challenges (new vocabulary and structures), and issues that require empathy and ethical thinking (the con-nection between literature and environmental responsibility), scaling back expectations in other respects seemed appropriate. In organizing the pro-gression of the course material, I looked to apply the scaffolding suggested by Bloom's taxonomy, particularly in the cognitive and affective domains.[3] So, whereas some goals were geared toward a fairly low level of learning on both the linguistic and conceptual levels (tasks such as defining, describ-ing, and giving examples), the more ambitious objectives included mid- to high-level learning that required higher competency in the language and sophisticated analytical skills (evaluating, justifying, and generating new knowledge—i.e., producing ecocritical readings of literary texts). In general, the instructor should always keep in mind that a course such as this one is expected to perform double duty: both expanding and enhancing the lan-guage competency of students while introducing new concepts and mate-rial in the target language. In the case of ecopedagogy, we can add a third, ethical-affective dimension: the goal is not only to give students new tools (both linguistic and conceptual) but also to transform attitudes as a result of that acquisition. How those ethical-affective goals are achieved is dis-cussed below in the context of working with the specific texts chosen for the course. Ultimately, whether the goals are reached can be measured by the degree to which, in course evaluations, students report acquiring certain skills or being affected by the course material.

Concerning the course design details, it was clear to me that in Latin American Literature in the Environment the main activities would be reading and discussing literature, journalism, and criticism, often contextualized with the aid of videos or films, along with relevant writing assignments. With regard to genres, I chose to work with shorter pieces (poetry, essays, and short stories) because they matched my expertise and seemed better suited to the close readings I targeted. When appropriate, I used excerpts from novels, providing students with summaries and context. The choice of materials and their organization (either as topics or a chronological survey), however, was far from obvious. Whereas English departments can rely on an established canon or corpus of nineteenth-century "pastoral" or "nature writing" as a starting point (Murphy), no comparable tradition exists in Latin America (Doman). There is no Latin American Thoreau, so to speak. And still, as Niall Binns notes, "[t]he weight of the natural environment—analyzed, anathematized, celebrated, rendered mythical—has been foundational in the Spanish American republics, from regionalist narratives to so many essayistic national identity quests" (132; my trans.). Celebrations of the landscape contrast with misgivings about nature, given the paradigms of nature versus culture and of civilization versus barbarism that have characterized literary history in Latin America. Thus, early European chronicles extolling the land and its indigenous population were initially read, not as environmentally oriented writing, but as the literal *pre-texts* of colonization and exploitation. Latin America's *sense of place*, to return to Heise's term, can be gleaned in these ubiquitous and conflicting references to nature.

Yet, what to include and how to group materials can be both a challenge and an opportunity. The lack of a Latin American canon of ecocritical literature demands ingenuity on the part of the instructor yet also affords more freedom. As I discuss below, there are many present-day texts and authors with a clear ecological orientation, but we are not limited to that period. Virtually any literary text can be analyzed ecocritically to discern human attitudes toward, and relations with, the environment writ large. Texts may be organized either as chronological survey or by topics, or through a combination of both. My objective was to give students some sense of the historical evolution of nature before plunging into contemporary works, so

I devised a brief survey of representative texts from the colonial, Romantic, and modern periods to chart changing attitudes and ideas about nature in those key moments in literary history. My thirteen-week course was divided into the following eight units: introduction to the course and general introduction to environment and literature: issues, debates, approaches; a sense of place: Latin America and the environment; pollution and toxic landscapes; endangered environments, endangered species; anthropocentrism, animals, and the nonhuman other; shamanism and indigenous views of nature; ecofeminism; and ecopoetics and planetary consciousness. The first unit was devoted to the considerations on ecocritical theory and methodology and ecological vocabulary and concepts discussed earlier in the essay. The second unit provided the brief chronological survey I describe. The remaining units focused primarily on contemporary texts (with the exception of some indigenous narratives).

A more comprehensive synthetic approach that follows a wider chronology combined with specific topics may also allow for more in-depth exploration of particular issues that emerge in each period. Here instructors have the freedom to decide which design fits their objectives and expertise better. I can imagine, for instance, a semester-long course devoted entirely to the colonial period or to the nineteenth century. For any and all of those periods, the choice of materials is wide (see appendix).

The colonial period is rife with texts that engage nature in a variety of ways: from awe-filled descriptions of landscape, flora, and fauna to accounts of harsh conditions and natural disasters as threats to human life and settlement. As an exemplary text, I assigned students the entries from 19–23 October in *Diario de a bordo* (*Diary*) by Christopher Columbus (in Spanish, Cristóbal Colón), asking them to identify phrases describing the natural world, noting the adjectives used, and evaluating whether the descriptions were positive, negative, or neutral. We discussed instances of cultural mediation (comparisons with known examples), and then moved to a consideration of Columbus's overriding instrumental vision (the perceived utility of natural resources for human purposes). As students read these texts, they can reflect on how the new landscapes inspired a sense of both wonder and pragmatic opportunity in European explorers, in great part, the driving force of colonization. As one critic puts it, in "[t]he literature of discovery and conquest . . . Nature as abundance is transformed into resource; discovery gives way to conquest" (Boling 245).

From the Romantic period to the Latin American wars of independence and throughout the nineteenth century, Latin American authors repeatedly probe the role of environment as constitutive of national identity, when "[n]ature (conceived as boundless) is set against nation (nature conquered through domestication)" (Boling 246). Responses range from Romantic praise and veneration to positivist fear, determinism, and the desire to tame. This period also witnessed the appearance of influential works by naturalist-travelers, such as Alexander von Humboldt (technically not considered part of Latin American literature), who record observations of nature and landscape. To represent this period, I chose chapter 5 of Domingo Faustino Sarmiento's *Facundo: Civilización y barbarie* (1845; "Facundo: Civilization and Barbarism"), the celebrated episode where Facundo Quiroga, the protagonist, encounters and fights a wildcat. A foundational classic of Latin America literature and culture, Sarmiento's part essay, part biographical narrative portrays the internecine wars plaguing Argentina in the nineteenth century and the lifestyle of the *gauchos* ("cowboys"), who inhabit the seemingly limitless *pampas* ("plains"), as embodied in their leader Facundo Quiroga. In positivist fashion, Sarmiento makes the larger argument that, in the allegedly barbaric *pampas*, nature is an obstacle to human progress, synonymous with the supposedly civilizing influence of the city. In the passage we read, students considered how the text argues for a deterministic relation of landscape to way of life: the dangers associated with the region, such as the *tigre cebado* ("man-eating wildcat"), Facundo's struggle with the animal, and Facundo's own apparently wild physiognomy. This selection exemplifies Sarmiento's anthropocentric civilization-barbarism binary that casts the environment as a hostile threat to humans while hinting at the unstable human-animal divide.

Regionalist narratives from the first half of the twentieth century depict nature as a force that humans must reckon with. Here Sarmiento's "civilizing" project is put into practice by taming the land (and its indigenous inhabitants) and exploiting natural resources in a way that anticipates contemporary notions of the Anthropocene. The influence of positivism carries over to novels such as *Doña Bárbara* and *Canaima*, by the Venezuelan Rómulo Gallegos; and *La vorágine* (1924; "The Vortex"), by the Colombian José Eustasio Rivera. This type of text, referred to as *la novela de la tierra* ("the novel of the land") for the role geography plays in constructions of national identity, can now be read ecocritically as *la novela de la Tierra* ("the novel of the Earth"), bringing out modern humanity's struggle to achieve mastery of nature (Boling 248). In contrast, the short narratives written by the Uruguayan Horacio Quiroga in the 1910s through the 1930s present a less sanguine view. Set in the wilderness of the Argentine province of Entre Ríos, where the writer spent the greater part of his life, Quiroga's short fiction reveals nature as a mechanism that acts dispassionately, relentlessly, and silently (Tittler 204), frustrating humankind's attempts to set itself apart from (even above) nature and escape mortality. "El hijo" ("The Son"), for instance, is a poignant tale about the fatal attempts of a man to teach his son how to survive by exposing him to the dangers of the wilderness. "El hombre muerto" ("The Dead Man"), "A la deriva" ("Drifting"), "La miel silvestre" ("Wild Honey"), "El desierto" ("The Desert"), and "Juan Darién" ("Juan Darién") can also be read as cautionary tales of the presumption of human superiority over, or independence from, nature.

Late twentieth-century works expand the panorama notably: from humans in relation to nature and the supernatural in Boom fiction; to indigenous *testimonio* narratives; and on to more self-conscious ecological poetry, essays, and fiction starting in the 1960s and beyond. These include futuristic dystopian narratives and what Barbas-Rhoden calls *ecotestimonio*, namely, texts that "prompt readers, and especially those readers removed from problems depicted, to confront the multiple facets of wicked problems of environmental degradation" ("Teaching"). Because of their sheer variety, present-day texts may be approached flexibly as a series of topics following the overview of earlier texts sketched above.

Grouping material under specific topics (as opposed to historically) also allows for more in-depth engagement with current issues in environmental thinking. In developing these topics, the figure of the environmental writer-activist emerged as an important guide for generating public environmental awareness. The topics often reflected the concerns of individual writer-activists, and the sequence moved gradually from concrete, familiar issues, such as pollution, to larger philosophical speculations, such as planetary consciousness. I chose to begin with air pollution in Mexico City for two reasons: first, because it is a common problem that many students might have heard of; second, because as an environmental success story, it was also a good way to learn about how writers and activists can bring about effective change. The key figure here was Homero Aridjis, a Mexican poet and tireless activist who, with his wife Betty, founded "El Grupo de los Cien" at a time when Mexico City had record-high levels of air pollution. Aridjis's group of one hundred intellectuals and artists lobbied for policy changes that led to a successful curbing of emissions. Environmental declarations and journalism gathered in Aridjis's volume *Noticias de la Tierra* (a wonderful title carrying both the sense of "News from the Earth" and "News *about* the Earth") can be read alongside reflective poetry written by his fellow countrymen José Emilio Pacheco and Octavio Paz.[4] The sequence allows students to move from activism to literature, from factual to figurative writing, and notice different ways of understanding through literature—witnessing the profound effect that metaphors can have in terms of communicating ecological values. For instance, Pacheco's "smog" poems specifically "foreground another level of complication: the conflict between the built environment and processes of Nature" (Dowdy 297).

A further environmental issue facing Latin America and familiar to students is endangered species, another of Aridjis's activist initiatives. *Noticias de la Tierra* contains articles on the sea turtle, the gray whale, and the monarch butterfly that can be studied alongside poems from *El ojo de la ballena* ("The Eye of the Whale"). I ask students to consider how Aridjis's contribution in activism is matched (or even surpassed) by his poetry and what it teaches us about the interconnectedness of humans, other forms of life, and the environment. Like Aridjis, Pacheco also is particularly attuned to the world of animals. A work such as *Album de zoología* (*An Ark for the Next Millennium*), writes Randy Malamud, constitutes one "of the most extensive treatments of animals by any modern poet, and one of the most sensitive and ambitious attempts to . . . approach animals on their own terms—representing their authentic existence and consciousness." In the Brazilian domain, Astrid Cabral's poetry focuses directly on the plant and animal world of her native Amazonia, a region where biodiversity faces challenges due to deforestation and overfishing. Documentaries on Amazonian wildlife can complement Cabral's collection *Cage* (introduced in English since no Spanish translation is available), where the poetic voice probes the kinship between the human and the nonhuman.

Discussing endangered species prepares students for consideration of more abstract, theoretical writings on anthropocentrism and animals. Provocative essays such as John Berger's *Why Look at Animals* and Greg Garrard's chapter "Animals" from *Ecocriticism* (146–80)[5] discuss animal representation and animal rights. These topics are large enough that they could constitute more focused and advanced courses in themselves, but I devoted only one unit to them. Berger and Garrard's respective ideas undergirded our discussion of animal-human interactions in creative works.[6] I asked students to reflect on the representation of humans versus animals in previously mentioned present-day works by Aridjis, Pacheco, and Cabral, as well as those in early-twentieth-century short stories, such as Horacio Quiroga's "Anaconda," "Juan Darién," and "La insolación" ("Sunstroke"). All these works feature animals, either observed by humans or as beings in their own right, in ways that problematize the human-animal divide.

The topic of anthropocentrism and animals can be followed by a unit on indigenous traditions of the Americas, which distinctly privilege nature, often questioning Western notions of human exceptionalism. Examining both literary texts and anthropological writings, we explored the Mesoamerican concept of animal souls. Gary H. Gossen's discussion of how Mesoamerican belief in *tonalli* ("animal souls"), *nagualismo* ("companion animals"), and shamanism, which explains connections between humans, animals, and destiny (86–89), can be compared to previously discussed Western notions of human-animal relations. The stories of Ixquic and of the works of Hunahpú and Ixbalanqué in the *Popol Vuh* (literally, the "Book of Counsel"), the sacred book of the Maya, provide rich textual illustrations of these pre-Columbian beliefs. In the twentieth century, the Nicaraguan poet Pablo Antonio Cuadra adopts the mask of the shaman to deepen his knowledge of the flora and fauna of Nicaragua in works such as *El jaguar y la luna* ("The Jaguar and the Moon") and *Siete árboles contra el atardecer* ("Seven Trees against the Dying Light") (White 49). A figure present in many indigenous cultures of the Americas, the shaman attempts to strike an ecological balance between humans and the landscape they inhabit (Abram 7). This search for balance is very much a part of celebrations of the earth-time deity Pachamama in the Mapuche worldview, wherein poetry also holds a special place. Chilean Mapuche poets Elicura Chihuailaf and Leonel Lienlaf (Vicuña) can be read against the background of two excellent documentaries, *La nación mapuche: Donde se cultiva la palabra profunda* ("The Mapuche Nation: Where the Deep Word Dwells") and *Punalka: El Alto Bío Bío*, both available on *YouTube*. I ask students to view these documentaries ahead of time in order to envision the setting and landscapes prior to analyzing the poetry's imagery in class. Shifting to the Brazilian context, we consider what the anthropologist Eduardo Viveiros de Castro calls *perspectivism*, "the conception, common to many peoples of the continent, according to which the world is inhabited by different sorts of subjects or persons, human and non-human, which apprehend reality from distinct points of view" (469). In perspectivism, and as a challenge to anthropocentrism, animals and other nonhuman elements of nature are people, or see themselves as people—not as a permanent inversion of the dichotomy human-animal, but rather as temporary positionality, a permanent flux of outward appearance with the underlying spirit remaining constant. I ask students to pay close attention to the many instances in creative works (indigenous or not) that emphasize transformation, nonhuman elements assuming human attitudes, and the primordial state of indifferentiation between human and nonhuman this entails.

The human-nature conflict can be brought into sharper focus with a unit on ecofeminism, which introduces gender into the discussion of environmental thinking through the examination of such issues as androcentrism and the connection between the exploitation of nature and the subordination of women. At this point in the course, students had built sufficient confidence reading foreign language materials, so selections of two representative longer works of fiction were introduced: *La loca de Gandoca* (1991; "The Madwoman of Gandoca"), by the Costa Rican Anacristina Rossi; and *Waslala: Memorial del futuro* (1998; "Waslala: Memorial of the Future"), by the Nicaraguan Gioconda Belli. Both feature strong female protagonists and broach ecofeminist themes, yet in very distinct ways. Rossi's semiautobiographical novel features a housewife-turned-environmentalist who struggles to protect a wildlife refuge in Costa Rica. Laura Barbas-Rhoden and Sofía Kearns suggest multiple ways of approaching Rossi's "polyphonic, testimonial discourse, [which] denounces the destruction of the refuge [by] Costa Rican neoliberal politicians allied with foreign investors who 'discover' the Caribbean lowlands for the exploding tourism industry" (169). In *Waslala*, Melisandra, the young female protagonist, sets out on a journey to reach a lost utopian community buried deep in the jungle of a Central American country devastated by drug trade, war, and the pollution First World consumerism generates. Belli's futuristic novel provides students with the opportunity to reflect on North-South environmental relations, utopia and dystopia, and the alternatives that ecofeminism might offer to androcentric social models (Zubiaurre 76).[7]

A concluding unit entitled Ecopoetics and Planetary Consciousness explored the work of two ecopoets avant la lettre: the Argentine Juan Laurentino

Ortiz, also known as "Juanele," who lived from 1896 to 1978, and the Nicaraguan Ernesto Cardenal, born in 1925. Juanele was deeply influenced by the forests and rivers of the Argentine province of Entre Ríos, where he spent most of his life. Long before formalization of ecological thought, his ecopoetic work articulates "a calling to the living matter of our connections, an aesthetic proposal that sees the human while recognizing its continuity and hybridity with the natural" (Forns-Broggi 35). Juanele's short poems (e.g., "Fui al río" ["I Went to the River"]) and his monumental epic *El Gualeguay* ("The Gualeguay") can be read alongside reports about this river's current state of decline due to deforestation and pollution ("El Río Gualeguay"). For his part, Cardenal illustrates what Bate called the historical move of intellectuals "from red to green" (*Romantic Ecology* 8–9). Following his involvement in the Marxist-inspired Sandinista Revolution, Cardenal traded revolutionary politics for wider planetary concerns. His four-hundred-page poem *Cántico cósmico* (1989; "Cosmic Canticle") incorporates scientific facts from quantum physics, astronomy, biology, anthropology, and geology into a dense poetic texture. Alluding in name and scope to Dante's *Divine Comedy*, Pablo Neruda's *Canto general* (*Canto General: Song of the Americas*), and Ezra Pound's *Cantos*, *Cántico cósmico* proposes how scientific evidence can contribute to the biological, social, and political betterment of humankind. Cardenal's ecological insistence on interconnectedness of all things is evident in a section tellingly entitled "Pluriverso," where he claims (quite literally) our human bodies are made of the same cosmic stuff as the stars. I invite students to consider how Cardenal's work employs direct reference to scientific facts (as opposed to their cultural signification) in an effort to renew poetry and create environmental awareness. This work recalls Laurence Coupe's suggestion that green studies, rather than a mere revival of mimesis, "queries the validity of nature as something which is 'produced' by language," and this for the purpose of changing our behavior (4).

The variety of materials discussed here and the many issues raised show that Latin American literature can teach us and our students unique lessons about the environment and about other ways of living with and in it. From early colonial texts to contemporary ecopoetry and self-conscious environmental fictions, Latin America has a wealth of perspectives to be added to the as yet unwritten canon of world ecocritical literature. Likewise, indigenous beliefs and epistemological attitudes can revise or complement Western understandings of our place in the universe, generating a different planetary consciousness. I hope that the preceding discussion of not only the challenges of integrating ecocritical concerns to the teaching of Spanish and of Latin American literature but also the practice of ecocriticism as interdisciplinary work will stimulate more debate on the subject. Joining environmental perspectives to the second language acquisition and literature-culture curriculum is a way to renew our course offerings and programs at a time when the humanities seem to be trailing in popularity compared to the STEM disciplines. This renewal also has larger goals that involve instilling in our students a sense of responsibility and purpose beyond our academic domain. Literature per se may not have the power to save the planet, but it does play a major role in educating us about our responsibilities therein. Bate, an early pioneer of ecocriticism, suggests that, although we learn a great deal from science about nature and the environment, the questions of value can only be answered by the humanities. He writes, "what ethical obligations we might have to future generations, to other species, or indeed to the planet itself, are 'humanities' questions, only answerable from within the framework of disciplines that are attentive to language, history, and philosophy" (*Public Value* 3). Latin American literature, no doubt, has much to add to that conversation.

NOTES

1. Excellent pedagogical volumes include *Teaching Environmental Literature: Materials, Methods, Resources*, edited by Fred Waage; *Teaching North American Environmental Literature*, edited by Laird Christensen et al.; and *Teaching Ecocriticism and Green Cultural Studies*, edited by Greg Garrard; none of these, however, specifically address Latin American literature taught in the target language. Laura Barbas-Rhoden and Sofía Kearns suggest approaches to teaching two Latin American novels from the theoretical vantage points of environmental justice and queer ecocriticism (167), and Barbas-Rhoden recently discussed integrating global learning with ecocriticism through the genre of *ecotestimonio* ("ecotestimony") ("Teaching").
2. Essential works for a basic understanding of the initial phase of ecocriticism, both in the United States and in the United Kingdom, include Jonathan Bate's *Romantic Ecology* and *The Song of the Earth*; Lawrence Buell's *The Environmental Imagination: Thoreau, Nature Writing, and the Formation of American Culture*; Greg Garrard's *Ecocriticism*; and Kate Soper's *What Is Nature? Culture, Politics and the Non-human*; as well as edited collections by Cheryll Glotfelty and Harold Fromm (*The Ecocriticism Reader*); Patrick Murphy (*Literature of Nature: An International Sourcebook*); and Lawrence Coupe (*The Green Studies Reader*). Spanish-language sources and works that specifically consider the Latin American context are listed in this essay's appendix. Currently, I am creating *ecopoesia.com* (set to launch in 2019), a trilingual (Spanish, Portuguese, English) online resource mapping the

relations between contemporary Latin American poetry and the environment, providing criticism, bibliographies, and a selection of poems in the original and in translation.

3. Though the concept of scaffolding has many implications for foreign language teaching (see carla.umn.edu/cobaltt/modules/strategies/ust.html), my concerns relate to scaffolding in the context of Bloom's taxonomy, particularly in the cognitive and affective domains (see "Bloom's Taxonomy"). In the cognitive domain, we begin with a low level of learning (remembering and understanding), move to a mid-level (analyzing and applying), and then transition to a high level (evaluating and creating). In the affective domain, the low level involves, among other skills, receiving and responding; the mid-level, valuing and organizing; and the high level, internalizing.

4. Aridjis's autobiographical piece "Los pájaros" ("The Birds") can be usefully contrasted with Quiroga's "El hijo" ("The Son")—both tell the story of a childhood hunting accident with life-changing consequences. "Literature and Environmental Activism," a *YouTube* video of Aridjis reading this piece in English, can bring the story closer to life. Pacheco's poems "Malpaís" ("Bad Land") and "Paseo de la Reforma" (from *Tarde o temprano: Poemas, 1958–2009*) ponder the effects of pollution on the atmosphere and landscape, whereas Paz's "Árbol adentro" ("A Tree Within") (from *Árbol adentro*) draws an analogy between human anatomy and tree biology.

5. The pieces by Garrard and Berger can be presented in their original English-language format for discussion in the target language, as suggested above, or can be read in translation. Berger's essay is included in the Spanish-language volume *Mirar*, and the first edition of Garrard's *Ecocriticism* is available in Portuguese (*Ecocrítica*).

6. The myriad topics that Berger and Garrard discuss include premodern and modern ideas about animals; anthropomorphic, zoomorphic, allomorphic, and mecanomorphic views of animals; zoos; pets; speciesism; animal liberation movements; the Disneyfication of animals; Donna Haraway's notion of "naturecultures"; and the connection between animal studies and disability studies.

7. Instructors who want to explore the topic of environmental dystopia further might want to include Homero Aridjis's novels *La leyenda de los soles* and *¿En quién piensas cuando haces el amor?*, both set in a postapocalyptic Mexico City fictionalized as Ciudad Moctezuma.

APPENDIX: SUGGESTED READINGS

Colonial Period (Fifteenth to Eighteenth Century)

Christopher Columbus, *Diaro de abordo* (*Diary*) (1492)

Pero Vaz de Caminha, *Carta* ("The Letter of Pero Vaz de Caminha") (1500)

Gonzalo Fernández de Oviedo, *Sumario de la natural historia de las Indias* (*Natural History of the West Indies*) (1526)

Alvar Núñez Cabeza de Vaca, *Relación de los naufragios* (*Castaways: The Narrative of Alvar Núñez Cabeza de Vaca*) (1542)

Pero de Magalhães Gândavo, *Tratado da terra do Brasil: História da Província Santa Cruz* ("The Histories of Brazil") (1576)

Jean de Léry, *History of a Voyage to the Land of Brazil* (1578)

Frei Vicente de Salvador, *História do Brasil* ("History of Brazil") (1627)

Romanticism to Independence (Nineteenth Century)

Alexander von Humboldt, *Views of Nature* (1808)

Andrés Bello, "Alocución a la poesía" ("Discourse to Poetry") (1823); "Silva a la agricultura de la zona tórrida" ("Ode to Tropical Agriculture") (1826)

Gertrudis Gómez de Avellaneda, *Sab* (1841)

Domingo Faustino Sarmiento, *Facundo: Civilización y barbarie* ("Facundo: Civilization and Barbarism") (1845)

José de Alencar, *Iracema* (1865)

Jorge Isaacs, *María* (1867)

Euclides da Cunha, *Os sertões* (*Backlands: The Canudos Campaign*) (1902)

Modernismo and Fin de siècle to Early Twentieth Century

Horacio Quiroga, "El hombre muerto" ("The Dead Man"); "A la deriva" ("Drifting"); "El hijo" ("The Son"); "La miel silvestre" ("Wild Honey"); "El desierto" ("The Desert"); "Juan Darién" ("Juan Darién"); "La insolación" ("Sunstroke"); "Anaconda" ("Anaconda") (1908–35)

José Eustasio Rivera, *La vorágine* ("The Vortex") (1924)

Rómulo Gallegos, *Doña Bárbara* (1929); *Canaima* (1935)

Juan Rulfo, *El llano en llamas* (*The Burning Plain*) (1953); *Pedro Páramo* (1955)

Alejo Carpentier, *Los pasos perdidos* (*The Lost Steps*) (1953)

Modern and Contemporary (Mid-Twentieth to Twenty-First Century)

Narrative

Luis Sepúlveda, *Un viejo que leía novelas de amor* (*An Old Man Who Read Love Novels*) (1989)

Anacristina Rossi, *La loca de Gandoca* ("The Madwoman of Gandoca") (1991)

Homero Aridjis, *La leyenda de los soles* (*The Legend of the Suns*) (1993); *¿En quién piensas cuando haces el amor?* (*Who Do You Think about When You Make Love?*) (1996)

Gioconda Belli, *Waslala: Memorial del futuro* ("Waslala: Memorial of the Future") (1998)

Eduardo Sguiglia, *Los ojos negros* (*Black Eyes*) (2001)

Poetry

Pablo Antonio Cuadra, *El jaguar y la luna* ("The Jaguar and the Moon") (1959); *Siete árboles contra el atardecer* ("Seven Trees against the Dying Light") (1980)

Juan L. Ortiz, "Fui al río" ("I Went to the River"); *El Gualeguay* ([1971] 2004)

Octavio Paz, *Árbol adentro* (*A Tree Within*) (1987)

Ernesto Cardenal, *Cántico cósmico* (*Pluriverse: New and Selected Poems*) (1989)

José Emilio Pacheco, *Tarde o temprano: Poemas, 1958–2009* (2010); *Nuevo album de zoología* (*An Ark for the Next Millennium*) (1998)

Homero Aridjis, *El ojo de la ballena* ("The Eye of the Whale") (2001); *Eyes to See Otherwise / Ojos de otro mirar* (2001); and *Los poemas solares* (*Solar Poems*) (2005)

Astrid Cabral, *Cage* (translated by Alexis Levitin) (2008)

Essays

Homero Aridjis, *Noticias de la Tierra* (*News of the Earth*) (2012)

Selected Secondary Sources

Anderson, Mark, and Zélia Bora. *Ecological Crisis and Cultural Representation in Latin America: Ecocritical Perspectives on Art, Film, and Literature.* Lexington Books, 2016.

Barbas-Rhoden, Laura. *Ecological Imaginations in Latin American Fiction.* UP of Florida, 2011.

Binns, Niall. *¿Callejón Sin Salida?: La crisis ecológica en la poesía hispanoamericana.* PU de Zaragoza, 2004.

DeVries, Scott M. *A History of Ecology and Environmentalism in Spanish American Literature.* Bucknell UP, 2013.

Fierro, Juan Manuel, and Orietta Geeregat V. "La memoria de La Madre Tierra: El canto ecológico de los poetas mapuches." *Anales de literatura hispanoamericana*, vol. 33, 2004.

Flys, Carmen, and Juan Ignacio Oliva, editors. *Ecocrítica.* Special issue of *Nerter*, vols. 15–16, 2010.

Flys Junquera, Carmen, et al. *Ecocríticas: Literatura y medio ambiente.* Iberoamericana / Vervuert, 2010.

Forns-Broggi, Roberto. "Ecology and Latin American Poetry." *Literature of Nature: An International Sourcebook*, edited by Patrick D. Murphy et al., Fitzroy Dearborn, 1998.

Kane, Adrian T., editor. *The Natural World in Latin American Literatures: Ecocritical Essays on Twentieth-Century Writings.* McFarland, 2010.

McNee, Malcolm. *The Environmental Imaginary in Brazilian Poetry and Art.* Palgrave Macmillan, 2014.

Miller, Shawn W. *An Environmental History of Latin America.* Cambridge UP, 2007.

Paredes, Jorge, and Benjamin McLean. "Hacia una tipología de la literatura ecologista en el mundo hispano." *Ixquic: Revista hispánica internacional de análisis y creación*, vol. 2, 2000, pp. 1–37.

Rivera-Barnes, Beatriz, and Jerry Hoeg. *Reading and Writing the Latin American Landscape.* Palgrave Macmillan, 2009.

Rojas Pérez, Walter. *La ecocrítica hoy: Nuevo paradigma.* San José, Costa Rica, 2004.

White, S. "Ecocrítica y chamanismo en la poesía de Pablo Antonio Cuadra." *Anales de literatura hispanoamericana*, vol. 33, 2004, pp. 49–64.

———. "Los poemas etnobotánicos de Esthela Calderón: Un enfoque ecocrítico." *Anales de Literatura Hispanoamericana*, vol. 38, 2009, pp. 95–110.

WORKS CITED

Abram, David. *The Spell of the Sensuous: Perception and Language in a More-than-Human World*. 1st ed., Vintage Books, 1996.

Aridjis, Homero. "Literature and Environmental Activism." *YouTube*, uploaded by The Public Mind Denver, 18 Nov. 2013, www.youtube.com/watch?v=WL5ueUGODmI.

Barbas-Rhoden, Laura. *Ecological Imaginations in Latin American Fiction*. UP of Florida, 2011.

———. "Teaching 'Global Learning' through the *Ecotestimonio*: *Ojos negros* by Eduardo Sguiglia in Class." *Studies in Twentieth and Twenty-First Century Literature*, vol. 39, no. 2, 2015, article 3, doi:10.4148/2334-4415.1833.

Barbas-Rhoden, Laura, and Sofía Kearns. "Questioning Modernity, Affirming Resilience: Eco-Pedagogies for Anacristina Rossi's *La loca de Gandoca* and Homero Aridjis's *¿En quién piensas cuando haces el amor?*" *Review: Literature and Arts of the Americas*, vol. 85, no. 45, 2012, pp. 167–74.

Bate, Jonathan. *The Public Value of the Humanities*. Bloomsbury Academic, 2011.

———. *Romantic Ecology: Wordsworth and the Environmental Tradition*. Routledge, 1991.

———. *The Song of the Earth*. Harvard UP, 2000.

Berger, John. *Mirar*. Gustavo Gili, 2008.

———. *Why Look at Animals*. Penguin, 2009.

Binns, Niall. "Ecocrítica en España e Hispanoamérica" ["Ecocriticism in Spain and Spanish America"]. *Ecozon@: European Journal of Literature, Culture and Environment*, vol. 1, no. 1, 2010, pp. 132–35.

"Bloom's Taxonomy." University of Waterloo, Centre for Teaching Excellence, uwaterloo.ca/centre-for-teaching-excellence/teaching-resources/teaching-tips/planning-courses-and-assignments/course-design/blooms-taxonomy. Accessed 28 June 2018.

Boling, Becky. "The Trope of Nature in Latin American Literature: Some Examples." *Studies in Twentieth and Twenty-First Century Literature*, vol. 30, no. 2, 2006, pp. 245–62.

Buell, Lawrence. *The Future of Environmental Criticism: Environmental Crisis and Literary Imagination*. Blackwell, 2005.

Colón, Cristóbal. *Diario de a bordo* [*Diary*]. Edited by Luis Arranz, Edaf, 2006.

Coupe, Laurence. General Introduction. *The Green Studies Reader*, edited by Coupe, Foreword by Jonathan Bate, Routledge, 2000, pp. 1–8.

DeVries, Scott M. *A History of Ecology and Environmentalism in Spanish American Literature*. Bucknell UP, 2013.

Doman, Danion Larry. *Latin American Liminality: Nature Writing in the Nineteenth Century, 1823–1867*. PhD dissertation, University of Colorado, 2001. *DAI*, vol. 67, no. 1, 2001, p. 2739.

Dowdy, Michael. "'Of the Smog': José Emilio Pacheco's Concussive Poetics of Mexico City." *Hispanic Review*, vol. 79, no. 2, 2011, pp. 291–316.

Forns-Broggi, Roberto. "El eco-poema de Juan L. Ortiz" [The ecopoem of Juan L. Ortiz]. *Anales de literatura hispanoamericana*, vol. 33, 2004, pp. 33–48.

Garrard, Greg. *Ecocrítica*. University of Brasília, 2006.

———. *Ecocriticism*. 2nd ed., Routledge, 2012.

Glotfelty, Cheryll. "Literary Studies in an Age of Environmental Crisis." Introduction. Glotfelty and Fromm, pp. xv–xxxvii.

Glotfelty, Cheryll, and Harold Fromm, editors. *The Ecocriticism Reader: Landmarks in Literary Ecology*, U of Georgia P, 1996.

Gossen, Gary H. "Animal Souls, Co-essences, and Human Destiny in Mesoamerica." *Monsters, Tricksters, and Sacred Cows: Animal Tales and American Identities*, edited by A. James Arnold and Derek Walcott, UP of Virginia, 1996, pp. 80–107.

Heise, Ursula K. "Globality, Difference, and the International Turn in Ecocriticism." *PMLA*, vol. 123, no. 3, 2013, pp. 636–43.

———. *Sense of Place and Sense of Planet: The Environmental Imagination of the Global.* Oxford UP, 2008.

Malamud, Randy. "The Culture of Using Animals in Literature and the Case of José Emilio Pacheco." *CLCWeb: Comparative Literature and Culture: A WWWeb Journal*, vol. 2, no. 2, 2000, doi:10.7771/1481-4374.1072.

Murphy, Patrick D. "The Varieties of Environmental Literature in North America." *Teaching North American Environmental Literature*, edited by Laird Christensen et al., Modern Language Association of America, 2008, pp. 24–36.

La nación mapuche: Donde se cultiva la palabra profunda. YouTube, uploaded by Salvador Díaz, 3 Feb. 2011, www.youtube.com/watch?v=Y5ZfbOlyReM.

Pons, Horacio, translator. *Palabras clave: Un vocabulario de la cultura y sociedad.* By Raymond Williams, Nueva Visión, 2003.

Punalka: El Alto Bío Bío. YouTube, uploaded by Néstor Fabián Lemunao, 18 Apr. 2013, www.youtube.com/watch?v=177OtR7x5-Q.

"El Río Gualeguay podría llegar a ser: el 'Riachuelo Entrerriano.'" *Ecología por Fundavida*, 14 Dec. 2008, fundavida.org.ar/web2.0//wp-content/uploads/2010/01/rio-gualeguay.pdf.

Rueckert, William. "Literature and Ecology: An Experiment in Ecocriticism." Glotfelty and Fromm, pp. 105–23.

Sarmiento, Domingo F. *Facundo: Civilización y barbarie.* Edited by Roberto Yahni, Cátedra, 2017.

TERMIUM Plus: The Government of Canada's Terminology and Linguistic Data Bank. Government of Canada, www.btb.termiumplus.gc.ca/tpv2alpha/alpha-eng.html?lang=eng.

Tittler, Jonathan. "Una relectura ecocrítica del canon criollista: Mariano Latorre y Horacio Quiroga" [An Ecocritical Re-reading of the Criollista Canon: Mariano Latorre and Horacio Quiroga]. *Tabula Rasa*, vol. 7, 2007, pp. 197–210.

Vasconcelos, Sandra Guardini, translator. *Palavras-chave: Um vocabulário de cultura e sociedade.* By Raymond Williams, Boitempo Editorial, 2007.

Vicuña, Cecilia, editor. *Ül: Four Mapuche Poets.* Americas Society / Latin American Review Press, 1998.

Viveiros de Castro, Eduardo. "Cosmological Deixis and Amerindian Perspectivism." *Journal of the Royal Anthropological Institute*, new series, vol. 4, no. 3, 1998, pp. 469–88.

White, Steven F. "Ecocrítica y chamanismo en la poesía de Pablo Antonio Cuadra" [Ecocriticism and Shamanism in the Poetry of Pablo Antonio Cuadra]. *Anales de literatura hispanoamericana*, vol. 33, 2004, pp. 49–64.

Williams, Raymond. *Keywords: A Vocabulary of Culture and Society.* Rev ed., Oxford UP, 1985.

Zubiaurre, Maite. "Discurso utópico, basura tóxica y reciclaje ecofeminista en Gioconda Belli: El Caso 'Waslala'/Goiânia." [Utopian Discourse, Toxic Waste and Ecofeminist Recycling in the Case *Waslala*/Goiânia]. *Letras femeninas*, vol. 30, no. 2, 2004, pp. 75–93.

An Intercultural and Ecocritical Approach to Teaching Turkish

Defne Erdem Mete

Environment is an intrinsic part of culture, influencing our ways of life, indeed even our language, so much so that learners of Turkish encounter it everywhere, from public gatherings in rural areas for the ritual Yağmur Duası ("Prayer for Rain") to nationwide protests against urban development plans that have geopolitical implications. In this sense, increasing environmental awareness is a global issue, because the values that emerge through such development further our understanding of many other aspects of culture. This essay examines how an intercultural approach to foreign language teaching intersects with ecocritical perspectives developed by literary and cultural studies and proposes a synthesis of the two dimensions for the teaching of Turkish as a foreign language.

The ecocritical orientation in foreign language teaching advocated here can be seen as an extension to the intercultural approach developed by Michael Byram, whose model of intercultural communicative competence (ICC) emphasizes three main components of competence (knowledge, attitude, and skills), as well as critical cultural awareness (*Teaching*). Using this model as a framework helps identify compatible objectives for both intercultural and ecocritical foreign language education. Whereas communicative language teaching practices have focused on the native speaker as a model, Byram's broader approach introduces the concept of the *intercultural speaker*, and thus regards learners' reflections about their own culture and their awareness of global issues as indispensable to language learning. Following discussion of this model, this essay turns to teaching practices that increase ecological awareness by fostering intercultural competence. These examples show that using the intercultural approach as a model to ask questions about the place of nature in Turkish culture reveals values involving the relations of human products and society to the environment today.

The Intercultural Speaker

Today's world conditions urge us to look for what we hold in common instead of focusing solely on our differences. As a result, we see the development of educational trends such as deep education (Tochon), values education (Robb), peace education (Reardon), and global education (Burnouf). New approaches to conceiving the foreign language curriculum according to types of literacies also advance such global perspectives. One of the crucial yet overlooked literacies is *intercultural literacy*, defined by Mark Heyward as "the understandings, competencies, attitudes, language proficiencies, participation and identities necessary for successful cross-cultural engagement" (10).

To prepare our students to be successful in our globalized world, we need to recognize that communication is a crucial element, not only for intercultural literacy but also for all types of literacies. Heyward concludes that a person who has cross-cultural literacy should have the "interpersonal and social skills required to interact respectfully with persons whose background and identity formation may differ substantially from their own" (8). Although respectful interaction seems to be mainly about skills, we also need to take into account factors, such as knowledge and attitudes, that influence the communication process. If an interlocutor does not sincerely feel empathy for another person, it is unrealistic to expect a successful display of cultural sensitivity in an interaction with that person. Therefore, the process of effective communication should be viewed as involving three interrelated dimensions: knowledge, attitude, and skills.

From the viewpoint of foreign language teaching, the competency model suggested by Byram in *Teaching and Assessing Intercultural Communicative Competence* is significant because it acknowledges that these dimensions contribute to the communication process itself. With the ICC model, Byram introduces the notion of the *intercultural speaker* to refer to the participant involved in complex interpersonal communication. In his view, judgment about whether such an interaction is successful can be made "in terms of the effective exchange of information, as has been the tendency in much communicative language teaching, but also in terms of the establishing and maintenance of human relationships" (32–33). The successful intercultural speaker is someone who speaks a foreign language to communicate effectively and build relationships with people from different cultural backgrounds. Byram emphasizes that the competencies of the intercultural speaker emerged out of a necessity in foreign language teaching:

> . . . [T]he aims and purposes of foreign language education have changed in the past few decades, with the much stronger emphasis on communication. Initially, this was conceived as the exchange of messages and information, but it was gradually realized that even in minimal exchanges of information, the presence of the people and their identities cannot and should not be ignored. The purpose of defining the competences of the intercultural speaker is, above all, to ensure that those teaching foreign languages can take this into consideration in a systematically planned approach to teaching and learning. ("Intercultural Speaker" 330–31)

What Byram claims, then, is that cultural patterns of awareness must play a key role in language teaching when we seek to engage language learners with global issues. This means the individual will become more broadly literate both by gaining linguistic proficiency in a foreign language and by developing the competencies of the intercultural speaker who has to engage with issues that have large-scale cultural dimensions, such as our human relation to the environment.

Arguably, the most pressing global problem today is the ecological crisis. As educators in general, and foreign-language teachers in particular, we can teach our students to be effective communicators in helping to address our world's problems. If we imagine what ecocritical pedagogy would look like, it would be the teaching of environmental concerns in the classroom. Greg Garrard observes, however, that "whatever innovations are practiced by ecocritics in their own teaching, published ecocritical pedagogy has remained both theoretically underdeveloped and empirically unresearched" (233). In the same way, foreign-language teachers who want to follow an ecocritical approach in their classes find few materials for this purpose. A relevant theoretical framework, such as Byram's, has praxis implications because it can provide guidance for an ecocritical approach to foreign language teaching.

Environment is a deeply cultural construct, as Uwe Küchler insists (445). Foreign-language learners' culturally determined understandings about the environment must be negotiated to focus on what is similar among students from different backgrounds and find common ground for offering appropriate solutions for ecological problems. Critical thinking on environmental issues can be fostered for foreign-language learners by attending to the critical cultural awareness dimension of the ICC framework.

Based on an understanding of communication as human interaction rather than as an exchange of information, the ICC model highlights the importance of respect, empathy, and tolerance as important global values. These ideals are also crucial in ecocritical pedagogy intended to develop students' sensitivity to the environment while fostering social responsibility for its protection. Recognizing that "we live in a world that has lost its deep values" (Tochon 3), we can reclaim those values by appropriate educational practices, such as those proposed in this essay.

In terms of the range of intercultural abilities discussed by Byram in *Teaching and Assessing Intercultural Communicative Competence*, the developing intercultural speaker has five competencies to master: attitudes, knowledge, "skills of interpreting and relating" (52), "skills of discovery and interaction" (52), and "critical cultural awareness [or] political education" (53). In the present discussion, the competencies that best enable learning about environmental issues are the primary concern. Hence, following Byram, we can see that *attitude*, which relates to "[c]uriosity and openness," pertains to "readiness to suspend disbelief about" another culture's understanding and practices related to nature, and leads to examination of one's own cultural understanding and practices (50). The dimension of *knowledge*, which refers to the knowledge "of social groups and their products and practices," likewise, can be related to nature in the learner's or the interlocutor's country and to "the general processes of societal and individual interaction" with the environment (51).

Skills of interpreting and relating support the "[a]bility to interpret a document or event from another culture" related to nature, as well as to make cultural comparisons (52). In contrast, *skills of discovery and interaction* demonstrate the "[a]bility to acquire new knowledge" about cultural understandings of nature, and the ability to transfer that knowledge to real-time communication about issues related to nature (52). The last dimension of the five competencies, *critical cultural awareness* or *political education*, which reflects the "ability to evaluate critically and on the basis of explicit criteria," comes into play in situations where connections are made between the "perspectives, practices, and products" related to nature of "[the learner's] own and other cultures and countries" (53).

Objectives for the Foreign Language Classroom: Attitudes, Social Knowledge, Interpretive Skills, and Critical Cultural Awareness

If we want learners to become more capable of using these skills, classroom practices need to be adjusted. We as teachers can help by recognizing that the content we choose to teach provides abundant opportunities for learners to become more proficient intercultural speakers, all the more so when environmental awareness as a key component of intercultural competency is taken into consideration. The objectives for teaching, learning, and assessment can, thus, be adapted from Byram for use in a dual curriculum of ecocritically and interculturally oriented approaches (*Teaching* 57–64). The specific topics that follow offer examples for learners of Turkish who aim to be not only proficient users of Turkish but also well-informed intercultural speakers who are sensitive to environmental issues.

For many learners of Turkish, encounters with unfamiliar cultural practices about nature occur most strikingly when they learn about the Yörük people, the nomads of Anatolia, who spend their lives in nature and seasonally change their habitats. Classroom activities focusing on the cultural dimensions of their daily life require careful planning to foster "willingness to seek out opportunities to engage with otherness in a relationship of equality," distinct from "seeking out the exotic" (Byram, *Teaching* 50). Similarly, discussions of earthquakes, which are familiar ecological phenomena in present-day Turkey and Turkish history, present opportunities for learning about their significance in other cultures. In rural areas of Turkey, a rich oral tradition still exists about the ecological signs that precede an earthquake, such as how the stars look in the sky and how the animals act, and one can also hear explanations for earthquakes as God's punishment for the people living in a particular region. For language learners, shifting cultural perspectives so dramatically starts with a receptive attitude, together with opportunities to make cultural comparisons that begin with a focus on language.

One topic that offers access to these comparisons for Turkish-language learners is Turkish proverbs, which are used frequently in daily life. Many proverbs refer to the environment in metaphorical terms. For example, *Ağaç yaşken eğilir*, whose literal translation is "a tree bends down when it is young," reflects Turkish presuppositions about youthful resilience. In terms of meaning, this Turkish proverb is equivalent to the English idiom *you can't teach an old dog new tricks*. To develop intercultural sensitivity in accordance with what Byram suggests, comparison and contrast of linguistic cultural practices like these proverbs can become a starting point for discussions. Other fruitful examples include forms of communication like the rituals performed in some ancient traditions, such as those during the festival of Hıdırellez, to celebrate the arrival of spring in Turkey. This celebration is accompanied by specific types of cultural communication, such as tying a golden ring to a rose bush, which is practiced especially by girls who want to get married. In this case, an objective for the Turkish-language learner would be to develop a "readiness to engage with the conventions and rites of verbal and non-verbal communication and interaction" (Byram, *Teaching* 50).

Such attitudinal readiness and flexibility as a goal of Byram's model functions in tandem with objectives related to the knowledge dimension of intercultural competence, which can be gained by exploring the historical and contemporary relationships to nature through comparisons across cultures. In this regard, students need to know about the international agreements for the protection of nature that Turkey has with other countries. Given that there are many institutions in Turkey that facilitate contact or help resolve problems related to nature, such as in the case of natural disasters, the Turkish-language learner should know the function of the voluntary organization named AKUT Arama Kurtarma Derneği ("AKUT Search and Rescue Association") and the public institution named Kızılay ("Red Crescent"), which aim to help victims of natural disasters.

Following Byram's recommendation that knowledge be gained about the "types of cause and process of misunderstanding" (*Teaching* 51), teachers may wish to foreground the diverse cultural perspectives that exist within Turkey, many relating to nature itself. Students of Turkish can be taught about the similarities and differences between the two traditional celebrations for the arrival of spring: Hıdırellez and Nevruz. Both have different cultural rituals, and hence a lack of knowledge about these rituals and their origins can cause misunderstandings that lead to learning opportunities. Similarly,

Turkish-language learners can study Yağmur Duası ("Prayer for Rain"), a ritual in which the public gathers with the aim of praying for rain, especially in
rural areas during a drought. This topic creates an opening for the discussion
of local cultural practices, ritual interactions, and deeply held beliefs.

A further example of this kind may be found in institutions of socializa-
tion and in policies related to the protection of the environment. It is important for the Turkish-language learner to understand how educational institutions try to foster environmental literacy and awareness in comparison
to the way other institutions, such as religious ones, approach issues related
to nature. More specifically, institutions that deal with environmental issues and the activities that they carry out for the protection of nature can be
discussed readily in the foreign language classroom, since learners can compare and contrast the influence of such activities on daily life in Turkey with
their own experiences in their home country. Good examples for learners to
investigate are the activities of the Turkish Foundation for Combating Soil
Erosion, for Reforestation and the Protection of Natural Habitats (TEMA).
The TEMA foundation carries out many projects under its well-known slo-
gan "do not let Turkey become a desert," including planting trees throughout Turkey. Boxes for the collection and recycling of used paper sponsored
by TEMA can be found in many public places and official buildings.

Byram's framework also points out the significance of having knowledge
on "the national memory of one's interlocutor's country and the perspective on [its events]" (*Teaching* 51), and these aspects are closely connected in
attitudes toward nature in Turkey. In his overview about the importance of
the Atatürk Orman Çiftliği ("Atatürk Forest Farm") in Ankara, John Vander-
Lippe states:

> The national architecture of the early Turkish Republic was a prod-
> uct of redefining space according to the Kemalist reform agenda
> of the young republic, including re-designating and disciplining
> of urban space as well as the natural environment. Ankara, as the
> new capital of Turkey, was at the centre of efforts, presented as an
> example to emulate, and a viable contrast to the old capital of the
> Ottoman Empire, İstanbul. The spatial and environmental restruc-
> turing of Ankara became a way to generate a physical representa-
> tion of *muasırlaşmak*, or "modernization", which was at the core of
> Kemalism, but also as a symbol for overcoming the Ottoman past
> and creating a new Turkish future.   (209)

Thus, the Atatürk Forest Farm in the national memory of the Turkish people has played a pivotal role in defining the capital city of modern Turkey by creating a role for nature that shapes cultural identity. Students of Turkish in the twenty-first century are interested to learn about what this farm symbolized in the past and what it signifies at present. The Turkish-language classroom is an ideal setting for discussions comparing and contrasting environmental issues from a transnational perspective.

Turning now to the two types of skills Byram refers to in his framework of intercultural competence—interpreting and relating on the one hand, and discovery and interaction on the other—we encounter equally complex possibilities for engaging learners in intercultural exploration. Byram locates interpreting and relating in learner tasks that depend on being able to "identify ethnocentric perspectives" and areas of misunderstandings in documents, events, and interactions, all of which relate to nature and our ability to contextualize our understanding of it through reference to cultural systems (*Teaching* 52). For example, some rituals related to nature in Turkish culture, such as the ones that take place during Hıdırellez for the arrival of spring, have origins in the shamanism of central Asia. After the influence of Islam in Anatolia, the celebration gained Islamic motifs by being associated with the holy figure Hızır and the prophet İlyas, whose names combined to form the word *Hıdırellez*. Misunderstandings or inaccurate overgeneralizations might occur if the concepts in the rituals of Hıdırellez are explained by references only to Islam. For students, this context would necessarily lead to discovery and interaction (Byram's second skill set), since negotiation of meaning and interpretation needs to occur.

Byram makes the point that the intercultural speaker should be expected to "elicit from an interlocutor the concepts and values of documents or events and develop an explanatory system susceptible of application to other phenomena" related to nature (*Teaching* 52), and in that sense it is worth considering the proximity of oral and written culture as experienced by learners of Turkish. A topic for study in formal Turkish instruction can be the Islamic belief in the historical story of the Flood of Noah and its application to the Aşure Ayı ("Month of Aşure") and its representation of environmental forces. It is a story of disordered nature that starts with severe rain and flood and ends with survival at the top of a mountain.

The event is presented as a punishment of God for those who did not respect God's orders. Instead of saving human beings, the prophet Noah rescued animals (the real natives of nature), from snakes to giraffes. Noah (who represents man as the master of nature) empathizes with the other species to restart life, just as God started life. Noah knows he will not survive without the other inhabitants of nature. Traditionally, it is believed that in the last days of the Flood when food was about to run out, Noah prepared a kind of dish by combining what was left of the dry legumes and fruits. Today this dish, with more or less the same ingredients, is a dessert known as *aşure*. Once a year during the Aşure Ayı, which is like a celebration of thanksgiving to nature, people cook this dessert in their homes and share it with the neighborhood. Thus, *aşure* symbolizes the abundance of God's gifts to human beings and is shared with others as an offering of peace and love. For the Turkish-language student, the complex conventions surrounding the sharing of *aşure* with neighbors, friends, and relatives mean that knowledge about the Month of Aşure depends on discovery and interaction.

Proficiency at discovery and interaction also helps learners "identify significant references" to nature and draw out their meaning "within and across cultures" (Byram, *Teaching* 53). Turkish-language learners, for example, may discover the ritual of tying colorful pieces of cloth on the branches of a tree and making a wish. This tradition dates back to the shamanism of central Asia again, where trees were regarded as sacred. According to the ancient description, the divine tree has roots reaching deep into the earth and branches that touch the sky, almost as if drawing a connection between God and life on earth. This Tree of Life is also found in Sumerian traditions. Muazzez İlmiye Çığ, a well-known Turkish Sumerologist, claims that Sumerians are a branch of Turks (*Sümerliler*) and that the motif of the pine tree and the placing of gifts under the tree for the gods originated with the Turks ("Noel"). Instead of decorations, Çığ explains, Turks used to tie pieces of cloth on the branches to represent their wishes. When Turkish culture encountered Islam, trees on which pieces of cloth were tied were frequently placed near the graves of Muslim mystics, even though such a belief is not supported by explicit Islamic religious practices. The sacred corpse lying near the tree was seen as a further means of making one's wish come true. As Galina Serkina explains, these are also the origins of the tree pattern commonly found in Turkish rugs today.

Beyond situations in which the present and past come together during the process of discovery and interaction, Turkish-language learners, like all contemporary students, experience real-time situations that require the use of "an appropriate combination of knowledge, skills and attitudes to interact with interlocutors from a different country and culture" (Byram, *Teaching* 53). In the classroom, role-playing can be used for this purpose and developed to center on environmental advocacy by Greenpeace, an international organization that is active in Turkey. In the real world, some of Greenpeace's demonstrations in Turkey have resulted in protestors being taken into custody. In such cases, Turkish-language learners, in effect, become witnesses to and potentially participants in history as they study contemporary events.

To do so, however, they need to exercise critical cultural awareness, an integral component of Byram's ICC framework. For the Turkish-language learners, the environmental protests that drew international attention can be a subject for discussion. One of these protests began as an effort to save trees in a small park. Soon afterward, the local protests turned into nationwide demonstrations. Different kinds of protests were observed in these events, one of which was called the *standing man*, where people simply stood still silently on the street. Based on this topic, class activities can be developed to contextualize this protest (in terms of origins, time, place, and relations to other events) and "demonstrate the ideology involved" (cf. Byram, *Teaching* 63). For these tasks, students would need to become aware of their own ideological perspectives and values to be able to evaluate the events. As Byram explains, learners need to be "aware of potential conflicts between [their] own and other ideologies and should be able to establish common criteria of evaluation of documents or events, and where this is not possible because of incompatibilities in belief and value systems, able to negotiate agreement on places of conflict and acceptance of difference" (*Teaching* 64).

A Turkish Lesson with an Intercultural and Ecocritical Approach

The way in which these five competencies interact can be seen through the discussion of a sample pedagogical treatment of a literary text. This lesson is designed around the Turkish poem "Ceviz Ağacı" ("The Walnut Tree"), by Nazım Hikmet. Although it may not be immediately clear what the connection is between environmental awareness and the understanding of language and culture, discussion of this poem illustrates why it is so important for learners to become knowledgeable about this association.

Nazım Hikmet, who lived from 1902 to 1963, is a well-known Turkish poet, playwright, and novelist who spent more than a third of his life in exile. His literary works were banned for decades, whereas today they are available in more than fifty languages. In this poem, the poet uses personification to challenge human-nonhuman dualism by letting the walnut tree speak to the reader. For this lesson, it would be useful to provide students with a brief background of the poem in order to help them have empathy for the poet's feelings.

The story of the poem at first seems mundane: Nazım Hikmet had an appointment with his beloved to meet under a walnut tree in Gülhane Park. When the day came, Nazım went to the park and started waiting under the walnut tree. At that moment, he saw some officers wandering in the park. In those days, as Turkish readers know, Nazım was one of those individuals who would have been arrested if he had been found. In an attempt to hide, he climbed up the walnut tree. When he was up in the tree, his beloved Piraye arrived and started waiting for him under the walnut tree, unaware of what was going on. Afraid of being heard by others, Nazım could not call out to his beloved. In despair, he took out his pen and a piece of paper, and started writing a poem called "Ceviz Ağacı" ("The Walnut Tree").

Bas,ım köpük köpük bulut, içim dıs,ım deniz,
ben bir ceviz ağacıyım Gülhane Parkı'nda,
budak budak, şerham şerham ihtiyar bir ceviz.
Ne sen bunun farkındasın, ne polis farkında.

Ben bir ceviz ağacıyım Gülhane Parkı'nda.
Yapraklarım suda balık gibi kıvıl kıvıl.
Yapraklarım ipek mendil gibi tiril tiril,
koparıver, gözlerinin, gülüm, yaşını sil.
Yapraklarım ellerimdir, tam yüz bin elim var.
Yüz bin elle dokunurum sana, İstanbul'a.
Yapraklarım gözlerimdir, şaşarak bakarım.
Yüz bin gözle seyrederim seni, İstanbul'u.
Yüz bin yürek gibi çarpar, çarpar yapraklarım.

Ben bir ceviz ağacıyım Gülhane Parkı'nda.
Ne sen bunun farkındasın, ne polis farkında. (Hikmet 1618)

My head is a foaming cloud, inside and outside of me is the sea,
I am a walnut tree in Gülhane Park,
An old walnut tree with knots and cracks.
Neither you are aware of this, nor the police.

I am a walnut tree in Gülhane Park.
My leaves are agile like fish in water.
My leaves are sheer like silk handkerchiefs,
Break one off, my rose, wipe your tears.
My leaves are my hands, I have one hundred thousand hands.
I touch you, İstanbul, with one hundred thousand hands.
My leaves are my eyes, and I am amazed at what I see.
I watch you, İstanbul, with one hundred thousand eyes.
My leaves beat like one hundred thousand hearts.

I am a walnut tree in Gülhane Park.
Neither you are aware of this, nor the police.   (my trans.)

This poem can be analyzed in the Turkish language classroom as a literary text, using intercultural and ecocritical approaches. If the lesson starts with an analysis of the poem's grammatical features, additional steps focusing on intercultural competency skills could be incorporated by the teacher in the following ways.

Explain how the reduplication of words in the poem is used to intensify the meaning and ask students to identify examples of this pattern. Reduplication is a grammatical feature of Turkish, one type of which is called *ikileme* ("repeating twice"). In this poem, examples of *ikileme* are "köpük köpük bulut"; "budak budak ceviz"; "şerham şerham ceviz"; "kıvıl kıvıl yapraklar"; "tiril tiril yapraklar." After identifying these examples, the students can work in groups to discuss how this grammatical feature enhances the meaning of the expressions used in the poem. Ask small groups of students to imagine the walnut tree described in the poem and answer questions involving empathetic responses: What does the walnut tree say to us? How does it feel? How does the walnut tree offer friendship to the human beings? What is the attitude of the human beings toward the walnut tree? How does the poem make you feel?

After classroom discussion on the questions, the students can then be asked to replace Gülhane Parkı ("Gülhane Park") in the original poem with names of other parks that are under the threat of urban development plans, making a kind of transposition discussed by Claire Kramsch (253). They can then try to imagine the walnut tree in the other park, this time answering the same questions and comparing their answers in discussion groups.

Address the objectives for this lesson that encourage students' development of intercultural and ecocritical thinking by emphasizing skill areas as follows.

Attitudes

Curiosity about what the walnut tree wants to say and the values involved leads learners directly to discussion of the social and environmental aspects of the situation.

The poet's identification with the walnut tree in a relationship of equality challenges the dualism of human-nonhuman by provoking empathy. Through reverse personification, the speaker, instead of giving human qualities to a tree, presents himself as a tree to the reader, giving himself the qualities of a tree, including leaves and branches. In mainstream dichotomies, the human is always superior to the nonhuman. In this example, however, the reverse happens: nonhuman parts are privileged over human qualities.

Contextualized Knowledge

To gain knowledge about the geographical space that the park occupies in İstanbul, learners can work with teacher-provided information about Gülhane Park and other parks, as well as the number of parks and green areas in İstanbul. Maps of the city (authentic materials) can be used by the teacher to design interactive activities for this purpose.

To gain knowledge about the national memory of the Turkish people regarding the time when the poem was originally written, additional prose texts can be assigned, and learners can compare Turkey with their home country. They can discuss whether there are any similarities between them, and whether the students know about similar periods in their own country's history.

Additionally, discussion may lead to inquiry into whether the education system in Turkey teaches students about nature starting from a young age, whether outdoor education is popular or not, and how the education system functions in general, creating options for Turkish-language learners to be directed to additional informational texts.

Skills of Interpreting and Relating, Discovery and Interaction

Learners can reflectively mediate by engaging with the contrast the poem establishes between the walnut tree and the unaware human beings in the form of a role-playing activity. They can also develop an appreciation for references related to nature within and across cultures that allows them to recognize the significance and connotations of these allusions. For example, the poet compares the leaves of the walnut tree to a silk handkerchief. One of the connotations of this simile is that a gentleman of İstanbul is offering his handkerchief to a lady who needs it. In the past, the nobles living in İstanbul were referred to as *İstanbul soylusu* ("the noble/elite of İstanbul"). Therefore, the walnut tree is also associated with nobility. From this perspective, the tree is given the qualities of a gentleman, as the tree itself is associated with nobility, which is a reflection of the cultural significance of trees in traditional Turkish society. Trees symbolize wisdom and generosity. In addition, the comparison of the leaves to the fish in the sea, from an ecocritical perspective, highlights the interdependence and interconnectedness of every creature in the world.

To develop skills for use in real time, learners can be encouraged to exercise "an appropriate combination of knowledge, skills and attitudes for interacting with interlocutors from a different country and culture" (Byram, *Teaching* 53). For this purpose, the teacher can organize a debate about a controversial topic regarding the protection of the environment.

Critical Cultural Awareness

As a follow-up to the previous activities, the teacher can refer to the objectives for raising critical cultural awareness or political education outlined in this essay. For example, in relation to the first objective Byram offers in this category, that of identifying and interpreting "explicit or implicit values in documents" (*Teaching* 53), learners could be asked to identify and interpret the connotations of the word *old* in the poem, where the walnut tree defines itself as an "old walnut tree." In Turkish culture, being old is associated with having wisdom, and therefore an important value is respecting the elderly. Age is linked to experience; thus, the older people are, the more experienced and wise they are held to be. Instead of focusing on the present, the wording emphasizes the guidance that would be provided by the past for present and future generations. Students can also compare and contrast the connotations of the word *police* in the poem with its implications in their own cultures. In this poem, from an ecocritical perspective, "the police" symbolizes the authority that students may associate with the human part of the human-nonhuman dichotomy, since the description reveals human blindness to the true nature of a single tree.

Suggestions for Other Topics to Explore in the Turkish Classroom

Other literary and nonliterary texts can also be used in the Turkish-language classroom to enhance intercultural and ecological awareness. Various activities can be designed for different levels. Turkish folk songs can be used, as they provide a rich resource for exploring how nature plays an important role in expressing the Turkish people's feelings (Parlak). The Turkish national anthem and other anthems that have national significance can also be studied in the language classroom. As an example, the well-known anthem "Gençlik Marşı" ("Youth Anthem"), which contains many references to nature, can be used for listening activities that focus on vocabulary development, especially for beginning-level students. For the intermediate and advanced levels, national anthem activities can be developed asking students to compare and contrast cultural values associated with nature and national identity. Where necessary, classroom discussions can be carried out in English rather than Turkish. In this way, learners can feel free to express themselves even if their Turkish proficiency is limited.

Turkish traditional rituals can also be studied through role-playing, which is suitable for all levels of learners. A well-known tradition involves throwing water with a glass or a cup behind a loved one who is setting out on a journey. This ritual has the meaning "have a smooth journey, as smooth as water." At the end of the activity, instructors can facilitate discussions about the cultural associations of water in different cultures in either English or Turkish.

As the discussion of Hikmet's poem and aspects of Turkish language and culture reveals, environmental awareness can be viewed as fundamental to intercultural communication issues. Foreign-language learners may not be aware of how deeply culture plays a role in shaping their attitudes toward nature. In the classroom context, activities such as the ones suggested in this paper can allow students not only to reflect on their own selves but also to realize how their cultural understandings influence the way they see nature. Developing environmental awareness in this way gives learners of Turkish, and indeed any language, the opportunity for the type of self-critique that can lead to a motivation to take action to protect nature.

On a broader scale, approaching environmental issues within an intercultural communication framework that puts emphasis on effective communication as well as on culture would help us to question our lives in fundamental ways: how can an effective balance be established between the human and the nonhuman on our globe? What does nature tell us, if we are willing to listen? How do we communicate with and about nature with respect and empathy, mindfulness and tolerance? Though nature seemingly has tolerated our disregard and ignorance, it is time for us to respect its wisdom, an attitude that has a deep relationship to Turkish language and culture.

WORKS CITED

Burnouf, Laura. "Global Awareness and Perspectives in Global Education." *Canadian Social Studies Journal*, vol. 38, no. 3, 2004, files.eric.ed.gov/fulltext/EJ1073942.pdf.

Byram, Michael. "The Intercultural Speaker and the Pedagogy of Foreign Language Education." *The Sage Handbook of Intercultural Competence*, edited by Darla Kay Deardorff, Sage, 2009, pp. 321–32.

———. *Teaching and Assessing Intercultural Communicative Competence*. Multilingual Matters, 1997.

Çığ, Muazzez İlmiye. "Noel Bayramı'nın Kökü Türklerde" [Christmas Originates from Turks]. *Bütün Dünya* [The Whole World], Jan. 2017, pp. 45–48.

———. *Sümerliler Türklerin Bir Koludur* [Sumerians Are a Branch of Turks]. Kaynak Yayınları, 2014.

Garrard, Greg. "Problems and Prospects in Ecocritical Pedagogy." *Environmental Education Research*, vol. 16, no. 2, 2010, pp. 233–45.

Heyward, Mark. "From International to Intercultural: Redefining the International School for a Globalized World." *Journal of Research in International Education*, vol. 1, no. 1, 2002, pp. 9–32.

Hikmet, Nazım. *Nazım Hikmet: Bütün Şiirleri* [Nazım Hikmet: All His Poetry]. Yapı Kredi Yayınları, 2016.

Kramsch, Claire. "The Challenge of Globalization for the Teaching of Foreign Languages and Cultures." *Electronic Journal of Foreign Language Teaching*, vol. 11, no. 2, 2014, pp. 249–54, e-flt.nus.edu.sg/v11n22014/kramsch.pdf.

Küchler, Uwe. "Linking Foreign Language Education and the Environment." Oppermann et al., pp. 436–52.

Oppermann, Serpil, et al., editors. *The Future of Ecocriticism: New Horizons*. Cambridge Scholars Publishing, 2011.

Parlak, Zafer. "Nature in Anatolian Mystic Poetry and Folk Songs." Oppermann et al., pp. 172–87.

Reardon, Betty A. *Comprehensive Peace Education: Educating for Global Responsibility.* Teachers College Press, 1988.

Robb, William. "What Is Values Education—and So What?" *The Journal of Values Education*, vol. 1, 1998, www.valueseducation.co.uk/articles/What-is-values-education-and-so-what.pdf. Accessed 10 May 2016.

Serkina, Galina. "Traces of Tree Worship in the Decorative Patterns of Turkish Rugs." Eleventh International Congress of Turkish Arts, Utrecht University, 23–28 Aug. 1999.

Tochon, Francois Victor. "Deep Education." *Journal for Educators, Teachers and Trainers*, vol. 1, 2010, jett.labosfor.com/index.php/jett. Accessed 20 May 2016.

VanderLippe, John. "The Statist Environment: Gazi Orman Çiftliği and the Kemalist Modernization Project." Oppermann et al., pp. 209–26.

Stepping Out of the Language Box: College Spanish and Sustainability

María J. de la Fuente

In 2007 the Modern Language Association (MLA) published "Foreign Languages and Higher Education: New Structures for a Changed World," a report advocating curricular reform for collegiate-level foreign language programs geared toward the creation of a broad disciplinary and interdisciplinary perspective on languages and cultures. The authors argued that this type of change was needed to support language learning outcomes at a more advanced level (241). A subsequent MLA white paper published in 2009, *Report to the Teagle Foundation on the Undergraduate Major in Language and Literature*, recommended connecting the goals and objectives of undergraduate concentrations in foreign languages to those of a liberal education. Since then, these calls for transformation have had a positive effect on many foreign language departments, where the inclusion of interdisciplinary and multidisciplinary perspectives has become common. Despite the increasingly abundant body of literature in the area, however, Spanish programs and departments have found it difficult to break through the firmly entrenched format and content of more traditional curricula. More initiatives are needed to stimulate curricular innovation in Spanish teaching and learning at all levels (Nuessel).

The transformation of foreign language curricula advocated by both MLA reports calls for coherent four-year sequences in which language study permeates all levels of the curriculum and where advanced courses address multiple content areas, with the overarching goal of cross-cultural literacy (see also Byrnes and Maxim; Swaffar and Arens; Swaffar and Urlaub). Any (re)design of courses and curricula under this approach requires a fundamental rethinking in terms of theory, learning outcomes, approach, delivery of course content, and assessment of learning. Above all, the design needs to integrate disciplinary content knowledge and language proficiency.

Without doubt, when considering the incorporation of interdisciplinarity into the language curriculum, we need to "look to content of important concern to the linguistic, social, or cultural life of communities represented in the areas we teach" (Melin 113). With Latin America at the forefront of current global debates about sustainable development, and with sustainability as one of the main goals of liberal arts education, Spanish programs are in a unique position to facilitate cross-lingual and cross-cultural perspectives related to sustainability.

This essay describes a curriculum redesign project that addresses transformation in advanced Spanish pedagogy through sustainability. With the help of a Green Leaf grant from the George Washington University Institute for Sustainability in 2013, a third-year Spanish conversation class was redesigned as an advanced oral communication course with a focus on environmental and social sustainability in Latin America. Redesigning the course in this way would align it with the institution's liberal arts educational goals while attracting a wider spectrum of students to Spanish.[1] This type of course can better prepare students for study abroad and careers crossing linguistic and cultural boundaries.

In this essay I argue for the relevance of sustainability as critical content in advanced language instruction. I first discuss the theoretical and pedagogical frameworks of this curricular redesign and then underscore the value of problem-solving tasks using case studies as optimal pedagogical tools in a sustainability-specific language classroom. Afterward, I describe the components of the curricular work that resulted in an interdisciplinary advanced Spanish course combining language and sustainability content. I emphasize the development of clearly articulated language and content learning outcomes as the central element of the curricular design. Finally, I describe and discuss the assessment of learning outcomes and the evaluation of the course.

Task and Content as Constructs
for Advanced Language Learning

The theoretical underpinnings of the present essay come primarily from the second language acquisition field, in particular three major strands. The first derives from the *interaction hypothesis* (Long), which assigns face-to-face interaction a crucial role in language development. The second, the *output hypothesis* (Swain), posits that learning takes place when learners encounter a gap in their linguistic knowledge, notice it, modify their production, and respond to feedback. The third strand is the construct of *focus on form* (Doughty and Williams), which emphasizes the value of instructed language learning, that is, the focus on formal features of the language within content-based instruction. These three constructs are realized in task-based pedagogy.

From a cognitive perspective, tasks are specific language-learning activities that facilitate optimal conditions for language learning by triggering processes that facilitate acquisition (Bygate 35; Bygate et al. 5; Robinson, *Cognition*). In other words, language development occurs while learners engage in the task (Skehan 95). Peter Skehan suggests four criteria for tasks: meaning is primary, there is a goal to be accomplished, the task is outcome-evaluated, and there is a real-world relationship (268).

Task-based research has largely focused on the concepts of negotiated interaction and focus on form. The interaction hypothesis predicts that tasks that promote learners' negotiation of meaning facilitate the development of a second language. At advanced levels of language study, sustainability topics provide meaningful and motivational content for such negotiations to take place. They also allow for advanced-level structures (argumentative) and lexicon to be the focus of interactions among learners. Indeed, most researchers agree that, although meaning processing should be primary to tasks, some focus on form is needed in order to acquire the second language (Doughty and Williams; Ellis, "Investigating" and *Task-Based Language Learning*; Robinson, "Attention"; Skehan). This focus on form causes learners to notice specific features of the input and compare them with their own production, which also induces them to reflect on language form (Swain 126). Merrill Swain's theoretical standpoint is that, without pushed output, learners engage in surface input comprehension (i.e. they process meaning), which does not guarantee further processing of linguistic form that leads to acquisition (128). Sustainability content provides opportunities for much-needed, complex language production to reach advanced levels of proficiency. The key idea is that language cannot be isolated from content.

Research has provided evidence of the positive effects of integrating content and language at all levels of instruction (Dupuy; Lyster and Ballinger; Rinner and Weigert; Stoller; Stryker and Leaver). Sandra Burger and Marie Chrétien demonstrate that students can make important gains in oral language proficiency by taking integrated content-language courses where "massive exposure to reading texts" is paired with extensive production of written and oral texts (98). Similarly, Betty L. Leaver and Christine Campbell analyze language programs that are successful in taking learners to advanced and superior levels of proficiency, identifying content-based instruction as a "key feature" in ensuring the success of the curriculum (13). Sustainability, and its multiple associated topics, is one of the most relevant areas to provide necessary content in advanced language instruction. Indeed, making students "sustainability literate" is arguably one of the key objectives of a liberal arts education (Bonnet 675). This literacy can come from many disciplines, including the study of foreign languages and cultures. In the case of this project, combining language and sustainability-specific goals produced a framework that allows learners to acquire critical content knowledge and terminology specific to environmental issues as they relate to Latin American countries, cultural practices, and social efforts to address sustainability. Through carefully designed problem-solving tasks, students encounter, interpret, analyze, and ultimately present information related to these ideas, practices, and values.

Problem-solving pedagogy provides an ideal framework for students to use the target language to explore solutions to basic or complex problems, depending on their language acquisition stage, and ultimately acquire higher levels of proficiency. In addition, problem-solving tasks are one of the most effective instructional strategies to promote higher-level critical thinking skills in a content-specific language classroom. When raising a thought-provoking issue, such tasks compel students to talk in the foreign language while requiring them to identify key points, choose and articulate positions, evaluate and reason courses of action, and argue different points of view. They also promote collaborative work (Barkley et al. 9; Duch et al. 6).

Sustainability Case Studies as Problem-Solving Tasks

One of the most effective ways to incorporate problem-based pedagogy in content-driven, advanced levels of foreign language instruction is through the use of case studies. A case study presents a real and complex situation, and often involves a dilemma, conflict, or problem that one or more "stakeholders" must negotiate. One strength of case methodology is that it encourages participants to defend their positions (Dunne and Brooks 72). A case study places students in an active role: they are faced with a problem that mirrors a real-world situation (Stover 9) and have to make decisions or judgments based on facts, logic, and rationalization. According to Daniel Stover, this type of problem-based learning "will increase retention of knowledge, help students transfer concepts to new problems, enhance their interest in the content and enhance self-directed learning" (2). Given the intrinsic nature of sustainability problems (for example, exploitation versus conservation of natural resources), cases related to sustainability have a particularly valuable function in the advanced foreign language classroom: they help students develop problem-solving, analytic, and decision-making skills and train them to cope with situations where there is no one right answer. The redesigned course, Advanced Oral Proficiency: Environmental and Social Sustainability in Latin America, combined language and sustainability components in cohesive pedagogical units, each culminating in a sustainability case study.

The Stages of Course (Re)Design

Course redesign is a circular process that moves from selection of content and themes related to sustainability (based on their potential to stimulate critical thinking: e.g., climate change, poverty), to assessment of learning outcomes, to decisions on how this assessment will improve the learning of our students.[2] There is unanimity regarding the interpretation of sustainability as the interaction of three systems: the ecological, the economic, and the social. The natural system and its resources are the infrastructure that enables economic progress and the development of society (Goodland and Daly 1005). A guiding principle for the selection of sustainability-related content was a commitment to ensuring that students could build on prior historical, political, social, and cultural issues studied in third-year Spanish courses, which guaranteed articulation and coherence. For this reason, I focused on ecological and social aspects of sustainability, that is, an orientation of sustainability that places human beings and the environment at the center of sustainable development. An introductory lesson to the content included the following: the multidimensional mode of sustainability, a brief history of sustainable development, and the United Nation's sustainable development goals related to our target region. After this, I identified the main environmental and social issues affecting Latin America's Spanish-speaking countries, and environmental sustainability challenges were selected accordingly: exploitation of natural resources, environmental degradation, conservation of ecosystems—all associated with the social challenges of poverty, economic and social inequality, and exclusion. These topics yielded five thematic units: natural resources: exploitation versus conservation, climate change, alternative sources of energy, social exclusion (ethnicity, gender), and poverty and inequality. Once content areas were selected, decisions were made on the main learning outcomes (LOs) for the course. It is important not to equate LOs to content: LOs are set considering what we want students to be able to know, think, and do at the end of the course. The measure is not what we will teach, but what our students will learn. Learning outcomes also provide students with a way to understand the overall purposes of their course work. With this in mind, three types of LOs were formulated: content-, language-, and skill-specific; all three, and the interactions between them, are needed for curricular projects that address literacy in an integrated manner.[3] All activities and tasks are designed to pay attention to these interactions. In what follows I use the unit on alternative sources of energy in Latin America and its corresponding case study (initiative for nuclear energy in Bolivia) to exemplify the stages of the redesign.

Learning Goals in the Sustainability Course

The main learning goal of this course was to be able to understand the relation between the environment and social, political, and economic factors and to apply this understanding to specific cases. For this reason, each unit's progression of learning culminates with a case study. The LOs of each case study are connected to the LOs of each unit. Each unit has four LOs, based on a psychocognitive framework of learning called Bloom's taxonomy (Bloom). They are the basis for design of the rest of the unit's elements. The learning sequence for each unit moves from lower-order LOs (recalling, understanding, and applying information), to higher-order LOs that require analysis and evaluation. All are needed to master target sustainability contents.

Integration of language LOs within each thematic area is arguably the most effective way to promote instructed development of advanced language skills in the classroom. Through constant exposure to and interaction in the foreign language, much higher task engagement and deeper processing of language occurs. Sustainability provides rich and significant learning content for the classroom. This significance makes language and content learning more efficient. With respect to the language-learning process, it is also important to have explicit language LOs, and pedagogical tasks where specific forms are objects of implicit and explicit instruction at some point. In determining language LOs, we used the American Council on the Teaching of Foreign Languages's *Proficiency Guidelines*, including all expected characteristics of an advanced level, and some of the superior level. The language LOs target the specific grammar and content-related vocabulary as well as the discursive and functional aspects of advanced Spanish (such as narrating, summarizing, introducing arguments or counterarguments, comparing and contrasting). The language LOs are as follows: describe and narrate in major past, present, and future time frames (LO 1); produce, in written or oral form, organized speech in paragraph-level length and discourse, and with enough structural control to avoid miscommunication (LO 2); explain and discuss an abstract topic, express opinions, and provide structured arguments and counterarguments to support opinions (LO 3); use specialized vocabulary (LO 4).

Finally, the development of intellectual and practical skills is considered a fundamental part of this type of course. The applied-skills learning goals for the sustainability course are for students to develop the ability to present information to an audience (LO 1); communicate effectively and persuasively (LO 2); and work collaboratively in decision-making and problem-solving tasks (LO 3).

Input as Content for the Sustainability Course

A sustainability-specific language course requires textual input to be extensive, authentic, cover a wide range of genres and discourse types (graphs, maps, digital mass media, documentaries, film), and offer different perspectives of the same theme, problem, or case study. Following Janet Swaffar and

Katherine Arens, the criteria for selecting input is to use multiple modalities of text for a similar thematic content; select cognitively challenging texts that can be exploited from a content and linguistic viewpoint, with content driving selection; and consider factors that affect the readability of the text, such as redundancy and concreteness (57–58).

For example, to address the unit LO1 in table 1 (knowledge and understanding), I selected a basic informational text describing the main types of alternative energy, a graph and a map to illustrate Latin America's energy consumption, and a video documentary on alternative energies in which an expert discusses the regional efforts and challenges to supply energy to the region. To address the same-level LO in the corresponding case study, I selected a map illustrating the countries with current nuclear plants, a video from an energy company's educational Web site explaining the functioning of a nuclear plant, a video in which two experts address the use of nuclear energy in Latin America, and a video of Argentina's president addressing the nation at the opening of a new nuclear plant. As the learning unit moves up in the LOs' cognitive demands, input sources showing specific problems and views of different stakeholders are used, as well as more complex linguistic input (e.g., argumentative or opinion pieces).

Table 1. Cognitive LOs for a Unit on
Alternative Sources of Energy in Latin America and a Case Study

LO	Unit: Alternative sources of energy in Latin America	Case study: Nuclear energy in Bolivia
LOWER-ORDER LEARNING OUTCOMES		
LO 1	Demonstrate knowledge and understanding of Latin America's energy consumption, a variety of alternative sources of energy, main stakeholders, and effects of relying on traditional forms of energy.	Demonstrate knowledge and understanding of some initiatives for nuclear energy.
LO 2	Apply knowledge to compare energy consumption in different countries.	Apply knowledge of the tridimensional sustainability model to identify problem: effects on social, environmental, economic sustainability.
HIGHER-ORDER LEARNING OUTCOMES		
LO 3	Analyze environmental, social, and economic repercussions of clean energies in specific countries.	Critically analyze the presence of nuclear energy in Bolivia and the main positions. Evaluate Bolivia's nuclear energy initiative from the point of view of different stakeholders.
LO 4	Evaluate current clean energy initiatives. Identify problems and propose solutions.	Use problem-solving and decision-making skills to propose a solution and reach an agreement.

Interactive Teaching in the Sustainability Course

The design of student-centered activities is crucial to content-based instruction. In the class, students participate in input- and output-based oral and written activities that promote, along with each of the thematic units, lower- to higher-order cognitive skills. During case studies they engage in decision-making and problem-solving tasks that provide challenging production opportunities as they work toward advanced proficiency. This design of materials is based on interactive teaching; that is, students are responsible for discovery of new material (through out-of-class activities), and the instructor uses the classroom to help them process material through application, analysis, argument, and problem solving (during in-class activities).

Out-of-class activities provide a first exposure to content to acquire necessary background knowledge. Students produce brief oral or written responses to materials (written and audiovisual). Materials also include topic-related vocabulary exercises and content-interpretation activities, such as expressing and justifying opinions. These initial tasks generally will target lower-level cognitive abilities (understanding) and four language-related LOs (discussed below). Before watching a documentary segment on alternative energies in Latin America, students need to describe a graph outlining the composition of the energy matrix in the region and formulate an initial opinion based on this graph. After watching the video documentary, they answer eight questions that address their comprehension of the information. The questions have a built-in focus on form component. For example, to respond to a question such as the one below, they need to follow a specific pattern requiring the use of subordinate clauses with the subjunctive and the expression of contrast relationships, which are target-language LOs:

Question: ¿Qué problema ambiental específico presenta la energía de biomasa? ("What specific environmental problem does biomass energy posit?")

Answer: Aunque es cierto que . . . sin embargo . . . ("Although it is true that . . . nonetheless . . .")

The activity ends with extension questions that require learners to think critically about the information and produce responses expressing their own ideas and opinions about nonrenewable versus renewable energy sources.

The extension part can then be shared in class, where students compare their responses and discuss different opinions.

The activity section of the case study targets two lower-level cognitive abilities: understanding and applying. Students work with two texts and a video from a news source. Students need to familiarize themselves with the main stakeholders and their points of view. The first part asks students to read a text and underline the parts where the viewpoints of the Bolivian government and the environmentalist organizations are expressed. Next, students read an article on nuclear energy use and identify economic, environmental, and sociopolitical arguments and counterarguments in the text by filling out a chart. Last, they watch a video about Bolivia's plan and identify the point of view and arguments of both the government and the political opposition. The extension part requires students to identify the problem and apply the sustainability model to decide if this initiative is viable, sustainable, and equitable.

In-class tasks (e.g., pair or group work and discussion, debates, and panels) target higher-level critical thinking, are connected to out-of-class activities, are student-centered, and involve a higher-level cognitive skill: analysis. Language LOs expand to include students' production of arguments and counterarguments. Applied skills such as collaborative work, decision-making, and problem solving are also target LOs (see below). Working in groups, students need to think about this sustainability case from the perspectives of several stakeholders (government, environmentalists, citizens, etc.). Each stakeholder's position needs to be explained from a social, environmental, and economic perspective. The activity ensures that all students understand the multiple points of view involved in any sustainability problem. This is compared and contrasted in a whole-class session. Following this, students work in groups, each assuming a specific role to defend their views in a panel or debate. For this panel or debate there are six stakeholders represented. Each group develops arguments and counterarguments to use during the panel, based on the social, environmental, and economic consequences of this initiative. The panel is held during the following class session.

Other out-of-class activities target high-level critical thinking LOs: a follow-up activity to the debate that requires each student to assume a stakeholder's identity, respond to a hypothetical situation, and give a possible solution that incorporates all parties involved via an online voice blog. A hypothesis is posited: if this plant could bring better salaries and schools and an improvement in the quality of life of the area, would you be in favor or not, and why? Linguistic production goals for this task include expressing hypotheses. Students prepare and record a four-minute response. This on-line blog is an effective venue for students to develop presentational skills, as they can work offline, listen to what they record, and repeat all or parts of their response. All of this helps them build confidence for in-class panels and discussions.

Assessing Students' Learning

Student learning is best assessed through performance-based tasks that rep-licate learning tasks and serve as a measure of students' success at achieving learning outcomes. *Direct* measures of work to assess student performance in relation to learning outcomes require evidence of performance. Some examples are voice blog assignments, oral exams, presentations, or debates. When provided to students in advance, rubrics for direct assessment that identify tasks and expected standards help them prepare for assessments, communicate what is being evaluated, and convey in what ways they have or have not achieved mastery. Analytic rubrics provide each student with a holistic evaluation. Benchmarks for LOs at three levels (below, approaching, and meeting the standard) allow for a fine-grain assessment of outcomes.

Indirect means of assessment, such as students' reflective statements, also provide insight into what they are learning. For example, in-class writing that connects daily work to course goals provides us with students' opinions or thoughts about their knowledge, attitudes, learning experiences, and per-ceptions, as well as inform us of any need for clarification. Another example of indirect measure is a self-evaluation tool where LOs are laid out for each case study. Students can self-assess their achievement of learning goals prior to and after a case study and identify trouble spots related to the material.

Evaluating the Redesigned Course

To address sustainability LOs, students' results in three end-of-semester di-rect assessment tasks were reviewed (see table 2). The results for level 2 and 3 LOs were less than satisfactory, as we had expected at least seventy-five per-cent of students to meet the standard. A decision was made, based on the results, to incorporate more activities that would help students establish

Table 2. Mapping of Sustainability-Specific LOs

LO	*Direct assessment*	*Component*	*Outcome relative to standard*	*Action*
LO1	Final oral presentation	Content and sources	Meets: 74% Approaches: 26% Below: 0%	None
LO2	Final oral exam	Content and application	Meets: 50% Approaches: 50% Below: 0%	Emphasize establishing connections between old and new situations or cases during the semester.
LO3	Voice blog 5	Analysis	Meets: 64% Approaches: 36% Below: 0%	Emphasize importance of exploring causes behind situations or problems.

connections between old and new situations or cases and explore causes behind situations or problems.

Similarly, to address language-acquisition LOs, students' results in three end-of-semester evaluative tasks were reviewed (see table 3). Language LO1 (*"describe* and *narrate* in major time frames"*) proved challenging to measure, as this goal appeared under the "grammar" or "language" category. A decision was made to make this a separate rubric category. The percentage of students meeting LO2 (addressing structural control and discourse ability) was low for both areas. A similar result was observed for LO3 (*"explain* and *discuss* a complex, abstract topic; express opinions, and provide structured arguments and counterarguments to support opinions"); no students met the standard.

In terms of indirect assessments, the students' weekly reflections on learning proved to be very beneficial to fine-tuning both out-of- and in-class activities and expectations. A focus group, conducted by a professor not teaching the class, provided extremely useful information for evaluating the course as well. Students underscored the importance of the round-table format to encourage whole-class, face-to-face discussions; they also reacted positively to the materials, considering them engaging, representative of different media, and, overall, effective. They thought the course provided plenty of opportunities to work toward the targeted LOs and engage at the appropriate cognitive level: they were active participants in their learning. Summative replies to the survey indicated that learning goals were achieved.

Table 3. Mapping of Language-Specific LOs

LO	Direct assessment	Component	Outcome relative to standard	Action
LO1	Final presentation	Language	Meets: 42% Approaches: 58% Below: 0%	Change rubric to incorporate language LO1 as independent category.
LO2	Final oral exam	Grammar, discourse	Meets: 33% / 17% Approaches: 58% / 83% Below: 9%	Integrate more explicit focus on form during activities and additional focus on form questions.
LO3	Debate	Discussion	Meets: 0% Approaches: 100% Below: 0%	Increase focus on formal aspects of argumentation in Spanish.
LO4	Final oral exam	Vocabulary	Meets: 92% Approaches: 8% Below: 0%	None

Students also valued the inclusion of case studies as a means of developing their understanding of sustainability issues in Latin America's Spanish-speaking countries and applying their comprehension of the issues to actual examples by taking on and rotating through different roles and examining the perspectives of different stakeholders (rather than simple discussion of pros and cons), which made debates more interesting. With respect to language development, students were satisfied with the increase in specialized vocabulary that the course content provided. Each unit incorporated a corpus of sustainability-related words and expressions that students had to understand and produce through the unit's activities. This increase in lexical acquisition is without a doubt one of the biggest benefits of sustainability-based language instruction, as students' constant exposure to and need to produce discipline-specific terms provides immersion-like vocabulary-building opportunities.

Students pointed out the benefits of the class for developing their oral communication skills, especially fluency; however, some thought accuracy (i.e., focus on form) and complexity were neglected. They seemed to agree that adding conversation about grammatical structures, including explicit explanations of language use, and providing more corrective feedback would be beneficial. This is consistent with the results of direct assessment discussed above in relation to advanced language learning LOs.

In terms of skills, there was a consensus that the class helped students develop their ability to work collaboratively, apply problem-solving and decision-making skills to propose a solution, and present information and arguments to an audience. These are all transferable skills that are important for students' success in college and beyond. According to students, the strength of the course was the amount of learning that took place as a result of the approach. The recurrent nature of the issues discussed reinforced both content knowledge and language use and allowed them to look for finer details.

Upon review of the results of the direct measures as well as the information obtained from indirect measures it was evident that the focus of the course had been much more directed to sustainability content than to language content. In content-based second-language instruction there is a continuum of content and language integration that spans from a high content-driven end to a high language-driven end. Fredricka L. Stoller points out that content-based instructional approaches "make a dual, though not necessarily equal, commitment to language and content-learning objectives" (59). The challenge of any content-based language course is to decide where on the continuum the course will fall and to design goals and material accordingly. In the foreign language classroom environment, language will not be developed without specific focus on form instruction. In this project, the sustainability nature of the course took a main focus, perhaps to the detriment of the language goals. Consequently, in the future, class activities should be better directed toward language-acquisition goals.

Lessons Learned and Final Remarks

Moving toward a broader interdisciplinary perspective on Spanish language and cultures is an effort worth pursuing. This essay illustrates one way to integrate Latin American environmental and social sustainability into advanced undergraduate Spanish studies, which contributes to the goal of sustainability literacy, since students will acquire the knowledge and skills needed to live sustainably. The influence of the sustainability-based language course cannot be underestimated. It has the ability to make advanced-level language study relevant to our students and enhance their employability. Through carefully designed course work, students engage with the materials because they appreciate their relevance; as a consequence, they acquire a deeper understanding of sustainability issues by seeing them through the lens of another language and culture and comparing them with their personal values and beliefs.

This type of curricular work is not free of challenges: it requires instructors trained in content-based and task-based pedagogy and assessment, and knowledgeable of the discipline. New imperatives in teaching and learning languages, however, mean the development of faculty expertise. It is expected that this work and the materials provided can be used and replicated by other Spanish-language practitioners in their own courses.

NOTES

For additional pedagogical materials related to this essay, please visit the Foreign Language Teaching and the Environment group on *Humanities Commons*.
1. At the time cross-listed in the Spanish and Sustainability minor, this was the minor's only course offered in a foreign language.
2. Students had completed at least six semesters of college Spanish, which in our program (based on final proficiency assessments) is equivalent to ACTFL's low- to mid-advanced proficiency. About half were familiar with the content area.
3. As noted by Short, content-based courses may present a lack of attention to language development in favor of attention to content (21).

WORKS CITED

ACTFL Proficiency Guidelines 2012. American Council on the Teaching of Foreign Languages (ACTFL), 2012, www.actfl.org/sites/default/files/pdfs/public/ACTFL ProficiencyGuidelines2012_FINAL.pdf.

Barkley, Elizabeth F., et al. *Collaborative Learning Techniques: A Handbook for College Faculty.* Jossey-Bass, 2005.

Bloom, Benjamin S. *Taxonomy of Educational Objectives: The Classification of Educational Goals.* Longmans, Green, 1956.

Bonnet, M. "Education for Sustainable Development: Sustainability as a Frame of Mind." *Journal of Philosophy of Education*, vol. 37, no. 4, 2003, pp. 675–90.

Burger, Sandra, and Marie Chrétien. "The Development of Oral Production in Content-Based Second Language Courses at the University of Ottawa." *Canadian Modern Language Review*, vol. 58, no. 1, 2001, pp. 84–102.

Bygate, Martin. "Task as Context for the Framing, Reframing and Unframing of Language." *System*, vol. 27, no. 1, 1999, pp. 33–48.

Bygate, Martin, et al. *Researching Pedagogic Tasks: Second Language Learning, Teaching, and Testing.* Longman, 2001.

Byrnes, Heidi, and Hiram H. Maxim. *Advanced Foreign Language Learning: A Challenge to College Programs.* Thomson/Heinle, 2004.

Doughty, Catherine, and Jessica Williams. "Pedagogical Choices in Focus on Form." *Focus on Form in Classroom Second Language Acquisition*, edited by Doughty and Williams, Cambridge UP, 1998, pp. 197–262.

Duch, Barbara J., et al. *The Power of Problem-Based Learning: A Practical "How To" for Teaching Undergraduate Courses in Any Discipline.* Stylus Publishing, 2001.

Dunne, David, and Kim Brooks. *Teaching with Cases.* Society for Teaching and Learning in Higher Education (STLHE), 2004.

Dupuy, Beatrice C. "Content-Based Instruction: Can It Help Ease the Transition from Beginning to Advanced Foreign Language Classes?" *Foreign Language Annals,* vol. 33, no. 2, 2000, pp. 205–23.

Ellis, Rod. "Investigating Form-Focused Instruction." *Form-Focused Instruction and Second Language Learning,* edited by Ellis, Blackwell, 2001, pp. 1–46.

———. *Task-Based Language Learning and Teaching.* Oxford UP, 2003.

Goodland, Robert, and Herman Daly. "Environmental Sustainability: Universal and Non-negotiable." *Ecological Applications,* vol. 6, no. 4, 1996, pp. 1002–17.

Leaver, Betty L., and Christine Campbell. "Experience with Higher Levels of Proficiency." *To Advanced Proficiency and Beyond: Theory and Methods for Developing Superior Second Language Ability,* edited by Tony Brown and Jennifer Bown, Georgetown UP, 2005, pp. 3–21.

Long, Michael H. "The Role of the Linguistic Environment in Second Language Acquisition." *Handbook of Second Language Acquisition,* edited by William C. Ritchie and Tej K. Bhatia, Academic, 1996, pp. 413–68.

Lyster, Roy, and Susan Ballinger. "Content-Based Language Teaching: Convergent Concerns across Divergent Contexts." *Language Teaching Research,* vol. 15, no. 3, 2011, pp. 279–88.

Melin, Charlotte. "Program Sustainability through Interdisciplinary Networking: On Connecting Foreign Language Programs with Sustainability Studies and Other Fields." Swaffar and Urlaub, pp. 103–22.

MLA Ad Hoc Committee on Foreign Languages. "Foreign Languages and Higher Education: New Structures for a Changed World." *Profession,* 2007, pp. 234–45.

MLA Teagle Foundation Working Group. *Report to the Teagle Foundation on the Undergraduate Major in Language and Literature.* Modern Language Association of America, 2009, www.mla.org/pdf/2008_mla_whitepaper.pdf.

Nuessel, Frank. "Curricular Changes for Spanish and Portuguese in a New Era." *Hispania,* vol. 93, no. 1, 2010, pp. 119–22.

Rinner, Susanne, and Astrid Weigert. "From Sports to the EU Economy: Integrating Curricula through Genre-Based Content Courses." *Educating for Advanced Foreign Language Capabilities,* edited by Heidi Byrnes et al., Georgetown UP, 2006, pp. 136–51.

Robinson, Peter. "Attention, Memory and the 'Noticing' Hypothesis." *Language Learning,* vol. 45, 1995, pp. 283–331.

———. *Cognition and Second Language Instruction.* Cambridge UP, 2001.

Short, Deborah. "Language Learning in Sheltered Social Studies Classes." *TESOL Journal,* vol. 11, no. 1, pp. 18–24.

Skehan, Peter. *A Cognitive Approach to Language Learning.* Oxford UP, 1998.

Stoller, Fredricka L. "Content-Based Instruction." *Second and Foreign Language Education,* edited by Nelleke Van Deussen-Scholl and Nancy H. Homberger, Springer, 2008, pp. 59–70. Vol. 4 of *Encyclopedia of Language and Education.*

Stover, Daniel. "Problem-Based Learning: Redefining Self-Directed Instruction and Learning." *The Forum Sharing Information on Teaching and Learning,* vol. 7, no. 1, 1998, pp. 9–10.

Stryker, Stephen B., and Betty Lou Leaver. *Content-Based Instruction in Foreign Language Education: Models and Methods.* Georgetown UP, 1997.

Swaffar, Janet, and Katherine Arens. *Remapping the Foreign Language Curriculum.* Modern Language Association of America, 2005.

Swaffar, Janet, and Per Urlaub, editors. *Transforming Postsecondary Foreign Language Teaching in the United States.* Springer, 2014.

Swain, Merrill. "Three Functions of Output in Second Language Learning." *Principle and Practice in Applied Linguistics: Studies in Honour of H. G. Widdowson,* edited by Guy Cook and Barbara Seidlhofer, Oxford UP, 1995, pp. 125–44.

Collaborative Teaching of a Japanese Content-Based Course: 3.11 and Nuclear Power Crisis

Nobuko Chikamatsu

Imagination—dreams of driving a flying car in the sky or living on Mars—is often taken as just futuristic fantasy in today's scientific, industrialized, utilitarian society. Imagination as manifested in creative works, however, may be the only force we can count on when we face an unimaginable disaster and struggle to recover from its aftermath. Such power of imagination may be necessary in Japan as the country faces one of the most critical moments in its modern history.

On 11 March 2011 the northern coastal Tohoku region of Japan was hit by the worst earthquake ever recorded in modern times. The following day, the Fukushima Daiichi Nuclear Power Plant exploded, and invisible radiation permeated the air. Unfamiliar lexical terms, such as *mizō* 未曾有 ("unprecedented") and *sōteigai* 想定外 ("beyond imagination"), suddenly became common expressions, as if we could not express the magnitude of damage and shock using ordinary terms. Years later, the recovery process still proceeds slowly and without any clear vision for the nation's new energy policy.

Surprisingly, however, Jonathan E. Abel argues that "in some significant ways Japan was already prepared," and "such preparedness can be read into Japan's long history of dealing with disasters, twenty years of economic stagnation and the growing prevalence of mysticism and eschatology in pop culture . . ." (297). In works such as Komatsu Sakyō's science fiction and the anime *Space Battleship Yamato*, predictions of disaster were made long before the latest crisis, and plans for the future were proposed (Gardner; Amano).[1]

Although these fictional events take place in text and visual media, such exercises in imagination and creativity prepare readers for natural disasters and encourage prevention of human-made ones. Using language learning to nurture this kind of imagination and creativity in students was an important goal of the content-based advanced Japanese language course entitled 3.11: Earthquake, Tsunami, and Nuclear Power Crisis, which was designed soon after the "unimaginable" disaster in Fukushima took place.

Theoretical and Pedagogical Rationales for Content-Based Instruction and Language Ecology Approaches

The course was developed based on two pedagogical and theoretical foundations: content-based instruction (CBI) and language ecology. Content-based instruction is a language-learning approach in which the target language is used to build academic content knowledge in areas such as history, culture, or literature. Viewed as effective for advanced language teaching, CBI has been widely adopted in North America for teaching English as a second language and Indo-European languages, such as Spanish, French, and Italian (Krueger and Ryan; Lyster and Ballinger). Although definitions vary, CBI is generally understood to have two primary goals: content learning and language acquisition. Stephen B. Stryker and Betty Lou Leaver define CBI as having three main features: *subject-matter core*, in which a course is developed based on subject matter rather than linguistic forms or functions; *use of authentic language*, where the core materials for a course are chosen primarily from those produced for native speakers; and *learner's needs*, in which content and learning tasks correspond to linguistic, cognitive, and affective needs. Thus, whereas CBI is designed for language acquisition, content learning should be a main goal, and the content should be challenging at the level of the learner's intellectual maturity.

With an increase in the number of learners of Japanese with higher proficiency, CBI is slowly emerging in Japanese-language instruction in North America (Chikamatsu, "Beikoku ni okeru," "Preparing," and "Language"; Kubota). A powerful rationale for such CBI use is to facilitate implementation of critical- and creative-thinking activities developed based on selected themes (Iwasaki and Kumagai). Furthermore, through CBI, individuals can develop a sense of purpose and responsibility for learning not only for its own sake but also in relation to their roles as productive and responsible members of society (Chikamatsu, "Communication"; Sato and Kumagai). Thus, language learning can be viewed as a social activity embedded in society beyond the classroom (Hosokawa).

So, what would be the best content or theme in such integrative language learning? *Language ecology*, a concept originally proposed by Einar I. Haugen, may help us understand the priorities and choices employed by instructors in their curriculum design as they select certain types of material and modes of instruction. Language ecology is a way of thinking about the linguistic dimensions of culture that explores the relations among human beings, the environment, and language. This framework allows for the analysis of interactions between a given language and its environment; that is, it attends to how language functions when users relate to others and to their physical, cultural, and social environment. Through language we define what the world is, how we human beings are connected to our world and other human beings, and, ultimately, who we are and what we do in our environment.

A first step toward answering these questions is recognizing that language is constantly changing and that a linguistic expression may lose its essential meaning as relations between humans and the environment change over time. As we reevaluate the connection between the world and ourselves, and between our current life and the future of the earth, we redefine language. For instance, the term mentioned above, *sōteigai* ("beyond imagination") came to be overused by government officials and Tokyo Electronic Power Company (TEPCO) executives in press conferences immediately after the Fukushima Daiichi plant was hit by the massive tsunami. But was the Fukushima disaster really "beyond imagination"? As Abel pointed out, similar situations had been predicted in apocalyptic science fiction in Japanese pop culture for years. Yoichi Komori also argues that warnings supported by scientific data regarding the danger of a tsunami hitting the Fukushima Daiichi plant had been reported officially by parliament and committee members for years, yet such warnings were ignored.[2] In short, *sōteigai* came to be used in a way that no longer carried its original or conventional meaning of "a condition beyond imagination," and thus the word lost its substance and reality (*naijitsu* 内実). As this example shows, linguistic expressions evolve, and so linguistic communities must constantly question and redefine language to build a better and more truthful relation among humans, nature, and language.

To develop such a mind-set, Toshio Okazaki, an advocate of language ecology in Japanese pedagogy, asserts that language learning must go beyond communicative skill development or a focus on merely the acquisition of linguistic skill. Accordingly, topics examined in Japanese courses employing the CBI approach should include complex issues, such as employment, welfare, economic crisis, globalization, and environmental destruction, that require the learner to make choices and decisions, and that foster the imagination and creativity needed to tackle these ongoing challenges. Okazaki stresses that such language teaching must be pursued across the curriculum to connect different disciplines and to address the time dimensions of past, present, and future. The Japanese CBI course described in the present essay was thus developed with these educational principles in mind and drew on collaborations with interdisciplinary faculty members for the purpose of examining the current environmental crisis in Japan. The following sections give a brief overview of the course and a description of its curricular design.

Advanced Japanese CBI Course: 3.11 Earthquake, Tsunami, and Nuclear Crisis

It can be challenging for language instructors to design content courses, because of a lack of subject expertise in other fields. With the multitude of ongoing issues and enormous number of available resources, it was especially difficult to design a single course on the 3.11 disaster to be taught in Japanese. Therefore, I polled fellow Japanese studies faculty members about topics and enlisted the help of three colleagues in ethics, history, and literature, who each agreed to give a lecture in the course. The resulting course outline reflected themes from these three disciplines (table 1).

The book *Mirai o tsukuru* 『未来をつくるBOOK：持続可能な地球と地域をつくるあなたへ』 ("Book for Building the Future: Building a Sustainable World and Community"; ESD-J Mirai o Tsukuru Book Team) was selected as the main Japanese textbook.[3] Intellectually challenging yet appropriate for the students' language proficiency, it was compatible with the core lecture themes and covered a variety of topics, including the scale and effects of the disaster as well as subsequent energy issues, recovery efforts, and domestic and international support.

With the core lectures and textbook identified, the course was designed as a ten-week class that met twice a week in sessions of an hour and a half

Table 1. Specialist Lectures: Themes and Materials

Week	Discipline	Main questions and themes	Materials used in the lectures
5	Ethics	Why is Fukushima our concern? Validity of scientific data Safety myth of nuclear power Ethical imbalance and sacrifice system	"The Panic over Fukushima" (J, E) "Panic over 'The Panic over Fukushima'" (E) *Blind* (J with E subtitles) *Atomic Age* (J, E)
7	History	How do we connect the past and the present? Earthquakes and subsequent social movements Role of folklore, media, and mass or pop culture	"Shaking Up Japan: Edo Society and the 1855 Catfish Picture Prints" (E)
9	Literature	Why does literature prevail over time even after a disaster? Disaster and literature Translation	*1Q84*, ch. 1 (J, E)

Note: J=Japanese, E=English

for fourth- and fifth-year Japanese-language students. Table 2 summarizes the course structure. From the first week to the third week, the magnitude of the disaster was discussed. Starting in the fourth week, the focus shifted to the nuclear power crisis, Japan's history of earthquakes, and subsequent social movements, followed by a unit of literary analysis. Each section was built around the three core specialist lectures. Thus, in terms of sequential work on intercultural competence, facts were presented at an early stage to engage learners, and then literary analysis was conducted at the end to offer them opportunities for reflection and cultural comparison.

Three Collaborations across Curricula and across Time

With this curricular structure established, units on ethics, history, and literature were developed in collaboration with interdisciplinary colleagues. These three specialists were bilingual in Japanese and English; two were native speakers of Japanese, and one a non-native speaker with near-native fluency. Each lecture was given in a bilingual format (Japanese and English), with the speaker switching back and forth depending on the familiarity and complexity of the content. Introductory readings, such as newspaper articles or scholarly papers, were assigned by the specialists and mainly in English. Apart from those readings, course work was generally conducted and completed in Japanese.

Table 2. Course Outline

Week	Topics	Sample learning activities
1	Introduction Ch. 10: Building the future	Presentation 1: Unforgettable image and video
2	Damage and aftermath Ch. 1: The great earthquake	Current issues post-3.11 (translation into Japanese) Anime: *Nausicaä of the Valley of the Wind*
3	Survivors and living Ch. 5: Life after the earthquake	Guest lecture: A survivor of 3.11 and former Japanese Exchange Teaching participant Meeting 1: Language evaluation
4	Fukushima nuclear power plants Ch. 8: Energy and economy	Presentation 2: Ethics and nuclear power
5	Nuclear and atomic powers Ethics and industrialization	Guest lecture: An ethics specialist Final project proposal due
6	Nuclear power in Illinois Sustainable energy	Presentation 3: Nuclear power in Illinois Meeting 2: Final project (proposal)
Chicago International Film Festival: *The Land of Hope (Kibō no kuni)*		
7	Earthquakes and social movements in Japanese history Ch. 9: Nature and Civilization	Guest lecture: A history specialist
On campus lecture: "After Fukushima: How Shall We Live?" (with an activist, a doctor, and a scholar)		
8	Mass media and creative work Poetry and music Ch. 3: Information communication	Presentation 4: Parody songs of nuclear power Meeting 3: Final project
9	Literature and disasters	Guest lecture: A literature specialist Translation of poems (from English into Japanese and vice versa)
10	Final project presentation	Meeting 4: Final project Presentation 5: Final presentation

Notes
Chapter numbers refer to the Japanese textbook, *Mirai*.
Meetings are with individual students outside class.

From the fourth through sixth weeks, discussion covered the ethical dimensions of nuclear power and energy issues in Fukushima and Illinois. This unit was developed based on a lecture given by a specialist in comparative ethics in the fifth week. Before the lecture, students were required to read a newspaper article written by the physicist Richard Muller (available in English and Japanese), along with a response to the article written by the ethics specialist (Miyamoto). Students were also asked to choose one article in Japanese or English from the *Atomic Age* Web site and to state the reason(s) for their choice (in Japanese). This lecture started with a short film, *Blind* (in Japanese with English subtitles), which depicts a fictitious post–3.11 Japan. Then a bilingual *PowerPoint* presentation explored questions of scientific research validity in terms of who conducts what research for what purposes, and why numbers pose a danger, something observed in Muller's article to downplay the radiation effects on victims. The safety myth that nuclear power is cheap, clean, and good for the environment was also discussed. Then utilitarianism was examined, focusing on trade-offs made in the nuclear energy business and their potential effects on different segments of society. Here comparisons of rural versus urban, farming and fishing versus corporations, and the interests of blue- versus white-collar workers helped focus discussion and introduced questions about rhetoric. For instance, questions surfaced about why *Fukushima* is transcribed as フクシマ, using syllabic katakana, the Japanese script commonly used for words of non-Japanese origin, instead of the original logographic kanji characters, 福島.[4]

Due to the complex nature of the issues addressed, students needed to prepare in advance to meet the linguistic challenges of the Japanese-language activities in this unit. To this end, students completed a worksheet before the specialist's lecture to familiarize themselves with Japanese energy policies and debates. Working with a chapter of the *Mirai* book that lists twenty common arguments in the debate between nuclear and renewable energy, students were asked to categorize each statement as a *pro* or *con* for each energy type, in terms of efficiency, stability, cost, global warming, waste, or other factors. They were also asked to justify their own stance regarding energy policy. Such learning tasks prepared students linguistically and conceptually to evaluate the nuclear safety myth.

After the specialist's lecture, each student was tasked with presenting a critical interpretation of assigned scientific statistical data from the *Mirai* book. This information showed cost comparisons of various types of electric energy, a cesium radiation map for the Tokyo metropolitan area, imports of energy resources, and current usage and future plans for renewable energy in major counties. Students were asked to analyze the data, paying attention to the source and time of publication (who conducted the research, when, and why), and to evaluate its validity, if possible by providing comparison data in English or Japanese. With bilingual skills explicitly incorporated into the task, students explored information in both languages and developed further questions.

In the seventh week, a specialist in Japanese history discussed historical disasters and their role as a catalyst for social movements. To address the question of how we connect the past to the present and future, this lecture explored the topic through the medium of mass culture and folklore. Students read Gregory Smits's article "Shaking Up Japan: Edo Society and the 1855 Catfish Picture Prints" in advance as an introduction to *namazu-e* ("catfish pictures") and the 1855 Great Ansei Edo earthquake. *Namazu* is a mythical giant catfish that, according to popular legend, was thought to cause earthquakes. *Namazu-e* were commercial prints distributed as leaflets to disseminate news and depict social and political issues in major cities like Edo (current Tokyo). When the Ansei earthquake hit the Edo area toward the end of the Tokugawa period (1603–1867), the power of the *bakufu* ("military government") had already been weakened by the visits of Commodore Perry's Black Ship (1853 and 1854), setting the stage for the rapid modernization and industrialization of the Meiji Restoration (1868) ten years later. Thus, Smits concludes that the earthquake "functioned as catalyst for growing doubts about the bakufu's ability to govern . . . [and] . . . an emerging vision of Japan as a natural political community blessed by the deities. The *namazu-e* were the means by which the common people adumbrated this new vision" (1071).

In a lecture given in English after a brief self-introduction in Japanese, the specialist encouraged students to apply the analysis of the Ansei case to other historical disasters, such as the 1923 Great Kantō earthquake and post–3.11 Japan. After considering the new forms of mass gatherings, protests, and activism that have emerged through hyperconnected social media and creative art forms in post–3.11 Japan (see Seto), students were urged to imagine the consequences of the next disaster and think about preparations that could be undertaken before it strikes. Japanese-language activities in this unit related closely to chapters in the *Mirai* book. Students completed a worksheet asking them to compile a list of the major earthquakes in modern Japanese history. In addition to indicating the scale and damage of each earthquake, they identified relevant postdisaster social movements and the medium of information processing, ranging from old hand-printed leaflets to twenty-first-century social media.

In the eighth week, students viewed *YouTube* clips of several antinuke parody songs. They were asked to choose one parody song from a preselected list, compare it with the original song, and identify keywords, satires, and the creators' respective messages. For instance, one student chose the parody song entitled *Tōden ni hairo*. The title of the song can be transcribed with two very different interpretations in Japanese: 東電に入ろう and 倒電に廃炉; the former means "let's get a job at TEPCO"; the latter, "nuclear decommissioning to overthrow TEPCO (or electricity)." Another song entitled *Zettai genshiryoku sentai suishinjā* 絶対原子力戦隊スイシンジャー ("Unconditional Supporters of the Nuclear Power Rangers"), a parody of the popular television superheroes, the Power Rangers, was also reviewed. These parodies provided opportunities for students to think about ambivalent attitudes toward nuclear power in post–3.11 Japan. On the one hand, they reflect corporate promotion of nuclear power, and, on the other, they signify protest by victims and the general public. Students analyzing satire and humor found in antinuke pop culture noticed ambivalence and abstractness, and they recognized the influence and popularity of such creative work across generations and over time.

In the ninth week, as the last unit of the course began, literary texts were examined to challenge students' imagination through fiction with overarching questions about the role of literature in our world. A specialist in Japanese literature discussed the relations among disaster, literary texts, and translation in Murakami Haruki's novel *1Q84*, published shortly before the events of 3.11. Students read the first chapter of *1Q84* in English (and optionally in Japanese) and completed several translation tasks: identifying a passage in the English translation for revision, retranslating it, reflecting on how the retranslation affects the interpretation of the chapter as a whole, and articulating the relevance of *1Q84* for the post–3.11 world.

Other Murakami short pieces, such as "All God's Children Can Dance" (originally published in 2001) and "Super-Frog Saves Tokyo" in *After the Quake,* closely relate to earthquakes in the past. The novel *1Q84* was chosen, however, because as a literary work it challenges students to contemplate why certain literary works prevail and are appreciated long after the historical moment in which they were written. If *1Q84* was Murakami's response to the post–9/11 world, how should we read it now in the post–3.11 world? Furthermore, through the translation tasks, students were encouraged to analyze and evaluate verbal and written texts closely and critically in both the original and translation and develop skills for understanding multiple meanings that might guide their inquiry.

In a lecture conducted in Japanese that employed translations of key phrases and sentences, the specialist led a discussion of these matters. Students identified the two passages as being related to the 3.11 nuclear power plant disaster. In the first scene, a cab driver is talking to the protagonist, Aomame, while they are stuck in heavy traffic on the highway. Here the Expressway Corporation could be seen as mirroring the Japanese government's mendaciousness in connection with the Fukushima nuclear power plant disaster, as Murakami writes, "'You can't trust them,' he said with a hollow ring to his voice. 'They're half lies. The Expressway Corporation only releases reports that suit its agenda. If you really want to know what's happening here and now, you've got to use your own eyes and your own judgment'" (*1Q84* 7). In the second scene, Aomame is talking to herself at the end of the chapter as she is about to descend an emergency stairway after leaving the taxi and observes, "'You couldn't begin to imagine who I am, where I'm going, or what I'm about to do. . . . All of you are trapped here. You can't go anywhere, forwards or back. But I'm not like you. I have work to do. I have a mission to accomplish. And so, with your permission, I shall move ahead'" (15). Students interpreted these passages as relevant to post–3.11 society and sensed that we each must take initiative on our own to step out of the norm and overcome challenges.

Japanese-language activities before and after the literature specialist's lecture supported extended reflection about these matters. Students read antinuclear poems (two Japanese and one English) in class, selected from the bilingual anthology *Farewell to Nuclear, Welcome to Renewable Energy* 『脱原発・自然エネルギー218人詩集』 (Suzuki et al.). In the first, entitled *Onagawa no obāchan no hanashi* 女川のおばあちゃんの話 ("A Story of an Old Woman in Onagawa"), by Yaguchi Yorifumi, an old woman ponders why a big factory (a nuclear power plant) was built in her beautiful little town as the plant "dances wildly each time an earthquake visits here" (34). The second, *Kona* 粉 ("Powder") by Mutō Yukari, is written in the voice of a child, who asks the mother whether the child is covered with an (invisible) powder (i.e., radiation) because the child's friends said not to come near them even after the child washed vigorously. The third poem, *Kyokun* 教訓 ("Lessons"), a short five-line prose work originally written in English, lists Hiroshima, Nagasaki, Chernobyl, and Fukushima and then ends with the final line "how slowly we learn" (67).

Before the lecture, students read the first two Japanese poems in class, analyzing their meaning, audience, and context. In this discussion it was startling how vivid and intense the images and emotions depicted in the poems were to students. The texts conveyed responses to devastation that resonated with feelings and perceptions about 3.11 despite being written before the Fukushima disaster. When the students were divided into two groups and asked to translate the second Japanese poem, *Kona*, into English, the act of rewriting in simpler terms familiar to them intensified the assignment of translating the heartbreaking emotion of the child making a plea to the mother.

After the literature lecture, students completed their translations in groups while discussing the power of creative work over time and beyond a particular disaster. The translation process became more meaningful, albeit more challenging, after the literature lecture, because students became more attentive to and creative in their formal, stylistic, and rhetorical choices. At the end of the class, each group's translation was shared in class, and students provided critiques before the instructor read the English translation published in the book. The students' final version of the poem in English was read and then translated back into Japanese in the following class session as the culmination of the unit.

Whereas the three core interdisciplinary lectures formed the basis for a wide variety of learning activities, for the course's final project, students were asked to write or create a work in any form or style of their choice to discuss what they could do for post–3.11 society in Japan, the United States, or elsewhere. One student conducted a bilingual survey with native speakers both of English and of Japanese—comparing their knowledge, feelings, and attitudes about nuclear energy—and made a proposal for new energy policies based on the results. Others translated Japanese original works into English, such as manga recounting children's experiences, antinuke poems, and a short story from Murakami's *After the Quake*. Through these projects, students confronted choices about environmental, ethical, energy, and social issues in the post–3.11 world.

The outcomes observed in this course reflected gains in language skills, cultural knowledge, and critical thinking. Learners discussed the current 3.11 disaster in terms of not only its scale and damage but also its function as a catalyst for social movements that address ethical imbalances in society. They negotiated the interconnections of past and present, fiction and reality, and individuals with others and the environment, in the process expanding their own visions for the future. Such learning in second-language Japanese became possible, despite the complex topic, because content knowledge had been built up through content learning about the course themes within the CBI framework (Stryker and Leaver). Learners read and critically analyzed resources in a variety of genres instead of focusing solely on mere comprehension of linguistic expressions. They were encouraged to apply ethical considerations to their own lives and experience (family background, academic major, local industry, etc.), recognizing the relevance of such an approach to any career or field they may pursue in the future. They learned to appreciate the power of imagination by examining the creation and preservation of works of art, literature, film, and other media in connection with protest and activism in social movements. With bilingual resources in Japanese and English, learners accessed sources with differing perspectives, enabling them to make judgments rather than relying on information provided by any single authority. Translation activities allowed students to analyze and evaluate verbal and written texts closely and critically, understand the multiple meanings and metaphors of literary expressions, and become aware of the importance of word or orthographic choice. Furthermore, the collaborative teaching format encouraged the educators involved in the course to acquire interdisciplinary knowledge across fields well beyond their specializations, transforming the language classroom into a setting for where language learners from various academic programs such as science, engineering, literature, and international studies met.

After this term ended, participants continued studies in classes with the guest speakers, more students joined the Japanese studies courses, and a film screening of *Live Your Dream: The Taylor Anderson Story* was organized. The following year saw a new Foreign Language Across the Curriculum (FLAC) pilot program focused on Japan's industrial disease and environmental ethics, including case studies of Fukushima and Minamata. For it, two courses were offered concurrently: a core content course taught in English by the ethics specialist and an adjunct Japanese language course taught by the language faculty, with a coordinated film screening event of *Tōhoku Tomo* organized by former students and the FLAC students during that quarter to discuss the ongoing recovery of the Tohoku region and voluntarism. Thus, collaboration among faculty, students, and the local community led to continuing reflection about our post–3.11 world. Although the repercussions of 3.11 on daily life in Japan are fading, people in the Tohoku region are suffering from the slow recovery, and the nuclear crisis has become more serious beyond the immediate Fukushima area, with news of nuclear contamination, spills, and waste reported daily. We as educators cannot stop discussing this legacy with our students.

In a recent book, *Shisha no koe, seija no kotoba* 『死者の声、生者の言葉：文学で問う原発の日本』 ("Voices of the Dead, Words of the Living: Nuclear Japan through Literature"), Komori reminds us of the crucial role literature plays for nuclear Japan today. Whether Miyazawa Kenji's utopian fantasy, *The Life of Guskō Budori*, or real-time poetry tweeted at a disaster site, literary work must be written and read continuously because "lying words (*uso no kotoba* 嘘の言葉) numb our sense of crisis, fear and even anger" (Komori 97).[5] We feel helpless and powerless in the face of "unimaginable" and "unprecedented" devastation, hearing the words *sōteigai* or *mizō* over and over again. Komori argues that we, as writers and readers, must feel, use, share, and spread words of truth among ourselves as an antidepressant and to suppress rhetorical fabrication. All of us, as human beings endowed with language, must continue to express fear, anger, hope, and imagination with words, because words last and remain powerful and truthful even after we are long gone, and our students as learners of Japanese and other languages can bear this responsibility across cultures.

NOTES

I thank Dr. Miho Matsugu, Dr. Yuki Miyamoto, and Dr. Kerry Ross for their collaboration and guidance in the development of the course. For additional pedagogical materials related to this essay, please visit the Foreign Language Teaching and the Environment group on *Humanities Commons*.

1. Komatsu Sakyō (1931–2011) was a Japanese science fiction writer well known for his 1973 seismic disaster novel, *Nippon Chinbotsu* ("Japan Sinks"). *Space Battleship Yamato* was a Japanese science fiction anime, released in the 1970s, first as a television animation series, and later as an animation film. They have been widely discussed as "allegor[ies] of apocalyptic post–3.11 Japan" (Amano 325), as published in a special issue of the *Japan Forum*, entitled *Beyond Fukushima: Culture, Media, and Meaning from Catastrophe*.
2. Komori reports at least two cases: the question posed by Mr. Hidekatsu Yoshii, a parliament member, to the Japanese Nuclear Safety Commission in 2006; and the warning made by Mr. Yukinobu Okamura to the Advisory Committee for Natural Resources and Energy in 2009.
3. In addition to the Japanese textbook, one English book was assigned, a collection of newspaper articles published in *The Japan Times*, entitled *3.11 One Year On: A Chronicle of Japan's Road to Recovery* 『英文版 東日本大震災1年—復興への道』.

4. Kanji are Japanese logographs adopted from Chinese characters into the Japanese writing system. Proper nouns, such as Japanese place names, are commonly written in kanji; for example, *Fukushima* is written 福島 in kanji. On the other hand, katakana, one of the two Japanese syllabic scripts, was derived from components of kanji, and is often used for loanwords in modern Japanese, with a connotation of foreignness or inter-nationality. Since the nuclear incident broke out in Fukushima, the katakana form, フクシマ, has been used deliberately in the media because the nuclear crisis in Fukushima is viewed as an international issue beyond Japan. This is also the case for Hiroshima, known as the first city in history to be targeted by a nuclear weapon. The name *Hiroshima* is normally written 広島 in kanji, but the katakana form, ヒロシマ, is often adopted in the debate on the world's nuclear proliferation.
5. The original quotation in Komori's book is "嘘の言葉は一人歩きし、私たちの危機感や恐怖心や、政府や東電の無責任さに対する怒りを、確実に麻痺（まひ）させていく。それを抗うには、嘘の言葉を押し返す、現実を正確に認識する言葉を手にし口にし、社会的に流通させ共有し続けなければならない。そして「三・一一」と、それ以後の日々の記憶を手放さないことである。" (97).

WORKS CITED

Abel, Jonathan E. "The Measures of Waves." Introduction. *Japan Forum*, vol. 26, no. 3, 2014, pp. 297–305.

Amano, Ikuho. "From Mourning to Allegory: Post–3.11 *Space Battleship Yamato* in Motion." *Japan Forum*, vol. 26, no. 3, 2014, pp. 325–39.

Blind. Directed by Yukihiro Shoda, 2011, www.blind-film.net. Accessed June 2015.

Chikamatsu, Nobuko. "Beikoku ni okeru kontento bēsu jugyō no kokoromi." *Japanese Language Education around the Globe*, vol. 19, 2009, pp. 141–56.

———. "Communication with Community: Connecting an Individual to the World through Japanese Content-Based Instruction of Japanese American History." *Japanese Language and Literature*, vol. 46, 2012, pp. 171–99.

———. "Language as an Essential Element for Human Thought Processes: Critical and Creative Thinking in Content-Based Instruction." *Journal of Canadian Association for Japanese Language Education*, vol. 12, 2011, pp. 1–22.

———. "Preparing Students for Life-long Learning of Japanese: Content-Based Language Instruction and Its Possibilities in Higher Education: Japanese American History in *Chicago* and *Hana's Suitcase*." *Proceedings of the Twenty-Second Annual Conference of the Central Association of Teachers of Japanese*, 2010, pp. 11–20.

ESD-J Mirai o Tsukuru Book Team. *Mirai o tsukuru Book.* Mikuni Shuppan, 2011.

Gardner, William. "Narratives of Collapse and Generation: Komatsu Sakyō's Disaster Novels and the Metabolist Movement." *Japan Forum*, vol. 26, no. 3, 2014, pp. 306–24.

Haugen, Einar I. *The Ecology of Language.* Stanford UP, 1972.

Hosokawa, Hideo. *Nihongokyōiku wa nani o mezasuka: Gengobunkakatsudō no riron to jissen.* Akashi Shoten, 2004.

Iwasaki, Noriko, and Yuri Kumagai. "Promoting Critical Reading in an Advanced-Level Japanese Course: Theory and Practice through Reflection and Dialogues." *Japanese Language and Literature*, vol. 42, no. 1, 2008, pp. 123–56.

The Japan Times. *Special Report: 3.11 One Year On: A Chronicle of Japan's Road to Recovery.* 2012.

Komori, Yoichi. *Shiha no koe, seija no kotoba.* Shinnihon Shuppan, 2014.

Krueger, Merle, and Frank Ryan. *Language and Content: Discipline- and Content-Based Approaches to Language Study.* D. C. Heath, 1993.

Kubota, Ryuko. "Memories of War: Exploring Victim-Victimizer Perspectives in Critical Content-Based Instruction in Japanese." *L2 Journal*, vol. 4, 2012, pp. 37–57.

Live Your Dream: The Taylor Anderson Story. Directed by Regge Life, www.thetaylor andersonstory.com Accessed 16 Jul. 2013.

Lyster, Roy, and Susan Ballinger. "Content-Based Language Teaching: Convergent Concerns across Divergent Contexts." *Language Teaching Research*, vol. 15, no. 3, 2011, pp. 279–88.

Miyamoto, Yuki. "Panic over 'The Panic over Fukushima.'" *Atomic Age*, U of Chicago, 26 Aug. 2012, /lucian.uchicago.edu/blogs/atomicage/2012/08/26/panic-over-the-panic-over-fukushima/. Accessed 3 Oct. 2012.

Muller, Richard. "The Panic over Fukushima." *The Wall Street Journal*, 18 Aug. 2012, www.wsj.com/articles/SB10000872396390444772404577589270444059332. Accessed 3 Oct. 2012.

Murakami, Haruki. *After the Quake.* Vintage, 2003.

———. *1Q84.* Knopf, 2011.

Okazaki, Toshio. *Gengo seitaigaku to gengo kyoiku.* Bonjinsha, 2009.

Sato, Shinji, and Yuri Kumagai. *Shakaisanka o mezasu nhongokyōiku.* Hitsuji Shobō, 2011.

Seto, Tomoko. "Incorporating 3-11 in a History Course on Japanese Social Movements." The Second Teaching Japan Conference, 28 Apr. 2013, Elizabethtown College, Elizabethtown, PA.

Smits, Gregory. "Shaking Up Japan: Edo Society and the 1855 Catfish Picture Prints." *Journal of Social History*, vol. 39, no. 1, 2006, pp. 1045–78.

Stryker, Stephen B., and Betty Lou Leaver. *Content-Based Instruction in Foreign Language Education: Models and Methods.* Georgetown UP, 1997.

Suzuki, Hisao, et al., editors. *Datsugenpatsu shizenenerugī 218nin shishū: Farewell to Nuclear, Welcome to Renewable Energy, A Collection of Poems by 218 Poets.* Coal Sack Publishing, 2012.

Tōhoku Tomo. Directed by Wesley Julian, 12 Mar. 2014.

Sustainability in "Post-communicative" Advanced Chinese Courses: Engaging Learners in Real-World Issues

Haidan Wang

Amid China's unprecedented explosive economic growth in recent decades, sustainability and environmental protection in the developing superpower has been the subject of great admonishment. It has then become our responsibility as higher education professionals to educate students in embracing a greener world and to present the discussion on sustainability in an inspiring and compelling way. Teaching foreign languages—especially Chinese—through the lens of sustainability combines content and language, providing for a more comprehensive and holistic overview of society and culture.

In 2010, when Advanced Chinese for Business Professionals (ACBP) at the University of Hawai'i at Mānoa (UHM) was reconstructed to create a course featuring a content-based, pragmatics-enhanced, culture-enriched, and technology-assisted curriculum that included a focus on sustainability issues, a process of educational change was set in motion that would have a transformative effect on the experiences of students (Wang, "Attaining"). As part of ongoing curriculum development, sustainability was identified as a topic of emphasis and was expanded from a single lesson chosen from the course textbook into a theme-based and self-designed comprehensive unit that included several related lessons. Initially this change altered the syllabus. The authentic listening and reading materials related to this topic—that is, materials created for Chinese native speakers, including "ideas, words, phrases, and expressions that are heard and read in real-life situations"

(Ciornei and Dina 275)—were carefully selected. These materials have been updated each semester based on the students' profiles and needs (Wang, "Toward" 253). Classroom activities, tasks, and assignments were similarly designed and implemented to enhance students' language proficiency, communicative skills, and cultural literacy. Ultimately, however, these changes had fundamental repercussions on the curriculum: this unit emphasizing a contemporary topic presented through regularly updated authentic materials shifted the focus of curricular planning to a student-centered design that connected classroom learning with the real world.

When the topic of sustainability was first introduced through a lesson in the Chinese textbook used for ACBP, the wider academic community at UHM had already started a campus-wide campaign to promote sustainability. Following the Board of Regents' explicit incorporation of sustainability into the university's mission in early 2014, an executive policy identifying "the importance of supporting sustainability research and scholarship, with appropriate integration into UH teaching and learning" was established (University of Hawai'i). In addition, the university began to hold an annual statewide sustainability higher education summit, encouraging cross-campus participation and student leadership in sustainability efforts as well as the sponsorship of local organizations, businesses, and individuals. With this institutional affirmation of sustainability principles, developing the original unit into a capstone component on sustainability became a way to shift higher education from static instruction to instruction focused on learners and engaged learning (Byrnes 267) while incorporating the university's educational priorities. This article presents the pedagogical principles, curriculum design, and content-based approaches used in developing the theme of sustainability in the advanced Chinese classes at UHM and discusses the results, student responses, observations, and implications of this practice.

Pedagogical Principles and Approaches

The original ACBP redesign adopted a "post-communicative approach," which differs from traditional communicative language teaching in that the latter emphasizes rich language input to develop proficiency with discrete communicative competence in four skills (listening, reading, speaking, and writing) and in three communicative modes (interpretive, presentational, and interpersonal). However beneficial the communicative approach might be in some regards, it has been shown that learners achieving good listening and reading competence may be relatively poor in the productive skills of speaking and writing. The post-communicative approach, or a modified version of communicative language instruction, overcomes these limitations by focusing on language use at the discourse level and emphasizing each learner's personal learning and discovery through task-based activities, collaborative work among learners, and the teacher as a vital facilitator (Paesani et al. 7). Throughout the instructional process, learners are not passive receivers of input but rather active participants who work on texts as researchers. Authentic listening materials, for example, are linked to learners' speaking activities; readings covering a variety of text styles are linked to learners' writing production. All this input facilitates the raising of learners' consciousness about the thematic topic and their attending to language forms and is accompanied by collaborative tasks and expectations about analytic learning outcomes ("Language Teaching"). Given these highly effective features, this discourse-based approach has been adopted in the advanced-level Chinese language courses at UHM and many other institutions.

One of the key features of this post-communicative focus on discourse competence is the use of the *inductive method*. In contrast to the rule-governed deductive method that concentrates on grammatical rules, the inductive method presents learners with examples and data and then provides opportunities for them to discover and induce the rules on their own. This method benefits learners of all ability levels in the acquisition of language forms and leads to higher performance scores on difficult concepts; it is especially preferable to use the inductive method in advanced-level courses where students have the proficiency to work with more data (Shaffer 399).

For reasons that will be explored in this essay, the post-communicative approach is also closely connected to project-based learning (PBL), as described by John W. Thomas (1), making it highly suitable to the sustainability content chosen for this course redesign. Project-based learning is a model for organizing learning around projects that are complex tasks and is also a discovery learning process. Students design, solve problems, make decisions, and investigate relatively autonomously over an extended period of time, utilizing technology tools. This learning model emphasizes authentic content, assessment based on authentic performances, and teacher facilitation, along with cooperative learning and reflection. The teacher assesses students' learning outcomes by evaluating the products of their projects.

The projects are formed around driving questions that students encounter throughout the unit. Capturing the heart of the project, these driving questions should be "provocative, open-ended, complex, and linked to the core" of what students are learning (Larmer and Mergendoller 53). This PBL approach culminates in realistic final products, such as oral presentations, illustrated posters, or research papers, in which issues are thoroughly investigated and students' voices and opinions are clearly presented.

Curriculum Components and Instructional Process

Since the ACBP curriculum is closely articulated with the fourth-level advanced Chinese courses at UHM, the teachers of the two proximate courses were invited to adopt the revised unit of sustainability and coordinate their teaching using the post-communicative approach. Students registering for these courses came from a wide variety of backgrounds. More than half of the students were Chinese majors; others included undergraduate and graduate students in business, marketing, and a variety of humanities disciplines.

The sustainability curriculum was taught over two to three weeks and was composed of five parts:

1. A preliminary survey of students' background knowledge was administered, followed by an introduction to the theme and student learning outcomes. During this lesson, project groups were formed and started brainstorming.
2. An intensive listening activity was conducted in class, followed by comprehension discussions, and then continued in online forums.
3. An intensive reading activity was conducted in class, followed by comprehension discussions, and then continued in online forums.
4. Parts 2 and 3 were repeated with extensive listening and reading activities.
5. A post-theme survey was administered, and students completed a project assignment that included an oral presentation of posters and a written report. Selected posters were displayed in the department hallway and were planned to be entered in the UHM sustainability fair held annually on campus. The structure of this unit is illustrated in this essay's appendix.

The interconnected design of these parts yielded opportunities for course participants to reflect on their understanding of sustainability concepts, engage in tasks targeting advanced language learning, and practice self-assessment. The preliminary bilingual survey used in part 1 was designed to reveal students' understanding of and interest in the theme as well as how they viewed the importance of studying sustainability in a Chinese language course. Students were also asked to provide their definition of this concept and their perceived knowledge about sustainable development in China, the United States, and locally. The purposes of this survey were to identify students' background knowledge and personal interest, create a reference point prior to starting the theme, help teachers determine the instructional foci, and reconfirm the student learning outcomes. Afterward, an introduction to the concept of sustainability was presented in Chinese, and the Chinese definition was compared with the English definition found on *Wikipedia*. The introduction was designed to establish common ground for teaching and learning for the subsequent steps in the course and, most important, to define customized and individualized student learning outcomes, that is, a comprehensive project including a formal oral presentation, poster, and written report, all in Chinese.

The intensive listening activity in part 2 included a three-minute video clip, 低碳生活重在选择 ("The Choices Needed to Live a Low-Carbon Life"), which was selected because it provides an overview of suggestions on how to live a low-carbon life. Guided oral discussion within small groups followed immediately after a listening comprehension exercise. Each group focused on one aspect of the issues covered in the video. Students discussed the feasibility of living a low-carbon life, in particular examining the relation between time efficiency and carbon footprint when choosing transportation and the feasibility of green transportation for residents of Hawai'i, as well as the pros and cons of using plastic versus reusable shopping bags, the affordability of consuming organic food, and the rationale for purchasing local products. Students continued these discussions on the online forums after the in-class listening and speaking session, meaning that cross-group interaction extended beyond the space and time of the classroom. The extensive listening exercises in part 4, which took place after the intensive reading exercise, followed the same procedure. One listening selection involved a text about Beijing residents who processed home waste using a new trash compactor; the other was about China's new population policy, allowing one more child for some families.

The intensive reading passage used was an editorial article titled 中国更环保还是美国更浪费 ("Is China More Environmentally Friendly, or the United

States More Wasteful?"). This text contrasts the perspectives of working and living practices in China and the United States, along with providing the author's suggestions regarding China's pursuit of a greener environment. The teacher-guided reading process used for this text followed a top-down method, incorporating activities to train students in the use of the prediction strategies. After reading, students responded to the comprehension activities, including a group oral discussion in the classroom and using online forums. The extensive reading in part 4 was an academic paper published in a Chinese academic journal, titled 夏威夷对海南国际旅游岛可持续发展的启示 ("The Implications of Hawai'i's Sustainable Development on Hainan's International Tourism Sector"). This paper analyses the geographic and economic situations and characteristics of Hawai'i in comparison to Hainan, China, and advocates a suitable model featuring the tourism economy in Hawai'i. Additionally, it discusses the implications of the Hawai'i model for Hainan's international tourist business development. Taking into consideration that this authentic article requires language abilities at the Superior level (*ACTFL Proficiency Guidelines*), use of scaffolding for the comprehension activities accommodated learners who had not yet reached that level.

Both intensive and extensive reading activities were introduced with questions that elicited the readers' reactions to the title, thus activating their background knowledge and establishing a personal connection with the readings. Postreading questions required readers to extrapolate from the text, probed readers' opinions about the writer's voice, and asked readers to express reflections on perspectives relating to themselves. Students also contemplated aspects covered in the readings that interested them. These student-generated discussion points were intended both to kindle students' interest in further exploration and to lead to research questions for the final projects.

Student groups were formed based on common interests, with consideration of students' diversified language proficiency and academic majors. These groups narrowed down the scope of interests and eventually came up with one or two self-selected topics for the required project. Following the PBL model (Larmer and Mergendoller), teachers used scaffolding for the learning process and monitored it on an ongoing basis. Rubrics for the project were reviewed during class and posted on the course Web site for student viewing. In general, the rubrics made students aware of the realistic nature of the project and the significance of the project to society and their own lives. In addition to raising and investigating questions through collaboration and communication among their group members, course participants had to organize their projects with arguments and supporting data, hypotheses, conclusions, or solutions to problems raised. When presenting their research projects orally, students were expected to elaborate on their ideas in response to questions, defend their stances when critiqued, and revise their posters and research papers by incorporating suggestions and feedback from the audience of teachers and peers.

At the end of the unit, a bilingual survey was conducted to find out whether students' knowledge, views, and interests regarding sustainability development in China had changed. They also redefined the concept of the unit, incorporating personal perspectives. The survey required students to elaborate on new knowledge they acquired regarding sustainable development in China and the United States (specifically in Hawai'i). Students were also asked to list related topics that they were interested in exploring but had not yet touched on. These perspectives were then used to inform subsequent curriculum planning. A final question sought to determine the confidence students had gained in learning about sustainability in a Chinese language class, with the aim of determining whether the approaches in this unit changed their attitudes toward learning Chinese.

Reflections and Discussion

Although sustainability has been a theme in the ACBP curriculum at UHM since 2007 and I have modified many components of the course on an ongoing basis, the creation of this unit and the updating of readings and listening materials with discussion prompts, assignments, and projects had a greater effect on the curriculum as a whole than isolated modifications did. As the pedagogical interventions described here were extended from the ACBP into the regular advanced Chinese curriculum, four transformative changes were observed. Students made gains in linguistic ability and critical thinking skills, while the teacher's role evolved in response to the multiliteracies and technology-enhanced approach.

Students' gains, including acquisition of critical thinking skills and understanding of the subject matter, are some of the most widely studied aspects of PBL research (Thomas 14). First, the most positive effect of assigning students a project is that they are engaged in questions of personal interest. During the process of forming questions, students examine many aspects related to the main concept, in this case the complex topic of sustainability. The introductory lecture on this theme combined authentic texts from multiple resources in Chinese supplemented with comparisons to similar content written in English. When answering the comprehension questions designed for the introductory readings, students were encouraged to reexamine the concept from multiple perspectives (i.e., environment, economy, population, and resources) and to find as many parallel practices as they could in both China and the United States. Teachers helped groups fine-tune the questions they proposed when they proved too broad or loosely related. Since students were encouraged to choose something relevant to themselves, they were able to come up with dynamic, specific topics. In subsequent course offerings, students' projects have covered a wide variety of topics that go beyond clichés that equate sustainability with environmental protection. A review of the projects shows that the Comparisons category defined in the American Council on the Teaching of Foreign Languages' national standards is particularly well-addressed ("Standards Summary"). Project topics have included Hawai'i's plastic bag laws; China's enlightenment from American solar energy; the Oahu rail project plan; a comparative analysis of the environment and energy: pros and cons of the Hoover and Three Gorges Dams; the debate on the construction of an Advanced Technology Solar Telescope on Haleakala (on Hawai'i Island); Beijing's waste-management system; facing the big "Car Wreck": the collision between China's economic future and the oil shortage; electronic waste in China; China's change in population policy and its relation to China's sustainability development; analyzing the benefit of a nuclear power plant in Taiwan; Hawai'i's solar energy; and the most livable cities in China.

Beyond greater understanding of the subject matter, students also demonstrated growing confidence about their capacity for sustainable thinking, as reflected in the self-assessment section of the two surveys. In the pre-unit survey of students' knowledge of sustainability, fourteen percent (out of $N = 45$) of students indicated that they understood "a lot," thirty percent indicated "somewhat," and forty percent "very little." After the two- to three-week unit, about twenty-eight percent of students indicated feeling that they understood "a lot" or "a great deal." More than half (fifty-six percent) indicated "somewhat," with only thirteen percent reporting "very little."[1] Many students indicated that "[they] got to delve deeper into the rich contents of this theme." Compared with the definition of *sustainability* given by students in the pre-unit survey, their redefinition in the post-unit survey shows richer content including more concepts and perspectives related to this theme. Generally, their understanding of sustainability is expanded, although this data only reflects students' impressions of their gains. One student's reflection is exemplary: "I used to equate 'sustainability' to more of an environmental or resource issue, e.g. save electricity, etc., but now I know it encompasses a lot more than that."[2] Another student commented that "this concept indicates the ability to have development that is maintained, which applies to many that I've thought about before, such as the economy, population, and social and political issues." Their interpretation of this concept goes beyond the definitions provided in the introductory text. As one student stated, it "is an issue of increasing importance across the nation and nations that innovators are constantly seeking ways to harness new forms of energy to power future development."

Expanded knowledge about sustainability changed student views of both China and Hawai'i. In the post-unit survey, one student acknowledged learning "more about sustainability from China's perspective" and about China's green energy industry, especially that "its photovoltaic sector is very competitive in the world." Before studying this unit, one student said, "my image of China was full of pollution, and overall quite negative." Another student commented, "it surprised me that the one-child policy in China was a political effort aiming for sustainability and to combat over-population despite its negative impacts such as gender imbalance. This is totally different from the aspects emphasized in the West about the violation of human rights." Course participants watched the news clip on China's new policy that allows a couple (with at least one individual being a single child from their family) to have a second child in order to promote long-term balance, particularly given the current aging population. In a follow-up discussion, students explored the repercussions of this new policy and speculated that it was unlikely to produce a baby boom with possible implications for social and economic development that would lead to a deteriorating living environment and other conditions. They concluded that for some couples, not having a second child is a form of societal choice in response to the increasingly high cost and pressure of raising more children in contemporary Chinese societies.

Study for this unit changed student views on local issues, as well. According to one student, "it's interesting to learn about eco-tourism, the sustainability of tourism in Hawai'i, and its referential value to China's tourism."

Another student also commented on learning more about the monorail project, which is a hot topic in Hawai'i currently, saying "I have different views on it from before." One student noted discovering that "Hawai'i is one of the nation's leaders in the innovative process of testing tide energy and ocean energy." Clearly students thought about global issues in terms of their local implications.

The post-unit survey also showed student gains in linguistic ability. Comparing the semantic differences of the word "sustainability" between Chinese and English, some students elaborated on their answers by writing that the English meaning focuses on the ability to sustain, whereas the Chinese meaning includes an additional concept of "development," emphasizing the process of maintaining and developing. "The Chinese term denotes a win-win for both economic development and environmental protection," one student claimed. Students also developed the ability to apply words with complicated meanings in their projects. Having just distinguished the differences between the Chinese word 悖论 and its English correspondence "paradox" in class discussion the day before, one group used the different senses of this Chinese word appropriately in their oral presentation, commenting on Hawaii Electric Company's monopoly and its suppression of the booming photovoltaic industry in Hawai'i.

Another important outcome was engagement in critical thinking through the projects.[3] After digesting the audiovisual and written materials, students discussed and applied concepts related to the theme. They subsequently analyzed, applied, negotiated, synthesized, observed, and evaluated information using reasoning and critique.

Multidimensional understanding was discerned in the discussion forums as well. After watching the video clip about choosing a low-carbon lifestyle, students all favored this sustainable approach at the macroscopic level. On further exploration of the possibilities for buying local products, such as agricultural products in Hawai'i, however, students realized the limited options Hawai'i residents have when making purchases. As one explained, "It's out of reach [for students] since buying local costs much more. This is because Hawai'i only produces very limited agricultural products that are essential to our daily life." Another student pointed out that sustainability "is both a trivial [packaging of household goods] and global issue, and can't be managed or controlled by one nation." While welcoming the plastic bag ban in Hawai'i, students praised its positive effect on the environment but also said it was too small in scale: "It would be great if the whole [United] States had established such a law." One group discovered that the Chinese government had started banning free plastic bags over a decade ago. Some of them were, however, "astonished at how wasteful the Chinese sometimes are about wrapping gifts in huge boxes or containers (luxury cartons with gilded decoration for tea, or moon cakes for the mid-autumn festival) for the last decade." One student noted that "business needs to take sustainability of natural resources into account in order to protect our environment." Their emotional investment in these discussions in Chinese was clearly a driving force in the class.

Even more robust critical thinking emerged in students' projects, some of which concerned controversial issues locally, nationally, and internationally. When studying the ongoing rail-transit project on Oahu, students voiced criticisms. One group contrasted information from the government of Hawai'i's Web site on the beneficial aspects of the rail system to much more abundant data from other sources, pointing out that the monorail would not resolve the problem as much as the government claims. By referring to their personal experience of commuting to UHM daily, they criticized the project as something that "has created more problems" than it would solve. Taking up critiques of the state government on its extension of extra state taxes in order to cover the huge expense of the monorail, this group suggested the construction of a less expensive, elevated highway, supporting this alternative idea with data of the costs of each project juxtaposed with government budgets and actual expenses, showing that their proposal cost less. They concluded that the monorail was just a face-saving project embraced by politicians pursuing their political legacy at the price of the whole state of Hawai'i, which will suffer for decades. They further suggested that "economic sustainability needs to be taken into account when looking at long-term financial decisions."

In a project comparing the Chinese Three Gorges Dam and Hoover Dam, a group concluded that "the intention to create a sustainable solution may have accidental impacts" on the environment, economy, and society. When disclosing the shocking state of pollution from e-waste in China, they protested the Chinese government's lack of restriction on e-waste imports and the rapaciousness of business profiteering. As an innovative recommendation, this group promoted the advantages of moving environmentally hazardous activities into space.

In terms of instructional practices, integrating post-communicative theory with PBL has thus shifted the teacher's role from that of sole authority to facilitator. With this change, the formation of productive project groups becomes crucial. When activating students' interest during the input phase, teachers can observe students' discussions in class and forums and then group students with diverse academic backgrounds, majors, and proficiency levels. When teachers review the initial project plans proposed by each group, they can provide suggestions for fine-tuning proposals that help learners transform their initial topics into suitable research questions. During the input phase and preparation for the project, teachers can explicitly discuss skills of collaboration, communication, and inquiry, encouraging coherent design among group members. Models and exemplary projects from previous cohorts can also be given as examples for students of later cohorts. When feedback and revision suggestions from teachers are provided soon after students deliver their oral presentations and submit the first drafts of their written reports, teachers can monitor revision with guidance that refers to the rubrics and examples, thus promoting the development for learners of their voices as authors and the refinement of their overall structure and organization.

In the case of this redesigned course, teachers played a facilitative role in this revision process through moderate intervention and by emphasizing the goals and expectations of the theme. By highlighting learning as the key component of the PBL approach, the teachers guided students to contrast the difference between work completion and learning at the beginning, as well as during the process of the project (Thomas 29). Throughout the project, teachers explicitly elaborated that learning was an inquiry into unknown areas, acquisition of knowledge, identifying problems and solutions, and producing oral or written products containing this knowledge, together with reflections that make their audiences learn. This particular perspective on learning directly influenced the students' working processes and determined the quality of their final product.

Focusing on literacy, which is the primary goal of both the post-communicative approach and PBL, was an important aspect of the overall curriculum redesign. The term *literacy* has evolved from a traditional, static, cognitive-psycholinguistic concept to a plural form in second-language education, expressed by the terms "literacies," "new literacies" (Leu), "biliteracies" (Wiley), or "multi-literacies" (Abdallah). These terms encompass many forms and variations of literacy, the most noteworthy being literacies gained from authentic text and through technology. In this unit, students develop their literacy using materials presenting the wider sociocultural contexts and social practices of the target language and culture that are made accessible through technology. The sustainability theme, as it has been described in the present essay, has moved from a textbook lesson to a much more comprehensive teaching-learning experience by incorporating entirely authentic materials for input. By allowing this, technology has made achieving multiliteracy more feasible, and student learning has shifted from "in-school" compartmentalization to real-world, "out-of-school" literacy (Street; qtd. in Abdallah; see also Barton and Hamilton; Gee, *Social Linguistics*).

This unit was taught in a blended environment, a format frequently used in higher education nowadays. The online platform *Brix* (a UHM-developed courseware) enabled teachers to arrange the course materials systematically, updating and revising input materials easily and in a timely fashion. Links in the course Web site made teaching materials and supplementary resources easily accessible. Students, moreover, often used online resources to enhance comprehension and conduct research for projects. When compared with my notes on students' in-class discussion, I observed more extended discussion and interactive negotiation of issues taking place in postings on the course online forums. The asynchronous online discussion made students read and analyze ideas and viewpoints shared by classmates, raise new issues for further exploration, and discover the silent language—culture—embedded everywhere they explored (Furstenberg and Levet). Technology also increased convenience and collaboration, since the project could be stored in the cloud and easily accessed by group members.

Two main aspects of such a multiple-literacies, technology-enhanced approach are worth mentioning here. First, reading a text from a published academic journal exposed students to Superior-level linguistic input. One student shared in the reflection, "I was 'suffocated' and a little mad when we received the lengthy reading on Hawai'i-Hainan sustainability at the beginning, but thrilled to realize that I can comprehend both the gist and details of it after the reading sessions guided by reading strategies." Another student stated, "I was so proud of myself, and, of course with my team, that we could complete such a long report containing our research IN CHINESE despite these many expressions that had to be re-worded [because of its academic nature]." This unit facilitated the mutual promotion of literacy skills and sustainability. The comprehension of Superior-level discourse, in turn, stimulated students to complete complex and linguistically sophisticated written products, as was also demonstrated in the practice of other languages (Ter Horst and Pearce).

Second, the social practice and ideological orientation of literacy observed throughout the process can become an explicit component of the curriculum. As Terrence G. Wiley points out, "literacy is first and foremost a social relationship among people, their ways with words, deeds, and things, and institutions" (534; qtd. in Gee, Foreword iv). Reflecting on the diversity of views on China's one-child policy in Chinese and Western media, students sensed the stereotypes that exist for others and themselves. They discerned how contemporary Chinese people regard their choice of not having a second child and discovered hidden dimensions related to culture and modern Chinese society. Another student pointed out, "my understanding of China's place in the world's path toward sustainability has changed . . . in research of electronic waste in China, it was interesting to discover that this country holds about 70% of the entire world's EEE [electrical, electronic, and electromechanical] wastes, because it is sent there by OTHER nations. Not all of the pollution in China is its own doing." Another commented on the same issue, saying, "[I]s it fair to solely blame China for 'creating' more and more pollution when Westerners can enjoy their new e-devices almost every six months!" Students' excitement in their forum discussion fluctuated when realizing that buying local in Hawai'i can be ideal but impractical to them. Knowing the perspectives of a sustainable tourism industry in Hawai'i versus Hainan Province, China, made local students reflect on their own environment and feel encouraged. One project group defended the Haleakala solar exploratory project after reading the updates on the project Web sites and hearing about the ongoing protests at the construction site of this project on Hawaii Public Radio. This live news eventually appeared as supporting materials in their final project presented in Chinese.

Such a multiliteracy orientation empowers teachers to "train students to reflect on the world and themselves through the lens of another language and culture" (MLA Ad Hoc Committee 237). Based on my own experience, multiliteracy can be achieved with the integration of a post-communicative approach and PBL implemented in a hybrid learning environment, where the contents are significantly related to students' lives and interests and students' achievements are comprehensively assessed with their apprehension of content, continuous linguistic and cultural comparison, and cross-cultural reflection contained in their project production. In sum, besides developing their language proficiency, students were able to deepen their understanding of the concepts and cultural issues related to sustainability through comprehending and producing texts with complexity and being involved in a local, national, and global community through this learning journey.

Incorporating the theme of sustainability into the advanced Chinese curriculum via the integration of post-communicative and PBL approaches proved successful in developing self-perceived gains and multiliteracies for those students taking advanced Chinese language courses at UHM. This practice situates Chinese-language learning in a geographic, cross-cultural, and contemporary frame, as advocated by the Modern Language Association and forward-thinking foreign language educators (MLA Ad Hoc Committee 236). It has therefore led to a unified language and content curriculum. The success and effectiveness of teaching and learning about the theme of sustainability in a language class can be gauged by the students' gains in both Chinese-language competence and knowledge of the subject matter. Students' reflections, class performance, pre- and post-unit surveys, and final projects have demonstrated the value and great potential for the approaches adopted. The integration of listening to and reading authentic materials with discussion and reflection on the subject matter, together with clear language and content learning objectives, made possible the implementation of post-communicative approach techniques, such as inductive instruction, inclusion of intellectual content, and use of a multiliteracy focus. Especially during inductive instruction, students drew their own conclusions from authentic materials provided by the teacher and those they identified from their own research. In short, in contrast with the instructing of language forms and skills in isolation typical of communicative language teaching, this post-communicative approach promotes language learning as various interconnected discourses, and distinguishes among types of sociolinguistic settings. It encourages learners to participate in diverse forms of discourse communication while collaboratively and critically thinking, with a focus on all types of texts, additional intellectual content, and comprehensive literacy skills. Ideally, this would not deter traditional teachers, since all four skills are addressed in balance. The PBL approach to this unit, comprising an oral presentation, essay, and poster, provided a guided environment in which students formed research questions, gathered data, created outlines, and composed presentations. Moreover, the potential for the utilization of the results of a final project for real-world purposes is a strong incentive, giving students a sense of personal involvement and achievement, thus enabling them to make contributions to social issues through their language-learning process.

With selected posters from previous cohorts covering the walls of the department hallways, the full breadth of the knowledge and achievement made by students from Chinese-language classes has been brought home to the whole department, and later to the university community at its annual sustainability fair. Inspired by these encouraging experiences with the sustainability unit, I, along with my colleagues, will continue the practice of holistically incorporating content and cross-cultural reflections with Chinese-language teaching and apply this model to the introduction of more new themes in advanced classes.

This essay has provided a post-communicative module of language instruction with the integration of content-based teaching and PBL. This practice and the analysis of students' reflections demonstrate that this unique combination can achieve promising learning outcomes. I see the potential for this module to be adapted to other content-based thematic instruction concerning real issues relevant to an interdisciplinary student body. Future curriculum design and instructional practices in line with this module could expand to include new domains of content knowledge or themes. Further research will continue to explore the effectiveness of this module quantitatively and qualitatively and give more attention to the assessment of learners' in-depth multiliteracies from both linguistic and sociocultural perspectives.

NOTES

I would like to thank Professor Song Jiang and Ms. Jing Wu for their cooperation. Professor Jiang contributed a significant amount of time in providing suggestions for revision and improvements in many aspects of this process.
1. The percentages do not add up to one hundred because some students did not respond to this survey question.
2. All quotations from students' forum discussions, reflections, or postproject surveys are either partly cited from their original postings in English or my translations of their Chinese postings.
3. I adopt the definition of *critical thinking* as a mode of thinking about any subject, content, or problem where the thinker improves the quality of thinking by skillfully analyzing, assessing, and reconstructing it ("Our Concept").

APPENDIX:
CONCEPTUAL MAP OF THE SUSTAINABILITY UNIT

Part	Contents	Activities
Part 1: Preparation	Students' background knowledge Introduction to the theme What is sustainability (什么是可持续发展)? The concept of sustainable development (可持续发展概念的提出)	Surveying Lecturing in class Grouping students for projects
Part 2: Input 1: Intensive listening	(1) Earth report: The choices needed to live a low-carbon life (地球宣言：低碳生活重在选择) (2) The focus on a low-carbon economy and the development of green energy (聚焦"低碳"经济 发展绿色能源)	Listening comprehension Class discussion: Speaking Continue online forum discussion: Writing Group discussion on topic options for group project
Part 3: Input 2: Intensive reading	Is China more sustainable, or the United States more wasteful? (中国更环保还是美国更浪费)	Reading comprehension Class discussion: Speaking Continue online forum discussion: Writing Deciding group project topic Starting research and data gathering for group project
Part 4: Recycling parts 2 and 3	Extensive listening (3) Beijing residents' DIY waste disposal facilities (北京居民自建垃圾处理设施) (4) The authoritative interpretation of China's reformed one-child policy ("单独两孩"政策权威解读) Extensive reading The implications of Hawai'i's sustainable development for Hainan's international tourism sector (夏威夷对海南国际旅游岛可持续发展的启示)	Listening comprehension Class discussion: Speaking Continue online forum discussions Lecturing on reading guide Facilitating students' reading with strategies Student independent reading Working on group project
Part 5: Group projects	Project presentations, essays, and posters	Post-theme survey: Students' reflections Oral presentation on projects Turning in essay Poster display to public

WORKS CITED

Abdallah, Mahmoud M. S. "Web-Based New Literacies: Revisiting Literacy in TESOL and EFL Teacher Education." *The Australian Council of TESOL Association (ACTA) International TESOL Conference, Surfers Paradise Holiday Inn, City of Gold Coast, 7–10 July 2010*, files.eric.ed.gov/fulltext/ED511725.pdf. Accessed 20 June 2015.

ACTFL Proficiency Guidelines 2012. American Council on the Teaching of Foreign Languages (ACTFL), 2012, www.actfl.org/sites/default/files/pdfs/public/ACTFL ProficiencyGuidelines2012_FINAL.pdf.

Barton, David, and Mary Hamilton. *Local Literacies: Reading and Writing in One Community.* Routledge, 1998.

Byrnes, Heidi. "Constructing Curricula in Collegiate Foreign Language Departments." *Learning Foreign and Second Languages: Perspectives in Research and Scholarship*, edited by Byrnes, Modern Language Association of America, 1998, pp. 262–95.

Ciornei, Silvia Ileana, and Tatiana A. Dina. "Authentic Texts in Teaching English." *Procedia: Social and Behavioral Sciences*, vol. 180, 2015, pp. 274–79.

Furstenberg, Gilberte, and Sabine Levet. "*Cultura*: From Then to Now: Its Origins, Key Features, Methodology, and How It Has Evolved: Reflections on the Past and Musing on the Future." *Cultura-Inspired Intercultural Exchanges: Focus on Asian and Pacific Languages*, edited by Dorothy M. Chun, University of Hawai'i, National Foreign Language Resource Center, 2014, pp. 1–31.

Gee, James P. Foreword. *Illegal Alphabets and Adult Biliteracy: Latino Migrants Crossing the Linguistic Border*, edited by Tomas M. Kalmar, Lawrence Erlbaum, 2001, pp. i–iv.

———. *Social Linguistics and Literacies: Ideology in Discourse.* 2nd ed., Taylor & Francis, 1996.

"Language Teaching in the 'Post-communicative' Era." Harvard University, Department of Romance Languages and Literatures, 2009, slideplayer.com/slide/4931448/. *PowerPoint* presentation. Accessed 3 Mar. 2015.

Larmer, John, and John R. Mergendoller. "Seven Essentials for Project-Based Learning." *Educational Leadership*, vol. 68, no. 1, 2010, pp. 52–55. Revised as "Eight Essentials for Project-Based Learning," Mar. 2012, static1.squarespace.com/static/530e32e2e4b02e9cbe11317b/t/54b044c9e4b0265c9838432f/1420838089897/8+PBL+Essentials.pdf. Accessed 17 June 2018.

Leu, Donald J. "The New Literacies: Research on Reading Instruction with the Internet and Other Digital Technologies." *What Research Has to Say about Reading Instruction*, edited by Alan E. Farstrup and S. Jay Samuels, 3rd ed., International Reading Association, 2002, pp. 310–37.

MLA Ad Hoc Committee on Foreign Languages. "Foreign Languages and Higher Education: New Structures for a Changed World." *Profession*, 2007, pp. 234–45.

"Our Concept and Definition of Critical Thinking." *The Foundation for Critical Thinking*, 2017, www.criticalthinking.org/pages/our-concept-of-critical-thinking/411. Accessed 17 June 2018.

Paesani, Kate, et al. *A Multiliteracies Framework for Collegiate Foreign Language Teaching.* Pearson, 2016.

Shaffer, Constance. "A Comparison of Inductive and Deductive Approaches to Teaching Foreign Languages." *The Modern Language Journal*, vol. 73, no. 4, 1989, pp. 395–403.

"Standards Summary." American Council on the Teaching of Foreign Languages (ACTFL), 1996, www.actfl.org/publications/all/world-readiness-standards-learning-languages/standards-summary. Accessed 16 Aug. 2016.

Street, Brian V. "Multiple Literacies and Multi-literacies." *The SAGE Handbook of Writing Development*, edited by Roger Beard et al., Sage Publications, 2009, pp. 137–51.

Ter Horst, Eleanor E., and Joshua M. Pearce. "Foreign Language and Sustainability: Addressing the Connections, Communities, Comparisons Standards in Higher Education." *Foreign Language Annals*, vol. 43, no. 3, 2010, pp. 365–83.

Thomas, John W. "A Review of Research on Project-Based Learning." Buck Institute for Education, 2000, www.bie.org/object/document/a_review_of_research_on _project_based_learning. Accessed 17 June 2018.

University of Hawai'i. "New UH Sustainability Policy Aims for Carbon Neutrality by 2050." 27 May 2015, www.hawaii.edu/news/2015/02/26/new-uh -sustainability-policy-aims-for-carbon-neutrality-by-2050/.

Wang, Haidan. "Attaining Sustainable Growth of a Business Chinese Program through Utilization-Focused Evaluation." *Global Business Languages*, vol. 18, no. 1, 2013, pp. 130–44.

———. "Toward Deepening Cultural and Language Understanding: The Design and Practice of a Hybrid Business Chinese Course." *Journal of Teaching in International Business*, vol. 25, no. 3, 2014, pp. 250–62. *Taylor and Francis Online*, doi:10.1080/ 08975930.2014.925750.

Wiley, Terrence G. "Second Language Literacy and Biliteracy." *Handbook of Research in Second Language Teaching and Learning*, edited by Eli Hinkel, vol. 1, Lawrence Erlbaum, 2005, pp. 529–44.

Interdepartmental Collaboration and Curriculum Design: Creating a Russian Environmental Sustainability Course for Advanced Students

Olesya Kisselev
and William Comer

In 2008, the newly funded Russian Language Flagship (RLF) program at Portland State University (PSU) partnered with the university's general education program to create a series of courses to provide general education content instruction and advanced language learning opportunities in the framework of language across the curriculum. One of the designated general education courses on the topic of environmental sustainability served as a parent content course to the Russian language adjunct course Readings in Russian: Environmental Sustainability. This essay summarizes our experience in designing this course: it explains the rationale behind choosing both the methodological approach and the topic of sustainability, discusses the challenges of developing and implementing a content-based course, and provides an instructive case study of interdepartmental collaboration in curriculum planning that can serve as a model for successful integration of language and content learning.

The main goal of The Language Flagship (www.thelanguageflagship.org) is to promote expertise in critical foreign languages and to educate a new generation of "global professionals," college graduates who, in addition to holding a major in any specialty, will possess a professional (i.e., Superior) competency in a critical language according to the proficiency scale of the American Council on the Teaching of Foreign Languages (*ACTFL Proficiency Guidelines*). Similar to flagship programs in other languages, the RLF at PSU seeks to prepare its students for expertly using their second language in professional settings by offering undergraduate students sequences of specialized language courses designed to allow them to pursue advanced subject matter studies in Russian. Advanced-track courses are pitched for students who have attained the Intermediate Mid level on the ACTFL scale, and they aspire to guide these students to the Advanced High level. The program is designed to accommodate students from diverse backgrounds: traditional classroom learners (who received instruction in Russian primarily at American schools and colleges), students who complete high school immersion programs, students returning from immersion experiences (such as the Peace Corps), and heritage learners of Russian (individuals exposed to Russian in the family or community). The advanced classes are mixed, meaning that they serve all these student populations in the same instructional setting. Recognizing the need to develop all learners' skills with both advanced-level general academic language and discipline-specific language, the program from its inception chose the content-based instruction (CBI) approach to language study.[1]

The effectiveness of a CBI approach is supported by more than thirty years of thorough second language acquisition research. In addition to greater exposure to the target language in CBI courses, many other benefits of this model have been recorded: higher levels of motivation among learners (Leaver 44–45; Wiesemes 46–47), increased learner interest in both the topic and the language (Leaver 44–45), increased learner output in the target language (Leaver 45–46; Dalton-Puffer 187; Wiesemes 47), better comprehension and tolerance of complex and unfamiliar language (Dalton-Puffer 188), and better-developed strategies for dealing with complex information in the target language (Brinton et al. 66–67; Dalton-Puffer 187–88; Leaver 46–47; Marsh viii; Wiesemes 46). This approach is particularly appropriate at advanced levels of foreign language study, since advanced proficiency calls for using academic and professional varieties of language, which are field- and genre-specific (Schleppegrell and O'Hallaron 3–5).

Although all flagship programs utilize some features of CBI pedagogy in their curricula (Freels et al. 51–52), the RLF took a comprehensive approach to integrating its courses with PSU's general education program, effectively laying the foundation for a Russian-across-the-curriculum model. This model was made possible by the willingness of PSU's award-winning University Studies program to partner with the Department of World Languages and Literatures in supporting the development of content-based Russian language courses.

University Studies, PSU's general education program, requires all first-year students to take a yearlong course called Freshman Inquiry, which addresses a single topic from multidisciplinary points of view. In their second year students complete Sophomore Inquiry, three ten-week-long quarter classes, each covering a different topic. The subject matter of these classes does not have to relate to the student's major, since the courses focus more generally on the four underlying goals of university education: critical thinking, social responsibility, communication, and appreciation of diversity of human experience. Inasmuch as these goals foster abstract thinking, argumentation, hypothesizing, comparing and evaluating different positions, and control of academic register about topics of broad public interest, they mirror the main goal of The Language Flagship, which focuses on educating "global professionals" capable of using the second language effectively (i.e., understanding the positions of interlocutors and formulating and expressing educated opinions) at the Superior level in a range of professional settings. Furthermore, the courses meet the ACTFL *World-Readiness Standards for Learning Languages* in that they develop students' ability to comprehend and present information, concepts, and ideas on a variety of topics and to obtain information and recognize different points of view and values (National Standards).

Myriam Met describes the CBI approach as a range of instructional models available in terms of a continuum, ranging from immersive models to partial-immersion and content-driven courses to more language-driven courses that utilize content as a unifying topic and context (40–41). The RLF faculty adopted a version of a CBI curriculum known as the "adjunct" format (Lyster 611). This model rests at the middle of Met's continuum and is often referred to as "sheltered instruction" (Lyster 611). Widely employed in the English as a second language (ESL) context in the United States, in this model classes integrate attention to language with content from a mainstream course to benefit second-language learners in terms of both linguistic and conceptual knowledge development.

In our case, we set out to create two-credit Russian language adjunct courses to correspond with the selected general education courses. We planned not to replicate the parent class in Russian but rather to augment it, both by introducing additional materials, viewpoints, and tasks that are unique to the Russian-speaking world and by comparing the subject matter taught in the parent course to that covered in the Russian section. We posited that the English-language general education classes would benefit from the existence of the Russian section, since RLF students bring additional perspectives and ideas that might not otherwise be available to monolingual students. Such a partnership between courses, we believed, would enhance the internationalization of the university curriculum, a stated goal at PSU and many other institutions.

When approached with this model, University Studies readily embraced our goals, helped identify courses and instructors, and consulted about the compatibility of the parent and adjunct courses in terms of content and assignment. One of the most successful collaborations led to the development of the partnered courses on environmental sustainability: the University Studies course Environmental Sustainability and the Russian adjunct course Readings in Russian: Environmental Sustainability.

Why Environmental Sustainability?

Following trends observable at all levels of education across the United States and the world, PSU began bringing issues of environmental sustainability and ethics into the center of many educational programs and majors in 2008 (Chapman; "Colleges"). Originally more at home in science and engineering programs, discussions of the environment and sustainable development are increasingly embraced in world languages programs, as the current volume illustrates so potently. The environment and sustainability are topics that all nations have to address, although responses to any particular environmental issue often reflect local cultural perspectives and practices. World languages departments are often the only units on campus linguistically capable of accessing research and opinions from other parts of the world and interpreting them within their original cultural contexts. The environment and sustainability are also highly appropriate topics for encouraging students to produce advanced-level academic language, since any aspect of these topics requires the average speaker to be able to use scientific academic discourse as well as describe complex problems, contemplate their implications and possible solutions (discussion of abstract topics), and recommend courses of action (argumentation and persuasion).

Although research literature on this trend in education is still rare, the topic of sustainable development is, in fact, uniquely suited to our current understanding of what students should know and be able to do in foreign language education (National Standards 11). The topic can serve as a platform to address all five Cs of the world-readiness standards for learning languages: Connections (linking language study to other disciplines—science, ethics, politics, economy), Comparisons (contrasting different national perspectives on environmental issues), Cultures (exploring cultural and societal views on the value and practices of the use of natural resources and environmental protection), Communication (encompassing interpersonal, interpretive, and presentational modes on scientific, ethical, and emotionally charged topics), and Communities (participating directly in environmental campaigns, educational projects, NGO work, and other activities).

Sustainable development continues to be an issue of great importance for the modern world, one that requires a sustained and concerted effort of various social institutions, including education, whose goal is to prepare a new generation of global citizens to successfully take on the most pressing problems that the world is grappling with these days. Language education can—and should—play an instrumental role in teaching young people about environmental issues and in engaging them in sustainable practices (Jacobs and Cates 46–47).

Despite all the potential positive outcomes of building an advanced language course around the issue of sustainability, such a course is not easy to implement. Content-based and content-integrated courses present language educators with significant challenges: crossing departmental and administrative borders (Brinton et al. 71), reimagining and refashioning teacher preparation (Brinton et al. 74; Schleppegrell and O'Hallaron 7–9; Wiesemes 53–54), negotiating content and curricula (Dalton-Puffer 188–89), and preparing new pedagogical materials and resources (Brinton et al. 92–95; Schleppegrell and O'Hallaron 13–14). One of the most difficult issues to navigate in developing a new content-based or content-integrated course is the question of expertise. On the one hand, foreign-language teachers are generally not prepared to be teachers of content and are not afforded opportunities to develop such expertise. Jing Li, for example, found that teaching environmental topics in English for foreign language courses in China was largely ineffective due to teachers' lack of understanding of the topics and lack of a coherent framework to guide the integration of challenging content and language (145). Administrators and colleagues from other departments also often question foreign-language teachers' authority to address subject matter other than a national language, literature, and culture, and the teachers themselves often question their capacity to work in such unfamiliar terrain (Creese 611–12; Lyster 613–14; Schleppegrell and O'Hallaron 7; Li 141).

On the other hand, research shows that when content experts teach courses in the target language that focus exclusively on mastery of content, there is often inadequate focus on learners' language development, resulting in learners who fail to increase their command of the target language (Swain 201–02; Dalton-Puffer 192–93; Lyster 612–14). Deborah J. Short observes that even trained ESL teachers devote no more than a fifth of their class time to language instruction, with an overwhelming majority of comments (up to 95%) focusing on vocabulary comprehension (21). The majority of CBI researchers now agree that explicit instruction in vocabulary, grammar, mechanics, and discourse patterns are required for successful learning of both content and language. After all, a comprehensive knowledge of discipline-specific language—which includes both general and specialized vocabulary, as well as genre- and text-specific grammatical and discourse patterns—has been found to correlate positively with learning outcomes in science, technology, engineering, and mathematics and leads to fuller participation in academic and professional communities (Halliday 11–12; Thorne 7). In light of these observations, it is not surprising that "programs that combine foreign language instruction with another discipline (content-based instruction) are relatively rare, although there is evidence that such programs lead to increased interest in language learning, as well as prepare students, whatever their area of specialization, to work in a global society" (Ter Horst and Pearce 368).

The challenges of implementing CBI courses in foreign language departments may be even more pronounced with regard to environmental topics, when scientific and public discourses are intertwined in heated and often controversial debates. The subject matter may overwhelm a language specialist not schooled in science. Yet these obstacles can and should be overcome: successful integration of environmental education and language development has been observed in many studies (Cates 71; Jacobs and Cates 46–48; Li 149–50; Ter Horst and Pearce 371–79; Yakovchuk 39–40). In what follows, we describe a model that successfully combined the expertise of language educators with that of sustainability experts and was implemented by the Russian Flagship Program at PSU.

Curriculum Design and Lesson Planning
in an Integrated Content-Language Course

The RLF is first and foremost a language-teaching program that accepts strictly prescribed goals for students' acquisition of high-level language skills. The RLF faculty, however, strongly believes that attainment of higher-level language competency is contingent on the development of students' general cognitive abilities to engage in critical thinking (analysis, comparison, and synthesis of information) and emotional abilities (the ability to empathize, accept differing world views, and respect diversity of opinions). Moreover, Advanced and Superior language skills (*ACTFL Proficiency Guidelines*), such as describing and narrating at paragraph length or longer, expressing and supporting opinions, and arguing and hypothesizing on a range of professional and abstract topics, are clearly context- and discourse-dependent. In such language use, grammar (especially discourse patterns) is tightly integrated with both topic and genre and is understood as an indispensible tool in creating meaning in a particular social and linguacultural context (Halliday 85).

With these considerations in mind, we believe that the best approach to achieve the goals of the program is Jeannette Bragger and Donald Rice's approach to CBI; it uses content not to "merely teach language forms and vocabulary items, but rather [it] presents learners with issues that are interesting and valuable to learn about in their own right" (qtd. in Hadley 167). The currency, urgency, and overall importance of the environmental sustainability movement in the modern world provide us with a topic that addresses the goals of language education and the education of global citizens. To implement the focus on language per se in our CBI instruction, faculty members targeted the areas of corrective feedback, language analysis, and the implementation of tasks tied to grammar and discourse patterns (Brinton et al. 89; Dalton-Puffer 192–93).

To integrate the language and content foci on equal footing, we chose the adjunct model of language across the curriculum, with a parent course on the topic of environmental sustainability in English and a separate class in Russian. This allowed us to overcome administrative boundaries and the trap of content expert versus language expert. The model keeps the goals of both programs intact and promotes a balanced development of content knowledge and language skills. This model resembles the approach proposed by Roy Lyster, known as counterbalanced instruction. Lyster suggests that counterbalanced content and language instruction avoids the pitfalls observed in some immersion classrooms, where teachers moved into traditional approaches to teaching language when attention to language was called for (615). Counterbalanced instruction proposes form-focused tasks embedded in meaning-based activities. These notions drove the creation of the Readings in Russian: Environmental Sustainability syllabus.

To make the adjunct model work, before the beginning of each term when the topic of environmental sustainability was taught, the RLF faculty member received detailed curricula and comprehensive descriptions of activities and assignments from the professor of environmental science who teaches the University Studies course. The Flagship faculty group then met for curriculum development meetings to design a matching curriculum for the adjunct course: at this stage of curriculum development, we focused on the selection of Russian-language materials and the development of compatible tasks. The RLF instructor teaching the adjunct language course then met with the environmental science professor again to go over the program for the Russian course and to discuss together the compatibility of topics and tasks in both sections. In fact, the syllabus for the adjunct course explicitly paired information from the English language course with the materials for the Russian adjunct course, so that students could relate the topics and activities in one course to those in the other. For instance, when the English-language course covered "Conservation science and management, the role of NGOs, and managing water systems," the topics in the Russian course were "Lake Baikal: Ecology of the lake, ecological threats to the lake, and the role of NGOs" (see appendix).

Given the feedback provided in this meeting, the RLF faculty created a more detailed course plan, which was then shared with the University Studies professor for additional feedback. The RLF faculty also held weekly lesson-planning sessions, in which we chose authentic (i.e., not pedagogically adapted) materials for the course, evaluating their fit within the topic, relevance to current events in Russia and the United States, representativeness for their genre, and applicability to our pedagogical goals. For example, when choosing the topic for the week cited above, we were governed by several considerations: Lake Baikal is at the forefront of Russia's ecological and nature conservation discussions; at the time the course was being developed, debates about the lake raged in the Russian-language press and public discourse, ensuring a copious array of authentic materials representing multiple genres and modes to choose from. Greenpeace Russia's campaign to protect Baikal was covered both on the official Greenpeace Web site and in other media sources; UNESCO issued an open letter to the Russian president at the time with a plea to support the conservation efforts, and this document provides a stellar example of an argumentative essay in the genre of an open petition.

Additionally, the RLF instructor teaching the Russian section audited the parent course during the first year of collaboration, and, through additional meetings with the parent-course instructor and extensive reading on the course topics, the RLF instructor gained a better grasp of the subject matter and the parent class's proceedings and progression. Moreover, the RLF instructor's presence highlighted the collaborative nature of the project for all the students involved in the program. The University Studies instructor heavily supported inclusion of the Russian theme into the syllabus, which culminated in a modified final project that students in the Russian section prepared and presented in the English section for credit and to the benefit of the rest of the group.

The language skills targeted in this advanced-level course on environmental sustainability included description and narration, expression of opinion, and argumentation on professional and other abstract topics at the level of coherent discourse. These abilities need to be developed in all four areas of language use (speaking, listening, writing, and reading), with a particular focus on writing. The challenge, of course, is to integrate language-focused tasks within meaning-based activities that incorporate authentic materials and real-life knowledge.

A typical lesson consists of a warm-up; a main activity, often divided into two or more tasks targeting different skills; and a wrap-up (see appendix). A warm-up is usually based on topics, such as local events or national and international news, with relevance to the overall theme of the course; it is intended to allow students to practice known vocabulary, structures, and concepts. In the sample lesson plan, for instance, the topic of the warm-up is an Earth Day Fair taking place on the university's campus that day; it includes an informal exchange, comparing various stations the students saw at the fair, and allows students to speak within their comfort zone (advanced functions of description and comparison) while practicing (recycling) known vocabulary and structures (*ACTFL Proficiency Guidelines*). Additionally, the warm-up is deeply situated in the course's content: the topic allows students to think aloud in the second language about many practical applications of sustainable practices to their everyday lives; another practical connection to students' lives is that they also wrote a short report on the fair for the English-language parent course, providing an additional incentive to talk about the fair and compare notes.

The main activity always targets a Superior level of language functions (e.g., supported opinion, argumentation) and aims to extend the students' vocabulary, grammatical knowledge, or understanding of genre above their current level. The sample lesson presented in the appendix, for example, proceeds with a listening comprehension activity based on an authentic video clip; the material is accompanied with tasks that introduce and practice novel vocabulary, develop listening comprehension skills, and practice short definitions and descriptions reflecting a formal register. In the vocabulary activities connected with the video, the instructor prioritized those words that would be useful in describing upcoming topics, such as a water-based ecosystem and the management of water systems. Working on this vocabulary in longer discourse allows students to review those scientific concepts in the second language and add to their knowledge about the topic.

After this, the sample lesson plan moves into a general discussion, the most frequent activity format in our curriculum. Discussions are usually split into two phases: a timed prediscussion writing activity and an open oral exchange. The writing activity is a key prerequisite for in-class discussions. This activity is designed to aid in writing fluency (the in-class writing samples are always collected and commented on by the instructor); more important, writing helps students organize thoughts, formulate ideas, and link those ideas sequentially, thereby preparing them to express complex opinions and arguments in subsequent academic speaking (Byrnes et al. 54–55).

The organized oral discussion that grows out of the preparatory writing exercise has the potential to be conducted on a more sophisticated level than completely spontaneous speech; in the sample plan presented in the appendix, the topics for discussion push students to express supported opinions and argumentation in coherent paragraph-length discourse. The topic of the oral discussion for this particular class serves as a stepping-stone toward a subsequent goal, namely, reading a petition to protect the lake, which will in turn lead to an assignment where the students compose a similar written document. The homework assignment from the sample class asks students to find specific content issues as well as note rhetorical and linguistic features of the petition genre. In a subsequent class, the students' underlining of these rhetorical and linguistic features allows the group to analyze the phrasing of various types of arguments, which they can incorporate into drafts of their own letters. In the later lessons, the learners polish both the argumentation and the style of their letters to the Russian president. That year students were encouraged to submit their final letter through a petition page on the Greenpeace Web site. The opportunity to produce work for purposes other than class activities motivated many students to engage with the topic with real passion, and they willingly engaged in the community-action aspect of the project.

The topics of the environment and sustainability quite naturally lead to multiple opportunities for classes to engage in community action and other kinds of volunteer and experiential learning. In the RLF, students evaluated such opportunities to connect their classroom environmental learning to life outside the classroom as "useful," "interesting," or "memorable." For example, some heritage students were particularly engaged with the petition described above, perhaps because they felt a stronger sense of social responsibility toward this situation in Russia. One such student mentioned that she shared her letter with her family and encouraged her family and her Russian-speaking friends to get on board. During another academic year, the class had an opportunity to host representatives of environmental protection agencies (both public and NGOs) from Russia. The group's visit was organized through the Open World Program, which chose Portland as one of the flagship green cities in the United States. The Russian section organized the group's tour of the PSU campus, during which the Flagship students were able to show and explain different aspects of the university's sustainability efforts to the Russian guests (drawing on class assignments that included a great deal of work on language). The students' ability to interact on these environmental topics in Russian with a group of interested guests produced a very strong impression on the nonheritage RLF students, who eagerly participated in the event and appraised it highly in their final reflections. Most important, all students appreciated the experiential aspect of learning, which we believe to be a crucial part of our curriculum. Experiential learning coupled with strong language instruction has been noted to result in a dramatic increase in target language skill (see, for example, Askildson et al. 424–25). At the same time, these outreach activities fit more appropriately with the main focus of environmental education, which, in recent years, has shifted from teaching the subject matter to engaging in environmental action.

Anecdotally, comments from students indicated that they all expressed satisfaction with their linguistic progress. Most stressed improvement in vocabulary skills (likely because they can easily perceive this quantitative change); some mentioned a newly acquired ability to think about critical issues and formulate complex thoughts and ideas in Russian. Many students suggested that they learned more about the environment in the Russian section than in the English-language one. Although this is unlikely to be true, it is possible that the additional cognitive effort of processing complex material in a foreign language creates a sense of more learning.

The Sustainability of Sustainability

One of the main advantages of this model for integrating environmental sustainability into foreign language study is its flexibility. Since the Russian language course curriculum stands on its own, it can be adjusted to the needs of the program and the needs of particular cohorts of students. As originally developed, the tandem course model works well for heritage speakers of Russian and for graduates of secondary school immersion programs entering the RLF program on the advanced track as first-year students. They can be advised to take a sophomore inquiry course in English when they are linguistically ready to complete the adjunct course in Russian. Students who start Russian in their first year of university, however, generally take the environmental studies course a year before they are linguistically ready to tackle the adjunct Russian course. As the percentages of heritage speakers and native-English speakers shift in the Flagship program, we are able to adjust the connection between the two courses and make the Russian adjunct less contingent on the everyday class procedures of the principal course.

The RLF curriculum, which capitalizes on hot topics in the Russian-language press in methodologically principled ways, has continued to evolve course content as circumstances change. At the time of the initial course development, Lake Baikal was much in the news, and controversies surrounding it could serve as a focus for that academic year. With fresh topics constantly entering the public sphere, new opportunities for active civic engagement emerge, and new course themes and materials can be introduced for students' consideration.

Changes in the structure of the Flagship program also have an influence on the development of the course: in fall 2014 the Russian Overseas Flagship program was moved from Saint Petersburg, Russia, to Almaty, Kazakhstan, where different political, cultural, and economic perspectives and practices shape the Russian-language discourse about the environment. This change has required the RLF faculty to rethink the content topics to be addressed in the environment and sustainability course. Although water is a concern in semiarid Kazakhstan, the booming oil and natural gas industries in the country raise major issues about sustainable development, global warming, fracking, and related industrialization. And with our new focus, we will continue to look for new opportunities to partner with other academic units inside the university, such as energy experts.

Any project that requires implementation of an innovative curriculum that crosses established conceptual and institutional boundaries requires the active effort of many individuals in addition to access to financial resources and crucial institutional support. It has been noted that successful CBI, both in foreign language and ESL contexts, is contingent upon continuous and mutually respectful collaboration between language and content experts (Lyster 613). Our case suggests that such collaboration is not only possible but also fruitful for all parties concerned. We are convinced that administrative support for content-integrated language courses will continue to grow. On the one hand, leading academic, social, and political organizations outside the field of language study strongly advocate interdisciplinary approaches to learning in general, stressing both the importance of connecting content to language and the importance of language to acquisition of professional skills (Ter Horst and Pearce 366). On the other hand, approaches to content and language integration, such as those presented in this volume, begin to provide convincing evidence of successful results in language learning and in acquiring general academic skills.

In an educational climate that supports the goals of both general education and language study, the topic of environmental sustainability should be considered a prime candidate for interdisciplinary teaching and learning. It allows students "to reinforce and further their knowledge of other disciplines through the foreign language" (standard 3.1), to "acquire information and recognize the distinctive viewpoints that are only available through the foreign language and its cultures" (standard 3.2), to "demonstrate understanding of the concept of culture through comparisons of the cultures studied and their own" (standard 4.2), and to "use the language both within and beyond the school setting" (standard 5.1), just to name some of the national standards for foreign language education (National Standards). In sum, studying the topic prepares the future generation for tackling one of the main challenges confronting the modern world: that of a sustainable future.

NOTES

We wish to express our gratitude to Dr. Sandra Freels, the first director of the Russian program at PSU, whose ideas and hard work laid the foundation for the Russian across Curriculum approach described in the essay.
1. Current literature identifies a number of different approaches to interdisciplinary language learning, including content-based instruction or content-based language teaching, content and language integrated learning, integrated content and foreign language, etc. The discussion of nuances of these various approaches is beyond the scope of this paper.

APPENDIX: SAMPLE LESSON PLAN

The following is a lesson plan for the first of two class sessions focused on Lake Baikal: this session covers the ecology of the lake, ecological threats to the lake, and the role of NGOs. The lesson takes place in the target language.

Lesson plan	Targeted skills
Warm-up: Earth Day topic. Teacher asks students what they know about Earth Day and what campus activities are happening in observance of Earth Day.	Speaking Description and narration; opinion Connecting class topic to real-life experiences Connecting Russian class topic to sustainability class assignment
Main activity. Students view and discuss video clip about Lake Baikal from the Web site of Greenpeace Russia.	
Task 1: Vocabulary. Students receive a list of challenging vocabulary from the clip, including metaphors (e.g., *the laboratory of biodiversity*), terms (e.g., *mammals*), abbreviations, etc. Students are encouraged to work in small groups and provide definitions for the vocabulary items.	General academic and field-specific vocabulary Definition Scientific concepts
Task 2: Video clip. FIRST VIEWING. Students answer factual questions (e.g., What percentage of the world's water resources does the lake contain?) SECOND VIEWING. Students answer questions ranging from factual to inferential (e.g., Who are the most vocal protectors of the lake?). Students are encouraged to use register-appropriate vocabulary and structures.	Listening Description and narration; paraphrasing Listening and speaking Description and narration; paraphrasing
Task 3: Five-minute in-class writing. Students must "think in writing" about one or two of the discussion questions: Is it important to protect the ecological health of the lake? Why? Who is responsible for protection of the lake? Do you know of any campaigns that aim to protect the lake? If not, can you think of ways to protect the lake?	Writing with focus on fluency at the level of cohesive paragraph Supported opinion, argumentation
Task 4: Discussion. Students are asked the discussion questions and prompted to extend their discourse to the level of coherent paragraph.	Speaking at the level of cohesive paragraph Supported opinion, argumentation
Wrap-up. Teacher pulls together the threads of students' comments from the discussion, makes final comments, and announces the homework assignment.	Listening
Homework. Students print out and read the official petition to the director general of UNESCO requesting protection of Lake Baikal. Students are asked to underline structures that are particular to the genre of petition; underline all metaphors and epithets that describe the lake or the ecological situation; underline all arguments against the reopening of the paper mill, the main polluter of the lake; and, if they choose to do so, sign the petition online.	Reading with focus on language (linguistic structures highlighted in this assignment are genre conventions, figurative language in formal discourse) Argumentation

WORKS CITED

ACTFL Proficiency Guidelines 2012. American Council on the Teaching of Foreign Languages (ACTFL), 2012, www.actfl.org/sites/default/files/pdfs/public/ACTFL ProficiencyGuidelines2012_FINAL.pdf. Accessed 22 June 2018.

Askildson, Lance R., et al. "Developing Multiple Literacies in Academic English through Service-Learning and Community Engagement." *TESOL Journal*, vol. 4, no. 3, 2013, pp. 402–38.

Brinton, Donna, et al. *Content-Based Second Language Instruction*. U of Michigan P, 2003.

Byrnes, Heidi, et al. *Realizing Advanced Foreign Language Writing Development in Collegiate Education: Curricular Design, Pedagogy, Assessment*. Special issue of *The Modern Language Journal*, vol. 94, no. s1, 2010.

Cates, Kip. "Teaching for a Better World: Global Issues in Language Education in Japan." *Citizenship and Language Learning: International Perspectives*, edited by Audrey Osler and Hugh Starkey, Trentham, 2005, pp. 59–73.

Chapman, Paul. "Environmental Education and Sustainability in U.S. Public Schools." *Project Green Schools*, Inverness, 2014, projectgreenschools.org/wp/wp -content/uploads/2014/08/USGreenSchools12114.pdf. Accessed 10 June 2015.

"Colleges and Universities Lead the Way in Sustainability." *Homeroom, The Official Blog of the U.S. Department of Education*, United States, Department of Education, 2013, blog.ed.gov/2013/01/colleges-and-universities-lead-the-way-in-sustainabil ity. Accessed 10 June 2015.

Creese, Angela. "The Discursive Construction of Power in Teacher Partnerships: Language and Subject Specialists in Mainstream Schools." *TESOL Quarterly*, vol. 36, no. 4, 2002, pp. 597–616.

Dalton-Puffer, Christiane. "Content-and-Language Integrated Learning: From Practice to Principles?" *Annual Review of Applied Linguistics*, vol. 31, 2011, pp. 182–204.

Freels, Sandra, et al. "Adding Breadth to the Undergraduate Curriculum: Flagship Approaches to Interdisciplinary Language Learning." *Exploring the US Language Flagship Program: Professional Competence in a Second Language by Graduation*, edited by Karen Evans-Romaine and Diana Murphy, Multilingual Matters, 2016, pp. 51–69.

Hadley, Alice Omaggio. *Teaching Language in Context*. Heinle and Heinle, 2001.

Halliday, M. A. K. *Language and Education*. Edited by Jonathan J. Webster, Continuum, 2007. Vol. 9 in *The Collected Works of M. A. K. Halliday*.

Jacobs, George M., and Kip Cates. "Global Education in Second Language Teaching." *K@ta*, vol. 1, no. 1, 2004, pp. 44–56.

Leaver, Betty Lou. "Content-Based Instruction in a Basic Russian Program." *Content-Based Instruction in Foreign Language Education: Models and Methods*, edited by Stephen Stryker and Leaver, Georgetown UP, 1997, pp. 30–54.

Li, Jing. "Environmental Education in China's College English Context: A Pilot Study." *International Research in Geographical and Environmental Education*, vol. 22, no. 2, 2013, pp. 139–54.

Lyster, Roy. "Content-Based Second Language Teaching." *Handbook of Research in Second Language Teaching and Learning*, edited by Eli Hinkel, vol. 2, Routledge, 2011, pp. 611–30.

Marsh, David. Foreword. Ruiz de Zarobe and Jiménez Catalán, pp. vii–viii.

Met, Myriam. "Curriculum Decision-Making in Content-Based Language Teaching." *Beyond Bilingualism: Multilingualism and Multilingual Education*, edited by Jasone Cenoz and Fred Genesee, Multilingual Matters, 1998, pp. 35–63.

National Standards Collaborative Board. *World-Readiness Standards for Learning Languages*. American Council on the Teaching of Foreign Languages (ACTFL), 4th ed., 2015.

Ruiz de Zarobe, Yolanda, and Rosa María Jiménez Catalán, editors. *Content and Language Integrated Learning: Evidence from Research in Europe.* Multilingual Matters, 2009.

Schleppegrell, Mary J., and Catherine L. O'Hallaron. "Teaching Academic Language in L2 Secondary Settings." *Annual Review of Applied Linguistics,* vol. 31, 2011, pp. 3–18.

Short, Deborah J. "Language Learning in Sheltered Social Studies Classes." *TESOL Journal,* vol. 11, no. 1, 2002, pp. 18–24.

Swain, Merrill. "French Immersion Research in Canada: Recent Contributions to SLA and Applied Linguistics." *Annual Review of Applied Linguistics,* vol. 20, 2000, pp. 199–212.

Ter Horst, Eleanor E., and Joshua M. Pearce. "Foreign Languages and Sustainability: Addressing the Connections, Communities, and Comparisons Standards in Higher Education." *Foreign Language Annals,* vol. 43, no. 3, 2010, pp. 365–83.

Thorne, Steven L. "Language Learning, Ecological Validity, and Innovation under Conditions of Superdiversity." *Bellaterra Journal of Teaching and Learning Language and Literature,* vol. 6, no. 2, 2013, pp. 1–27.

Wiesemes, Rolf. "Developing Theories of Practices in CLIL: CLIL as Post-method Pedagogies." Ruiz de Zarobe and Jiménez Catalán, pp. 41–62.

Yakovchuk, Nadezhda. "Global Issues and Global Values in Foreign Language Education: Selection and Awareness-Raising." *English Language Teacher Education and Development,* vol. 8, 2004, pp. 28–47.

Imbibing Russian Language and Culture in Siberia: Wellesley College's Lake Baikal Course

Thomas P. Hodge

Since 2001 the course Lake Baikal: The Soul of Siberia has been offered biennially at Wellesley College, cotaught by faculty members from the Departments of Biological Sciences and of Russian. Baikal, the world's most voluminous and biotically diverse lake—declared a UNESCO World Heritage Site in 1996—was the focus of efforts in the 1960s that started the modern Russian environmental movement. This essay describes the educational experience, with an emphasis on the benefits of combining formal and informal language learning. Following an intensive predeparture seminar devoted equally to Siberian culture and the science of the lake (limnology), the program sends a group of twelve undergraduates to the biological field station in a small village on the shores of Lake Baikal for a month of scientific and cultural fieldwork under the aegis of Irkutsk State University's Department of Biology. While there, participants study the environment in situ before collaborating on a scientific project. At the remote field station, language learning takes place organically and incidentally as students work on culture journals, interact with Russian students housed at the facility, converse with guest speakers, interview local residents, and pursue research.

A key outcome is that students with widely varying initial competence readily increase proficiency when given opportunities to employ Russian while engaged in immersive study of this ecologically critical site, gaining confidence that encourages many to continue language study later. Courses of this kind help language programs argue their centrality to the overarching goal of producing educated undergraduates who become global citizens. Although such offerings may not boost language proficiency to the degree achieved by long-term study abroad, they actively engage all three dimensions of "intercultural effectiveness through study abroad" identified by Jeffrey R. Watson et al. (64): knowledge of language, culture, and region. Courses focused on environmental treasures provide the benefits of informal interaction (incidental learning) as opposed to what has traditionally been counted as academic experience (formal or structured learning). Incidental learning (Allen and Dupuy 481–82), though hard to track, does indeed yield long-term benefits that have a clear influence on students, as the later successes of our Baikal alumnae suggest. Although many researchers have concluded that extended, intensive study is best (e.g., Davidson 17–23), such programs are not practical for all students, and other types of study abroad experiences offer excellent opportunities to promote cultural competence.

The legendary twentieth-century Russian philologist Dmitrii Sergeevich Likhachev has summarized the Russian field known as *kraevedenie*, which is a foundational element of the Wellesley Baikal course:

> [G]eography, unlike *kraevedenie*, does not accord such great significance to noteworthy individual people, the history of science, literary history, or art history . . . *kraevedenie* lacks "two levels," one for scholarly specialists and another for "the general public" and is instead popular in and of itself. It exists as a field to the extent that the broad masses participate in its creation and reception (its use). . . . It teaches people not only to love their regions, but also to love knowledge about their (and not only "their") regions . . . it demands knowledge in the fields of history, art history, literary analysis, natural history, and so on. . . . The participation of all age groups in the activity of *kraevedenie* itself has the most enormous educational significance. . . . *Kraevedenie* introduces into the human sphere a high degree of spirituality without which a person cannot exist in a state of awareness.   (3–4)

The intellectual and language-learning benefits of Wellesley's Baikal course derive in large part from its systematic incorporation of eclectic *kraevedenie*, a term translated in many ways, including "regional studies" and "local lore." By combining the comprehensive gains described by Watson et al. with the irresistible appeal of the *kraevedenie* approach, courses that focus on environmentally precious sites offer tremendous potential for language learning.

History and Structure of the Course

Because the natural and serendipitous way this course evolved can serve as a model for similar efforts, some background is in order. Our Baikal course had its genesis at an informal lunch meeting with fellow professor Marianne Moore in the spring of 1993, soon after I arrived at Wellesley College. By July 2000, we had made an initial one-week site visit to determine the feasibility of mounting a course and found that conditions, though rugged, were otherwise ideal. We offered the course for the first time in the spring-summer of 2001 and have repeated it every two years, for a total of nine offerings through 2019. Over ninety students have taken the course, with six different faculty members participating from the Wellesley side over the years (see Bartlett; "Lake"). Two limnological articles coauthored during the course by its students have been published in Russia. To date, alumnae of the course have gone on to earn eight Fulbright scholarships, a Watson Fellowship, a Gates Scholarship, a Greater Research Opportunities fellowship from the Environmental Protection Agency of the United States, and numerous in-house accolades; many are in (or have completed) top-tier graduate degree programs in Russian language and literature or scientific fields related to their experience at Baikal.

From the outset, and as it evolved over the years, the Baikal course was envisioned as offering students an equal combination of science and culture, including language. Because Baikal has long occupied a special place in the Russian national consciousness, we set a goal of using the lake as a point of interdisciplinary convergence for biological research and the study of Russian language, literature, music, history, and religion. Once we had completed our initial reconnaissance visit, we also understood that, though the journey would at times be arduous, the natural and cultural treasures offered by the lake would consistently attract students.

Russians know and revere Baikal in much the same way that Americans prize Yellowstone, Yosemite, or the Grand Canyon. There is a nationally known song about the lake ("Glorious sea, sacred Baikal") that serves as a Baikal anthem, and some of the most revered Decembrists—highly educated, progressive rebels against autocracy—lived out their exile in the mid-1800s near the lake. Baikal's outsize role in Russian cultural life and science directly informed the structure of the course, which has always been team-taught by one faculty member from the Russian Department and one from the Biological Sciences Department. The multifarious richness of Baikal necessitates careful preparation before students and faculty visit the site. For this reason, the course is divided into two phases: preparatory (on the Wellesley campus in spring) and on-site (at the lake in August). The preparatory phase is organized around a weekly two-hour seminar-style course meeting for the entirety of the spring semester immediately preceding the summer in which the on-site phase will take place. The on campus seminar is itself subdivided into two parts: Siberian culture and lake science.

Prerequisites directly reflect the hybrid essence of the course. All students must have taken at least one semester of Russian language and one semester of organismal biology with laboratory. These requirements impel the course's undergraduate Russianists to stretch to take science and science majors to stretch to take Russian. The result is a salutary blend of students pushing the boundaries of their usual intellectual pursuits. Although language teachers would welcome a language requirement beyond the minimum, it is likely that demanding more than one semester of Russian would perilously reduce the number of applicants. Though it is challenging at times to instruct students with extraordinarily divergent language backgrounds, this configuration is one of the Baikal course's defining features, as it creates a heterogeneous group united by devotion to a single natural wonder.

From the start, admission to the course has required instructor permission. Aspiring participants must complete a written application that elicits information about outdoor skills, health issues, environmental interests, experience with Russian language and culture, and scientific proclivities. This documentation process is followed by a forty-five-minute personal interview with both instructors, who also carefully check applicants' references. The goal is to arrive at a roster of academically talented and personally compatible students that is well balanced between scientists and Russianists.

In our experience, it is beneficial to have students from a wide range of social strata and ages, from first-years to seniors, and coming from urban and rural homes, advantaged and disadvantaged economic backgrounds, international families as well as those from the United States, and so on.[1] The registrar has helpfully adopted a policy of allowing seniors to take the course, even though they graduate before the August fieldwork phase; course grades are simply suspended until they complete the fieldwork in Siberia.

Predeparture Seminar Work

The science and culture portions of the preparatory phase of course work on campus could be undertaken in any order, but New England weather requires that we start with culture (January to mid-March) and finish with science (mid-March to May), since limnological training requires hours of wading and specimen gathering in our local lake (Lake Waban). This instruction offers a serious foundation in Siberian culture, which is crucial if students are to comprehend the people, places, and policies they encounter once they reach Baikal six months later. In keeping with the concept of *kraevedenie*, cultural materials span anthropology, religion, history, music, and film, as well as Russian literature. Although the instructional approach follows a relatively traditional model, due to its format as a single meeting each week, demands on students are intensive. Each week they are expected to read approximately two hundred pages of primary and secondary sources in English and post a response paragraph on the reading electronically by the morning of class, followed by two hours of lecture and discussion in the classroom (see appendix 1). Thanks to their excitement about Baikal, students do this work with a high degree of independence. The first class hour is devoted to one topic; after a short break, a second topic concludes the day's meeting. For instruction, I illustrate the material with abundant realia (slideshows, videos, and sound recordings), many of which are already available to students through the hyperlinked syllabus. In-class discussion is lively, as students become energized to make queries and venture hypotheses about the cultural information in their readings. Students quickly develop genuine concern for the ecological stewardship of a precious resource, which motivates frank, passionate exchanges in class.

When the course began, no suitable textbook existed, so readings had to be gathered from disparate sources. This changed dramatically in late 2003, when Peter Thomson contacted the instructors regarding a project he was just starting. Thomson, the founding editor and producer of National Public Radio's *Living on Earth*, planned a book based on his personal experiences at Baikal. He hoped we could provide him with background material. We gladly obliged, and Thomson independently read the same sources we had developed for our students. As he worked on the book, Moore and I lined up Wellesley Baikal alumnae to work as Thomson's research assistants, and we commented on his manuscript drafts. The resulting publication, *Sacred Sea: A Journey to Lake Baikal*, published in 2007, is a much-praised account that engagingly conveys the scientific, cultural, and environmental importance of the lake. Since that time, we have used *Sacred Sea* as the basic textbook for the course, because it knits together precisely the sources we had always deemed necessary in the first place. Because we were open to collaborating in public intellectual work, a textbook ideally tailored to our course was created, and faculty, students, and author all benefited from it enormously.

With Thomson's book as the backbone, the course can begin with the prehistory of the Baikal region, including the shamanistic religion that dominated the area up to half a millennium ago, before moving on to Russia's conquest of North Asia from the sixteenth through the nineteenth centuries (Naumov; Reid). Students then scrutinize the arrival in the Baikal region of Buryat Mongols in the early medieval period and use the archpriest Avvakum's rich autobiography (generally held to be the first example of that genre in Russian) to explore Siberia's role as both a refuge and place of punishment for Russian religious sectarians (Old Believers) starting in the late seventeenth century (Forsyth; Avvakum; Ware; Robson). As the Russian Empire expanded, it used Siberia as a zone of imprisonment for criminals and of exile for dissidents and rebels. In the early nineteenth century, Irkutsk, the most important Russian city near Lake Baikal, received the celebrated Decembrist exiles (Rasputin, *Siberia, Siberia*; O'Meara). Fedor Dostoevsky and Aleksandr Solzhenitsyn were incarcerated in Siberia's vast expanse, and students read their fictionalized autobiographical accounts in, respectively, *Notes from the House of the Dead* and *One Day in the Life of Ivan Denisovich*. The environmental and cultural violence caused in Siberia during the late twentieth century by the Soviet regime is deftly encapsulated in Valentin Rasputin's novel *Farewell to Matyora*, the pinnacle of the Russian Village Prose movement; this work concludes the cultural half of the spring term.

These basic readings are constantly illuminated by further explorations in Galya Diment and Yuri Slezkine's excellent English-language anthology. To make the material come alive, public lectures by outside experts are timed to complement the Baikal syllabus as well.[2] As technology has improved, we have added sessions with Siberian stakeholders via videoconference, as when the Buryat lawyer and scholar Vladimir Munkhanov engaged the 2013 and 2016 classes in discussion from his home in Irkutsk. In addition to weekly response paragraphs, participation in class discussions, and guest lectures, students are also required to submit a two-thousand-word essay in English by the end of the seminar's culture segment. This essay on a theme of the student's own choosing may connect to any of the cultural topics we have covered. Native speakers and students with advanced Russian skills are encouraged to quote from sources in the original language whenever possible.

The subsequent scientific half of the on campus course employs an authoritative biology textbook (Bronmark and Hansson) but, like the cultural half, features a wealth of articles and materials from a wide variety of sources. From the outset, students learn that the peerless biodiversity and grandeur of Baikal persist under myriad anthropogenic threats, including industrial pollution, unbridled development, overfishing, forest fires, erosion, oil pipelines, and damming. The first session (led by Moore) begins with a discussion about the role of science in Russian life and the history of the Soviet environmental movement, which began with grassroots efforts to protect Lake Baikal when the Baikal'sk Pulp and Paper Plant was constructed on the lakeshore in the mid-1960s. Students go on to tackle Baikal's aquatic communities, food webs, biodiversity, and environmental threats and receive hands-on training in sampling, specimen gathering, and measurement techniques.

Fieldwork at Baikal

With their newfound cultural, biological, and environmental expertise, students are keen to move on to the phase they relish most: a nearly month-long visit to Lake Baikal itself. The opportunity to live and work in intimate contact with one of earth's environmental treasures is without doubt the main attraction for students, and they are not disappointed. Baikal works its magic on all of them, and the experience they have at the lake is one they never forget. Their direct exposure to this precious resource, however, depends on a large number of logistical steps.

Travel to Russia is not simple, and typical study abroad complications are compounded by the fact that Baikal is located on the other side of the globe, deep in the Siberian hinterland, just north of Mongolia, and about twelve hundred miles from the Pacific Ocean. As we travel through chaotic airports in Europe, Moscow, and Irkutsk on what for most in the group is the longest journey they will ever undertake, students remain at least in pairs at all times. Unexpected delays are frequent, and language knowledge is crucial as we endeavor to make our travel connections. Careful planning, far in advance, is essential. Over the years we have compiled a handbook containing detailed information on itinerary, phone numbers, climate, clothing, equipment, medical supplies, social customs, and basic language etiquette.

The Wellesley team arrives in Irkutsk early in the morning of the third travel day. The following morning, the group boards a speedy public hydrofoil and, after a two-hour water journey, is dropped off at Bol'shie Koty, located in the boreal forest of Pribaikal'skii National Park. The lakeside village has a year-round population of under fifty but swells to about two hundred in the summer months, thanks to its popularity among hikers and campers. Facing the dock are the grounds of the biostation belonging to Irkutsk State University (ISU), which includes laboratory spaces, bunkhouses, a dining hall, and the tiny ISU Baikal Museum. We are met at Bol'shie Koty by ISU biologists, the facility director, and the three or four ISU undergraduate biology majors who live in the bunkhouse with the Wellesley group.

After a brief tour of the facility the next day, the group falls into its fieldwork schedule, which consists of working on scientific field problems in the mornings and early afternoons and hosting a series of local stakeholders in the late afternoons and evenings (see appendix 2). Those activities, which unfold over three weeks, are interspersed with a series of field trips. While living and working at the biostation, Wellesley students have two main academic tasks: to formulate and test a limnological hypothesis, and to keep a scientific and cultural journal. Performance on these two tasks, combined with their marks from the on campus phase, determine overall course grades.

For the limnological field problem, students are divided into three small groups, and each cohort sketches out a problem worthy of investigation. Groups come back together and, in consultation with the biology instructor, decide which problem is most likely to produce valuable, publishable results. Field problems have included the effect of lakeshore docks on biodiversity in the littoral zone, the relation of pelagic and littoral food webs, and the nocturnal vertical migration of endemic fish species. In all cases, students must disperse along the shore and into the village in order to carry out an extensive sampling regime that will yield enough data to make the study meaningful. The scope of this project necessitates frequent interaction with Russian-language speakers at the biostation, in the village, and along the shoreline, where tourists frequently congregate.

Journal writing likewise leads to intimate communication in Russian with local speakers. Students keep daily notes on biological observations as well as on cultural topics. Guidelines for the cultural notebook are designed to boost language skills (see appendix 3), since they encourage students to probe issues that are best explored by informally interviewing Russians. Students also work in pairs to create and upload a daily blog in English, with occasional Russian interpolations, that contains photographs and a summary of the day's activities.

Fieldwork ends with a four-day, five-hundred-mile round-trip excursion by boat to experience some of the lake's most famous features: Sandy Cove, Ol'khon Island, Shaman Rock, the geothermal springs at Snake Cove, and the famous Baikal seal colonies at the Ushkan'i Islands. The excursion serves as a reward for the hard scientific work the students have just completed; it also affords them ample opportunity to have informal interactions with our Russian hosts, to reflect on what they have experienced, and to record those thoughts in their journals.

Language Learning: Campus, Transit, Baikal

The Baikal course is taught in English and not designed specifically to function as a language course, yet it affords a multitude of opportunities for participants to learn Russian. Such opportunities first arise gradually during the on campus phase. Once students begin fieldwork in Siberia, however, they naturally imbibe and employ the Russian language in order to achieve their goal of studying and understanding one of the world's most fascinating environmental resources.

Because many of the students with science backgrounds have not previously taken Russian, they tend to enroll in the section of Russian 101 taught intensively during a three-week January term immediately preceding the start of the Baikal course. This timing means that many of the Baikal students have completed a challenging course of intensive Russian just days before they begin the cultural portion of the on campus seminar, and their enthusiasm is infectious: they ask many questions about the language that kindle the interest of their Russianist classmates, and remarkably lively discussions of Russian ensue. Although most of these exchanges take place in English—a tolerable practice among learners of what the Foreign Service Institute defines as a category 4 language, which has significant linguistic and cultural differences from English ("Language Assignments")—others take place in the target language and involve entire conversations that showcase features about which the students are curious. In terms of Milton J. Bennett's model of intercultural competence (7), learners have already moved beyond rejection and minimization of intercultural difference and into a stage of being open to new experiences, which leads to adaptation. As their teacher, I attempt to build on this whenever possible. For example, a question about the Russian word for "Siberia" (*Sibir'*) provokes further queries about the Russian nouns for "Siberian" (*sibiriak, sibiriachka*), the adjectival form (*sibirskii*), and the disputed etymology for the root of all these terms. From there, students often ask about regional Siberian accents, at which point they can role-play with simple, everyday phrases they have learned in Russian class, but pronounced with the staccato rhythm and lack of intervocalic *j* that frequently characterize the mode of speech they will hear at Baikal. Such moments generate laughter and genuine fascination; before they know it, students have spent ten minutes speaking Russian and deepening both their intellectual grasp of the language and their practical ability to employ it.

The on campus classroom experience emphasizes the inquiry and discovery that are possible when a diverse student group has access to basic linguistic tools. Because all twelve students have studied some Russian, everyone knows the alphabet, and we can dispense with transliteration. Our discussions encourage all students to comment actively on aspects of the Russian language they find noteworthy in the readings. I am able to comment in much more detail on the linguistic intricacies of the literature we read together than in other courses in translation. I frequently read aloud short passages from Dostoevsky, Solzhenitsyn, and Rasputin in the original language. Relying on activated receptive abilities, students clearly grasp the details of dialect and lexicon with little explanation from me. In class, we enjoy a spirited exchange of linguistic information between the Russianists and the scientists, which the former are happy to oblige. Those roles are reversed in the second half of the semester, when the scientists share their expertise with the humanities-oriented Russianists. This symbiosis is precisely what we want to create as educators: situations in which linguistic negotiation and exchange of ideas are necessary. From the second language acquisition perspective, such exchanges act as vibrant examples of Lev Semenovich Vygotskii's famous "zona blizhaishego razvitiia" ("zone of proximal development") theory (42).

With regard to interdisciplinary symbiosis, it cannot be overemphasized that the Baikal course serves as a magnet for science- and environment-oriented undergraduates who might otherwise never have considered studying the Russian language. Some of the most talented and ardent Russian majors found themselves in our courses solely because Baikal tempted them there. Once they sampled the language and literature, they stayed for more.

For most Westerners, air travel to and within Russia is a daunting experience: airports are overcrowded, signage is unreliable or absent, check-in and passport procedures can be opaque, public-address announcements are muffled and lightning-fast, staffers can be brusque, personal space is nonexistent, and queues are amorphous. Students, therefore, tend to be in a state of hypervigilance, alert to all linguistic cues that can help smooth their passage. Lengthy layovers become an opportunity for impromptu seminars on crucial travel language: lexicon (words for *exit, entrance, gate, baggage claim, ATM, flight, delay, bathroom, electrical socket*), conversation (how to ask directions, what to do when lost), etiquette (polite methods for getting attention, what to say after bumping into someone, how to ask to squeeze by people in a crowd), and so on. On board the aircraft, similar opportunities arise: what do the signs in the lavatory mean? How do you ask the flight attendant for a glass of juice? What do the terms on the safety card mean?

Such situations continue on the small bus that takes the group from the airport to the dormitory and finally to the dock where students catch the hydrofoil. Russian verbs of motion (e.g., "to go") are complex, and classified by type of motion: pedestrian, ground-vehicular, aquatic, aerial. In addition to the expected vocabulary questions (Why do Russians call hydrofoils "boats on underwater wings"? Why do the workers on boats use ground-vehicular verbs of motion?), students spontaneously ask about and practice their *going* verbs, because they have immediate practical reasons to do so.

Once they reach the biostation, students' receptivity to and motivation for language learning are multiplied by a number of factors: they have finally arrived at a scenic destination; they are surrounded by Russian-speaking students and staff; they have important scientific work to do in and around the laboratories, in the village, and on our research vessels; and they want to understand all they can about the lore of the world's largest lake. The two student-translators from ISU are present to help, but they are not professionals, and neither they nor the group's leaders can be everywhere at once. Students, therefore, do the vast majority of the language teaching and learning on their own, spontaneously, either by asking newfound Russian friends or by reaching out to more advanced learners, who thus become part of the instructional team.

This experience is immersive learning at its best, driven by wonder at spectacular natural beauty and a genuine desire to make authentic scientific progress in the effort to preserve that beauty. Some of the most important ways in which students make linguistic progress at Baikal result from situations that never occur in a classroom: singing around evening campfires on the beach, steaming together in the rustic Russian bathhouse, learning Russian card games, drawing deepwater samples by moonlight at three o'clock in the morning, sketching endemic medicinal plants, and asking Russian undergraduates to help select the best photos for the blog.

To cite one illustrative example, in 2013, when the students were hard at work taking samples and making measurements to define the deleterious effects of dock building on shoreline organisms, a pair had the job of interviewing villagers about the frequency with which the half-dozen docks dotting the shoreline were used by watercraft. One student returned from such a foray, beaming:

> I just had the most amazing experience. I walked up to a Russian I'd never met before, said hello, and asked him how many boats pulled up each day at the dock by his house. He told me two or three. I thanked him, said good bye, and he wished us well. When I took Russian 101, I never, ever dreamed I would be able to talk to a real Russian, ask a real question about a real problem, and have a conversation in which the Russian didn't think I was crazy or stupid.

This student, who had until that time only experienced Russian in a classroom in Massachusetts, was now intellectually on fire. After Baikal, she enrolled in the fall Russian literature course and excelled; she was accepted into Wellesley's Albright Institute that winter; she studied in Saint Petersburg, Russia, for a semester that spring; she interned at a nonprofit organization in the Republic of Georgia over the summer. In her senior year she graduated with a double major in Russian and political science and won a coveted fellowship at the Carnegie Endowment for World Peace in Washington, DC, as a research assistant to one of the Russia fellows there, and she is now working for the Peace Corps in Ukraine. Baikal was of course not the sole reason for her success, but it dramatically influenced the direction of her academic interests. Her impressive trajectory is not an isolated example among Baikal alumnae.

Exporting the Baikal Course Model

The learning that takes place in Wellesley's Baikal course suggests the approach could work well in other language contexts and involve many scientific disciplines besides biology. The key is to offer direct, serious scientific access to an irresistibly attractive and rugged natural treasure. Twenty-first-century students crave world travel and have an authentic thirst to engage in environmentally focused experiential learning, especially when they can have meaningful contact with local stakeholders. Though the site is legendary, the travel is not simply touristic. It is an intellectually rigorous, physical adventure dedicated to conducting actual scientific research that has long-term benefits for the Baikal region. An experience that inspires students to make career choices that unite environmental and language work, it raises profound awareness of the interconnectedness of the twenty-first-century world. Though access to unique natural beauty is a crucial element, this kind of course goes far beyond detached pleasure travel by instilling empathy for and a sense of service to the global environment.

The list of World Heritage sites identified by the United Nations is an excellent starting point for contemplating similarly designed courses. In Europe, such offerings might focus on Ötzi the iceman (German, French, Italian; anthropology, geology), the Lascaux Caves (French; anthropology, geology), Pyrénées–Mont Perdu (Spanish, French; biology, geology), or the prehistoric pile dwellings of Lake Constance (German; anthropology, biology). In Asia, Japan's Mount Fuji (Japanese; biology, geology) and Shiretoko National Park (Japanese; geology, biology) and China's Sichuan Giant Panda Sanctuaries (Chinese; biology) and Huanglong site (Chinese; biology) present abundant opportunities. In the Western Hemisphere, Mexico's El

Pinacate y Gran Desierto de Altar Biosphere Reserve (Spanish; biology, geology) was recently named a World Heritage site.

Such courses require a great deal of organizational effort from faculty, especially during the first few offerings. The vagaries of contemporary geopolitics, including global terrorism, are likewise a constantly evolving concern. Funding, too, can be a challenge, as instructors work to keep the supplemental fees charged to students under control. Partnerships between the humanities and sciences, and between United States and international colleges, however, are something that most institutions in the United States are eager to encourage. And the opportunity for faculty members to immerse themselves in natural wonders of which local speakers of the target language are intensely proud is a powerful motivation for potential instructors. Because of the tremendous intellectual, social, and environmental benefits they generate, ecologically oriented courses that blend language, culture, and science are more than worth the effort they entail.

In the end, endeavors such as Wellesley's Baikal course are a source of intense satisfaction for all participants, thanks to some of the less tangible, but no less real, benefits of the syncretic approach described by Likhachev:

> [When we engage in *kraevedenie*] the city, whose history we come to know, is transformed. And if we know what sort of events occurred there, what battles played out there, whose fate was decided there, the landscape too is transformed. The natural environment of [the Russian city of] Plyos takes on a special beauty when we know that it was painted by Isaak Levitan in particular. We especially value places connected with the writings of Gogol' or Shevchenko, Pushkin or Baratynskii. And so in essence the same thing happens when we come to learn about the flora of a particular area, about its fauna, geology, climate, and so forth. . . . There are thus two kinds of ecology: biological ecology and cultural (or moral) ecology. Violating the laws of the former can kill a person biologically; violating the laws of the latter can kill a person morally. And there is no great chasm between them. Where is the precise boundary between nature and culture?   (4)

Likhachev's musings on these two "ecologies" remind us that academic work, including the teaching and learning of languages, nourishes the moral core of students and instructors when that work is rooted in the study, admiration, and preservation of precious environmental resources.

NOTES

For making the Baikal course possible, special thanks go to Marianne Moore, who is an ideal colleague in every conceivable way. I am also grateful to the late Debbie Chapman, Nina Tumarkin, Nicholas Rodenhouse, Liudmila Nedospasova, Liudmila Riapenko, Liubov' Izmest'eva, Adam Weiner, Alla Epsteyn, Jeff Hughes, Mary Pat Navins, Jessica Gaudreau, Peter Thomson, Andrew Shennan, Katie Sango-Jackson, the late Kathryn W. Davis, the Davis Fund for Russian Area Studies, and the French Family Fund. Sincere thanks also to Charlotte Melin for her extraordinarily helpful comments on earlier drafts of this essay. The comprehensive course Web site is at sites.google.com/a/wellesley.edu/bajkal/. All translations are mine.
1. It is usually the case that at least one of the admitted students is a native speaker of Russian, which can be very helpful, especially during travel to and from Siberia, though the same is largely true of advanced non-native students of the language.
2. We have hosted lectures by such social scientists and literary scholars as Douglas Weiner, Paul Josephson, Nicholas Breyfogle, Tatiana Nomokonova, Jane Costlow, and Kate Pride Brown; science lecturers have included Loren Graham, Harley Balzer, Olaf Jensen, Marina Rikhvanova, and Ted Ozersky.

APPENDIX 1: CONDENSED SAMPLE SYLLABUS
FOR WELLESLEY COLLEGE'S LAKE BAIKAL COURSE

Required Texts

Fyodor Dostoevsky, *The House of the Dead*
Valentin Rasputin, *Farewell to Matyora*
Aleksandr Solzhenitsyn, *One Day in the Life of Ivan Denisovich*
Peter Thomson, *Sacred Sea: A Journey to Lake Baikal*
Lake Baikal chrestomathy (course reader)
Scientific readings about Baikal

Course Requirements

Daily reading of e-mail and the messages on the *Google* group
Weekly one-paragraph critique posted to the *Google* group
One two-thousand-word essay on issues covered during first half of course
One exam on material covering latter half of course
Field journals in Russia (due when we depart Russia)
Field problem write-ups in Russia (due during stay at biostation)

Schedule

Note: Readings are excerpts from the works listed.

WEEK 1: Introduction
    Orientation slideshow; introduction to the class; Baikal geography, history, architecture, biology; personal equipment needs for summer fieldwork
WEEK 2: Thomson on Baikal; early Russian inroads
    Readings: Thomson; Naumov; Reid; Diment and Slezkine

Week 3, Part 1: Old Believers
  Readings: Thomson; Avvakum; Ware
Week 3, Part 2: Buryats: Video conference with Vladimir Munkhanov, live from Irkutsk
  Readings: Thomson; Reid
Week 4: Decembrists; Irkutsk; Dostoevsky in Siberia, part 1
  Readings: Thomson; Dostoevsky; O'Meara
Week 5: Dostoevsky in Siberia, part 2; Solzhenitsyn in Siberia
  Readings: Dostoevsky; Solzhenitsyn
Week 6: Rasputin's *Farewell to Matyora*
  Readings: Rasputin, *Farewell to Matyora*; Parthé
Week 7: Discussion of Lake Baikal and its meaning in Russian and world culture, with special guest Peter Thomson
  Readings: Rasputin, *Siberia, Siberia*; "Lake Baikal"
Week 8: Science in Russia and the history of Russia's environmental movement
  Readings: Sher; Horton; Weiner
Week 9: Introduction to limnology and physicochemical processes in lakes
  Readings: Bronmark and Hansson; Martin; Thomson
Week 10: Aquatic communities and food webs in lakes
  Readings: Bronmark and Hansson; Crane et al.; Burgis and Morris
Week 11: Baikal's biodiversity and its origins
  Readings: Wilson; Goldman; Sherbakov
Week 12: Threats to lakes and Lake Baikal
  Readings: Bronmark and Hansson; Thomson
Week 13: Environmental threats to Lake Baikal and its protection
  Readings: Thomson; Dean; Moore et al.; Brown

APPENDIX 2:
SAMPLE FIELDWORK SCHEDULE AT LAKE BAIKAL

Day	Morning	Afternoon and evening
1	Breakfast; depart for Bol'shie Koty	Settle in at Bol'shie Koty; tour of biostation with Evgenii Zilov
2	Hike to Chernaia Creek; work at biostation	Collect samples at Chernaia Creek; discuss student hypotheses
3	Trip to Listvianka; visit Museum of Baikal, Limnological Institute	Dry suit divers collect benthic samples; discussion of samples
4	Guided tour of Kadil'naia Valley Preserve with ISU botanists	Discussion with Svetlana Sizykh and other botanists from ISU Botanical Garden
5	Guided tour of Bol'shie Koty valley with botanists	Collection of samples; discussion
6	Visit site of Great Baikal Trail; discussion with Great Baikal Trail leader	Ecotourism discussion with Tat'iana Klepikova, Great Baikal Trail
7	Boat trip across the lake to Baikal'sk, site of the Pulp and Paper Mill	Visit mill's sludge ponds; meet town administrator, local people; dinner and discussion with several town residents
8	Work at biostation in groups	Develop hypothesis and collect samples
9 and 10	Data collection	Lecture by National Park ranger Liudmila Bol'shikova
11	Data analysis; write up field problems	Home visit with local resident Ada Veshcheva; lecture on Buryats by Vladimir Munkhanov
12	Write-up of field problem	Pack for the next day's excursion
13 to 17	Long boat trip to Ol'khon and Ushkan'i Islands, Snake Cove; across lake to Chivyrkuiskii Bay	Town of Khuzhir; regional museum; lecture by shaman Valentin Khagdaev; lecture on fishing and navigation
18	Return to Bol'shie Koty	
19		Farewell dinner at Bol'shie Koty
20	Depart Bol'shie Koty; transfer to bus and drive to Tal'tsy Open-Air Museum of Wooden Architecture	Tal'tsy; drive to dorm in Irkutsk; dinner at dorm
21	Breakfast; tour of Irkutsk	Lunch in Irkutsk; lecture by environmental activist Jennie Sutton on ecological problems of the Baikal region
22	Breakfast; Volkonskii and Trubetskoi Decembrist house-museums	Attend evening folk concert, Irkutsk
23	Free day in Irkutsk: shopping, sightseeing	Dinner at dorm; depart for Moscow next morning

APPENDIX 3: CULTURAL NOTEBOOK GUIDELINES

Economic and Sociological Issues

Students address questions about how Siberians live, how they make a living, and what they do for recreation, as well as their behavior, dress, rules of etiquette in various contexts, and discrete social strata.

Art

"High art": students describe any artifacts of so-called high culture they observe, for example, music, architecture, painting, sculpture, or formal literature.

"Folk art": students discuss such topics as folk music, legends, oral tales, domestic architecture, crafts, and local mythology.

Religion, Philosophy, and Law

Religion: Students write about rituals or other religious observances they have witnessed, along with other evidence of spirituality they encounter. They consider how religious views seem to affect Siberians' regard for the natural world.

Philosophy: Students explain personal philosophies and worldviews that have intrigued them and consider what manifestations of political beliefs they have witnessed (e.g., international relations, nationalism, chauvinism, egalitarianism, communitarianism, etc.).

Law: Students comment on what legal practices and rules they have observed and discuss people's attitudes toward complying with them.

History

Students review what evidence of Siberian history they have seen and how Siberian history is packaged and manipulated for locals and tourists. They also discuss their impressions of the history of local scientists and their families.

Language

Students keep a running list of noteworthy Russian and non-Russian vocabulary and take notes on idioms, place names, and local terminology.

Technology

Students take note of the use of any manual (i.e., low-technology) tools they have observed, whether modern or archaic. They also write about high technology and discuss what means of locomotion they have seen.

Medicine

Students address the form and extent of modern, Western medicine available in the Baikal region and identify evidence and types of traditional, non-Western medicine they have seen.

WORKS CITED

Allen, Heather Willis, and Beatrice Dupuy. "Study Abroad, Foreign Language Use, and the Communities Standard." *Foreign Language Annals*, vol. 45, 2012, pp. 468–93.

Avvakum. *The* Life *Written by Himself.* Edited and translated by Kenneth N. Brostrom, Michigan Slavic Publications, 1979.

Bartlett, Thomas. "A Course That Ends in a Siberian Odyssey." *The Chronicle of Higher Education*, 21 February 2003, chronicle.com/article/A-Course-That-Ends -in-a/11231.

Bennett, Milton, J. "A Developmental Approach to Training for Intercultural Sensitivity." *International Journal of Intercultural Relations*, vol. 10, no. 2, 1986, pp. 179–96.

Bronmark, Christer, and Lars-Anders Hansson. *The Biology of Lakes and Ponds.* 2nd ed., Oxford UP, 2005.

Brown, Kate Pride. *Saving the Sacred Sea: The Power of Civil Society in an Age of Authoritarianism and Globalization.* Oxford UP, 2018.

Burgis, M. J., and P. Morris. *The Natural History of Lakes.* Cambridge UP, 1987.

Crane, Kathleen, et al. "Hydrothermal Vents in Lake Baikal." *Nature*, vol. 350, no. 281, 1991, p. 281.

Davidson, Dan E. "Study Abroad: When, How Long, and with What Results? New Data from the Russian Front." *Foreign Language Annals*, vol. 43, 2010, pp. 6–26.

Dean, Cornelia. "Family Science Project Yields Surprising Data about a Siberian Lake." *The New York Times*, 6 May 2008, p. F3.

Diment, Galya, and Yuri Slezkine, editors. *Between Heaven and Hell: The Myth of Siberia in Russian Culture.* St. Martin's, 1993.

Dostoevsky, Fedor. *The House of the Dead.* Translated by David McDuff, Penguin, 1985.

Forsyth, James. *A History of the Peoples of Siberia: Russia's North Asian Colony, 1581– 1990.* Cambridge UP, 1994.

Goldman, Erica. "Puzzling Over the Origin of Species in the Depths of the Oldest Lakes." *Science*, vol. 299, no. 5607, 2003, pp. 654–55.

Horton, Richard. "The Virtues of Russia." *The Lancet*, vol. 383, 2014, p. 1532.

"Lake Baikal." *The Wellesley One Hundred*, Wellesley College, w100.wellesley.edu/ lake-baikal.

"Language Assignments to 3/3 LPDs." U.S. State Department, www.state.gov/docu ments/organization/247092.pdf.

Likhachev, Dmitrii Sergeevich. "Kraevedenie kak nauka i kak deiatel'nost'" [Regional Studies as Science and Activity]. *Istoricheskoe kraevedenie v SSSR: Voprosy teorii i praktiki*, 1991, pp. 3–4.

Martin, Patrick. "Lake Baikal." *Archiv für Hydrobiologie–Beiheft Ergebnisse der Limnologie*, vol. 44, 1994, pp. 3–11.

Moore, Marianne, et al. "Climate Change and the World's 'Sacred Sea': Lake Baikal, Siberia." *BioScience*, vol. 59, no. 5, 2009, pp. 405–17.

Naumov, Igor. *The History of Siberia.* Routledge, 2006. Routledge Studies in the History of Russia and Eastern Europe.

O'Meara, Patrick. *K. F. Ryleev: A Political Biography of the Decembrist Poet.* Princeton UP, 1984.

Parthé, Kathleen F. *Russian Village Prose: The Radiant Past.* Princeton UP, 1992.

Rasputin, Valentin. *Farewell to Matyora.* Translated by Antonina W. Bouis, Northwestern UP, 1991.

———. *Siberia, Siberia.* Translated by Margaret Winchell and Gerald Mikkelson, Northwestern UP, 1996.

Reid, Anna. *The Shaman's Coat: A Native History of Siberia*. Walker, 2002.

Robson, Roy. *Old Believers in Modern Russia*. Northern Illinois UP, 1995.

Sher, Gerson. "Why Should We Care about Russian Science?" *Science*, vol. 289, no. 5478, 2000, p. 389.

Sherbakov, Dmitry. "Molecular Phylogenetic Studies on the Origin of Biodiversity in Lake Baikal." *Trends in Ecology and Evolution*, vol. 14, no. 3, 1999, pp. 92–95.

Solzhenitsyn, Aleksandr. *One Day in the Life of Ivan Denisovich*. Translated by Ralph Parker, Signet, 1974.

Thomson, Peter. *Sacred Sea: A Journey to Lake Baikal*. Oxford UP, 2007.

Vygotskii, Lev Semenovich. "Dinamika umstvennogo razvitiia shkol'nika v sviazi s obucheniem." *Umstvennoe razvitie detei v protsesse obucheniia*, by Vygotskii, GIZ, 1935, pp. 33–52.

Ware, Kallistos [Timothy]. *The Orthodox Church*. Penguin, 1963.

Watson, Jeffrey R., et al. "Assessing Gains in Language Proficiency, Cross-Cultural Competence, and Regional Awareness during Study Abroad: A Preliminary Study." *Foreign Language Annals*, vol. 46, no. 1, 2013, pp. 62–79.

Weiner, Douglas R. *A Little Corner of Freedom: Russian Nature Protection from Stalin to Gorbachev*. U of California P, 1999.

Wilson, E. O. *The Diversity of Life*. W. W. Norton, 1992.

Gikinomaagemin Gichigaming: Teaching Anishinaabemowin and Ecology in the Great Lakes

Margaret Ann Noodin

Niibnanchingsh maaba gii-bbaa-zhizhaa waa nji-mshkikiikeng,	Many times afterward he went out to pick medicine,
gaagwan waa-nji-ndane'e'aad, waa-nji-giigoonke'aad miinwaa waa-nji-niiwge'aad.	where they can search for porcupine, where to fish and where to trap.
Mii maaba gaa-nankiid na'aa Giiwse-niniins gaa-ni-mbigid,	So this is what he did, Little Hunter Boy when he grew up,
miish wi gaa-nj-maajsenig wii kinoomowind. . . .	from there it started, his teachings, his instruction. . . .

—Leona Nahwegahbow (my trans.)

Anishinaabemowin, one of the languages indigenous to the Great Lakes area that has experienced a dangerous decline in the United States and Canada, is now undergoing a revitalization in homes and classrooms. As Leona Nahwegahbow reminds us in her story, which she tells both in Anishinaabemowin and in English, learning has long been connected to the world around us in the Great Lakes. This essay examines the breadth of contemporary Anishinaabemowin picture books created for learners of all ages as a means for communities' work to reconnect linguistic systems and living spaces. What I hope to demonstrate is that when these multimodal stories are used from preschool to university levels to combine lessons in grammar, culture, and ecology using the target language, the encounter with narratives leads to a more complex and nuanced Anishinaabe understanding of both the language and the natural world. Teaching ecology through Anishinaabemowin works against idealized stereotypes about American Indians and nature by allowing literature to be read as part of scientific belief systems, which construct "a meaningful and useful contemporary American Indian land ethic" (Schweninger 15). Ultimately, such teaching about the patterns of life on the planet through Anishinaabemowin offers a new framework for both quantitative and qualitative analysis of life that has important implications for all language educators. As Donelle N. Dreese suggests in her book *Ecocriticism*, "Place is not only physical, but also ideological" (19). Although any language could be used to communicate location and provide a description of life, the differences between languages create new perspectives from which to view the world around us. The Anishinaabe outlook is one of action, energy, and reciprocity, which invites exploration of survival as an interconnected communal act—a grammar of environmentalism.

To understand this focus in Anishinaabe culture, it is important to know the region where the language has been spoken for centuries. *Gichigaming*, which means "the Great Sea" in Anishinaabemowin, is known in English as five separate lakes: Superior, Michigan, Huron, Ontario, and Erie. Together they hold over twenty percent of the world's surface water and cover nearly 100,000 square miles. Formed by glaciers fourteen thousand years ago, the lakes changed size and shape several times before settling into the current configuration around eight thousand years ago. Evidence of hunting, harvesting, storytelling, and gathering to celebrate or bury loved ones can be found in the earth and written or carved on stones. The Anishinaabeg, who originally lived east of the Great Lakes, migrated west to surround the watershed approximately three to four thousand years ago. One of over twenty-five Algonquian languages, Anishinaabemowin is used by the Potawatomi, Ojibwe, and Odawa peoples in over two-hundred tribal nations in the United States and Canada. Differing colonial histories have given each community its own dialect, slight variations in vocabulary, and nuanced orthographic preferences, but in the twenty-first century, as this indigenous language has become a subject more commonly taught on a region-wide basis, teachers and students are learning to focus on how to work together to keep the linguistic heritage vital.

For hundreds of years Anishinaabemowin was one of several dominant languages of trade in North America, especially south of Hudson's Bay, a history that left many rivers, lakes, towns, and communities with names that provide an Anishinaabe description of the landscape. The Mamaceqtaw and Ho-Chunk were known for years by the Anishinaabe as Menominee and Winnebago. These names referenced the valuable *manoomin* ("wild rice") near the Mamaceqtaw and the dark waters of Lake Winnebago where the Ho-Chunk lived. Other words that became part of American English include *Mississippi, Michigan, Wisconsin, moose, toboggan,* and *moccasin.* When the American colonies declared—and began to defend—their independence, the people of the woodlands continued to trade in the center of the continent. Later, as the United States grew, the Anishinaabeg, along with their culture and language, struggled to survive. After the bitter and decisive war of 1812, treaties and government policies led to an increase in both forced and voluntary assimilation. As states formed and became united, more Anishinaabeg people were killed or removed from their original territories.

Throughout the 1800s, removal and erasure continued, with another increase in both forced and voluntary assimilation at the close of the century and into the first decades of the 1900s. The combined cultural effects of land lost to allotment and identity dissolution as a result of the creation of boarding schools and the granting of citizenship of the United States had deep repercussions, since these changes moved traditional languages and earth-oriented practices out of physically grounded, lived practices and into the realm of ethnography and archiving. Lives that once focused on land and water became focused instead on ownership, capital, and industry. Homes where an indigenous language flourished became less and less common and only a few native and non-native intellectuals dedicated themselves to saving Anishinaabemowin. Many speakers were forced to give up their first language in order to survive. Then in the 1960s, in both the United States and Canada, global pressure to protect human rights began to create space for reclamation. Several prominent leaders of the American Indian Movement were Anishinaabe, which likely helped empower the large diaspora to revitalize the endangered culture. Eventually, aided by social services mandated by treaty agreements and new policies at a federal level, language and culture classes were founded, first at urban and rural community centers, and then in a number of universities in the United States and Canada, as well as tribal colleges.

Any introduction to Anishinaabemowin—indeed, to every North American indigenous language—must include mention of the modern struggle to recognize and reconcile these languages within the context of nations where English is now dominant and where other European languages, including French and Spanish, are the ones most frequently spoken after English. On 11 June 2008, the then prime minister of Canada Stephen Harper asked his thirty million Canadian citizens to tune in to Parliament for a live, nationally broadcast apology to their country's First Nations peoples. The task was specific and long overdue. "The Government of Canada sincerely apologizes and asks the forgiveness of the aboriginal peoples of this country for failing them so profoundly. We are sorry," said Harper (*Statement*). He then launched the Canadian Truth and Reconciliation Commission. By contrast, on 19 December 2009, the then president of the United States Barack Obama signed the Native American Apology Resolution into law with very little media attention. Senator Sam Brownback, Republican from Kansas, had successfully added the resolution to the Defense Appropriations Act, HR 3326, after five years of effort. The approved document "apologized on behalf of the United States to all Native Peoples for the many instances of violence, maltreatment, and neglect" and urged the president to "acknowledge the wrongs of the United States against Indian tribes in the history of the United States in order to bring healing to this land" (King). Neither apology had a direct effect on the number of fluent speakers, but both laid the groundwork for respect, recovery, and the kind of collaboration that recognizes the potential for innovation across languages, cultures, and scientific perspectives, which becomes increasingly important as all nations face climate change and other environmental challenges.

Although my brief summary does not begin to address the complex social and economic history of the many sovereign nations in the United States and Canada, or the connection, now clearly documented, between language use and overall well-being, this glimpse of the Anishinaabe linguistic landscape charts the loss and continuing attempt to recover Anishinaabemowin. Despite forty years of effort to revitalize the language, by the year 2000 nearly all Anishinaabe communities were English-speaking. Only a minority of elder speakers, who either survived or averted boarding school, remember a time when Anishinaabemowin was the dominant language in the home and community. Gradually, the proficient second-language speakers of younger generations have become linguists and teachers, while immersion schools for Anishinaabemowin have opened (and sometimes subsequently closed). Lexicons became dictionaries in print and then online. Scholarly papers on grammar have begun to merge and create standards or have facilitated divergence to allow for definition of dialects and other differences between community vernaculars. Slowly, collective proficiency has been increasing, yet many challenges remain due to the precarious situation of the language in terms of linguistic community. One of the most enduring and effective strategies for enhancing the comprehension of this community has been the creation of picture books to teach the language and culture. Like ancient scrolls and pictographs that can still be deciphered today, these graphic-format texts, which make use of diverse combinations of words and images, are often published specifically for language classrooms, offering clear examples of both the language and the cultural view of the world shared by Anishinaabemowin speakers.

Mazinai'dibaajimowinan: Picture-Stories

One of the most important conceptual strands found in Anishinaabemowin picture books, along with basic grammar and vocabulary, is scientific knowledge derived from direct experience of the environment, especially as expressed in stories that clarify the networks of life in the Great Lakes region. Stories containing ecological knowledge convey aspects of the culture well beyond mere subject and setting. Texts that correctly communicate the complex relation between geography and the construction of community are able to move beyond using culture as a theme. These place-based texts can help students recognize authentic narratives and more easily learn complex linguistic patterns. Furthermore, the picture books discussed in this essay reaffirm the power of storytelling and soft skills in the classroom as useful tools for interpreting data sometimes viewed only through the lens of the hard sciences. Adding an affective dimension to learning one's language and culture can raise overall cultural competency, as students experience new dimensions of sound, meaning, and knowledge production.

Whenever possible, modern teaching resources have relied on stories generated within Anishinaabe communities as a source for authentic content. In some cases, these texts include long-ago stories about times very different from now that call for reflection about the past and critical comparison with the present. In other cases, the texts include stories of practices that, like the language, are in a state of revitalization, such as rice harvesting, spearfishing, birch biting, and ethnobotany. These land- and water-dependent activities were curtailed in the 1800s by loss of access to traditionally shared spaces and further diminished in the 1900s through the effects on the region of immigration and industrialization.

Frequently, however, such eclectic curricular material also includes both more recent stories that record changes to the land, water, and culture and direct translations of popular stories originally written in English and then translated. Whereas the former unquestionably have value in terms of the representation of the natural environment they provide, the latter raise questions about what we regard as authentic texts that can be used for learners. In my own files I found two translations of the Book of Genesis and four versions of "The Three Little Pigs," but tales about the Garden of Eden and the homeless descendants of the Eurasian wild boar have dubious value in terms of teaching about the way the Anishinaabeg people understand connections between woodland and water organisms and their sustaining systems. Teachers of modern languages for which authentic materials are plentiful rarely confront the instructional dilemmas raised by these kinds of extreme examples. For experts in the field it can be fascinating to see how such translations still reflect a verb-based viewpoint, and how concepts from other continents are filtered through the Anishinaabe linguistic lens, yet these perspectives do not help us teach an authentic Anishinaabe aesthetic. Exacerbating the situation is that the most common forms of these materials, board books or concept books, typically use a constrained format for the linguistic presentation that focuses on one word to an image, and thus usually contain more nouns than verbs. Bilingual Anishinaabemowin-English publications frequently attempt to follow the English, French, or Spanish syntactical patterns. This kind of interlinear translation results in the use of adjective and adverb prefixes as separate words, which confuses learners because Anishinaabemowin is comprised mostly of verbs. Properly translated, these words should be verbs with prefixes and suffixes based on categories of animacy or inanimacy. One perspective is always privileged in translation, which demonstrates the importance of uncovering ethnocentric attitudes in language instruction.

In light of these limitations, the picture books that clearly have the highest value are those written first in Anishinaabemowin and based on culturally relevant content that incorporates rich environmental subject matter. When we survey these materials, it becomes apparent that they share a common design: they are books with interdependent text and images, and all of those mentioned here tangibly reflect the ecology of the Great Lakes by identifying forms of life and activities that take place in North American lakes, rivers, beaches, swamps, savannahs, and woods. These narratives are not stories of distant prairies, deserts, or sea coasts. They are stories of what is sometimes called the inland coast or the Sweetwater Sea. Many of the tales allude to early exemplary community practices of oral and communal pedagogy where students learned together, and elder storytellers made clear that they were merely the present speaker in a long line of speakers envisioned as extending in both directions to past and future. Although the stories are now taking shape in writing, the oral origins are easily recognized. Coauthorship is common, and introductory rhetorical protocols are still employed. Certain elements are fixed, while others are expected to change with the season, location, and historical moment. Not least important are the aural patterns of internal rhyme, syncope, and discourse markers. Oral stories, which are often considered a traditional form of education, include petroglyphs; pictographs; prayer, song, and recipe sticks; birch scrolls; and other forms of visual reinforcement that have a very long history of use in Anishinaabemowin and other cultures where they appear. Anishinaabe stories typically introduce indigenous animals and settings, help with identification of local places, and encourage intergenerational memory. In them, complex facets of ecological networks emerge as the narratives blur contemporary genres of fiction and nonfiction to include scientific concepts with culturally relevant lessons in morality and spirituality. Given that there are numerous resources created by teachers in the United States and Canada, many for local audiences, let us analyze the work of four specific publishers whose multiple titles have proved defining for this educational field, because they represent a broad geographic range and are widely available beyond the area where they are created. Because the authors and publishers discussed here are students and speakers of Anishinaabemowin, their representation of the language and culture differs from mainstream attempts. A language and culture viewed from the outside as exotic and endangered is celebrated as a spectrum of vibrant active interpretation by members of the community.

The first, the Kwayaciiwin Education Resource Centre (KERC), is located in Sioux Lookout, Ontario, on the Mishkeegogamang Ojibway First Nation. A time line on KERC's Web site offers a detailed review of aboriginal education in Canada that emphatically connects the center's work with "millennia of education based on wisdom, teachings, practices of Anishinine." This statement of mission is followed by a long outline of residential schools and treaties, with the current organization surfacing in 2003 as a part of the Northern Nishnawbe Education Council, which began in 1978. The description of this arc of political injustice, inhumane treatment of Native students, and surge of resistance in the late 1970s, followed by continued organized efforts to revitalize language, is echoed across other publishers' Web sites. The primary goal of the organization is to provide educational resources—including professional development and curriculum in three languages: Ojibwe, Oji-Cree, and Cree—several of which will be discussed here since they are among the twelve Ojibwe and English picture books printed by KERC. Notably, Ojibwe stories are presented as monolingual books with up to three versions: Ojibwe in Roman orthography, Ojibwe in syllabics, and English.

A second publisher, Kegedonce Press in Neyaashiinigmiing, Ontario, is located on the traditional territory of the Chippewas of Nawash First Nation. Established in 1993, Kegedonce Press publishes a wide range books with a commitment to aboriginal authors, illustrators, and editors. The two titles relevant to this survey are from the Anishinaubaemowin series, by Basil Johnston: *Anangoog Meegiwaewinan* (*Gift of the Stars*) and *Mino-nawae-indawaewin* (*Living in Harmony*). The books are edited by Kateri Akiwenzie-Damm and illustrated by Adrian Nadjiwon, who are both Anishinaabe. Each book includes ten stories about Anishinaabe life that appear first in Anishinaabemowin and then in English. These stories stretch the definition of *picture book* by having only one summarizing image, but the modern woodland-style images are so engaging they are sold as separate prints and offer students an opportunity to consider the way a single image can capture multiple narrative moments.

A third source, the Wikwemikong Heritage Organization (WHO), publishes books and other resources exclusively in Anishinaabemowin and has hosted an annual cultural festival for over fifty years. Located on the Wikwemikong Unceded Indian Reserve on Manitoulin Island in Ontario, WHO serves the Ojibwe, Odawa, and the Potawatomi of Wikwemikong, celebrating and helping to preserve Anishinaabe language and lifeways. More diversified in terms of media forms than KERC, WHO has created books, book-and-audio sets, videos, and apps to support the revitalization of Anishinaabemowin. The aural component of learning has long been a focus of WHO, and all twenty of the picture books currently in print come with a compact disc so that learners can experience the sound of first-language speakers.

In Minneapolis, Minnesota, Wiigwaas Press, the fourth publisher under consideration, was established in 2010 with well-known Ojibwe poet Heid Erdrich as the press director. Although the press has several other titles, its primary publications have been heavily illustrated books targeted to audiences and learners at a level higher than beginning readers. For reading instruction in general, with first-language speakers, the goal is usually to move along a continuum from emerging readers to experts able to read complex texts. In second-language classrooms, the challenge is to offer a range of texts that allow students to learn basic grammar and vocabulary while still attending to higher levels of cognitive skill. For languages such as Anishinaabemowin, where the balance between oral traditions and print texts means that linguistic and cultural competency develop in unique ways, distinct challenges emerge. Although it might be imagined that older readers regaining the use of a heritage language already have access to cultural knowledge, that precondition is not always the case. The goal at Wiigwaas, thus, has been to support language learning by also re-presenting those traditions in Anishinaabemowin-only literature. No English versions are available, and all the stories that have been created are the result of collective efforts involving extensive collaboration between fluent first-language speakers and highly proficient second-language speakers. All these storytellers, along with their translators, illustrators, and publishers, have a role in supporting Anishinaabe language and culture. The praxis of storytelling depends on publication, which can be viewed as a form of preserved performance. It also depends on the deep understanding of the language, which can be explored in the texts as they are archived for view and review by current and future generations. Without intentionally creating a curriculum, the creators of picture books are allowing experiences of environment and culture to be made available for detailed examination, which fosters both scientific and linguistic curiosity.

Ezhi-bakise Anishinaabemowin: Anishinaabe Linguistic Systems

Making a connection between teaching environmental relations and the language of instruction requires an understanding of the complex dimensions of diverse linguistic systems that goes beyond explanations having to do with linguistic influence or determinism. Simply put, there are always a number of ways to make comparative observations—no element exists in a vacuum. Offering students a system of complex verb structures versus an analysis of the linear syntax of subject-verb constructions in sentences with multiple nouns that require semiotic interpretation, for example, requires an alternate set of analytical tools. It is not likely that someone will love the water more if they simply learn to say "I love water" compared to how they might feel when they say *niibi gizaagi'in*. The Anishinaabe version is, however, animate and more literally translates as "water, I love you," which raises a very different set of questions about our relation to natural resources. Even if the speaker chooses to use an inanimate construction, *niibi nizaagitoon*, translated as "water, I love it," the morpheme *zaag-* connotes opening and outward motion. Consider the following Anishinaabe words, which create a classification of semantic associations that differ from those in English: *zaagi* ("to love someone"), *zaagajiwe* ("to come out"), *zaaga'igan* ("lake"), *zaagakii* ("to sprout"), and *zaag'am* ("to exit" or "to urinate"). Thinking about how love, lakes, and pee relate to survival certainly takes students in unexpected directions.

In an ideal setting, like an immersion or partial-immersion classroom focused on language revitalization, high-impact lessons can be designed to present the full range of linguistic and cultural information. Presentation of the Anishinaabemowin vocabulary and grammar can be combined with an introduction to the Anishinaabe system of perception, observation, and description. Although there are many ways for students to build vocabulary by studying pictures and words, complete sentences rather than isolated examples are required to understand the semantics, structure, and aesthetics of a language. For this reason, the teaching of traditional Anishinaabe ecology requires not only an emphasis on verbs but also a solid understanding of the patterns they create. The primary way to indicate who is doing something or how it is happening is by describing observed action and adding prefixes and suffixes to verbs to provide detail. For example, *ginitaaniibaakwazhiwemin* means "we are all paddling well at night." This Anishinaabemowin word is equivalent to several words in English and, consequently, requires a speaker to focus on the central root verb to decode the meaning. Carefully selected texts combined with images can offer samples of such complex grammar, which can then be absorbed by young learners or explored later through analysis in more advanced classes. Thus, one reason picture books

have made such an enduring contribution to Anishinaabemowin revitalization is their elastic ability to fit into many settings: the materials can be
recycled and repurposed at multiple levels. It takes time for students to fully
absorb what they are learning, to see the pronoun, adverb, and compound
verbs in that single word: the image of a group navigating the water under
the cover of darkness helps to make both linguistic and cultural connections memorable.

Ideally, the range of picture books for any classroom should model fluent speech and use all four of the main Anishinaabemowin verb forms,
and, when they are introduced, connections between the formal features of
the language and environmental content emerge immediately. In the past,
curriculum worked its way through the verb types sequentially and rarely
offered a full exploration of the most complex form. More recently, instructors have shifted to story-based instructional materials and devised new approaches to teaching, limiting discrete instruction, with beneficial effect.
When traditional stories are told to very young learners, they will typically
incorporate correct use of all four verb forms without hesitation. Although
such an approach requires careful planning in order to ensure that exercises
for any single text include the full range of pronouns, tenses, and modifiers,
it is quite easy to move through diverse forms and content. In doing so,
the situated experience of the environment becomes the focus of linguistic
instruction. Learners explore the type of intransitive inanimate verbs used
to describe climate and atmosphere, the intransitive animate verbs used
whenever any animate action takes place, and the transitive inanimate and
animate verb forms that involve beings responding to their surroundings
and to other beings. Using the complex Anishinaabe verb system to describe
what the sun does or the way a pack of wolves hunts, or is hunted, demonstrates layers and levels of animacy and interdependence that are simply not
communicated the same way in noun-based English sentences.

To appreciate the importance of verbs in Anishinaabemowin and how
they relate to teaching science or other environment content, let us consider
the KERC's book *Ma'iinganag* ("Wolves"), by Laurence Hay. This twenty-six-
page book has thirteen pictures, seventy-three words, and nineteen total
sentences. The narrative introduces the habitat and life cycle of wolves in
North America. Only four nouns are used in the entire text. By contrast,
four intransitive inanimate verbs describe meteorological phenomena; four

transitive inanimate verbs clarify ways the wolves interact with their food and the environment; six transitive animate verbs explain various roles, including offspring, adults, prey, and predators; and twenty-nine intransitive animate verbs make up nearly one-third of the book, detailing exactly what the wolves and everything living around them do. In contrast to the roles of wolves in English storybooks, the wolf in Anishinaabe stories is not a dangerous loner; rather, the wolf is an active part of a complex environment, and thus stories of wolves focus on patterns of interaction and interdependence. For example, the wolf in this story explains:

> Ni-naagaji'idimin amii dash wenji-zoongiziyaang. (10)
> We watch out for one another so that we are stronger.

> Ni-maamaanaan nin-gikino'amaagonaan.   (11)
> Our mother teaches us.

> Ngoding wiinge ni-wii-wiisinimin. Gaawiin dash nindayaasiimin
>   miijim.   (17)
> Sometimes we really eat. Other times, we have no food.

> Ngoding gii-dibikag gii-giizhigaateg, ni-nitaa-oonomin
>   e-ganoonindiyaang.   (19)
> Sometimes when it is night, after the day, we howl well to call
>   out to each other.[1]

The wolf narrator finds strength in numbers, illustrating the dependence of life on variable systems of resources and alluding to methods of communication across communities and generations. This attitude expresses fundamental ecological concepts needed for survival and sustainable communities.

Closely related to the verb types just described are the pronouns indicated by various conjugations of each root verb. Several pronouns in Anishinaabemowin simply do not exist in English, and others are used in radically different ways. When presented correctly, these contrasts offer students an alternative way to view relations in the environment. The most striking differences are the lack of gender in the third-person pronoun *wiin* and the inclusive or exclusive option of the second-person plurals *niinawind* and *giinawind*. As students read in Anishinaabemowin, they notice that gender is not specified by use of *he* or *she*, as it is in English. Additionally, *we* can indicate "just some of us" or "all of us." For instance, in the monolingual Anishinaabemowin book *Awesiinyensag* by Nancy Jones and a small community of coauthors, there is no definite way to know which animal is a boy or a girl, although the story always clearly indicates who is engaged in each activity. Each reader has interpretive freedom to use the cues familiar to their family for determining gender roles. For teachers, such openness helps engage more listeners, since it is well recognized that sometimes just the name of a protagonist can cause one gender to feel less connected to the story. Research has shown that gender biases in early readers can lead the less-represented gender to have lower self-esteem, while the overrepresented gender feels a sense of entitlement (Hamilton 758). In *Awesiinyensag*, as *Nigigoons* ("Little Otter"), *Migiziins* ("Little Eagle"), *Mikinaakoons* ("Little Turtle"), and *Gaagoons* ("Little Porcupine") make plans to harvest rice, readers must work to sort out their roles. As the story begins, Gaagoons asks, "Nashke awe, aaniin ezhichiged Mikinaakoons? Obiidoonan giizhikaatigoonsan" ("Look there, what is Little Turtle doing? He/She is bringing cut sticks"; Jones et al. 19). Later, when Migiziins says to the entire group, "Mikinaakoons wii-poodawed, giga-gaagiizhoozimin" ("Little Turtle will light the fire and we all will be warm"; 21), whether the animals are male or female does not really matter; what is important is who will be warm along with the speaker. It is, however, possible to say to someone *inga-gaagiizhoozimin*, meaning "I will be warm, along with some other people, but you will not be part of that group." The tension between inclusive and exclusive clarity is, in fact, the dominant binary in Anishinaabe speech.

By teaching students to consider the subject and audience of any statement, teachers can introduce a level of required observation and classification that relies on the kind of precision that underlies scientific methods and academic rigor. The nongendered third person provides an alternative way of thinking about feminine and masculine binaries under which only one gender produces and nurtures life. Additionally, in stories where animals and parts of the landscape commonly speak for themselves, the awkward practice of anthropomorphizing is superseded by an attitude that places humans in context in the environment rather than in control of it. This system, which demands careful observation of human-nonhuman relations, is extraordinarily well-suited to teaching about the environment, the biological universe, and our own place in the web of life.

Ezhi-maadiziyang Anishinaabeg Akiing:
Anishinaabe Life Systems on Earth

In Anishinaabemowin the root verb for both teaching and learning is *(a)kinomaage*, which Johnston translates as "the earth's teachings in all directions" (*Gift* 11). By placing the earth at the center of the definition in Anishinaabemowin, a connection to life sciences is implied. Increasingly, educators working in this area are, thus, involved in a project to develop complementary learning about Anishinaabemowin and science. Through what we might call biology, botany, zoology, microbiology, physiology, biochemistry, and environmental studies, people come to know the networks of life and their own place within those networks. As Johnston observes,

> Our grandfathers and grandmothers took in what they needed to know in the meadows, forests, mountains, valleys, rivers and lakes; listened to the thunders and the calls of birds and insects and animals; watched the clouds and heavenly bodies, the sun, the moon and the stars. They saw the objects of their observations not in isolation unto themselves, but as members and parts of the habitat of that quarter of the land giving meaning to, and receiving meaning from, their environs.   (*Gift* 7)

By infusing Anishinaabemowin instruction with science, teachers are continuing traditional pedagogical practices and stretching the boundaries of scientific inquiry. Stories often begin with basic identification of plants and animals and then move on to make connections between actions, seasons, and the landscape. In many cases, these stories include qualitative information about community history, beliefs, and practices related to the environment that would otherwise be inaccessible. In this way, stories that begin with science merge with philosophy and psychology, offering an example of teaching where the separation of language and culture, or the environment and ethics, simply is not possible. For instance, the Kegedonce Press series by Johnston suggests a genre of environmental stories that position humans as learning from, not learning about, animals and other forms of life:

> Maewizhah kakinah waesseehnuk w'gee weekau-inaendiwuk, w'gee weedjigaendauiwuk, w'gee-weedoopindiwuk. Kakinah w'aendatchiwaut w'gee mino-waendiwuk. Iwih apee waugooshuk, myeengunuk gayae w'gee-weedji-gaendaudiwuk weemb-aubi-

kaunik kemauh waushiwumoong. Bae-pekaun w'gee inundjigaewuk w'ae-izhi-ningudiziwaut; bae-pekaun w'gee izhi-geewi-ossaewuk w'd'geewi-ossaekauning; ae-izhi-bae-baezhigoowaut w'gee mino-audjitoowuk.

There was a time, a long time ago, when all the animals lived in friendship. They sometimes shared the same dens, the same food. Everyone, insects, birds, animals and fish, lived in harmony, the way it was meant to be. In those days foxes and wolves often lived together in caves or dens. Each had his own food to eat, each had his way of hunting, each had his own hunting territory, and each respected the other's habits and comings and goings.   (*Living* 92)

Johnston translates the term "w'gee-weedji-gaendaudiwag" (written in his singular folk phonetics) as the nouns "friendship" and "harmony." The equivalent in Anishinaabemowin adds the verb *wiiji* ("to be with"), a term for respect and protection that can be used in all four verb forms:

ganawendaagwad	it is taken care of, respected, or protected
ganawendaagozi	to be protective
ganawendan	someone cares for something
ganawenim	someone cares for someone

These words operate differently in Anishinaabemowin than approximate equivalents work in English, thus framing the narrative differently as well. The animals do not share friendship and harmony as they might share other commodities or qualities—they actively *ganawenindiwag*, or "befriend and harmonize with one another," a strained combination of six words in English but a single dynamic concept in Anishinaabemowin.

Similarly, other narratives that can be used to teach about the linguistic, scientific, and social dimensions of Anishinaabemowin also emphasize relations to the environment and others. The story *Amikwaanowan* ("Beaver Tails") by Laurence Hay and Patricia Ningewance describes the relations between predators, prey, and the larger landscape. The beavers "mitigoon odamwaawaan biinish e-giishkamaawaad e-gawised awe mitig" ("eat the [animate] trees until they bite through and the trees fall"; 13). However, the narrative explains, "Waniiwaaganiwiwag amikwag. Giizizwaaganiwiwag, e-amwaaganiwiwaad. Minopogwan amikwaanow!" ("Beavers are trapped.

They are cooked. They taste good!"; 5). Questions of producers, consumers, carnivores, herbivores, omnivores, and the food chain necessarily arise as students clarify the meaning of conjugations for eat, trap, cook, and other verbs throughout the story. For students learning these words for the first time, the pictures on each page clarify and aid in remembering the new root verbs and pronoun combinations.

In *Ngo-ki-noon-win Aanh-so-kaanh-en-san* (*Short Stories for Each Season*), told by Wikwemikong elders Phyllis Williams, Madeline Wemigwans, Steven George, and Dwayne Animikwan, the subject is the relation between the climate and the animals. *M'kwa Giizis* ("Bear Moon") is the month of February and, as the story explains, "Pii ga gwe-daakji-maad m-koonh-san owa kit-chi m-kwa maan-da pii, mii en-ji zhin-kaa-deg m-kwa giizis" ("When the cubs are tested by their mother is the reason for the name of this month"; 8). *M'kwa Giizis* is a time for watching the activity of bears, for recognizing that cold *biboon* ("winter") is a time to *booni* ("to pause") and, like the bears, take time away from others. The story also sets up the end of hibernation as a *gagwedinan* ("a tactile test"), which can be used as a verb to show how the mother bears teach the young cubs about the end of winter and arrival of spring.

With many forms of modern employment separated from a direct relation to the land, the signs of spring seem less significant today, but Anishinaabemowin reminds us that *ziigwan* ("spring") is a time of *ziigwebin* ("pouring"), and therefore an essential part of our environmental experiences. In the same set of stories, *Aanhdek* ("the Crow") offers another sign of spring:

> Pii gwa non-daa-ji-gaaz-waad de-bwe-daa-ma-waad ge-we aanh-deg-waak mii gwa gi-ken-daag-wak wii mino-ka-mik. Mii dash we-pii non-dood-waa ge-we aanh-deg-waak, maa-jii aa-bwaak dash m-kwen-dan awi ge-yaa-bi ngo-ding wii n-ka-we kit-chi ksi-naa.

> When the crows are heard in the distance, it is usually the first sign that Spring is coming. So when you hear the crows and it starts warming up, remember there is another cold spell coming.   (5)

Along with accurate meteorological advice comes a warning about variable cycles. As in many Anishinaabe stories, this particular observation can lead to more specific discussions of environmental issues on a number of levels. As acknowledged by the word *giizhigad* ("day"), which is closely related to *giizhitaa* ("to finish"), the language uses morphemes to connect concepts related to the passing of time to acknowledge the motion of the Earth's non-circular orbit and the gravitational tug of other bodies in space, which cause the start of spring to vary each year.

Waa Dibaajimowinkewaad: Future Story-Making

By creating a content-rich, story-based curriculum in Anishinaabemowin that combines linguistic systems and environmental content, teachers are able to reflect the core epistemology of a people and a place. In this model the language is alive and ever evolving to meet the communicative needs of speakers who are part of a diverse and interdependent universe. Using the pictures and words, novice speakers make verbal and visual connections while intermediate speakers become storytellers engaged in learning and retelling or redrawing the elements of narrative. Together teachers and students can consider the complex issues of sustainable ecosystems and how partnership with these systems of land and water might be more appropriate than management of resources for profit. As students advance, they build linguistic, cultural, and social capacity across generations through creative reexpression of living stories about the world around us.

NOTE

1. Unless otherwise noted, translations in this essay are mine.

WORKS CITED

Dreese, Donelle N. *Ecocriticism: Creating Self and Place in Environmental and American Indian Literatures.* Peter Lang, 2002.

Hamilton, Mykol, et al. "Gender Stereotyping and Under-representation of Female Characters in Two Hundred Popular Children's Picture Books: A Twenty-First Century Update." *Sex Roles*, vol. 55, no. 11, 2006, pp. 757–65.

Hay, Laurence. *Ma'iinganag.* Kwayaciiwin Education Resource Centre, 2011.

Hay, Laurence, and Patricia Ningewance. *Amikwaanowan.* Kwayaciiwin Education Resource Centre, 2011.

Johnston, Basil. *The Gift of the Stars: Anangoog Meegiwaewinan.* Edited by Kateri Akiwenzie-Damm, illustrated by Adrian Nadjiwon, Kegedonce Press, 2010.

———. *Living in Harmony: Mino-nawae-indawaewin.* Edited by Kateri Akiwenzie-Damm, illustrated by Adrian Nadjiwon, Kegedonce Press, 2011.

Jones, Nancy, et al. *Awesiinyensag: Dibaajimowinan Ji-Gikinoo'amaageng.* Wiigwaas Press, 2011.

King, Lise Balk. "Does a Silent Apology Really Say 'We're Sorry'?" *Indian Country Today Media Network*, 3 Dec. 2011, newsmaven.io/indiancountrytoday/archive/

does-a-silent-apology-really-say-we-re-sorry-gqsuGX9BSEmUxpwcOqfJqg/. Accessed 6 Sept. 2018.

Kwayaciiwin Education Resource Centre (KERC). "Historical Timeline." 2016, www.kwayaciiwin.com/?page_id=221. Accessed 29 June 2018.

Nahwegahbow, Leona. "Giiwse-nini." *Dibaajimowinan: Anishinaabe Stories of Culture and Respect*, edited by James St. Arnold and Wesley Ballinger, Great Lakes Indian Fish and Wildlife Commission, 2013, pp. 130–35.

Schweninger, Lee. *Listening to the Land: Native American Literary Responses to the Landscape*. U of Georgia P, 2008.

Statement of Apology to Former Students of Indian Residential Schools. Government of Canada, Office of the Prime Minister, 2008, www.aadnc-aandc.gc.ca/eng/110010 0015644/1100100015649. Accessed 6 Sept. 2018.

Williams, Phyllis, et al. *Ngo-ki-noon-win Aanh-so-kaanh-en-san: Short Stories for Each Season*. Wikwemikong Heritage Organization, 2007.

PART THREE | *Institutional Structures*

Environmental Literacy as a Global Literacy in Modern Languages: Lessons from a Liberal Arts College

Laura Barbas-Rhoden,
Beate Brunow, and
Britton W. Newman

Starting in 2003, grassroots interest in environmental realities on the part of faculty members led to the integration of environmental literacy threads in the Wofford College modern languages curriculum. Though we did not set out at that time to make transformative changes in our teaching, we shared an understanding that environmental challenges demand intercultural approaches, and over time this common understanding led to much more comprehensive work in our curriculum and in institutional conversations than we initially imagined. This essay explains how the threads of intercultural competence and environmental awareness have been interwoven with other competencies through the curricular experimentation of faculty members. It also shares our rationale for exploring environmental literacy topics from the novice through the advanced levels of the foreign language curriculum and explains techniques we have found effective for integrating environmental literacy at different levels and across languages.

Meaningful incorporation of assessment work into our academic routine has led us to improve our curriculum, and so we also discuss assessment instruments we have used effectively, such as the proficiency rubrics produced by the American Council on the Teaching of Foreign Languages (ACTFL) and the Association of American Colleges and Universities (AAC&U) VALUE (Valid Assessment of Learning in Undergraduate Education) rubrics. This assessment work, and in particular the lively debate and frequent reflection about it on the part of our faculty members, has in turn allowed members of our department to contribute innovative ideas to campus-wide curricular and institutional work, forge new collaborations, and articulate the contributions we make in a language accessible to multiple constituencies in higher education. In our discussion, we explain the assessment and curricular design challenges we have faced and the desired outcomes we wish to see in the future, both in terms of student learning and in light of the evolution in our own understanding of interrelationships between intercultural competence, language proficiency, and an understanding of the ways diverse human communities imagine and inhabit the material world.

Fundamentally, we believe that teaching environmental literacy is one of the best ways to demonstrate to students that meaningful interaction with diverse others is critical to address complex social challenges, and that such teaching affords us the opportunity for meaningful dialogue with colleagues across a range of disciplines. We also recognize that the dialogue we have enjoyed with students and colleagues on our campus takes place in a specialized niche in American higher education, for Wofford College is one of only approximately 130 liberal arts institutions in the United States with an exclusive focus on undergraduate education (Baker et al.). Wofford is a nationally ranked liberal arts college located in Spartanburg County, South Carolina, with an enrollment of 1,600 students, most of whom are full-time and of traditional age. The small size of our private institution and our focus exclusively on undergraduate education allow us to pilot transformational curricular work without burdensome layers of complexity and to share transferable lessons and models with colleagues at different institutions.

Like many other modern languages departments, ours is a heterogeneous one. The Modern Languages, Literatures, and Cultures Department offers majors in Chinese, French, German, and Spanish; minors in Arabic, Chinese studies, francophone studies, and German studies; and an interdisciplinary certificate in Latin American studies. For the twenty-first century, however, it is in a remarkably privileged position: all students must take a modern language course in their first semester, and a robust language program has long been part and parcel of what makes Wofford College unique. Nearly forty percent of students continue beyond the language requirement, fifteen to eighteen percent of each graduating class finishes with a degree in a modern language, and eighty-five percent of majors department-wide who take the ACTFL Oral Proficiency Interview (OPI) rate at or above the Intermediate High level in oral proficiency according to the ACTFL scale, with significant departmental effort now directed at enabling students to reach a goal of Advanced Low.[1] Our strength as a department has in many ways been a by-product of highly collaborative faculty members willing to partner with one another, and with colleagues in departments and programs across campus, to advance student learning and weave education in cultural and language studies into the experiences of many on our campus. Since the creation of an interdisciplinary environmental studies major in 2008, our department has integrated environmental literacy threads in the language curriculum in courses that satisfy both the general education language requirement and course work toward the major.

Since the 1990s, there has been a tradition in our department of connecting departmental goals explicitly with the college mission. When we explore changes, those articulated goals and institutional mission serve as a point of reference. That practice has allowed innovation in the field of environmental literacy, as well as in other areas (such as educational technology and assessment), to unfold in alignment with an overarching purpose from the outset and to take form by means of an iterative process driven by individuals and teams at the practitioner level rather than on the administrative plane.

We wish to emphasize that implementation of new ideas, with the risk-taking that it implies, has been steady, incremental, and supported by our departmental culture. Restraint regarding implementation pace has in our case been informed by the desire to acknowledge and respect the diversity of language and cultural traditions taught. For that reason, we have opted for incorporation of environmental literacy threads in ways that are variable across language programs. Idea development and implementation has required all of us to understand and respect the diverse strengths and interests of faculty members during the process of intradepartmental faculty development of new initiatives. Collectively as a department we build mechanisms for collaboration among ourselves and with faculty and staff colleagues outside our department (in the Office of International Programs, the Center for Global and Community Engagement, or the Center for Innovation and Learning, for example). Collaboration is particularly important with regard to the direct and indirect, qualitative and quantitative assessment tools we use to demonstrate outcomes and identify areas where we would like to develop new approaches and content. Scaling up pockets of innovative, successful work that has advanced the focus on literacies has been possible because we have found ways to develop similar, but not uniform, strategies across five very distinct programs (Arabic, Chinese, French, German, and Spanish). The challenges presented by this kind of collaboration have been rewarding: the approach has created a collegial culture in which more recently hired colleagues have been able to work collaboratively with faculty members with longer tenures at the college and take leadership roles in discussions of teaching and learning in both the department and college.

Environmental Literacy in Our Course Work: Why and How

Our language programs began exploring ways to introduce environmental literacy at multiple levels of the curriculum, including novice and intermediate levels, when the environmental studies major formally launched. The French program hosted a green film series to complement textbook work, and the Spanish program introduced a faculty-curated thread of environmentally related media clips from Spanish-language news outlets as multimedia course materials for the intermediate level in the course in which most first-year students enroll. Rather than share the particulars of the evolution of this work, we want to describe the connection between the labor-intensive, exploratory process of an evolving curriculum and overarching educational goals.

What, then, are the arguments for incorporating environmental literacy threads at the novice, intermediate, and advanced levels of modern languages curricula, as well as in courses taught in English that focus on the geographical areas associated with foreign languages departments? Fundamental to developing intercultural competence is understanding how diverse human communities, as well as groups within those communities, imagine material space and exist in it. As practitioners we must frame that understanding early and build on that knowledge. According to the 2007 Modern Language Association (MLA) report "Foreign Languages and Higher Education: New Structures for a Changed World," translingual and transcultural competence is imperative for twenty-first-century foreign language education in the United States (MLA Ad Hoc Committee). Emphasizing the need for students not only to acquire "functional language abilities" but also to learn "critical language awareness, interpretation and translation, historical and political consciousness, social sensibility, and aesthetic perception," the report takes the firm position that understanding other cultures has to be a core value of higher education if higher education is to remain relevant. Similarly, in a 2009 white paper to the Teagle Foundation, the MLA stresses the contribution of language arts to literacies relevant in the twenty-first century, as well as to cross-cultural communication.

Our departmental goals explicitly articulate that we want students to develop a sense of self in relation to diverse others whom they encounter through various gradations of displacement from their own lived (and imagined) reality. As faculty members have undertaken work in environmental literacy, we apply these goals to the work at hand; we want our students to begin to understand how humans of diverse cultures use, inhabit, and imagine physical spaces and landscapes, and to relate an understanding of the environment to their own intercultural learning and awareness. At the course level, faculty members have worked to design instructional units and assignments that allow students to begin to imagine the complexity of global structures and interdependencies and to cultivate self-awareness and curiosity.

For the millennial and subsequent generations, for whom environmental topics and sustainable practices play an important role in their lives (Rickes 15; Klahr 19), language study that provides insights into other cultures and knowledge is especially relevant. The ACTFL goal areas of Connections and Cultures are crucial to accessing and integrating environmental literacy as part of intercultural learning and awareness. The Cultures standard calls for students to demonstrate an understanding between the products, practices, and perspectives (termed the three Ps) of a culture; the Connections standard requires them to use a foreign language to reinforce and further knowledge of other disciplines and to recognize different viewpoints through the lens of language and culture (Summary 1).

Similarly, environmental literacy relates to two AAC&U goal areas for liberal education: Intercultural Knowledge and Competence (which includes elements such as cultural self-awareness and empathy) and Global Learning.[2] In broad institutional and national discussions about environmental literacy, it is critical to underscore the need for students to understand environmental topics as areas of knowledge, belief, and experience mediated by diverse cultural perspectives. As they implement and assess environmental literacy threads, modern languages faculty can readily connect AAC&U's Intercultural Knowledge and Competence VALUE rubric with ACTFL's five goal areas, or five Cs (Communication, Comparisons, Connections,

Communities, Cultures), that are now articulated in the world-readiness standards.[3] The examples below from the Novice through Advanced levels in language courses, as well as those from a global learning course taught in English, show how we develop those connections throughout our programs.

Although the tension between the teaching of language and culture remains unresolved for many instructors, it should not cause practitioners to shy away from incorporating environmental content into the curriculum. This apparent tension results partially from language-proficiency expectations and defined standards and assessment tools for language proficiency, but it also arises from the complexity of what experts mean by culture and the difficulty instructors face in assessing the process of intercultural learning in the modern language curriculum. The introduction of environmental literacy threads, thoughtfully implemented, can in fact offer a means by which instructors can design curricula for productive tension. Environmental literacy topics lend themselves readily to students' natural exploration of the complexity and range of cultural heterogeneity, even among target-language speakers, and can also offer opportunities for integrative reflection and critical thinking.

Considering the development of intercultural competence and environmental literacy as ongoing processes of inquiry, learning, and reflection necessitates designing a curriculum that reinforces the notion of process and allows students to develop dispositions that enable them to explore and build their competencies and literacies continuously from the beginning of their foreign language education. Virginia Scott and Julie Huntington challenge the notion of the monolingual classroom as the only accepted teaching model in foreign languages. They argue that some curricular goals, such as interpreting literary texts written in the target language, can be accomplished in the native language and lead to more critical thinking about a cultural aspect of the target language. Their study shows that guided classroom discussions in the native language further the development of the interpretive mode through critical thinking (12). In their work on intercultural competence Renate A. Schulz (18) and Aleidine Moeller and Kristen Nugent (8) acknowledge the language barrier for novice learners as well and propose using English at lower levels to provide opportunities for deeper thinking. Similarly, Glenn S. Levine contributes to a growing body of second language acquisition research that advocates for the value of mixed language use in novice-learner classrooms. Although students are able to use isolated words and familiar phrases to describe and compare images that represent cultural differences, beginning learners cannot speculate about different cultural perspectives that inform the products or practices they describe because they lack control of the linguistic structures needed to express their perceptions. Since our courses aim to build the foundation for intercultural learning at the beginning levels of our curricula, the intentional, limited, and judicious use of students' native language was identified as the most effective means to help them interpret and evaluate differences in perspectives, knowledge, and experiences through critical thinking and form a habit of integrating these kinds of questions into their foreign language learning experience and their second-language production.

Specifically, in the context of our German program, in 2015 sixty-one percent of majors and minors were students who started in our novice-level, first-year sequence, which provides us with the tremendous opportunity to shape students' cultural literacy from the beginning. At the novice level of our German curriculum, we emphasize intercultural competence from the earliest levels and integrate activities in German and English to introduce students to the three Ps through activities that develop cultural self-awareness and prepare learners to investigate cultural differences, including green issues, between their native cultures and the cultures of the target language. A growing body of work on the integration of green issues already exists for German college and high school curricula (see Melin; Berg; Ryshina-Pankova; Eppelsheimer; Levine et al.). Few proposals exist for the integration of green issues into classes with novice-level learners, however, as we have done at Wofford. In the second-semester German class, students post responses in English in online forums about texts they read in English and German on a variety of topics that connect intercultural learning with environmental topics. By supplementing textbook materials with these outside sources, such as Web sites and online articles on cultural topics, the forums prompt students to integrate intercultural learning with an analysis of environmental practices. Coordination of these materials with the textbook through guiding questions and pre- and postclassroom activities helps students acquire second-language vocabulary. Such assignments connect the teaching of language and culture and enable students in novice-level language classes to apply critical thinking within an exploration of green issues. Recognizing the three Ps when dealing with environmental questions is a precursor to engaging with these questions on a deeper level and understanding their connection to intercultural competence. Noticing the three Ps as manifestations of culture moves students toward our desired proficiencies in the goal areas of the ACTFL world-readiness standards and the development of the cultural self-awareness and integrative learning outlined in the AAC&U VALUE rubrics. Each forum post is preceded by classroom activities to build basic vocabulary and brainstorm existing ideas (prior knowledge, stereotypes) for the specific topic; the posts are followed by an in-class debriefing in the form of short partner interviews or classroom assessment techniques, such as minute papers or muddiest point questions (Angelo and Cross 151–58). The pre- and postforum activities sustain and strengthen the connection between the teaching and learning of language and culture.

In the Spanish curriculum, the connection between the teaching and learning of language and culture, and its exploration in the context of hands-on work, happens intentionally in the last course (fifth semester) of the language sequence, Advanced Spanish with Community-Based Learning. Until the 2010s, this course served almost exclusively sophomore students who had previously completed two semesters of intermediate Spanish in the department. Increasingly, it serves as an entry point for advanced first-year students (about one-third of course enrollment in 2015). Nonetheless, the function of the course as a bridge into content work in literature and culture for the major remains consistent; it emphasizes the ability to narrate and describe in Spanish and covers introductory content related to the cultural diversity; human geography; and economic, social, and political history of the Spanish-speaking world. This course in particular provides students an opportunity to build proficiency and connect their learning to engagement opportunities in neighborhoods with a high density of first-generation Hispanic and Latino immigrants who arrived in Spartanburg County in waves of immigration from Mexico and Central America beginning in the early 1990s.

The course challenges students to expand their understanding of the imbrication of their own lives and those of others in a global context, a concept many of them have explored in previous courses, even in high school, where local concerns motivate discussion of our dynamic global context in which environmental pressures often are a proximate cause of immigration. In advanced Spanish, the idea of healthy, dynamic, and sustainable communities serves as an umbrella concept for student exploration of instructor-curated content about local Latino communities, their places of origin, and traditional textbook units on issues such as diversity in the Hispanic world, gender, human geography, and relations between the United States and Latin America. Class discussions, group activities, and writing prompts invite students to explore connections, for example, among the historical movements of commodities and peoples across borders (with their environmental and human implications), geopolitical developments, and the positionality of individuals vis-à-vis political and economic events. The course thus invites students to understand themselves and the community in which they study in terms of global systems while they take discrete local action, in the form of research and service, to learn in and from the community. Class activities are largely instructor-generated and encourage global, integrative, and civic learning competencies explicitly articulated in course goals and objectives. Environmental literacy threads run throughout a series of inquiry-based learning activities, such as a global supply chain group project, which traces the movement of export commodities from Latin America to other world destinations and reinforces a textbook lesson on geography. Although the aim is to increase functional second-language competence in the production of paragraph-length discourse in both written and oral formats, the outcome is reflection on sustainable production and consumption. Weekly group research and individual writing projects related to readings and community work revolve around environmental topics (trade agreements, agriculture, and migration; urban infrastructure; food deserts and health) such that the environmental dimensions of content topics are constantly considered.

Nationwide, advanced courses centered on literary and cultural topics represent the level at which environmental learning has been most frequently introduced into language curricula. Our curricular experimentation began with the exploration of environmental topics in courses like Literature and the Environment, offered as a special topics course in Spanish. Over time, we have found that because environmental topics are introduced early in the curriculum, and across multiple languages, students have the opportunity to revisit topics, reflect on how their own understanding has deepened as they have progressed through the curriculum, and dialogue about matters of environmental concern with peers studying different languages. Environmental topics also often surface quite spontaneously, for example, as students perceive tensions between Daoism and materialism, or

Chinese state communism, as happens often in upper-level Chinese courses. Because our faculty members have engaged in intentional conversations with one another about environmental literacy threads and intercultural competence, we are better equipped to turn those spontaneous, student-generated inquiries into rich and productive discussions and extended reflections about the way humans live in material space and in relation to one another. Faculty members often sponsor cotaught or independent January-term student projects that involve travel by groups of students drawn from multiple majors, and they also advise students developing research topics to be pursued abroad, many of which have an environmental orientation. This ability to create a space that fosters and supports students' creative engagement with environmental topics, and to do so with increasing agility, is one of the transformative impacts that the environmental curricula in modern languages have had on student learning on our campus.

Beyond our major programs, our department has productively engaged with an institutional structure in the form of the general education requirement of Cultures and Peoples (CP). The CP requirement, calling for at least one course on non-Western cultures, was instituted in 2003 and championed by many across campus, including faculty members in our department. That same year, our department established the course currently called Seminar in Global Perspectives. Although each language major contains courses that meet the CP designation, we have found considerable benefit in relating to the campus community through this English-language CP course. In the common space of this seminar, we address the intercultural and related competencies that flow throughout our language programs and that resonate with Wofford's mission to prepare students for "extraordinary and positive contributions to society" ("Wofford College Mission").

Global Perspectives provides a forum in which students from a variety of majors can come together to discuss global challenges and bring to the table the expertise of their particular disciplines. As a panoramic offering open and appealing to non–language majors, this course has enabled us to move toward precisely what the MLA has recommended—that is, highlighting "language departments as valuable academic units central to the humanities and to the missions of institutions of higher learning" (MLA Ad Hoc Committee). The seminar builds by design on the intercultural competence initiated in general education language sequences and developed with greater depth throughout the language programs. It also nurtures other humanities and social science course areas, such as religion, sociology, and history. The course's unique contribution to the college curriculum is that it creates space in which intercultural and related competencies are brought to the foreground and their development is made the center of attention rather than presented as a tangential component of another subject matter.

In Global Perspectives, students grapple with many of the challenges and problems they have seen in language courses or elsewhere but with the liberty to focus precisely on intercultural cooperation and problem solving, as opposed to second-language proficiency or other disciplinary expectations. This English-language course prompts students to explore the interdisciplinary and integrative nature of work in modern languages at a depth that only the most advanced second-language course work can attain, providing this experience overwhelmingly to students who, as non–language majors, would not get it elsewhere. Our professional training in the areas of overlap between language pedagogy, literary criticism, and sociology makes us well suited to guide students through these interdisciplinary zones. One of the frequent results of having students wade into complex problems and disagreements in various parts of the world is to see them come to the realization that they themselves do not know how the problems can be solved. If nothing else, such exploration encourages a sense of humility, which may in turn make students more willing to seek out other perspectives.

Environmental issues that can only be addressed through collaborative responses across multiple (cultural) groups constitute one major global challenge studied in the course. Framing environmental literacy as a companion skill to intercultural competence, the seminar presents environmental challenges as an arena in which intercultural competence must be deployed in order for social actors to achieve their desired results. A primary example is river systems, used to illustrate interdependence between different cultural groups. The simple, but very concrete and visible, fact that river watersheds do not fit within national boundaries reinforces the point that humans are connected by their natural environment and must interact with each other along these lines of connection. Environmental connections, thus, became a way for the students to reimagine communities (borrowing the language of Benedict Anderson, one author the class reads): they see lines of interdependence and responsibility not previously visible.

Environmental Literacy and
the Challenges of Collaborative Assessment

Environmental literacy as a form of cultural literacy requires practice. Todd W. Reeser stresses that "students need training in the active interpretation of culture—in the process of cultural analysis—at least as much as in cultural knowledge per se" (774). We have integrated this practice by emphasizing the process of developing cultural literacy throughout the foreign language curriculum. An important part of our practice is the process of assessment, including student-centered assessment, such as students coding their own portfolios of work, and other classroom assessment techniques. An important challenge we face is how to bring different assessment programs and practices across languages into dialogue with one another and how to build spaces for collaboration with those developing and conducting campus-wide assessment programs. We also face an articulation challenge with high school standards and curricula that the MLA is now addressing, and it would be helpful to have regular, campus-wide discussions of incoming student survey data—including interest in environmental issues—and changing standards in high school instruction for different content areas, including modern languages.

As Nicole Mills and John Norris point out, assessment can function as an essential heuristic for innovation and accountability (11). In that spirit, department members have identified and piloted assessment instruments to tease out areas of student learning, including environmental literacy, across the curriculum. In this work, the practice of our department as a whole has been to acknowledge and embrace the tensions associated with innovation and organizational change, that is, that coming to consensus on new practices and instruments to adopt uniformly is a laborious process and that experimentation by a few, and sharing of results among all, is often the first step in lasting curricular change. Among the most valuable tools for our department are the AAC&U VALUE rubrics. An additional tool for us is the Socratic-Hermeneutic Shared Inquiry Interview (Dinkins), which elicits meaningful content and also provides opportunities for qualitative assessment by students themselves in the form of interview reports. Irrespective of which instruments are used to assess student learning, adapting and implementing generic assessment tools and practices requires faculty training or at least active collaboration with institutional support centers, such as a teaching center.

Assessing student learning at the program level and compiling meaningful measurements across the department is even more challenging. We have developed a senior survey as one in-house assessment instrument, using questions that can be targeted precisely toward such proficiencies as environmental literacy and intercultural competence, and the development of these targeted questions is a next step in the survey's ongoing refinement. At this level, after the creation of a department-specific instrument, programs will find that struggles are operational, with the main concern being timely delivery of the survey in formats that yield a sufficiently large sample.

More generic quantitative instruments, even those that are widely used, are problematic. The National Survey of Student Engagement (NSSE) has engagement indicators that are not specific enough to serve as an effective tool for assessing environmental literacy. The National Assessment of Service and Civic Engagement (NASCE) survey, given at Wofford for the first time in 2014, relates to civic engagement and student involvement in various topic areas, including the environment, and contains promising data for faculty and staff. The NASCE scope is limited, however, and the most meaningful targets for assessment lie in qualitative work at the program, department, and campus level.

Mixed methods assessment is critical when evaluating learning related to environmental literacy, and faculty need timely and regular access to information, often collected by different administrative units, in order to pull together data from the course, program, and department levels and marry it to institutional data. When requests for such information are generated at the department level, as they have been in our case, we find that fears about the intrusion of assessment into faculty work are mostly allayed, and discussions equip faculty to engage in conversations about institutional priorities. In our case, department members emphasized the role of learning about topics like environmental literacy in language classes and international study in the strategic plan development and implementation work of 2014 through 2016, which included commitments to new initiatives in sustainability and global learning, and in the general education reform that began in 2015.

Scaling Up Work on Environmental Literacy and Intercultural Competence

Involvement by modern languages faculty in interdisciplinary and integrative learning, around environmental literacy threads and other topics, means that department members often participate or lead in broad institutional conversations around curriculum development, grant initiatives, and community engagement. To scale up the integration of environmental literacy in our programs, we have identified areas that represent opportunities for further development and collaboration. Most important, and most practically, our department can formally articulate a shared commitment to environmental literacy threads with differentiated focus and approaches across language programs. Though informed by efforts outside our department, this work can be done exclusively within it. Discussion about the language with which to express a shared commitment is in itself a valuable process in that it creates further opportunity for open dialogue about what terms like *environmental literacy* mean, and what that literacy looks like when demonstrated by students at a variety of levels of cognitive development and second-language proficiency. Similarly, the development and implementation of rubrics that correlate with a shared statement will allow for direct and indirect assessment to guide and measure student progress in these multidimensional proficiencies over the course of the undergraduate career, including through international study.[4]

Active collaboration with academic leadership in a variety of centers on campus is a precondition for advancing in two additional areas for scaling up environmental learning. One area is the development and implementation of assessment instruments at the institutional level that reflect a fine-grained understanding that intercultural competence and environmental literacy are intertwined. Regular, inclusive discussion of information gleaned from such instruments would underscore the institutional commitment to environmental literacy explicitly stated in the strategic plan, emphasize its relevance to multiple spheres of student learning, and highlight areas for continued innovation. An additional area, which flows logically from the previous, is the cocreation with others on our campus of further curricular and cocurricular endeavors that bring the interweaving of intercultural learning and environmental literacy to the fore.

The process charted here has been one of steady collaboration in changes within language programs, across the department as a whole, and throughout the college and has led to the engagement of the modern languages faculty in the creation of new, intellectually ambitious curricula for the college. This evolution has taken place over a number of years and has offered colleagues at a variety of career stages meaningful opportunities to participate—from those who contributed as they phased into retirement to those who, as newcomers, arrived late in the process. The intentional incorporation of environmental literacy, combined with collective willingness to experiment, has been critical in helping our department remain relevant and vital. By embracing iterative, collaborative processes of innovation, our department has continuously adapted practices that engage with new institutional, national, and international conversations in higher education about teaching and learning.[5] With ever more acute environmental challenges in the real world that require ever more complicated and collaborative responses, modern languages departments have an important niche to fill.

NOTES

We extend our many thanks to our departmental colleagues and to our college archivist, Dr. Philip Stone, all of whose help made this chapter possible.

1. Throughout the early 2000s, nearly all modern language majors elected to take the OPI, paid for by the college as part of program assessment. Rates of participation have dropped substantially, however, and there has been considerable departmental discussion about incorporating the OPI into post-study-abroad course work to make the assessment more meaningful to students and part of a conversation about lifelong learning for proficiency. To encourage students to work to gain Advanced-level proficiency, the department voted to make study abroad a requirement (rather than an expectation) and to specify that students must take the majority of course work abroad in the target language.

2. AAC&U's Intercultural Knowledge and Competence VALUE rubric is informed directly by Darla K. Deardorff's research on intercultural competence ("Assessing" and "Identification"). Other relevant VALUE rubrics may include Civic Learning and Integrative Learning, as they also emphasize the need for self-awareness.

3. An innovative approach from the University of Minnesota applies the four areas of intellectual development from the Liberal Education and America's Promise (LEAP) Essential Learning Outcomes together with ACTFL's modes of communication as a framework for intellectual and language-proficiency development to their undergraduate language curriculum.

4. One-credit, elective predeparture and reentry courses began to be offered by our department in 2016 to help students make connections between their experiences abroad and their curricular and cocurricular learning at Wofford. By bracketing the study abroad experience in this way, we aim to integrate intercultural

and environmental literacy beyond the program and even the departmental level in the same way we have integrated them throughout the curriculum in our particular programs. A guiding question is, "How might our curriculum and cocurricular orientation for study abroad prepare students to read landscapes and spaces (ways of living in space) intentionally when they go abroad, from an environmental-cultural literacy perspective?"

5. These conversations include those conducted in relation to the Degree Qualifications Profile work, spearheaded by the Lumina Foundation; the Bologna Process; and the work of the AAC&U. They also include disciplinary conversations, such as those shaped by the MLA and the ACTFL.

WORKS CITED

ACTFL Proficiency Guidelines 2012. American Council on the Teaching of Foreign Languages (ACTFL), 2012, www.actfl.org/sites/default/files/pdfs/public/ACTFL ProficiencyGuidelines2012_FINAL.pdf.

Anderson, Benedict. *Imagined Communities*. 1983. Verso, 2006.

Angelo, T., and P. Cross. *Classroom Assessment Techniques: A Handbook for College Teachers*. Jossey-Bass, 1993.

Baker, Vicki L., et al. "Where Are They Now? Revisiting Breneman's Study of Liberal Arts Colleges." *Liberal Education*, vol. 98, no. 3, 2012, pp. 48–53.

Berg, Bartell M. "Perspectives on the German *Energiewende*: Culture and Ecology in German Instruction." *Die Unterrichtspraxis / Teaching German*, vol. 46, no. 2, 2013, pp. 215–29.

Deardorff, Darla K. "Assessing Intercultural Competence." *New Directions for Institutional Research*, vol. 2011, no. 149, 2011, pp. 65–79. *Wiley Online Library*, doi:10 .1002/ir.381.

———. "Identification and Assessment of Intercultural Competence as a Student Outcome of Internationalization." *Journal of Studies in International Education*, vol. 10, no. 3, 2006, pp. 241–66. *Sage Journals*, doi:10.1177/1028315306287002.

Dinkins, Christine Sorrell. "Shared Inquiry: Socratic-Hermeneutic Interpre-Viewing." *Beyond Method: Philosophical Conversations in Healthcare Research and Scholarship*, vol. 4, 2005, pp. 111–47.

Eppelsheimer, Natalie. "Food for Thought: 'Exotisches und Hausmannskost' Zum Interkulturellen Lernen." *Die Unterrichtspraxis / Teaching German*, vol. 45, no. 1, 2012, pp. 5–19.

Klahr, Douglas. "Sustainability for Everyone: Trespassing Disciplinary Boundaries." *Teaching Sustainability / Teaching Sustainably*, edited by Kirsten Allen Bartels and Kelly A. Parker, Stylus, 2011, pp. 19–30.

Levine, Glenn S. "The Case for a Multilingual Approach to Language Classroom Communication." *Language and Linguistics Compass*, vol. 7, no. 8, 2013, pp. 423–36. *Wiley Online Library*, doi:10.1111/lnc3.12036.

Levine, Glenn S., et al. "Global Simulation at the Intersection of Theory and Practice in the Intermediate-Level German Classroom." *Die Unterrichtspraxis / Teaching German*, vol. 37, no. 2, 2004, pp. 99–116.

Melin, Charlotte. "Climate Change: A 'Green' Approach to Teaching Contemporary Germany." *Die Unterrichtspraxis / Teaching German*, vol. 46, no. 2, 2013, pp. 185–99.

Mills, Nicole, and John Norris. "Innovation and Accountability in Foreign Language Program Evaluation." *AAUSC Issues in Language Program Direction*, 2014, pp. 1–14.

MLA Ad Hoc Committee on Foreign Languages. "Foreign Languages and Higher Education: New Structures for a Changed World." *Profession*, 2007, pp. 234–45. Modern Language Association of America, 2007, www.mla.org/Resources/Research/Surveys-Reports-and-Other-Documents/Teaching-Enrollments-and-Programs/Foreign-Languages-and-Higher-Education-New-Structures-for-a-Changed-World.

MLA Teagle Foundation Working Group. *Report to the Teagle Foundation on the Undergraduate Major in Language and Literature*. Modern Language Association of America, 2009, www.mla.org/content/download/3207/81182/2008_mla_whitepaper.pdf.

Moeller, Aleidine Kramer, and Kirsten Nugent. "Building Intercultural Competence in the Language Classroom." *Unlock the Gateway to Communication: Selected Papers from the 2014 Central States Conference on the Teaching of Foreign Languages*, edited by Stephanie Dhonau, Crown Prince, 2014, pp. 1–18.

Reeser, Todd W. "Teaching French Cultural Analysis: A Dialogic Approach." *The French Review*, vol. 76, no. 4, 2003, pp. 772–85.

Rickes, Persis. "Make Way for Millenials! How Today's Students Are Shaping Higher Education Space." *Planning for Higher Education*, vol. 37, no. 2, 2009, pp. 7–17.

Ryshina-Pankova, Marianna. "Understanding 'Green Germany' through Images and Film: A Critical Literacy Approach." *Die Unterrichtspraxis / Teaching German*, vol. 46, no. 2, 2013, pp. 163–84.

Schulz, Renate A. "The Challenge of Assessing Cultural Understanding in the Context of Foreign Language Instruction." *Foreign Language Annals*, vol. 40, no. 1, 2007, pp. 9–26. *Wiley Online Library*, doi:10.1111/j.1944-9720.2007.tb02851.x.

Scott, Virginia, and Julie Huntington. "Literature, the Interpretive Mode, and Novice Learners." *The Modern Language Journal*, vol. 91, no. 1, 2007, pp. 3–14.

Summary of *World-Readiness Standards for Learning Languages*. American Council on the Teaching of Foreign Languages (ACTFL), www.actfl.org/sites/default/files/publications/standards/World-ReadinessStandardsforLearningLanguages.pdf.

VALUE Rubrics. Association of American Colleges and Universities (AAC&U), 2013, www.aacu.org/value/rubrics.

"Wofford College Mission." Wofford College, 1998, www.wofford.edu/about/mission/.

Local, International, and Environmental Community Engagement in West Africa

Patricia W. Cummins

The humanities, indeed foreign languages, have the potential to play a pivotal role in addressing global challenges. Virginia Commonwealth University (VCU) encourages faculty research that engages with the community, as well as student experiential learning, internships, and interaction with international partner schools and organizations. After teaching the advanced topics course French for International Relations, where students explored in French the intersections of political, socioeconomic, and cultural issues, including health care and environmental sustainability, I joined the Richmond Sister Cities Commission, which lacked a French-speaking commissioner for the Ségou, Mali, relationship and which sought the involvement of university interns to work for the commission. Focused on culture, education, youth, sports, and economic development, the mission of Sister Cities International (SCI) promotes peace and prosperity in ways that complement or go beyond activities of the United States Department of State. The centrality of language and culture makes sister cities an ideal community-engagement venue for language faculty members and their students.

Environmental and sustainable development initiatives in African sister cities all require community, regional, and national connections like the ones Richmond developed for both our water project and health care initiatives. Mayors, city council members, medical professionals, university faculty members, national ministries, ambassadors, and business leaders all worked together to make things happen. Ségou is a small city in the heart of an agrarian economy, and clean water and women's health were just the first two projects my students and I addressed. In 2017 students reported that their experiences had helped them gain admission to graduate school and find employment with nonprofits, agribusiness, government and environmental offices, schools, and various technical or medical employers. Although the two grants had ended, the interdisciplinary structures created with African institutions and among VCU schools developed further. During the 2015–16 school year, students of VCU in one international studies class did projects with English learners in Mali, as described below, and those in another applied their expertise to a VCU School of Business cocoa project with an international student team from a grant-partner school in Côte d'Ivoire. In spring 2017 my French civilization class worked with English learners in Côte d'Ivoire to put together French-language *YouTube* videos whose topics included the environment, agriculture, and sustainability, alongside other civilization subjects. In fall 2017 my students were serving as interns for a bilingual conference titled Doing Business in Africa. The structures described below had both short-term and long-term repercussions.

Virginia Commonwealth University has a support system to encourage innovation and to connect teaching, research, and service to our local, national, and international communities. A Division of Community Engagement encourages faculty members to engage with the community at home and abroad. A Global Education Office (GEO) promotes international collaboration across disciplines. A Division of Inclusive Excellence seeks to diversify curricula and cocurricular activities as well as international research initiatives. The city of Richmond is VCU's laboratory. In this case, the Richmond Sister Cities Commission expanded my research, engaged students in curricular and cocurricular activities, and increased opportunities for language faculty members to collaborate with professional schools at home and abroad. These experiences are consistent with the best practices described by the contributors to Omobolade Delano-Oriaran's recent volume, *The SAGE Sourcebook of Service-Learning and Civic Engagement*, and are tailored to foreign languages as a discipline.

For students who will work across languages and cultures in their focus on the environment and sustainability, knowing how to get business done is critical, something reinforced by the American Academy of Arts and Sciences (AAAS) Commission on Language Learning report. In the following pages this essay describes the three types of contacts that sister cities commissioners typically make, using the example of Richmond's sister city in Ségou, Mali. The sister cities relations that resulted made it possible to engage in new interdisciplinary faculty research and to integrate into my teaching all five Cs of language learning defined by the American Council on the Teaching of Foreign Languages (Communication, Cultures, Connections, Comparisons, Communities). Although other language faculty members who join sister cities commissions will have different experiences, they will all participate in cultural events, and some will promote sports and educational opportunities, while others will encourage economic development. The Richmond experience is a model for humanitarian efforts, with attention given to health care, economic development, and sustainable development.

Types of Contacts:
Government, Medical Community, and Civil Society

Environmental challenges were the focus of the Gates Foundation's program with SCI entitled the Africa Urban Poverty Alleviation Program (AUPAP). The goals of the program were to increase access to clean water, promote world health, and respond to humanitarian crises. The seven-million-dollar Gates grant funded twenty-three water, sanitation, and health projects in Africa from 2010 through 2011.[1]

The Richmond Sister Cities Commission partnered with the Ségou Sister Cities Commission to construct latrines at a kindergarten, a community health center, and a public market. They also renovated the Médine Community Health Center in Ségou, which included a new maternity ward and doctor's office. The February 2012 *Festival sur le Niger,* an international music festival hosting twenty thousand people for three days of music on the Niger River in Ségou, brought together the three groups that worked on the water project from 2010 to 2011, namely government, medical community, and civil society. My research, teaching, and service from 2012 through 2015 were directly affected by these three groups of people. Furthermore, after terrorist attacks in Mali made activities with students unsafe, we began working with university partners in Côte d'Ivoire, where once again we built on person-to-person contacts between people in the United States and people in Mali.

Government Representatives

The mayor of Ségou was our main 2012 host and provided housing, a chauf-
feur-driven automobile, and lunch on four separate occasions during our
week in Ségou. He greeted me every day in Bamanankan, saying "Ika kené,"
and I learned to respond with "Toro cité." When he later came to Richmond
to commemorate Mali's Independence Day on the VCU campus in September 2012, he gave me my Malian name, Rokia Traoré; a famous singer by
that name is popular in France and West Africa, and I owned one of her
CDs. The mayor brought to Richmond with him the Malian ambassador to
Washington along with a delegation of four people from Ségou. The mayor
and the ambassador had roles in my service learning class, described below
in the section on student engagement and the five Cs of language learning.

The chair of the Sister Cities Commission was also our Ségou host in
February 2012 and accompanied us on visits to the medical community,
where we planned how to equip the new facility. He organized photo sessions with the local press and a national television session with Office de
Radiodiffusion-Télévision du Mali. Serving as project director for the Gates
water project, he negotiated with contractors and assured delivery of materials. He later became instrumental in carrying out a new VCU Gates-funded
research grant involving a clinical study on women in Ségou testing positive
for HIV.

We paid a courtesy visit to the governor of the region. The governor
during colonial times was responsible for the safety of the region, and today
he wears a military uniform and assures delegations from Richmond that he
will protect them. If terrorists tried to harm us, he would keep us safe. He
led a seven-member delegation to Richmond in 2014 and joined in the VCU
public presentation on clinical trials for Malian women. The transformation of the role of governor is comparable to elsewhere in French-speaking
Africa, where sister cities commissioners keep the governor informed about
their activities.

In Bamako, we visited with the minister of health, who thanked us for
our work with the Médine clinic. His ministry and personal involvement
were critical in obtaining permission to conduct medical research. This role
for health ministers is also typical elsewhere in Africa.

Finally, we met with the United States' ambassador to Mali in Bamako,
and we saw her again in Ségou when she sat behind us at the *Festival sur le*

Niger. The embassy controlled funds for ten-thousand-dollar grants to pro-mote interaction between Americans and Malian residents. Our plans for small grants were all put on hold after a coup d'état in March 2012, but we maintained ties with the ambassador, who later entertained six students in her home. Richmond sister cities commissioners received a special welcome because of their role in citizen diplomacy.

Medical Community

Applying for grants in the United States means following rules and require-ments established by government agencies, such as the National Institutes of Health and the National Science Foundation, as well as those of private foundations that award grants, like the Gates Foundation. In Africa rela-tionships play a greater role. Medical community members at three levels became critical to VCU's clinical study involving women in Ségou testing positive for HIV, and without our sister cities contacts, we might not have received the necessary approvals. The doctor and medical staff at the com-munity center we had renovated were at the most decentralized level of care, and they were strong supporters. Present at the inauguration were doc-tors and administrators from the regional center (a medium-level medical facility) and the Ségou Hospital (with higher levels of care). Several of them served on the Malian Ethics Review Board, a group consisting of local, re-gional, and national medical representatives, whose subcommittees must approve all clinical studies. This included VCU's HIV clinical study through the Gates Foundation from 2012 to 2018. As a language teacher, I instinc-tively built relationships with the medical community, something that later became important as I navigated intercultural challenges.

Community Members and Civil Society

Members of the community in Ségou—business leaders, heads of nonprof-its, and members of the press—interact routinely with sister cities commis-sioners. The organizer of the music festival was a business leader I had met in Richmond, where Virginia Friends of Mali members had provided him lodging and Richmond Folk Festival tickets. His generosity to our delegation included tickets to the festival in Ségou and to a balafon festival in the city of Sikasso. (A balafon is an instrument much like a marimba but made from gourds.) Because of these musical connections, my students know about the annual festival in Ségou, they have seen *YouTube* videos of a balafon concert, and they do presentations on West African music and musical instruments. We were interviewed by the local and national press. French-language interviews were heard on the local radio and shown on national television, and the contacts with the press made it easier the following year, when I was asked to explain whether clinical trials on Malian women were being conducted with the same code of ethics we would use in the United States. We were a known quantity through sister cities, and our goodwill toward Mali was appreciated.

New Interdisciplinary Directions in Faculty Research

As a result of connections I had made as a sister cities commissioner in February 2012, VCU successfully applied for two grant projects later in 2012. One addressed health care, and the other an expansion of the research and teaching interests of language and international studies faculty members. Both grant teams carried out activities in Ségou and elsewhere in West Africa. There were both face-to-face and distance components, as described below. VCU did not have a course focused solely on the environment or agriculture, but the language for special purposes instruction used in these projects applies to multiple disciplines. From 2014 on, expanding our use of social media, we held classes connecting English learners in Mali or the Côte d'Ivoire to French learners and international studies students at VCU, with a range of topics that included twenty-first-century skills (Mali) and the cocoa industry (Côte d'Ivoire).

Language for Special Purposes and Interdisciplinary Approaches to Health Care

American medical teams do little research in French-speaking Africa, and VCU's HIV project in Ségou was an exception. Leaving out forty percent of the continent because of language barriers occurs easily when no one on the research team speaks French at a level where it is possible to get things done. Although VCU's collaboration between language faculty and scientists in Mali was not unique,[2] it was the sister cities connection that brought together faculty members from the School of Medicine and the School of

Nursing, as well as from anthropology and foreign languages. The wealthiest foundations are American, and when they think of Africa, they turn to English-speaking partners in South Africa, Nigeria, or Kenya, not French-speaking partners in Madagascar, Mali, or Cameroon. The woeful lack of foreign language study in medical, business, and engineering professional schools in the United States leads to the exclusion of anything that requires a language other than English from so-called global research. As an expert on language for special purposes, I proposed a solution.

Round nine of the Gates Grand Challenges competition targeted HIV, malaria, and tropical diseases. The Institute for Women's Health provided space for me to host faculty members from French, anthropology, medicine, public health, and nursing. Over our West African lunch we discussed the call for proposals. After lunch, the group decided on a clinical study of women testing HIV-positive in Ségou. Women whose T cell count was too low to justify antiretroviral drugs would be chosen for our study and given probiotics instead of drugs to retard the progression of the disease. The head of the HIV center became the principal investigator, while I was co–principal investigator. Roles were identified for anthropologists and other faculty from the School of Medicine and the School of Nursing. Only one of every 133 proposals was funded, and our interdisciplinary team was one of them.

Putting together the Malian team came next. Working with the Virginia Friends of Mali, we identified a Malian doctor to serve as the VCU faculty member in Mali. She spoke English, French, and Bambara, and she had worked at Johns Hopkins University in Baltimore as well as with the United States Agency for International Development (USAID). We identified six doctors in Ségou who would identify patients for the study, and the chair of the Ségou Sister Cities Commission oversaw the distribution of payments to doctors and patients involved in the study. He also facilitated the purchase of a special freezer for blood and stool samples. Facilitating the transfer of funds from a VCU account to one in Mali, however, had many hurdles, both culturally and linguistically. Standards for record keeping differed, and many transactions involved cash rather than credit cards. In addition, interactions with the medical community and the press required sensitivity. Being able to assure each audience in Mali that the ethical standards used in the United States were the same as those being applied in Mali took significant time, as did being able to provide translations for accounting staff at VCU and at City Hall in Ségou.

The director of the HIV center wrote the one-hundred-page protocol document in its English version, and we hired a medical translator to do the French translation. Women's health experts from the School of Medicine and the School of Nursing at VCU participated in data analysis coming from blood and stool samples.

My role was more extensive. I served as an interpreter or translator when there were e-mail exchanges between Malian doctors and the HIV center's director at VCU, and I often provided a cultural framework for why questions were asked or how they were answered. Other challenges involved shipping supplies to Mali and returning the blood and stool samples. The chair and two members of the Richmond Sister Cities Commission personally transported supplies to Ségou. Mali follows protocols established by the United Nations, and they work with the United States Center for Disease Control office in Bamako as well as equivalent offices for the European Union when it comes to shipping blood and stool samples. VCU's affiliate Malian doctor was expected to make sure all rules were followed. When there were cultural misunderstandings, I was expected to resolve them in a timely manner.

As the author of two books on business French, I was equipped to work out budget details, shipping requirements, international wire transfers, and customs problems. My intercultural skills and sister cities connections were also critical. When we met with the minister of health, the governor of the region, or medical personnel at any level, I was expected to accomplish all formalities in a manner that was culturally correct. With the earlier AUPAP experiences, I was able to build on relationships that were already established. Even in press conferences where reporters sought assurances on the clinical study, I already had a positive context from AUPAP. I knew, for example, that they wanted assurances we would use the same standards for Malians as we did for American human subjects, because in the past drug companies from the United States had not always behaved ethically. Just prior to the start of the clinical trials, after medical staff had been trained and the final review of the protocol document was being presented, I was on-site in Mali and worked beside the Malian doctor giving the presentation. I answered budget questions, and I called the VCU principal investigator from Mali to get answers to technical questions I could not answer.

Faculty research with one student fit perfectly with her unique skills. Double majoring in French and nursing, she translated eight forms for patient medical charts into French. This was more than simple translating, as we frequently navigated cultural approaches and practices of the French-speaking medical system—for example, blood pressure recorded as 120 over 80 in the English-speaking world would be noted as 12 over 8 in a French-speaking environment. Whereas in American clinical studies doctors seeing patients can find a chart for how to describe stool samples on their computers, in Mali computer access during patient visits is not common, so we decided instead to reproduce the chart in the form in which doctors would be asked to complete it. Since the language expert must understand all terms before translating, there were also occasions where I helped the principal investigator decide whether he should revise the wording of forms for patients on the original English forms. Perspectives of culture were a part of our discussion when I worked with the French major who was also a nursing student. After this experience, she said that she was interested in working with a nonprofit in Africa following nursing school, and she has language tools to do this. (Unfortunately, nursing program structures did not allow this, and completing two degrees took her an extra year.)

Malian women did not always have refrigerators, and anthropologists with experience working in French-speaking West Africa identified a solution based on their knowledge of the practices of the culture. To store probiotics at the right temperature, patients received a *canari*, which is an earthen jar that can keep food and drinks cool when it is placed in the ground. The result was that all patients were able to store probiotics in their homes.

In another intercultural challenge, we were surprised by what we considered to be an inappropriate, if not an illegal, request when we were asked to pay for insurance for our probiotics study. We had already received approval to begin our study from both the minister of health, the Internal Review Board at VCU, and the Malian Ethics Committee, but a new minister of health had been appointed, and he wanted us to get insurance. Since probiotics are approved and on the market, the manufacturer is assumed to guarantee their safety. This is how we learned that the term "clinical trial" (*essai clinique*) is different from a "clinical study" (*étude clinique*). In Mali, a clinical trial involves drugs that are not yet on the market and requires insurance, whereas a clinical study does not require it. In the United States, neither clinical trials nor clinical studies require insurance. We had no acceptable justification to give VCU accountants if we wanted to pay for insurance. Sister cities connections resulted in a solution: we spoke with Ségou city officials, Ségou regional officials, and the Ségou deputy to the Malian

National Assembly. The deputy, who was also the president of a Ségou-based nonprofit that works to provide medical assistance to hospitals, clinics, and individuals who cannot pay for medical care, simply asked the Haidara Foundation to pay the insurance. After the fact, we were told by a source near the minister that the demand to pay insurance had been manufactured by someone who was hoping to scuttle this study so that he would be put in charge of a future probiotics study. Although we considered this to be a case of ethnorelative ethics, we simply noted the cultural differences and then moved on.

My current research includes language for special purposes, both English and French. I expect to develop African examples for modules in French for business and English for business, and I will add modules in engineering and medical fields. I plan to develop classroom activities for science students as well as continuing education for scientists and their staffs who already have some knowledge of French. Having language faculty members serve in clerical roles as translators for scientists with no language background, however, is a poor model to follow.

Hiring grant staff and accountants who speak French and other languages is the right solution if scientists are serious about global research. At the time I was finishing this essay, the Institute for Women's Health hired an employee who both speaks French and understands basic accounting and spreadsheets: we recognized the language dimension in every area (see Fleming). If we produce foreign language majors who develop applied skills, they will qualify for well-paying jobs with universities, nonprofits, and businesses that have international partners around the world. This project illustrates why employers who work internationally need to include language skills in the job descriptions for their staff.

VCU's French West Africa Project

The VCU French West Africa Project, a $450,000 grant from the United States Department of Education's Title VI program, sent eight VCU grant faculty to our sister city in Ségou and to Bamako, the capital of Mali, in 2013.[3] The Université des Lettres et des Sciences Humaines de Bamako (ULSHB) taught our students Bambara language and civilization, both in person and through distance learning. When VCU administrators became concerned about student safety in 2014, the Bamako instructor taught his course in Abidjan (Côte d'Ivoire). And the French West Africa Project came to include both

Mali and Côte d'Ivoire in its initiatives. The initiatives with the ULSHB continued with online opportunities for VCU students, while faculty members continued to travel to Ségou and Bamako in 2014 and 2015. A ULSHB faculty member came to VCU in fall of 2015, and he served as a visiting scholar in both French and international studies classes. This grant had implications for K–16 language and social studies education, and faculty members and students attended statewide language and social studies conferences. Virginia Friends of Mali, affiliated with the Richmond Sister Cities Commission, was an official grant partner providing cost share during all three years. Public events like Malian Independence Day in 2012 and the Women, War, and Peace in Africa conference in 2013 were tied to grant goals and jointly sponsored by VCU and its community partners in Richmond and Ségou. As I describe below, class assignments, study abroad, internships, and opportunities for student research resulted from this grant activity.

Student Engagement at Home and Abroad: The Five Cs of Language Learning

Third-Year Advanced Grammar and Composition Course

In the fall of 2012 I taught a section of French grammar and composition as a service learning course, and one of its projects was overseen by the Virginia Friends of Mali. While my syllabi usually include goals for the five Cs of language learning, this course had a heavier emphasis on communication, involving West African culture with connections to the community at home and abroad. In service learning courses, students have the guidance of a community mentor and apply the regular course language content to a specific setting. Most students already knew something about Mali, whether because *The Lion King* took place there or because of their elementary school education in Virginia. The medieval Kingdom of Mali is studied by all third and sixth graders in Virginia. This includes not only modern Mali but also portions of nine present-day West African countries. The reason for this requirement is that over half the children living in Virginia cities can trace their heritage to the medieval Kingdom of Mali as a result of the slave trade between West Africa and the New World. Children learn about Gorée in Senegal, where the slave ships left for North America and the Caribbean. Richmond was home to a large slave market, from which slaves were shipped throughout the Southeast. Having a college course that gives them firsthand experience with a culture they have studied and to which they can relate made this service learning course especially relevant to most class members. On 22 September 2012, we had a Mali Independence Day celebration, where the Malian ambassador came to Richmond, and we hosted a Malian griot and his orchestra, who held a public performance at VCU. The event was cosponsored by the Virginia Friends of Mali, the VCU Division of Community Engagement, and the VCU French West Africa Project. Students in my class were assigned to present individual work highlighting Malian music, history, and art, as well as the political and social issues they had studied about modern Mali. Their work was exhibited for the Malian ambassador, Virginia Friends of Mali members, and K–16 students attending the event. The Virginia Friends of Mali president Ana Edwards had supervised class projects from her office in Byrd Community Center, which was frequented by children who traced their ancestry to the Kingdom of Mali.

My syllabus mentions the three Ps of culture found in the National Standards of Foreign Language Learning: products, practices, and perspectives. Cultural topics in this course focused on the products of culture, and student research connected to other disciplines in the arts, humanities, and social sciences. Interacting with members of an international community in Ségou and with the Virginia Friends of Mali locally lent relevance to what students were studying and allowed for a discussion of cultural practices and perspectives when students interacted with the West African community inside and outside the classroom.

Students covered the first six grammar chapters in their textbook as they would normally. Since communication was the prime target, they also used checklists to self-assess their levels on the Common European Framework of Reference (CEFR) for Languages (Council of Europe Modern Languages Division).[4] Most of them self-assessed at the A2 or B1 level of the CEFR in reading, writing, conversational speaking, presentational speaking, and listening. The service learning activities were designed to give them opportunities to improve in all five skills on the checklists. The CEFR self-assessments also required students to develop personal strategies to improve their ability in each skill, one of the ways the CEFR is used in teaching. Others attempting a similar approach might find it equally useful for students to track themselves on the ACTFL scale (see "LinguaFolio").

Students improved their speaking and listening skills with native speakers when they interacted with the mayor of Ségou and the chair of the Ségou

Sister Cities Commission, as they and other delegation members came to my classroom and asked and answered questions for class members. On the day of the Mali Independence Day event, students stood by exhibits of their work and answered questions from the Malian ambassador and members of the Virginia Friends of Mali who came to the event. One city official from Ségou stayed in Richmond for six weeks to take courses at VCU, and he became a conversation partner for two students.

Students improved their reading, listening, and writing skills when they prepared their service learning projects. The project for the Mali Independence Day event served as the first service-learning project and included online research in French reading texts designed for native speakers. They also listened to music and heard presentations from Malian and French sources. If they had questions, they raised them either during class or with the community leader to whom they were assigned. Writing skills also improved, as students did two drafts of their presentation on Malian culture before putting it on display. Another service learning assignment involved formal letter writing, and among the letters students translated were the three that the mayor of Ségou had written to Richmond City officials. For business letters, students worked with the West African author and with me. Two drafts were again required to allow better learning outcomes. Throughout the class students used strategies requiring direct interaction with native speakers like those they had encountered through our sister city in Ségou. (In subsequent classes we identified other native speakers, both French and West African.)

Initiatives Using Skype *or* Google Hangouts

Another faculty member involved in the French West Africa Project required students to exchange English conversation for French conversation with English Club students at ULSHB in Bamako. They explored cultural differences in their perspectives of gender roles, health care, social justice, and the environment. Students from VCU thus connected to other disciplines through a French-speaking online community abroad.

Students' communication skill levels as reported by the faculty member were mostly at the A2 level in French (VCU) and the B1 level in English (ULSHB). Faculty provided vocabulary words and phrases for them to use as needed. When unsupervised, students reported spending more time speaking in English, in which communication was easier.

Study Abroad and Preparation of a Conference Workshop

The French West Africa project funded six VCU students to go to West Africa in 2014, and they went to Côte d'Ivoire instead of Mali after administrators expressed concerns about violence in Timbuktu and north Mali. They were hosted by families of students from the Agitel Formation business school in Abidjan, where they took Bambara language and culture classes in French with the faculty member we flew in from Bamako, Mali. He delivered in French a course in West African civilization and provided several lessons that introduced students to Bamanankan, the local language. Two VCU affiliate faculty members who led the group provided orientation sessions and cultural visits in French as well. Students stayed overnight with families of students from Agitel Formation in Abidjan and in the residence halls of another partner school, the Institut National Polytechnique—Houphouët Boigny (INP-HB). INP-HB is a prestigious engineering and business school located in Yamoussoukro, and INP-HB began to work with VCU faculty members and students as part of planning to become a bilingual campus by 2020.

On their return from Africa, VCU students spoke of a life-transforming experience, and all reported staying *Facebook* friends with African students. They prepared a three-hour 2014 workshop for the Foreign Language Association of Virginia, where they distributed educational materials to K–16 teachers of French. They delivered their workshop entirely in French after a single rehearsal with faculty feedback. Before leaving for Africa, five of the six had already performed at the B2 level in two skills, but all made progress in each skill during study abroad, which ranged from three to four weeks, depending on their time in West Africa after the two weeks of grant funds ended. Their progress in presentational speaking was outstanding, with all of them functioning at either the B2 or C1 level. They spoke comfortably to their audience and responded with ease in French to questions from an audience of secondary and college French teachers. They received outstanding ratings from the more than fifty teachers in the workshop.

Summer Employment

In June through July of 2015 two students went to Côte d'Ivoire as INP-HB English assistants. The INP-HB funded their travel, met them at the airport, provided housing and meals, and offered a generous stipend. The administration wanted very much to have Americans on campus, and the summer experience for these students in French became an opportunity to do comparisons across languages. In the 2016–17 academic year, one of the two students participated in the Teaching Assistant Program in France funded by the French government, and in the 2017–18 academic year, the other returned to Côte d'Ivoire as a Fulbright scholar.

Internships and Cocurricular Activities

Five student interns and eighty-two student volunteers participated in the 2013 Women, War, and Peace in Africa conference held on the VCU campus and cosponsored by the Richmond Sister Cities Commission, VCU, the Richmond Peace Education Center, and the Virginia Friends of Mali. Conference sessions included an update in two languages on water projects funded through Sister Cities International, health projects, and sustainable development initiatives. Students were able to use their written and oral communication skills to discuss a wide variety of topics. They interacted with people from other cultures and connected to many disciplines, often comparing their experiences with those of West African communities. The mayor of Ségou explained how the Médine clinic projects had helped his city welcome internally displaced persons from North Mali, and he pleaded for additional assistance, as indviduals driven from the North and affected by war came down to Ségou. The conference highlighted initiatives to bring medical supplies to Ségou. Researchers and practitioners from three continents described ways to promote peace through different disciplines, including through good medical care and safe water. Interns and volunteers were majors in French, social justice, and other internationally oriented fields. The French speakers from VCU classes helped French-speaking visitors from our sister city and elsewhere. For those planning careers in nonprofits, government agencies, and international businesses, this was an opportunity to work in an international setting. All five Cs of language learning were integrated into the conference and the preparations leading up to it.

Sister Cities Roles and Grants Supporting
Global Community Engagement

World languages and intercultural communication enhance interdisciplinary research and are critical to international community engagement. The

Modern Language Association (MLA) has long argued for new structures in a changed world where the undergraduate language major will be more appreciated (MLA Teagle Foundation; MLA Ad Hoc Committee). Sister cities relationships provide opportunities for language faculty and students to remove language and cultural barriers, as in the Ségou-Richmond relationship. Global medical research needs members of grant teams to speak a local language and adapt to the local culture. Roy Lyster and Susan Ballinger previously described content-based language instruction in "divergent" contexts, and these VCU contexts, building on sister cities connections, expand into new directions for language learning. When international students learning English interact with Americans learning their language, both groups benefit from hearing native speakers and from talking about differences in cultural practices and perspectives. Language faculty experts in film studies, literature, and civilization routinely do research on—and with the right support can involve students in—programs related to social justice, sustainable development, and peace building. Mary Ellen O'Connell and Janet L. Norwood argued in favor of continuing Title VI and other international education programs funded by the government of the United States in 2007, and I advocated the same in 2014 (Cummins, "Internationalization"). VCU's French West Africa Project and sister cities connections offer outstanding examples of how such grants prepare future leaders with the necessary language competence to assure our national security, economic prosperity, and social cohesion.

Language faculty often work with colleagues in professional schools and the social and natural sciences, and at national meetings of language teachers, participants hear about increasing numbers of degree programs where students can combine language majors with other disciplines. Janet Swaffar and Per Urlaub discuss transforming postsecondary language teaching in the United States, as does Michael Gueldry in his volume on globalization and cultural conflict. Experiences in this essay contribute additional models for faculty research and student learning in community engagement that is international, interdisciplinary, and inclusive of cultures that use the target language in a West African sister city.

NOTES

1. Projects are described in the 2013 SCI publication *Africa Urban Poverty Alleviation Program*; its fifty-six pages provide photos and recognize African and American sister cities partners.

2. When the biologist Florence Dunkel visited VCU in 2013, she praised the contributions of experts who spoke French and understood the local culture when she led a biology student group to rural Mali for a water project funded by the United States Department of Agriculture. Dunkel and Sidy Ba tell the story to scientists in S. J. Halvorson et al., and to French teachers in Thomas.
3. The French West Africa Project (2012–15) was a consortium with Northern Virginia Community College and included joint participation of students in events and initiatives.
4. The Council of Europe provided the basis for the CEFR levels and their descriptors, and it recommended how to use the framework for learning, teaching, and assessment ("Publications List"). Speakers at levels A1 and A2 are termed "basic users," while those at the B1 and B2 levels are "independent users," and those at the C1 and C2 levels are "proficient users." National rating scales disappeared during Europe's higher education reforms known as the Bologna Process (Cummins, "Reform"). During the 1980s the American Council on the Teaching of Foreign Languages (ACTFL) and the Center for Applied Linguistics adapted the United States Government's rating scale for an academic setting, and in the 1990s and 2000s the Standards Collaborative, involving American associations of teachers of specific languages, and ACTFL developed the national standards; under Communication, the first of the five Cs, descriptors were included to rate five language skills from the Novice to the Distinguished levels (NSFLEP). ACTFL worked with the Council of Europe to adapt what are known as ACTFL scale descriptors to CEFR descriptors. In order to use the same rating scales as African partners, VCU language students rated themselves on the CEFR scale. Europeans require Europass language assessment for admission to joint and double degree programs and to other student mobility programs (see Europass). (Kuder et al. suggest that students need a language level that is almost bilingual—officially C1 on the CEFR scale—to be successful in many programs [9]. English is the foreign language needed by most students in such programs, but French, German, and other languages are also targeted.) French-speaking Africa has adopted the new Bologna degree system with a three-year bachelor degree or *licence*, a two-year master's, and a three-year doctorate. When francophone African students are admitted to English-language universities in Europe, the level required for admission is B2 or even C1.

WORKS CITED

AAAS (American Academy of Arts and Sciences) Commission on Language Learning. *America's Languages: Investing in Language Education for the Twenty-First Century*. American Academy of Arts and Sciences, 2017.

Africa Urban Poverty Alleviation Program. Sister Cities International (SCI), 2013, user-2221582232.cld.bz/SCI-Africa-Urban-Poverty-Alleviation-Program#1.

Council of Europe Modern Languages Division. *Common European Framework of Reference for Languages: Learning, teaching, assessment*. Cambridge UP, 2001.

Cummins, Patricia W. "Internationalization of U.S. Education." *Richmond Times Dispatch*, 27 Aug. 2014, www.richmond.com/opinion/their-opinion/columnists-blogs/guest-columnists/internationalization-of-u-s-education/article_7c1f2c4d-6f2e-5372-856a-78a0c30948b3.html. Accessed 20 June 2015.

———. "Reform of Higher Education in France." *France in the Twenty-First Century: New Perspectives*, edited by Marie-Christine Koop and Rosalie Vermette, Summa Publications / American Association of Teachers of French, 2009, pp. 247–66.

Delano-Oriaran, Omobolade, et al., editors. *The SAGE Sourcebook of Service-Learning and Civic Engagement.* Sage, 2015.

Europass. *Common European Framework of Reference: Self Assessment Grid.* 2004–16, europass.cedefop.europa.eu/sites/default/files/cefr-en.pdf.

Fleming, Michael. *Report: Seminar on the Language Dimension in All Subjects.* Council of Europe, 27–28 May 2015, rm.coe.int/0900001680731509. Accessed 20 June 2015.

Gueldry, Michael, editor. *How Globalizing Professions Deal with National Languages: Studies in Cultural Conflict and Cooperation.* Mellen Press, 2010.

Halvorson, S. J., et al. "Water Quality and Waterborne Disease along the Niger River, Mali: A Study of Local Knowledge and Response." *Health and Place,* vol. 17, 2011, pp. 449–57.

Kuder, Matthias, et al., editors. *Global Perspectives on International Joint and Double Degree Programs.* Institute of International Education, 2013.

"LinguaFolio." National Council of State Supervisors for Foreign Languages, www .ncssfl.org/LinguaFolio/index.php?linguafolio_index.

Lyster, Roy, and Susan Ballinger. "Content-Based Language Teaching: Convergent Concerns across Divergent Contexts." *Language Teaching Research,* vol. 15, no. 3, 2011, pp. 279–88.

MLA Ad Hoc Committee on Foreign Languages. "Foreign Languages and Higher Education: New Structures for a Changed World." *Profession,* 2007, pp. 234–45.

MLA Teagle Foundation Working Group. *Report to the Teagle Foundation on the Undergraduate Major in Language and Literature.* Modern Language Association of America, 2009, www.mla.org/pdf/2008_mla_whitepaper.pdf. Accessed 8 Jan. 2015.

NSFLEP (National Standards in Foreign Language Education Project). *Standards for Foreign Language Learning in the Twenty-First Century.* 3rd ed., Allen Press, 2006.

O'Connell, Mary Ellen, and Janet L. Norwood, editors. *International Education and Foreign Languages: Keys to Securing America's Future.* National Academies P, 2007.

"Publications List." Council of Europe, 2014, www.coe.int/t/dg4/linguistic/ Publications_EN.asp.

Swaffar, Janet, and Per Urlaub, editors. *Transforming Postsecondary Foreign Language Teaching in the United States.* Springer, 2014.

Thomas, Jacqueline. *Étudiants sans Frontières: Concepts and Models for Service-Learning in French.* American Association of Teachers of French, 2012.

When Sustainability Means Understanding: Modern Languages and Emory University's Piedmont Project

Vialla Hartfield-Méndez, Karen Stolley, and Hong Li

Sustainability is frequently defined in terms of the common good by leading voices in the area of sustainable development (Day and Cobb; Dannenberg et al.). Yet, as the Emory University professor of French Catherine Dana puts it, "one of the main conundrums [of sustainability studies] appear[s] to be that the planet is common to all but that the countries and the people are not."[1] Understanding local contexts and relations to the environment is critical to the global project of sustainable living and development. The study of modern languages, cultures, and literatures provides access points to our comprehension of human activity and complex, often conflicting notions of what it means to live on Earth. For this reason, faculty members in languages, literature, and culture departments have a great deal to contribute to critical conversations on university campuses about sustainability. One of these critical conversations has taken place in the Piedmont Project at Emory University with significant participation by faculty members from the so-called foreign language departments—that is, from departments that study how the majority of humans on the planet who speak a language other than English conceive of, write and talk about, and live out cultural practices, including those related to the environment.

The Piedmont Project is a multidisciplinary faculty-development and curricular innovation program organized around issues of sustainability. Begun in 2001 and modeled after the Ponderosa Project at Northern Arizona University, the Piedmont Project has become a national model in its own right and is part of a larger, award-winning commitment to sustainability at Emory.[2] As of 2016 the Piedmont Project had completed twelve years of multiday workshops offered annually, with participants numbering 215 faculty members and 197 graduate students. Over three hundred Emory courses—in fifty-seven percent of departments—were identified by faculty members in 2013 to engage sustainability issues, and many of those were developed through the Piedmont Project. Funding for participating faculty members has been provided by different Emory sources, including three teaching innovation awards (from competitive all-university funds), the Program in Science and Society (a grant-funded interdisciplinary effort to promote engagement of science faculty members and students with broader societal challenges), the Office of the Provost, Emory College's former Center for Teaching and Curriculum, the Center for Faculty Development and Excellence, the Office of Sustainability Initiatives, and contributions from the deans' budgets of six professional schools and Oxford College.[3] Support to the program, which is led by a faculty liaison, has also come in the form of workshop-space access, donated supplies, and staff time.

Participants in the Piedmont Project explore approaches to teaching sustainability through an introduction to sustainability studies, guest speakers from Emory and the Atlanta area, an Emory database of resources and syllabi (including, for example, resources available through the Association for the Advancement of Sustainability in Higher Education), and ongoing conversations among faculty members from across the university. More than a dozen faculty members who teach courses in various modern languages throughout the full range of the curriculum, from beginning language and culture courses to advanced undergraduate and graduate seminars, are Piedmont Project participants. Their involvement expands the interdisciplinary horizons of the Piedmont Project, while the resulting courses are enlivened by the synergy among disciplines that the workshop fosters. This essay traces the development of sustainability-focused curricula in modern languages at Emory as a result of these efforts, with attention to cross-disciplinary idea sharing, innovative course designs, and strategies for infusing courses across the continuum of learning with sustainability-focused content. It highlights courses in a variety of languages that challenge the traditional binary between language and literature through the teaching of sustainability.

Grounded in David Orr's admonition that "It is not education, but education of a certain kind, that will save us" (qtd. in Barlett and Chase 1), the Piedmont Project encourages innovation in teaching materials, methods, and paradigms. That goes beyond merely addressing sustainability in a token way to weaving it into the fabric of a course and even into a whole curriculum. Place-based learning is a recurring theme, including questions of urban design and built environments and their relationship to social justice. This theme lends itself particularly well to the study of cultures across the globe. As a result, tenure- and lecture-track faculty members (and participating graduate students) in Chinese, Japanese, Spanish, French, German, Italian, and Portuguese have taught a diverse array of classes either wholly devoted to sustainability or enhanced with content-rich modules focused on sustainability.[4] The highly interdisciplinary nature of the Piedmont Project workshop has from the outset made it attractive to faculty members in many different fields, with the arts and humanities welcomed as valued contributors to the conversation. Peggy F. Barlett and Ann Rappaport note that, in comparison with a similar program at Tufts University, "[t]he goal of the Piedmont Project readings has been less to bring faculty [members] to familiarity with environmental literacy than to stimulate the imagination around possible issues that might connect with each person's field" (75). Faculty leaders "see their role as facilitating cross-fertilization among the people in the room—all of whom are 'the experts'" (Barlett and Rappaport 75).

For faculty members in modern languages, this campus conversation has fostered creativity and opened possibilities for new courses, course revisions, and broad rethinking of pedagogical goals. Additionally, faculty members who have not participated in the multiday Piedmont Project itself have been engaged through interactions with Piedmont Project alumni and Piedmont Project–focused events organized by the Emory College Language Center. In this way, the program has had a multiplier effect that reaches beyond the immediate participants. A review of the syllabi of more than a dozen courses in modern languages at Emory reveals thematic threads of the Piedmont Project—place, food cultures, and the relation of humans to nature—that reach across the full range of the curriculum.

Thematic Threads: Place, Food, Nature

The gravitation in language, culture, and literature classes toward subject matter that explores the sites where these cultures and languages have evolved, combined with the emphasis on place in the Piedmont Project workshop, led to the development of multiple place-based courses. The Piedmont Project responds to research that shows that "rebuilding a sense of place and reweaving connections to ecosystemic awareness are essential components of a more sustainable national (and global) culture" (Barlett and Rappaport 79). Thus, workshop participants go on guided walks (either in wooded areas or on the main campus) and take trips to nearby places significant for their environmental history or for contributions to sustainable living; in addition, local environmental advocates, directors of nonprofit organizations, and representatives of governmental agencies from the Atlanta area are invited to talk about their efforts in the community. Commenting on how this emphasis on place and one's relation to place transformed his pedagogy, the professor of German Hiram Maxim notes that "I came to see place within the language classroom as analogous to context. . . . [T]he Project's emphasis on being aware of and sensitive to place renewed my desire to work with my students on understanding how context shapes and is shaped by language use." He adds:

> [A] related point of emphasis . . . was the need for increased awareness of and sensitivity to our relationship to others and how our choices and behaviors affect those relationships. This aspect of sustainable living struck a chord with me because foreign language learners can have the tendency to impose their own world view on the target culture . . . without recognizing slight, yet significant differences.

Consequently, Maxim continues, "sustainable practices, such as recognizing the centrality of context and respecting one's impact on others, are actually central principles of a successful language user." This awareness of the pedagogical link between place-based sustainable practices and language and culture learning is an underlying instructional principle in many of the new courses and course modules developed through the Piedmont Project.

With the local environment as the focus, place became a key component of community-engaged learning courses. Two courses at different levels in the Department of Spanish and Portuguese provided opportunities for students to understand local geographies and their transformations through successive waves of human habitation. A senior seminar titled The Mexico-US *frontera* and Its Stories (Hartfield-Méndez) conceived of *border spaces* as multiple in form, ranging from the international border between the two countries to urban areas in the United States that reflect dividing lines, such as parts of the Atlanta area where immigrants from Mexico and other Latin American countries have settled. In one iteration this course facilitated student work for service organizations located in these border spaces or contact zones along an area of Buford Highway, a multiethnic main travel artery between the northern suburbs and downtown Atlanta, which alternately resembles the street corners of Mexican, Central American, Vietnamese, and Korean cities. Students incorporated interactional experiences, which occurred in Spanish and English, into several reflection papers written in Spanish. Another semester, the experience of border spaces was accomplished through guest speakers and a field trip to a local clinic and a mall that has undergone radical transformation from an abandoned collection of stores to a vibrant hub for Hispanic residents with the look and feel of a traditional Mexican plaza. Students learned about shifting notions of *border* by reading excerpts from Charles C. Mann's *1491: New Revelations of the Americas before Columbus* as a frame for discussion of the narrative of Alvar Núñez Cabeza de Vaca's ten-year journey walking from present-day Florida across the southern United States to the borderlands that would later be contested in the US-Mexican War.

Place-based learning that incorporates the local and the global was also essential to a first-year seminar, How We Learn, that compared "Italian and American educational systems with the aim of facilitating community engaged learning and inspiring a lifelong commitment to education" (Ristaino). Here, focus on sustainable practices in the Italian pedagogical philosophies of Montessori and Reggio Emilia framed a discussion of the public education system in the United States, and specifically in Atlanta. Taught in English, the seminar engaged Emory first-year students in various local educational partnerships to offer school-aged children activities focused on nutrition, exercise, and sustainable living, among other topics.

Food cultures and food ways also became important thematic foci in the curriculum, allowing for cross-cultural analysis of food practices. Noodle Narratives on the Silk Road: A Cultural Exploration of China and Italy through Noodles, a first-year seminar course that exemplifies the Piedmont Project's aim to "make connections" among faculty members across disciplines (Barlett and Chase 18), considered food studies through a comparative multicultural sustainability lens. Throughout history, the noodle has sustained livelihoods in China and Italy in different yet intersecting ways. The course introduced students to a theoretical framework that looked at food cultural practices, forms of cooking, and cultural variations of shared ingredients as important and often undervalued vehicles of cultural memory and communal identification. By focusing on a microcosmic view of each culture as reflected in the production and consumption of the noodle, the course considered how food influences and even changes the trajectory of a nation or culture ("Noodle Narratives"). After studying sociological and anthropological perspectives on food studies, students visited an Italian and a Chinese restaurant in Atlanta. Sampling the noodle dishes, they closely observed the cultural symbolisms manifested in the settings and atmospheres of the restaurants and discussed how local environments redefined and reinvented those dishes. In the final weeks, students followed the food practices of Italian and Chinese American families in the Atlanta area by conducting interviews to explore how the noodle holds onto the culture of the mother country and then breaks away into new forms once it is in the United States.

Just as Maxim found the place-based inquiry helpful in guiding students to a more nuanced understanding of culture, Hong Li (professor of Chinese) and Christine Ristaino (professor of Italian) used food as the entry point for engaging students in analyses of how common daily practices shape and transform cultures. Another first-year seminar, At the Italian Table: Sustainable Food and Culture of Italy, focused on the slow food movement, which has its roots in Italy but has ramifications worldwide. As first-year seminars, both At the Italian Table and Noodle Narratives on the Silk Road were taught in English, which raises an important consideration for teaching language and culture. Incorporating cultural and linguistic references critical to the understanding of the topic, both courses were designed to stimulate thinking about how the study of language and culture gives unique access to knowledge not otherwise accessible. Such an approach does not always translate into student enrollment in additional language classes, but it does make clear the value of the study of language and of culture through language. Since first-year seminars—most taught in English—are now a staple of undergraduate programs in the United States, foreign language departments have a role to play in contributing courses; sustainability-focused offerings are one example of where a strategic response to this double imperative can be made.

Beyond first-year seminars, content courses in the target language allow for deeper access to culture through language. Thus, a senior seminar
topically similar to At the Italian Table but taught in Italian, L'Italiano nel
piatto: Italian Food in Literature, Film and Culture, was developed to include informational readings about the slow food movement and the Medi-
terranean diet and nutrition, as well as related fiction, poetry, and films,
with a community-engaged learning component for which students prepared presentations for local high school students (Muratore). Such articulation with public schools provides an additional opportunity to reflect on
the convergence of local and global, expands the sustainability conversation across the K–16 spectrum, and introduces K–12 students to new ways of
thinking about the study of language and culture.

As we can see, food provides multiple access points for understanding
culture and attitudes toward sustainable practices that lead to diverse forms
of place-based inquiry, many of which also lead to the third thematic thread
here: the cultural construction of nature. Indeed, researchers and teachers of
literature and culture can fully own discussions of how depictions of nature,
manipulations of nature (including the built environment), and human response to natural events play out in literature, film, and art. An underlying
assumption of the Piedmont Project and similar programs is the conviction
that a nuanced understanding of human interactions with nature and the
environment forwards the agenda of establishing and maintaining sustainable practices. If we are to embrace the proposal that "higher education has
a key role to play in the move toward a more sustainable world" (Barlett and
Chase 1), heightened awareness of culturally based concepts and the history
of ideas regarding the relation of humans to the environment must become
central to our teaching. Exemplary courses tap directly into the ability of
the humanities to advance the common good for our shared planet.

Two such courses at Emory focus on understanding human responses
to disaster. Life After the Great East Earthquake is an advanced seminar in
Japanese focused on the 2011 earthquake, subsequent tsunami, and Fukushima nuclear disaster and the many ethical, cultural, and public policy
responses to the disaster (Takeda). An upper-division comparative literature
course, Literature of Disaster in the Americas, is organized around representations of disaster in writing from the United States and the Caribbean (and
cross-listed in English and French).[5] Historically grounded in disaster narratives of the Middle Passage and the Haitian Revolution, it also considers

representations of Hurricane Katrina and the 2010 earthquake in Haiti. Explicitly interrogating representations of disaster written in English, French, and Creole (these last translated into English), it crosses multiple cultural boundaries to confront questions such as the "problematic distinction between 'natural' and 'human-made' disaster; the intersection between individual and collective experience; the agency of land and sea; the vulnerability of the planet in the Anthropocene; the status of humanity and human rights in the face of disaster; the position of the witness, the survivor, the reader, and the spectator; and remembering and memorializing" (Loichot). This course was further developed as a University Course, offered through the Center for Faculty Development and Excellence to undergraduate, graduate, and professional students from across the entire university.

Other courses have focused on representations of nature in literature, painting, and film through a comparative lens. A first-year seminar, The Rise and Fall of Nature, taught by a professor of German, introduced first-year students to environmental issues in North American and German literature and film. "Rather than accept a certain type of landscape as backdrop or metaphor for human emotions and actions," the course challenged students to observe the "staging of the non-human world as a central element to story and plot." The course considered literary texts in light of scholarly work on the Anthropocene, "the myth of pastoral nature, the 'trouble with wilderness,' environmental damage and catastrophes, animal studies, and food studies" (Schaumann). A third-year survey course in German, Screening Nature (cross-listed with film studies), applied a similar approach with a series of films by directors from Germany and the United States. Finally, a senior seminar taught in French, titled The Caribbean and Its Environment, led students through examinations of "race, gender, colonialism, and postcolonialism" specifically as they related to the environment and sustainability (Loichot).

As a result of the involvement of language faculty members in the Piedmont Project, boundaries between languages and cultures are blurred, as faculty members and students from different departments work across languages. Linguistic and national boundaries are reified by our institutional and professional structures, with English as the default language for debates about sustainability or ecocriticism. Yet access to local cultures and the ability to do sustainability work on the ground are often possible only through local languages. Since a number of the Piedmont courses were allowed to count toward the sustainability minor, links between so-called foreign languages and other areas of the curriculum were further strengthened. When faculty members collaborate to bring together different linguistic and cultural traditions around a single theme, or when various iterations of a course are taught in English and another language, the institutional cross-pollination creates its own curricular ecosystem, one that replicates the border crossing inherent in discussions of sustainability.

Each of the many sustainability-focused learning experiences that have resulted from participation in the Piedmont Project or related workshops offers valuable lessons in pedagogical approaches and design, as well as opportunities for engaging in institutional initiatives and increased visibility for languages other than English.[6] To explore the transformative influence of such work, let us now turn to one example that shows the multiple effects of a single course.

One Course, Multiple Constituencies

The course Chinese Language Internship allowed advanced undergraduate students in Chinese the opportunity to work for one semester with students in a local middle school on a community-engaged learning project focused on traditional Chinese gardens. This is one of several courses with ties to the Piedmont Project that have incorporated engagement with community partners, including an Emory partnership with a nearby cluster of public schools known as Graduation Generation (Li). This particular course involved the Emory University Center for Community Partnerships, a public middle school, and the Edgewood neighborhood in Atlanta (with a Seed to Plate grant from the State of Georgia) to leverage Emory faculty and student resources through service activities. It also built on an existing partnership with the Confucius Institute.[7]

During the semester, under guidance of the professor, the Emory students researched the history and principles of traditional Chinese scholarly gardens and instructed seventh graders on the differences, historical and cultural, between American and Chinese diets and gardens. In traditional China the central goal in building a scholarly garden was to create an abstraction that could help the human soul escape to moods of contemplation in nature.[8] Thus, Chinese scholars built their houses with gardens to be in harmony with the spiritual and the natural worlds. According to Confucius, "the wise find pleasure in water; the virtuous find pleasure in hills" (Legge 32). By considering the philosophical beliefs embodied in the scholarly gardens, the Emory student interns understood that learning about and planning the construction of a scholarly garden offered an ideal way for the middle school students and their communities to benefit for at least two reasons: first, although grounded in Daoist principles, the scholarly garden provides essentially nonreligious yet spiritually enlightening and intimate connections to nature; second, such a garden could provide a place of inspiration and withdrawal from the often challenging state of urban life in Atlanta, especially in high poverty areas such as the one surrounding this school. The Emory students created and taught six lessons to seventh grade students at Coan Middle School. These lessons explored Chinese food production and dietary habits and compared vegetable gardens in the United States with scholarly gardens in traditional Chinese culture. The middle school students learned Chinese expressions related to nature and foods and, as a final project, created preliminary designs for a future Chinese garden at the school with traditional elements such as a bridge, a pathway, a lake, flowers, and trees. The academic experience of the Emory students was enhanced by their own research of classical Chinese poems on nature and presentations of their findings to the Emory community. This internship allowed for a consideration of place in a cross-cultural context, providing an experience of local geographies for the Emory students, a heightened awareness of natural spaces around them for the seventh graders, and for both an appreciation of how natural spaces can be transformed by cultural ideas.

Sustainability Woven into One Department's Curriculum

When multiple members of the same department are Piedmont Project alumni, significant changes in the departmental curriculum result. By 2015 in the Department of Spanish and Portuguese six tenure- and lecture-track faculty members, as well as several graduate students, had participated in the Piedmont Project and incorporated sustainability in courses across the entire learning spectrum. These courses included a first-year seminar on the Amazon Basin offered in Portuguese, a Spanish language and culture course at the advanced intermediate level on the local Atlanta Latino community, a foundational course on academic writing in Spanish, senior seminars on various literary and cultural topics related to the environment, and a graduate seminar. A departmental conversation about sustainability was continually renewed as colleagues brought back what they learned through various iterations of the Piedmont Project to the evolving curriculum. In that process, the themes discussed earlier in this essay became an integral part of the undergraduate and graduate programs in Spanish. Moreover, as we have seen in previous examples, the sustainability conversation offered opportunities for moving beyond the two-tier curricular structure that divides "language" and literary studies, with its corresponding two-tier teaching hierarchy, by means of interdisciplinary curricula and a commitment to collaborative practice that included members of both the lecture- and tenure-track faculty. Sharing a commitment to a common theme (sustainability) and a common pedagogical conversation through the Piedmont Project created points of contact among both faculty members and students along the continuum from introductory to advanced courses and the doctoral program. This work is a highly generative process that could be mobilized with regard to other issues, such as human rights and social justice, which also can be interpreted within the broad framework of sustainability. Moreover, the theme opened up the language and literature curriculum to innovative restructuring that positioned the teaching of language, literature, and culture at the center of campus conversations.

One approach was to interweave sustainability into the Spanish-language curriculum as part of existing courses students take for general education requirements or as foundational courses for the major. A colleague who participated in the Piedmont Project offered a modified version of the intermediate (fifth-semester) course that serves as one entry point into the major and is most frequently taken by first-year students as they begin their university-level study of Spanish.[9] The professor used the same grammar workbook as the other sections of the course used but, instead of the standard readings from the textbook, she incorporated selected texts— short stories, scientific or journalistic essays, and film—focused on environmental issues, alternative medicine, agriculture, water rights, and slow food. Experiential learning was also a key aspect of the course. Students walked through their campus environment in order to read the landscape (observe closely and interpret details) and then report on the mix of gardens, woods, buildings, and sidewalks in later discussions and writing assignments. They traveled to the Buford Highway and Plaza Fiesta neighborhood (also called the Capital Latina de Georgia), paying special attention to the built landscape for cars and pedestrians and exploring the food and commodities offered in local markets (Dillman). As in many urban areas outside city centers in the United States, the Buford Highway corridor grew up around a connector highway with residential developments on either side that were accessed initially by car, with no planning for pedestrian traffic. The immigrants who moved into this area beginning in the 1990s brought cultural habits that included walking and public transportation as a normal part of life. The lack of infrastructure to support these habits, which continued to be necessary for many for economic reasons, resulted in numerous pedestrian deaths.[10] As a result, local and state governments eventually responded with new sidewalks, and the built environment thus slowly began to reflect the presence of immigrant communities whose cultural habits included walking everywhere possible, with an attendant improvement in safety and (as a by-product) encouragement of environmentally friendly practices. By the time they visited this area, students were equipped to interpret the landscape and look for clues related to the environment and culturally based sustainability practices.

Using content-rich sustainability topics to develop writing skills in Spanish is another approach. Critical Writing in Hispanic Topics is one of a cluster of foundational courses for the major offered at the advanced intermediate level. The course aims to develop students' academic writing competency; each instructor who teaches the course chooses a topic that serves as a prompt for discussion and a range of in-class and out-of-class writing assignments. One version focuses on narratives of health, illness, and well-being in the Hispanic world—a topic that lends itself to the incorporation of sustainability, as students explore the relation between traditional and Western medicine, the importance of botanical remedies, or the role of the shaman (Stolley).

Advanced-level seminars, including the seminar on border spaces between the United States and Mexico, also become opportunities for addressing sustainability. In the advanced course titled Green with Love: Sustainability Discourse in Latin American-US Media, developed in the Piedmont Project, students were challenged to consider sustainability as the convergence of environmental, social, and economic forces and to develop an awareness of sustainability as a cultural story told in both hemispheres as a microcosmic representation of broader global discourse (Reber). Examples were drawn from film, television, advertising, and other forms of cultural and political discourse, including María Victoria Menis's 2008 film *La cámara oscura* ("The Darkroom"), James Cameron's 2009 blockbuster *Avatar*, and green urban planning projects, such as La Felicidad Ciudad Parque in Bogotá, Colombia. The use of materials in both Spanish and English serves as a reminder of a shared hemispheric concern with issues of sustainability but does not detract from the focus on students' written and oral interventions in Spanish as the target language of the class.

Another undergraduate seminar, Nature in the New World, explored how the geography, flora, and fauna of the New World inspired and challenged the imagination over time (Stolley). Separate units focused on the ways in which nature and natural history figured in sixteenth- and seventeenth-century geographical, commercial, and cultural expansion; the role that enlightened science played in eighteenth-century debates about the alleged inferiority of New World species; nineteenth-century polemics about *civilización y barbarie* ("civilization and barbarism") and the struggle between *ciudad y campo* ("city and countryside"); and contemporary narratives about the commodification of nature, from mining to ecotourism. Students studied representations of nature in texts ranging from Christopher Columbus's 1493 letter to Charles Darwin's *Voyage of the Beagle* and Pablo Neruda's "Alturas de Machu Picchu"; they analyzed the filmic treatment of nature in Werner Herzog's *Fitzcarraldo*, Terrence Malik's *The New World*, and Icíar Bollaín's *También la lluvia* ("Even the Rain"). They learned about non-Western approaches to nature through visits to the Ancient Americas galleries of Emory University's Michael C. Carlos Museum, where a colleague from the Department of Art History helped students see nature through Amerindian eyes as they studied artifacts such as a two-thousand-year-old bat-shaped ceramic flute from Central America, a Mesoamerican incense burner adorned with a figure of a sun god or jaguar god, and a paccha (ritual watering vessel from the Andes).

Graduate students in Spanish, meanwhile, have found the Piedmont Project extremely beneficial in providing an introduction to sustainability studies and literary ecocriticism, offering opportunities for pedagogical training such as course development, and granting additional professional credentials. One student was able to use her Piedmont syllabus on early modern Spanish representations of the *hortus conclusus* ("enclosed garden") as a point of departure for a course she later developed as an assistant professor, titled Gardens, Justice, and Sustainability in Early Modern Spain (Boyle).

This course explored the relations between early modern Spaniards—Jews, Muslims, and Catholics—and their natural world and was later redesigned to focus on gardens, herbs, and healing, the subject of a second book project.

A graduate version of the Nature in the New World seminar described above provided doctoral students with an overview of the key topics and theoretical issues in ecocriticism, or green cultural studies (Stolley). A joint meeting with faculty and students from another doctoral seminar, on Metropolitan Cultures and the Urban Imaginary, offered by Hazel Gold, was an opportunity to consider the convergence and divergence of ways of viewing the relation between urban and natural spaces in Spanish America and Spain. Final projects for the graduate seminar included syllabi for courses that students would offer at future points in their careers; others led to professional presentations. Continuing the sustainability focus into the graduate curriculum serves to train the trainers; in other words, graduate students are encouraged to develop competency in a topic of relevance and importance for today's students, thus positioning them to compete more successfully on the job market.

Thinking Sustainability in Many Languages

The development of sustainability-infused curricula in modern languages at Emory as a result of faculty involvement in the Piedmont Project has led to cross-disciplinary idea sharing, innovative course designs, and strategies for imbuing courses across the continuum of learning (from language-acquisition classes to advanced undergraduate and graduate seminars in literature and culture) with sustainability-focused content. This initiative has served as an impetus to revise and reenergize the curriculum along the lines advocated by the Modern Language Association (MLA) report, "Foreign Languages and Higher Education: New Structures for a Changed World," by encouraging faculty to experiment with approaches that are both instrumentalist (in the best sense of the world) and constitutive, by breaking down divisions between the language curriculum and the literature (or upper-level) curriculum, and by encouraging collaboration between tenure- and lecture-track faculty. Translingual and transcultural competency is encouraged by using sustainability as a lens through which to explore "differences in meaning, mentality, and worldview" (MLA Ad Hoc Committee), and this carries over into courses taught in English, including in the social sciences and sciences. These courses provide expanded visibility for the study of language and culture, and they generate new collaborations and initiatives that strengthen our shared teaching and research mission.

Heidi Bostic, writing in *The Chronicle of Higher Education* about the important role the humanities can play in increasing ecocultural awareness, concludes, "The world needs new narratives capable of situating and conveying to a global audience the challenges we share. Such narratives could direct and motivate action, foster solidarity, and help us reimagine who, when, and where we are: earthbound, sharing a fragile planet and an uncertain future." The Piedmont Project has supported us in writing a new narrative about the teaching of languages and cultures at all levels at Emory: undergraduate and graduate education; faculty teaching, research, and service; and community outreach. Although not every institution has the human and material resources to mount such an effort, our experience encourages us to believe that similar initiatives are possible within a wide range of institutional structures. The key elements are collaboration, interdisciplinarity, and a willingness to experiment. In the process, existing courses are retooled, pilot courses evolve into regular offerings, and small courses may be scaled up or taught collaboratively between different language programs. New faculty relationships are forged, and community partners bring outside energy and increased visibility to the modern language curriculum and to the campus at large.

"Verde que te quiero verde" ("Green, how I want you green"), wrote the Spanish poet Federico García Lorca. His words capture the energy and passion that the Piedmont Project has brought to Emory's exploration of how local contexts and relationships, lived through cultures and languages, inform our understanding of global sustainability.

NOTES

1. Unless otherwise noted, references to syllabi and reflections on the experience of the Piedmont Project are based on information available at the Emory University Web site for the Piedmont Project (piedmont.emory.edu), augmented through commentary and updated or additional syllabi supplied to the authors by the professors. The syllabi that can be accessed through this Web site are included in the works-cited list ("Participant Statements"), and others are available on request.

2. Among the accolades: the university was most recently recognized in 2015 by *BestColleges.com* as one of the greenest universities in the United States based on its sustainability-related academic offerings and its eighth-place ranking (of

240 schools) by the Association for the Advancement of Sustainability in Higher Education ("Greenest Universities").

3. Oxford College is a two-year college located on Emory's original campus in Oxford, Georgia. Once students complete their time at Oxford, they continue their studies at Emory's main campus in Atlanta, and faculty at both campuses work closely together to ensure the continuity of students' academic experiences.

4. The graduate student version of the Piedmont Project, funded mainly by the Laney Graduate School, consists of a one-day workshop (and in some years, a follow-up field trip) for ten to seventeen participants who develop a sample syllabus or laboratory exercise, connecting material from their own fields with sustainability issues.

5. French majors and minors have the option to turn in their papers in French (two short response papers and a longer final research paper).

6. Institutions of higher education benefit greatly from faculty development programs such as the Piedmont Project, as evidenced by the study by Condon et al.

7. The Confucius Institute in Atlanta was reconfigured in 2012, and the partnership with Atlanta Public Schools was discontinued.

8. Note that historically these scholarly gardens were accessible to men only, thus creating gendered and exclusionary spaces for this kind of contemplation, whereas modern versions open up the experience to wider participation, a move that is consonant with the project described here of introducing middle school students in Atlanta to these concepts.

9. In some ways, the course functions like a first-year seminar taught in Spanish.

10. A Public Broadcasting System (PBS) report from 2010 highlights the problems of infrastructure on Buford Highway that led to thirty deaths in the previous decade and explores the ongoing efforts to retrofit an area built to accommodate cars. See *"Blueprint."*

WORKS CITED

Barlett, Peggy F., and Geoffrey W. Chase, editors. *Sustainability in Higher Education: Stories and Strategies for Transformation.* MIT P, 2013.

Barlett, Peggy F., and Ann Rappaport. "Long-Term Impacts of Faculty Development Programs: The Experience of Teli and Piedmont." *College Teaching,* vol. 57, no. 2, Spring 2009, pp. 73–82.

"Blueprint America Special Report: Dangerous Crossing." *Need to Know,* Public Broadcasting System (PBS). *YouTube,* uploaded by PBS, 26 July 2010, youtu.be/rqIVBI -QJek. Accessed 5 May 2016.

Bostic, Heidi. "The Humanities Must Engage Global Grand Challenges." *The Chronicle of Higher Education,* 30 Mar. 2016, www.chronicle.com/article/The-Humanities -Must-Engage/235902.

Boyle, Margaret. "Piedmont Project." E-mail message to Karen Stolley, 17 June 2015.

Cabeza de Vaca, Alvar Núñez. *Chronicle of the Narváez Expedition: Translation of La Relación.* Edited by Ilan Stavans, translated by David Frye, W. W. Norton, 2013.

Condon, William, et al. *Faculty Development and Student Learning: Assessing the Connections.* Indiana UP, 2016.

Dana, Catherine. "Sustainability in France and the French Caribbean." *Piedmont Project,* Emory University, 2011–14, piedmont.emory.edu/documents/2011/ Dana_2011.pdf.

Dannenberg, Andrew, et al. *Making Healthy Places: Designing and Building for Health, Well-being, and Sustainability.* Island Press, 2011.

Day, Herman E., and John B. Cobb, Jr. *For the Common Good: Redirecting the Economy Toward Community, the Environment, and a Sustainable Future.* Beacon Press, 1989.

Dillman, Lisa. "Sustainability and the Environment." *Piedmont Project*, Emory University, 2011–14, piedmont.emory.edu/documents/2008/Dillman.pdf.

García Lorca, Federico. "Romance sonámbulo." *Poets.org*, Academy of American Poets, www.poets.org/poetsorg/poem/romance-sonambulo. Accessed 13 Sept. 2018.

"Greenest Universities." *BestColleges.com*, 2018, www.bestcolleges.com/features/greenest-universities/. Accessed 13 Sept. 2018.

Hartfield-Méndez, Vialla. "Drawing the Line: The Mexico-U.S. Frontera and Its Stories." *Piedmont Project*, Emory University, 2011–14, piedmont.emory.edu/documents/2007/Hartfield-Mendez.pdf.

Legge, James. *The Teaching of Confucius.* El Paso Norte Press, 2005.

Li, Hong. "Noodle Narratives on the Silk Road: A Cultural Exploration of China and Italy through Noodles." *Piedmont Project*, Emory University, 2011–14, piedmont.emory.edu/documents/2017/Li2017.pdf.

Loichot, Valérie. "Caribbean Literature and the Environment." *Piedmont Project*, Emory University, 2011–14, piedmont.emory.edu/documents/2009/Loichot.pdf.

Mann, Charles C. *1491: New Revelations of the Americas before Columbus.* Alfred A. Knopf, 2005.

Maxim, Hiram. "Intermediate German I: Coming of Age through the Ages." *Piedmont Project*, Emory University, 2011–14, piedmont.emory.edu/MaximComing-of-age.pdf.

MLA Ad Hoc Committee on Foreign Languages. "Foreign Languages and Higher Education: New Structures for a Changed World." *Profession*, 2007, pp. 234–45. Modern Language Association of America, 2007, www.mla.org/Resources/Research/Surveys-Reports-and-Other-Documents/Teaching-Enrollments-and-Programs/Foreign-Languages-and-Higher-Education-New-Structures-for-a-Changed-World. Accessed 13 Sept. 2018.

Muratore, Simone. "Italian Food in Literature, Film and Culture." *Piedmont Project*, Emory University, 2011–14, piedmont.emory.edu/documents/2010/Muratore.pdf.

"Noodle Narratives on the Silk Road: A Cultural Exploration of China and Italy through Noodles." *ECLC (Emory College Language Center) Newsletter*, Winter 2014–15, p. 8. *ScholarBlogs*, scholarblogs.emory.edu/noodles. Accessed 13 Sept. 2018.

"Participant Statements and Syllabi." *Piedmont Project.* Emory University, 2017, piedmont.emory.edu/syllabi.html.

Reber, Dierdra. "Ecological Imperialism: Nature and Power in Latin America." *Piedmont Project*, Emory University, 2011–14, piedmont.emory.edu/documents/2007/Reber.pdf.

Ristaino, Christine. "How We Learn." *Piedmont Project*, Emory University, 2011–14, piedmont.emory.edu/documents/2010/Ristaino.pdf.

Schaumann, Caroline. "Screening Nature." *Piedmont Project*, Emory University, 2011–14, piedmont.emory.edu/documents/2010/Schaumann.pdf.

Stolley, Karen. "Nature in the New World: Reading Green in Latin America." *Piedmont Project*, Emory University, 2011–14, piedmont.emory.edu/documents/2011/Stolley_2011.pdf.

Takeda, Noriko. "Advanced Language and Cultural Studies II: Life after the Kanto-Tohoku Earthquake in 2011." *Piedmont Project*, Emory University, 2011–14, piedmont.emory.edu/documents/2011/Takeda_2011.pdf.

Charlotte Ann Melin
and Maggie A. Broner | # Coda

What does it mean to be a truly global citizen in the twenty-first century, and how does a commitment to the future that term implies challenge us to transform higher education, in particular foreign language programs? As the essays in this collection compellingly explain, one answer to this question begins with the recognition that foreign languages and environmental thinking belong together at every level of the curriculum. Although the aspiration of supporting learners in the development of "translingual and transcultural competency" has contributed broadly to a revisioning of the educational landscape since the Modern Language Association (MLA) Ad Hoc Committee report "Foreign Languages and Higher Education: New Structures for a Changed World" (237), the present volume attests that we have seen only the start of this revitalization process. New ways of teaching and learning that are collaborative, digital, experiential, and interdisciplinary are fostering educational initiatives open to the creative experimentation of teachers and the active agency of students. These transformative efforts, in turn, lead to a deeper understanding of the practices and perspectives of other cultures while strengthening the connection between classroom praxis and overarching learning outcomes (see Melin, "Speaking" 108). The emphasis the collection's essays place on literacies (both language and environmental literacy) acknowledges a defining shift in perspective on the part of faculty members in all areas of disciplinary expertise toward multiliteracies frameworks that acknowledge the deep interdependence of our world—its language, culture, society, history, and environment. The projects described here offer ways of learning and teaching that promote the development of complex thinking in tandem with language learning and that respond to calls circulating in the profession since the 1990s for educational change (see Kramsch, *Context*; Byrnes; Kern; Swaffar and Arens; Paesani et al.). Their granular perspective on foreign language education reveals the intellectual resilience of faculty members, the strengths of reflective teaching practices, and the benefits of ongoing curricular refinement.

These essays present a rich array of initiatives that arose largely in the aftermath of the 2008 financial crisis. Strikingly, however, it is not the rhetoric of higher education that defines them (e.g., accountability, assessment, career readiness, liberal education requirements, lifelong learning, engagement, student learning outcomes), nor fear that the humanities occupy a precarious position, but the spirited conviction that foreign languages have an important role to play in creating a sustainable world—they grow in the space where the local and global converge. The essays offer a wealth of new models for teaching and learning oriented to technology and authentic materials to study abroad, group projects conceived for millennial students, individualized tasks, and place-based assignments. Many of the authors voice deeply personal as well as professional commitments to asking difficult questions that engage us in conversations about social values and the "slow violence" Rob Nixon has incisively critiqued. These discussions expand cultural and intellectual diversity on campus and make possible the work of the humanities in the world.

In other words, teaching for and about foreign languages and the environment brings out the best the humanities have to offer: the capacity to engage with the grand challenges society faces today without losing sight of their historical underpinnings or ethical dimensions. It emphasizes that language is fundamental to what it means to be human and recognizes that different ways of knowing indelibly shape how we see our world. It is often said, frequently with reference to the academic divide recognized by C. P. Snow in *The Two Cultures*, that the humanities ask questions and prize soft skills, whereas the sciences look for answers and hard evidence. Though this paradigm simplifies the actual complexity of disciplines, the first decades of the twenty-first century have made clear that the world we inhabit is profoundly relational, shaped by networks, intersectionality, and media of every kind—and thus in great need of humanities perspectives.

As Stephanie LeMenager and Stephanie Foote observe, "The humanities are especially suited to speak to the rhetoric of crisis and to problems of futurity and scale because they demand that we understand how narratives about place, about value, and about the relation of social actors to those ideas are made" (576). For this process, a more robust focus on content at all levels of language learning (in this case environmental thinking and sustainability literacy) is crucial to transforming the curriculum.

The essays in this volume make a strong case for the foreign languages as a place to develop sustainability literacy in a way that addresses fundamental educational issues raised in the documents and reports of our profession. Tangentially or overtly, many refer to the American Council on the Teaching of Foreign Languages (ACTFL) national standards, as well as MLA white papers and reports on student enrollments and majors (NSFLEP; MLA Ad Hoc Committee; MLA Office of Research; MLA Teagle Foundation; Goldberg et al.). In particular the MLA report, published more than a decade ago, "Foreign Languages and Higher Education: New Structures for a Changed World" challenges programs to break free from disciplinary silos and close the gap between language courses and those at the major level. Offering a number of suggestions to entice students to enroll in advanced language courses and develop expanded linguistic and cultural competencies, it recommends a number of steps, among them that language programs should involve more subject areas and encourage interdisciplinary collaboration (239–40). A central claim in the report is the need to replace the "two-tiered language-literature structure with a broader curriculum in which language, culture, and literature are taught as a continuous whole" (237). Despite early cautionary notes that it could have gone farther and done even more to address student needs (Grabe 11), the report on foreign languages in higher education has been a catalyst for conversations about reforming departmental structures and curricula, crossing interdisciplinary boundaries, and changing student demographics. Two years later, the MLA released its *Report to the Teagle Foundation on the Undergraduate Major in Language and Literature*, which likewise cites the need for language majors to reach beyond the traditional literature curriculum and across disciplinary boundaries (MLA Teagle Foundation 3) and include at least one interdisciplinary course (8). At the same time, the number of students with a second major in a foreign language was increasing (MLA Office of Research 2). This trend, plus the movement at some institutions toward minors and alternative credentialing (certificates, online learning, and career-related experiences), call us to rethink how and what we teach in our classes. The essays in this collection have taken on the task of making those aspirational calls more real.

The urgency for change now emerges from the trends documented by the MLA Office of Research report, *Data on Second Majors in Language and Literature, 2001–2013*, which addresses the impact of changing enrollment patterns in foreign language programs. This report notes a general increase from 28.0% to 38.6% between 2001 and 2013 of second majors in foreign languages (1), showing that they "outstrip other disciplines significantly in the number of second majors" (2). These national trends confirm what has been widely seen elsewhere: more than ever, students who study foreign languages bring a multidisciplinary lens to the foreign language classroom, and yet it is not clear, as Maggie A. Broner suggests in her essay in this volume, whether our courses attract students to bring "their whole selves" into our classes and programs.

Students, and indeed some faculty members and administrators, continue to view languages as silo disciplines disconnected from other areas of study. When asked about the likelihood of achieving the goals of the national standards' five Cs (Communication, Cultures, Connections, Comparisons, and Communities), many undergraduates in their first two years consider language study a discrete experience (Magnan et al. 102). Incoming college students ranked the Connections standard as the one they are least likely to achieve, because they did not expect to learn anything new in the foreign language since "the information they needed was readily available in English" (Magnan et al. 121). And while it has been noted that what students want does not necessarily coincide with the goals of foreign language instructors in higher education (Kramsch, "Teaching" 302), nor should it, program viability depends on alignment with institutional mission and, ultimately, enrollments. When we talk to students intentionally about the "imperative for interdisciplinarity" in a foreign language (Melin, "Program Sustainability" 113), we openly invite them to bring their expertise in other areas into our classrooms. The case studies presented here offer an alternative approach: students can be engaged in and excited about foreign languages when the endeavor is tied to a genuine need to communicate with others about big questions. Such work involves the study of multimodal and interdisciplinary content. When learning occurs in this way, students develop empathy for others and are empowered to become agents of change in their own communities.

More broadly, students who come from the natural and social sciences are pushing language faculty members to move beyond traditional offerings in literature, culture, and linguistics. The challenge is how to address the needs of that changing student population with the expertise we currently have in our departments, where most faculty members have training and experience in literature, and a few in linguistics, cultural studies, or second language acquisition (VanPatten). Adapting to this paradigm shift requires faculty members to embrace a "culture of experimentation" (Brown 36) and to develop student-oriented curricula and courses (Firth and Wagner), where teachers step away from the role of expert and manager into that of active collaborator and guide to students as they learn to carry out research, analysis, and interpretation (Kramsch, "Teaching" 308; Byrnes et al. 21).

Recently many discussions in higher education have focused on creativity and innovation (NSFLEP; Kramsch "Teaching"; Byrnes et al.; Pfeiffer and Byrnes), often in relation to a multiliteracies approach (Swaffar and Arens; Paesani et al.). Beyond the academy, creativity has been identified as a high-priority skill for future leaders as well ("Capitalizing on Complexity"). Echoing these discussions, the *Framework for Twenty-First Century Learning* considers "communication, collaboration, critical thinking, problem solving, creativity and innovation" to be essential skills that students will need to live and work in a complex world (3). The revised *World-Readiness Standards for Learning Languages*, too, reflects this trend with the Connection goal and specifically includes creativity.[1]

Although higher education seems poised to become a locus for innovation and the development of creativity, with Claire Kramsch stating that we are more innovative than ever ("Teaching" 296), academia is not above reproach for stifling creativity at times (Robinson). As Joyce Hwee Ling Koh and coauthors note, despite changes in curriculum and pedagogies, the current educational system is still set up to develop deep subject knowledge before students are encouraged to "embark in knowledge creation enterprises. . . . Where the overemphasis on learning may hinder the development of creativity" (10). This reluctance to "break with some disciplinary legacies" (Halberstram 10), however, reinforces students' tendencies to view their subjects as compartmentalized. The essays in this collection show how disciplinary silos can instead be transcended—at the course level (Broner;

Carrico; Chikamatsu; Cisneros; Fuente; Erdem Mete; Wang), in departmental and interdepartmental curricular offerings (Cummins; Kisselev and Comer; Hodge), and on the institutional plane (Barbas-Rhoden, Brunow, and Newman; Hartfield-Méndez, Stolley, and Li).

A major challenge to the development of creativity in foreign language classrooms is how to operationalize its practice. Development of the kind of innovative curriculum proposed in the MLA reports requires a fundamental revamping of course design and realignment of learning outcomes with theory, method, and approach. Such revisions culminate in new principles for structuring the delivery of course content. Broner, María J. de la Fuente, and Haidan Wang speak directly to the reality that teaching environmental topics leads us to innovative pedagogies that intentionally and overtly develop critical as well as creative thinking. These approaches include design thinking (Broner), systems thinking (Fuente), place-based learning (Noodin), project-based learning (Wang), and other experimental practices that transform the curriculum. Such innovative pedagogies address the needs of users (students), because they employ learner-centered teaching. Broner describes in detail one such model (design thinking) of how a pedagogy that centers on teaching students ways to unearth the unmet needs of users develops student agency by inviting them to be producers of knowledge and become agents of change in their own communities. Other essays in the collection (Carrico, Cisneros, Erdem Mete), meanwhile, propose expanding tools for analysis and interpretation through the incorporation of ecocritical perspectives and emphasis on the literary and cultural dimensions of environmental awareness. Several of these essays link environmental literacy with intercultural competence as well (especially Erdem Mete).

What becomes clear when the collection is viewed as a whole is that complementary perspectives transcend the diverse initiatives the authors describe and bridge differences in subject expertise. While it is true that the vast majority of authors in this collection have literary backgrounds, they are open to relating their curricular initiatives to second language acquisition (SLA) perspectives, and Fuente in particular spells out how SLA constructs (like the interaction and output hypotheses) can serve as guiding principles. This approach presumes a broad, professional community of practice; it is a promising trend and one way to bridge the SLA and literature gap identified by previous researchers (Byrnes; VanPatten). What emerges from these reciprocal forays into SLA and literary-cultural studies by the authors in this book is the recognition that we are all deeply invested in teaching languages and in helping our students acquire high levels of communicative and critical thinking competency. Familiarity with the documents of our profession (MLA Ad Hoc Committee; MLA Office of Research; MLA Teagle Foundation; *ACTFL Proficiency Guidelines*; *College Learning*) creates common ground and expansively affects the way we approach foreign language teaching. A concurrent commitment to interdisciplinarity and holistic thinking about the role of the humanities in education is equally essential.

There is no question that our field is coming to the realization that the future is in interdisciplinary thinking and teaching, and this volume presents a myriad of ways in which it can be accomplished. In SLA circles, the focus on transdisciplinary thinking has recently come to the forefront in the Douglas Fir Group report, which calls on researchers "to think integratively" in crossing disciplinary boundaries (38). Although the report does not encompass pedagogical innovation of the kind proposed here, the challenge of interdisciplinary and transdisciplinary thinking, teaching, and research that it recognizes remains the same for faculty members active in other areas: the fear of taking risks may lead to avoidance at the prospect of acquiring new theories (e.g., ecocriticism, SLA), new methods (e.g., design thinking, systems thinking, place-based study, and engaged learning), new content (e.g., environmental studies), and the like. In response, this volume presents an ambitious agenda that shows how small pilot initiatives can be extended beyond individual course experimentation to the curriculum as a whole. It proposes to do so by reshaping the perceived rigidity of the foreign language curriculum, and by focusing on our common enterprise as educators.

In *Remapping the Foreign Language Curriculum*, Janet Swaffar and Katherine Arens make a convincing case for educational reform through a transformation of the curriculum that fundamentally changes the way we conceive of ourselves as teacher-scholars. Much is at stake in their argument that "the professional face of teaching literature, culture, and language needs to be rethought as the teaching of multiple literacies: the ability to engage with culture, with its forms of knowledge and communication, and with its various publics" (xii). Such an approach defines the identities of foreign language programs by establishing aspirations for their work that go beyond the study of language for purely communicative or instrumental purposes or for the teaching of literature as traditional canon. The special concern

Remapping has with staging learners' encounters with texts through careful scaffolding enables critical thinking about sociocultural and aesthetic dimensions and has important implications in terms of both daily praxis in the classroom and, more broadly, the overall vertical articulation of the curriculum. The endorsement Swaffar and Arens give to an expanded notion of texts urges foreign language programs to look beyond high-culture literature in designing curricula. It includes multiple genre types and diverse media forms while emphasizing the centrality of texts to the humanities.

What is becoming increasingly clear, however, is the need for foreign language programs to adapt in ever more nimble ways to changes in higher education and pressures on the humanities. Higher education in the twenty-first century is increasingly characterized by a so-called mosaic curriculum, which makes it difficult to maintain extended sequences of tightly coordinated courses. These structural challenges point to a need to develop new forms of educational coherence that will allow for further evolution. Instead of advocating a particular institutional or programmatic curricular structure, the present volume, *Foreign Language Teaching and the Environment*, places emphasis on tested practitioner perspectives and transferrable practices of teaching and learning. Reflective teaching and professional development for teachers is vital for this evolution. From the essays, and from our individual experiences as teachers and collaborators, four principles emerge that can support educational transformation: work toward high levels of language ability involves complexity and leads to an emphasis on content, English has a role in our classrooms, experiential and engaged learning play an intrinsic role in teaching about the environment and sustainability issues, and it is vitally important to transcend silos by embracing interdisciplinary perspectives and methodologies.

One issue that surfaces in many of the essays is the question of how, when, and why to use English in the classroom. As Glenn S. Levine convincingly argues, the use of English in the foreign language classroom is both common and appropriate as a means to enable learners to engage with intellectual, conceptually difficult content that exceeds their linguistic ability at a given point in time. Rather than stigmatizing the use of English in foreign language courses, Levine recommends educators regard it as a tool to be judiciously used—a means to give learners access to background and context, to enable communication in ways that will eventually lead to communication in the target language, and to facilitate students' agency in their own learning. Levine's conclusions about the realities of the conditions that surround second language acquisition complement our understanding of what authentic communication involves in teaching and learning contexts by broadening the definition to take into account the perspective of inter-cultural communicative competence proposed by Michael Byram. Open-ness to mixed language use in the classroom follows from the conclusions reached by Kramsch that our students experience the materials they are learning through perspectives and collaborative negotiation (*Context*) and are immersed in the process of developing identities as multilingual speak-ers (Kramsch, *Multilingual Subject*). Furthermore, Ofelia García proposes that *translanguaging* in our classrooms—that is, using more than one language and symbolic code—is part of the natural practices of bilinguals (42–72). Although the authors in this collection do not refer to translanguaging per se, part of the tension and challenge caused by the use of English would be mitigated by acknowledging that what we are doing in our classrooms is an enactment of practices that should be normalized.

Numerous essays in this collection touch directly or indirectly on this point, all the while reaffirming the importance of maximized use of the target language. Thomas P. Hodge, in describing the opportunities afforded by Wellesley's Lake Baikal course, makes clear that the dual English-Russian target language adds depth to the overall learning experience and opens the course to students who have not attained advanced language skills at a point when they can be inspired to pursue further studies. Nobuko Chikamatsu describes a model for a team-taught course that builds on the expertise of instructors from multiple disciplines and includes comparative work with bilingual materials. Patricia W. Cummins provides rich examples of how student involvement in a transnational sister cities project, medical transla-tion, and community outreach situates learners in a real-world context in which multilingualism (and fluid English–other language interactions) is the norm. Vialla Hartfield-Méndez, Karen Stolley, and Hong Li show how Emory's Piedmont Project, which includes robust options for community-engagement activities, serves students by creating connections between their academic learning and the real world. Meanwhile, other essays in the collection emphasize just as strongly the importance of engagement with authentic materials through extensive target-language use as foundational to the development of higher-level linguistic skills applicable to the study of literature, culture, and languages for special purposes (Wang for business Chinese; Kisselev and Comer in a Russian flagship program).

The candor of these essays about the discussions that led to the authors' initiatives reveals the salience of several factors for success: pragmatism in conceiving initiative scope (identifying potential funding sources and possible obstacles), backward design (starting the planning process with desired outcomes), needs assessment (identifying student, institutional, and community interests), strategic planning (determining needs for projects of varying lengths), collaboration (finding allies who can build a support system in a department or program, at the institutional level, or through the wider profession), and advanced decision-making about how to monitor the success of the initiative (developing student learning outcomes or other metrics). The essays also highlight three dimensions we consider crucial to combining foreign language teaching with a focus on the environment: getting started, content, and stories.

Getting Started

The collection offers an abundance of ideas and entry points for creating environmentally focused and sustainability-infused courses that can become fertile ground for experimentation. Such pilot initiatives can serve as models to be adopted and expanded. Special topics courses seem to be relatively easy points of entry into well-established program curricula (e.g., for Spanish, see Broner; Fuente; for French, see Carrico). For Broner and Abbey Carrico, this opening occurred on purpose, since these courses were already envisioned to accommodate different topics, one of which could be sustainability. The ubiquitous conversation class that Fuente redesigned thus became a place for experimenting with ways of teaching sustainability in order to emphasize content without sacrificing skills development. Wang found a more modest opening by redesigning a unit rather than a whole course. Cisneros posits the challenge that literature texts can be analyzed through an ecocritical lens, hence changing the theory as opposed to the texts themselves. Hodge found his opportunity in an off-campus interdisciplinary team-taught course at Lake Baikal in Russia. Chikamatsu recognized the opening that developed in the wake of the Fukushima earthquake, which prompted the design of an advanced Japanese language course around the topics of the 2011 tsunami and nuclear plant disaster. Olesya Kisselev and Bill Comer located their chance by inserting their course on environmental sustainability into a Russian flagship program through general education curriculum requirements.

Place of Content

A common thread running through the essays is renewed emphasis on content. Content is not just a conduit to present grammar or functional language; rather, content becomes the central feature of courses that are delivered and processed through a foreign language. If the goal of the foreign language course is to infuse more environmental topics (ultimately with the intent of developing sustainability literacy), content cannot stay on the periphery of foreign language instruction. To this end, several authors frame their projects in terms of content-based instruction models and deal with the challenge of teaching content while at the same time focusing on language (Carrico; Chikamatsu; Fuente). Kisselev and Comer propose Roy Lyster's "counterbalanced instruction" as one promising model for this approach. All the essays stress the importance of infusing more content into foreign languages, even at the earliest levels (Barbas-Rhoden, Brunow, and Newman)—a priority that Heidi Byrnes has continuously stressed. This emphasis on content requires a rethinking of how authentic texts are used in foreign language instruction—as well as of materials written in English; it asks us to pay particular attention to the role of textbooks and assumes the need to supplement with additional material (Wang). All these examples highlight the importance of engaging students not only with language work but also with content.

The Power of Stories

The centrality of content also necessitates a renewed emphasis on vocabulary acquisition and listening-reading skills and ultimately highlights the efficacy of narratives for teaching and learning. In particular, Noodin; Erdem Mete; Chikamatsu; and Wang remind us of the power of words in cultivating sustainability literacy. Noodin makes a compelling case for the importance of understanding language differences as they relate to a "grammar of environmentalism," which creates new ways of looking at and understanding concepts. Illustrating this notion with one very compelling case, she explains what it means for language teaching to make the distinction between "I love water" and the contrasting term in Anishinaabemowin, "niibi gizaagin," which denotes "water, I love you." In the same vein, Defne Erdem Mete reminds us of the power of idioms and proposes teaching Turkish proverbs as one way to instill intercultural competence while fostering empathy and environmental literacy. Chikamatsu highlights how, in the aftermath of the 3/11 earthquake in Japan, rare words like *mizo* ("unprecedented") or *sotegai* ("unimaginable") have become part of the everyday lexicon of Japanese speakers, helping Japanese people to imagine the "unimaginable." In discussing the Comparison standard, Wang shows how students in a Chinese class that included environmental literacy came to see the word "development" as having broad implications for both economic progress and environmental protection in China.

Whether the stories reside in words and phrases, or in the kinds of deep metanarratives that Patricia Anne Simpson and Marc Mueller show to be an underlying feature of German culture, their historical dimensions, social complexity, and memorability make them fascinating to curious students. Underscoring the importance of stories for the human-centered work of interpretation, Broner describes how oral interviews changed the perspectives of students learning about sustainable food practices in Latin America. Finally, Annette Sampon-Nicolas shows how in a course that begins with the "stories" of historical French and contemporary francophone literature, students end up through a Kiva microfinance activity as active participants in human stories in the present.

Language, literature, and culture are at the core of what it means to be human and of humanities perspectives, which more than ever in the twenty-first century will need to engage with the forms of knowledge present in other fields rather than remaining in isolation, as *Foreign Language Teaching and the Environment* proposes. Interdisciplinarity is a true imperative, and yet such interdisciplinarity constitutes a challenge to foreign language education, because we as teachers, and our students as learners, begin our work together in the intensely disciplinary context of language. The essays in this collection seek to demonstrate the tenets that by starting small, working collaboratively, and persisting, foreign language programs can accelerate far-reaching transformations. The viability of our programs depends on our very ability to adapt and change, as the examples of curricular innovation represented here abundantly show.

NOTE

1. "Learners build, reinforce, and expand their knowledge of other disciplines while using the language to develop critical thinking and to solve problems *creatively*" (Summary of *World-Readiness Standards*; our emphasis).

WORKS CITED

ACTFL Proficiency Guidelines 2012. American Council on the Teaching of Foreign Languages (ACTFL), 2012, www.actfl.org/sites/default/files/pdfs/public/ACTFL ProficiencyGuidelines2012_FINAL.pdf. Accessed 6 Jan. 2015.

Broner, Maggie A. "Sustainability, Design Thinking, and Spanish: Unleashing Students' Creativity to Understand Sustainability." Center for Second Language Studies, Vanderbilt University, Nashville, TN, 2015. Lecture.

Brown, Tim. *Change by Design.* Harper Business, 2009.

Byram, Michael. *Teaching and Assessing Intercultural Communicative Competence.* Multilingual Matters, 1997.

Byrnes, Heidi. "Constructing Curricula in Collegiate Foreign Language Departments." *Learning Foreign and Second Languages: Perspectives in Research and Scholarship,* edited by Byrnes, Modern Language Association of America, 1998, pp. 262–95.

Byrnes, Heidi, et al. *Realizing Advanced Foreign Language Writing Development in Collegiate Education: Curricular Design, Pedagogy, Assessment.* Special issue of *The Modern Language Journal,* vol. 94, no. s1, 2010.

"Capitalizing on Complexity: Insights from the Global Chief Executive Officer Survey." *IBM,* 2010, www.ibm.com/downloads/cas/1VZV5X8J.

College Learning for the New Global Century. Association of American Colleges and Universities (AAC&U), 2007, www.aacu.org/sites/default/files/files/LEAP/Global Century_final.pdf. Accessed 5 May 2015.

The Douglas Fir Group. "A Transdisciplinary Framework for SLA in a Multilingual World." *The Modern Language Journal,* vol. 100, supplement, 2016, pp. 19–47.

Firth, Alan, and Johannes Wagner. "On Discourse, Communication, and (Some) Fundamental Concepts in SLA Research." *The Modern Language Journal,* vol. 81, no. 3 1997, pp. 285–300.

Framework for Twenty-First Century Learning. Partnership for Twenty-First-Century Learning, 2016, www.p21.org/our-work/p21-framework. Accessed 15 May 2015.

García, Ofelia. *Bilingual Education in the Twenty-First Century: A Global Perspective.* Wiley-Blackwell, 2009.

Goldberg, David, et al. *Enrollments in Languages Other Than English in United States Institutions of Higher Education, Fall 2013.* Modern Language Association of America, 2015, apps.mla.org/pdf/2013_enrollment_survey.pdf. Accessed 28 Dec. 2015.

Grabe, William. "Revisiting the MLA Report on Reconfiguring Foreign Language Programs: The Role of Reading." *Reading in a Foreign Language,* vol. 22, supplement 1, 2010, pp. 11–14.

Halberstram, Jack. "Unlearning." *Profession,* 2012, pp. 9–16.

Kern, Richard. *Literacy and Language Teaching.* Oxford UP, 2000.

Koh, Joyce Hwee Ling, et al. *Design Thinking for Education: Conceptions and Applications in Teaching and Learning.* Springer, 2015.

Kramsch, Claire. *Context and Culture in Language Teaching.* Oxford UP, 1993.

———. *The Multilingual Subject.* Oxford UP, 2009.

———. "Teaching Foreign Languages in an Era of Globalization: Introduction." *The Modern Language Journal,* vol. 98, no. 1, 2014, pp. 296–311.

LeMenager, Stephanie, and Stephanie Foote. "The Sustainable Humanities." *PMLA,* vol. 127, no. 3, 2012, pp. 572–78.

Levine, Glenn S. *Code Choice in the Language Classroom.* Multilingual Matters, 2011.

Lyster, Roy. *Learning and Teaching Languages through Content: A Counterbalanced Approach.* John Benjamins Publishing, 2007.

Magnan, Sally Sieloff, et al. *Goals of Collegiate Learners and the Standards for Foreign Language Learning.* Special issue of *The Modern Language Journal,* vol. 98, supplement, 2014.

Melin, Charlotte. "Program Sustainability through Interdisciplinary Networking: On Connecting Foreign Language Programs with Sustainability Studies and Other Fields." *Transforming Postsecondary Foreign Language Teaching in the United States,* edited by Janet Swaffar and Per Urlaub, Springer, 2014, pp. 103–22.

———. "Speaking the Languages of the Humanities." *A New Deal for the Humanities: Liberal Arts and the Future of Public Education,* edited by Gordon Hutner and Feisal Mohamed, Rutgers UP, 2016, pp. 101–14.

MLA Ad Hoc Committee on Foreign Languages. "Foreign Languages and Higher Education: New Structures for a Changed World." *Profession,* 2007, pp. 234–45.

MLA Office of Research. *Data on Second Majors in Language and Literature, 2001–2013.* Modern Language Association of America, Feb. 2015, www.mla.org/content/download/31117/1320962/2ndmajors200113.pdf. Accessed 13 May 2015.

MLA Teagle Foundation Working Group. *Report to the Teagle Foundation on the Undergraduate Major in Language and Literature.* Modern Language Association of America, 2009, www.mla.org/pdf/2008_mla_whitepaper.pdf. Accesssed 18 July 2013.

Nixon, Rob. *Slow Violence and the Environmentalism of the Poor.* Harvard UP, 2011.

NSFLEP (National Standards in Foreign Language Education Project). *Standards for Foreign Language Learning in the Twenty-First Century.* American Council for the Teaching of Foreign Languages (ACTFL), 2006.

Paesani, Kate, et al. *A Multiliteracies Framework for Collegiate Foreign Language Teaching.* Pearson Education, 2016.

Pfeiffer, Peter C., and Heidi Byrnes. "Curriculum, Learning, and the Identity of Majors: A Case Study of Program Outcomes Evaluation." *Toward Useful Program Evaluation in College Foreign Language Education,* edited by John N. Norris, National Foreign Language Resource Center, 2009, pp. 183–208.

Robinson, Ken. "How Schools Kill Creativity." *TED,* Feb. 2006, www.ted.com/talks/ken_robinson_says_schools_kill_creativity.

Snow, C. P. *The Two Cultures.* Cambridge UP, 1998.

Summary of *World-Readiness Standards for Learning Languages.* American Council on Teaching of Foreign Languages (ACTFL), www.actfl.org/publications/all/world-readiness-standards-learning-languages/standards-summary.

Swaffar, Janet, and Katherine Arens. *Remapping the Foreign Language Curriculum.* Modern Language Association of America, 2005.

VanPatten, Bill. "Where Are the Experts?" *Hispania,* vol. 98, no. 1, 2015, pp. 2–13.

Kiley M. Kost and
Charlotte Ann Melin Key Terms and Concepts

Anthropocene, from the Greek prefix *anthropos-* ("human being") and the marker for recent geologic epochs *-cene*, is a term that describes the current geologic epoch as characterized by human-induced change on a geologic scale. First coined in 2000 by the ecologist Eugene Stoermer and the atmospheric chemist Paul Crutzen, the label has been widely used by humanities scholars and was officially accepted by international geological societies in August 2016. The term itself is often criticized for its overgeneralization of how people contribute to climate change, because it does not take into account the unequal distribution of environmental consequences, but it has proved salient for conceptualizing large-scale human effects on the environment.

Content-based instruction (CBI) and content and language integrated learning (CLIL) are designations for language-teaching approaches that promote the teaching of content parallel to language instruction. In North America, CBI is associated with diverse instructional contexts, including immersion education settings; in Europe, the term CLIL is used similarly to advance outcomes sought in the Common European Framework of Reference for Languages (CEFR). Content-based approaches emphasize the use of authentic materials (those produced for native speakers) to promote purposeful language use, understanding of complex meaning, and extended learning activities as beneficial to learner discovery of the multiple dimensions of language and culture.

Design thinking is a process-oriented approach to problem solving that has been used in education settings and a wide range of business and nonprofit sectors to identify needs and develop solutions that can be progressively refined. It applies the concepts and methodologies of dynamic analysis and planning to solve complex problems. Through the Stanford University Institute of Design, the methodology was extended to K–12 reform initiatives and has attracted attention as a means to revitalize the liberal arts in higher education settings. Design thinking seeks to overcome the limitations of conventional planning protocols by turning to a human-centered approach to problem solving that encourages creativity, intuition, and questioning.

Ecocriticism, an interdisciplinary approach of literary studies that first emerged in the 1990s, explores the relations between literature and the nonhuman environment. Ecocritics examine the various ways the nonhuman world (e.g., nature) is depicted in, and shaped by, literary and cultural texts. Because of its interdisciplinary origins, ecocriticism scholarship uses eclectic methodologies with widely varying practices and approaches. First-wave ecocriticism is exemplified by Lawrence Buell's work on the environmental imagination in literary texts where nature is the object of study, whereas second-wave ecocriticism calls the very concept of nature and what it means to be human into question. The term *ecopoetics*, for example, may be used to foreground the hybrid interrelation of literary and scientific discourses, writerly reflection about the interdependence of culture and nature, or innovative creative work that engages with questions of ecological sensitivity.

Ecopedagogy is a movement associated with critical pedagogy that emphasizes the value of educating planetary citizens. The approach derives from the thinking of Paulo Freire, Moacir Gadotti, Richard Kahn, and others. It advocates forms of education that cultivate practices of sustainability, participatory dialogue, and activism.

Engaged learning (*see also* **service learning**) refers to an educational approach that serves to develop capacities for critical analysis, complex thinking, and contextual awareness. Its features typically include active learning, recursive reflection about the learning process, and work explicitly connecting formal academic study with the real world by means of assignments that encourage the development of civic identity and involvement with the wider community beyond the classroom.

Environmental humanities is the umbrella term used to refer to research fields that consider environmental issues and the complex relations between humans and the environment conducted from the perspective of humanities disciplines. It includes such subfields as ecocriticism and environmental history, as well as inquiry into the ontological, ethical, and social dimensions of environmental issues. Scholarship in this area is characterized by openness to modes of knowledge discovery and methodologies for knowledge production employed in scientific environmental research.

Five Cs: Communication, Cultures, Connections, Comparisons, Communities are goals outlined in the world-readiness standards for learning languages developed by the American Council on the Teaching of Foreign Languages (ACTFL). Used widely in K–12 settings in the United States to establish learning outcomes, they have received increasing attention in higher education. In addition to offering guidance in coordinating achievement expectations with abilities at all proficiency levels, these national standards also recognize the many dimensions of language learning and encourage development of interpersonal, interpretive, and presentational abilities.

Foreign languages across the curriculum (FLAC or **LAC)** is an integrative approach to education that combines course enrollment in diverse disciplines (e.g., the arts, humanities, social sciences, and sciences) with language study. Like writing across the curriculum initiatives, FLAC moves learning into contexts beyond the discrete language-classroom setting. Arrangements usually involve additional course work or certification requirements (e.g., participation in discussion sections, readings in the target language, and additional assignments) designed to facilitate content-rich language use. These practices are promoted by the Consortium for Cultures and Languages Across the Curriculum (CLAC) and regarded by many educators as an important component of an internationalized curriculum.

Genre-based foreign language instruction is an approach to instruction that is effective in raising learner awareness of discourse and usage conventions through exposure to linguistic models. By explicitly introducing common text types (genres) and emphasizing the relation between meaning and content, instructors using a genre-based curriculum can be effective in encouraging complex language by learners and coordinating (i.e., vertically articulating) course content and skills development, particularly with regard to writing and reading.

In the United States, the Georgetown model pioneered by Heidi Byrnes exemplifies a principled genre-based approach to curriculum planning.

Intercultural competence or literacy relates to an individual's capacity to respond to cultural difference in ways that demonstrate flexibility to the cross-cultural encounter. The model for intercultural sensitivity developed by Milton Bennett recognizes that intercultural sensitivity depends on having not only linguistic skills and cultural knowledge but also empathy, though learner attitudes range from ethnocentric perspectives to tolerance. In multicultural environments, intercultural literacy translates into the ability to act in appropriate ways: awareness of identity and power relationships function in concert with linguistic ability. Accordingly, the Association of American Colleges and Universities (AAC&U) includes intercultural knowledge and competence in its VALUE rubric as an essential learning outcome.

Language ecology, a concept proposed by Einar Haugen, is a branch of ecolinguistics that focuses on the relation between language and the environment. It provides a framework for considering human interactions (such as those associated with migration, hybridity, and precarity) in terms of their ecological and linguistic dimensions.

Languages for special or specific purposes (LSP) describes the context of studying language and culture in relation to specific disciplines or professional fields. Examples include the teaching of language for business, engineering, law, medicine, and social work. Interpretation and technical translation offer examples of LSP work.

Multiple literacies as an approach refers to language teaching that emphasizes the fundamental importance of texts as the central subject of learning, together with the development of learners' ability to interpret their meaning in terms of social, historical, and cultural dimensions. Here texts are understood to refer to a wide range of print, multimedia, audio, and visual materials. Departing from earlier curricular frameworks that tended to privilege the role of interpersonal speaking skills for communicative purposes as the objective of instruction, the multiple literacies approach emphasizes the importance of reading and writing—skills necessary for the development of strong interpretive and presentational abilities.

Nature, in common parlance, is often used to refer to the nonhuman, physical environment. Many scholars note that this definition of nature as separate from human environments creates a false dichotomy that has led to the misuse and poor treatment of the material world. Most scholars agree that nature as such does not exist as a space entirely separate from human influence and argue instead for hybrid concepts like *naturecultures* or *cultural landscape* to describe the physical world and the complexity of interactions between humans and nonhumans.

Place-based learning, which has roots in the educational philosophy of John Dewey, emphasizes modes of perception and learning that draw on local resources. Using proximate natural, cultural, and historical assets as the starting point for educational practice, environmental educators have developed a wide range of place-based strategies designed to move learning out of the classroom and into the natural environment. Salient examples include nature walks, mapping assignments, and projects related to local heritage. These tasks focus on the development of high-level cognitive skills through observation, analysis, and systems thinking.

Post-communicative language teaching, a phrase describing the increasingly diversified landscape of teaching approaches, implies critique of the communicative language teaching (CLT) method, which developed as a reaction against traditional grammar-translation language study. Emphasizing real-world communication, CLT became the basis for proficiency-oriented instruction that took as its objective the development of reading, writing, listening, and—especially—speaking skills. Although CLT changed the way in which languages were taught, it is no longer dominant. Rather, post-communicative language-teaching models, which acknowledge the role of situated practice (e.g., learning context, linguistic variation, and sociolinguistic factors), are becoming more influential.

Process-oriented approach describes a strategy for writing studies and language education that recognizes that assignments should engage learners in the creation of texts that are developmental in character. Instead of focusing simply on correctness, process-oriented assignments encourage learners to focus on production of meaning, experimentation with language, and practice of recursive editing skills. Pedagogical techniques for process-oriented writing assignments include peer editing, writing multiple drafts, correction coding, and using targeted guidance for reformulation.

Project-based learning, an assignment form applicable to many subject areas, involves extended work by students on problem-solving and research. Assignments of this type encourage investigation, analysis, negotiation, and interpretation. They usually culminate with a presentation or written assignment, or with a nontraditional submission (e.g., digital storytelling). Examples include group projects, simulations, and other activities that incorporate active learning.

Second language acquisition (SLA) is a scholarly field that explores how learners at any life stage begin to master and use a language other than their first. The field of SLA emerged in the 1960s out of the disciplines of linguistics and psychology and is informed by an increasingly wide range of research areas. Its research makes use of both quantitative and qualitative study methods for describing and analyzing the language acquisition process.

Service learning, together with **engaged learning**, is widely regarded as a means to involve students in real-world experiences that complement in-class learning and enhance their sense of civic responsibility by using local resources. These types of learning may include internships, individual or group service-learning projects, and fieldwork assignments. Such opportunities help develop personal qualities of independence, creativity, and empathy.

STEM is an acronym for science, technology, engineering, and mathematics that originated in discussions surrounding education policy in the United States. The push for more STEM education is frequently justified as necessary to prepare students for future careers by equipping them with technical expertise to address environmental and other problems.

Sustainability describes the ability of goods and practices to endure in continued use without depleting necessary resources. Sustainable practices must address environmental health, social justice, and economic prosperity across generations.

Systems thinking is a term that represents complex, interconnected thought processes focused on the links between individual things and the larger systems of which they are part rather than singular problems. Systems thinking is often invoked in environmental discussions as a principled way to address ecological issues or social systems with multiple actors and outcomes.

Task-based learning and instruction (TBL, TBI) focus on the use of authentic language in texts written for native speakers and the accomplishment of an outcome that follows from a specific task. In practice, instructors utilizing TBI first introduce key vocabulary and grammar, then facilitate task completion (e.g., information-gap activities for partner or small-group work), and lastly help students consolidate learning through review. The emphasis on communicative language, negotiation of meaning, and student-centered learning encourages learner autonomy while allowing instructor control of the structures taught.

Translingual and transcultural competence, a key concept in the 2007 MLA Ad Hoc Committee on Foreign Languages report "Foreign Languages and Higher Education: New Structures for a Changed World," challenged educators to reconceive fundamentally the work of language programs. The term *translingual* emphasizes that individuals move within and across cultures using multiple linguistic capacities. The word *transcultural*, in contrast, draws attention to the ways individuals and societies negotiate the boundaries of language and culture in the present and across time.

NOTES ON CONTRIBUTORS

LAURA BARBAS-RHODEN is professor of Spanish at Wofford College. She is founder and coordinator of the community-based learning partnership for the Spanish program and author of numerous articles on Latin American environmental humanities, literature, and pedagogy, as well as two books, *Ecological Imaginations in Latin American Fiction* (2011) and *Writing Women in Central America* (2003).

MAGGIE A. BRONER is associate professor and chair of the Romance Languages Department at St. Olaf College. Her research interests include second-language learning and content-based instruction, and she has published in *The Modern Language Journal* and *Foreign Language Annals*. She has cotaught (with Charlotte Melin) a Center for Advanced Research in Language Acquisition (CARLA) Summer Institute called Going "Green": Bringing Sustainability and Environmental Themes into the Language Classroom. Broner received the Minnesota Chapter of the American Association of Teachers of Spanish and Portuguese (AATSP) Teacher of the Year award in 2013.

BEATE BRUNOW is director of academic partnerships and initiatives at the University of Georgia. Her research interests focus on the scholarship of teaching and learning, foreign language pedagogy, and the integration of intercultural competence into foreign language and study abroad curricula.

ABBEY CARRICO is assistant professor at Virginia Military Institute, where she teaches French language and culture, writing, conversation, and literature courses and has codeveloped a new French curriculum that emphasizes communicative competence in students across all levels. A nineteenth-century specialist and ecocritic, she has presented and published on Gustave Flaubert,

Guy de Maupassant, and George Sand, focusing on literary representations of water.

NOBUKO CHIKAMATSU is associate professor in the Department of Modern Languages and director of the Japanese Language and Studies Program at DePaul University. She teaches Japanese language, Japanese linguistics, and translation. Her research interests include second language acquisition, Japanese pedagogy, translation, and Japanese-American history. Her articles have appeared in *Foreign Language Annals, Japanese Language Education around the Globe, The Modern Language Journal,* and *Studies in Second Language Acquisition.*

ODILE CISNEROS is associate professor in the Department of Modern Languages and Cultural Studies at the University of Alberta. She coauthored the *Historical Dictionary of Latin American Literature and Theater* (2011) with Richard Young and coedited *Novas: Selected Writings of Haroldo de Campos* (2007) with A. S. Bessa. She specializes in Latin American literature with a focus on Mexico and Brazil. In 2016 and 2017, she was the recipient of faculty and university-level awards for excellence in undergraduate teaching. Her current project is *ecopoesia .com*, an online resource on the environment and poetry from Latin America.

WILLIAM COMER is professor and director of the Russian Flagship Program at Portland State University. His main research interests include input processing and structured input approaches for teaching Russian grammar and the pedagogy of reading in Russian as a foreign language. His edition of Viktoria Tokareva's short story *A Day without Lying* (2008) won the American Association of Teachers of Slavic and East European Languages prize for Best Book in Language Pedagogy in 2010. He is coauthor of *Mezhdu Nami,* an online, open-access textbook for elementary Russian.

PATRICIA W. CUMMINS is professor of French at Virginia Commonwealth University. Her publications cover topics ranging from literature to language for special purposes to second language acquisition. *Commercial French* was the first textbook in the United States targeting Paris Chamber of Commerce exams. She has edited *Foreign Language Annals,* served as a national vice president of the American Association of Teachers of French (AATF), and received several teaching and service awards. She holds officer rank in the Order of the French Academic Palms and inaugurated a Gates Foundation–funded water project in Ségou, Mali. Her French students work with West African English-language learners on projects related to business, education, agriculture, and medicine.

DEFNE ERDEM METE is assistant professor at the Department of English Language and Literature at Selçuk University, Turkey. She received a Fulbright scholarship and taught intermediate Turkish at Syracuse University in the United States as a Foreign Language Teaching Assistant (2006–07). Her research interests include the teaching of Turkish as a foreign language, intercultural competence in language teaching, and approaches to developing the environmental awareness of language learners.

M A R Í A J. D E L A F U E N T E is professor of Spanish and applied linguistics at the George Washington University. Her research interests are the role of interaction in second-language vocabulary acquisition, the role of the first language in instructed second-language learning, and content-based approaches to the foreign language curriculum. Her publications have appeared in *Studies in Second Language Acquisition, Computer Assisted Language Learning, The Modern Language Journal,* and *Language Teaching Research.* She is author of two Spanish textbooks: *Gente* and *Puntos de Encuentro: A Cross-cultural Approach to Advanced Spanish.*

V I A L L A H A R T F I E L D - M É N D E Z is director of engaged learning in the Center for Faculty Development and Excellence and professor of pedagogy in the Department of Spanish and Portuguese at Emory University. She is author of *Woman and the Infinite: Epiphanic Moments in Pedro Salinas's Art* and articles on twentieth-century Spanish poetry and narrative. Her work on community engagement has appeared in *Hispania* and *PUBLIC,* and she has coauthored several articles on issues in higher education. Leader of Emory's Community Engaged Learning Initiative, she has also collaborated closely with the national consortium Imagining America and the Cultural Agents Initiative at Harvard University.

T H O M A S P. H O D G E is professor of Russian at Wellesley College. On the faculty at Wellesley since 1992, Hodge has taught a wide range of Russian literature and language courses. He cofounded Wellesley's Lake Baikal course with Marianne Moore in 2001. He specializes in nineteenth-century Russian literature and culture with a current research focus on the nature writing of Ivan Turgenev.

O L E S Y A K I S S E L E V is assistant professor in the Department of Bicultural-Bilingual Studies at the University of Texas, San Antonio. She completed her PhD in 2018 at Pennsylvania State University in the Department of Applied Linguistics. Her dissertation, *Word Order and Information Structure in the Writing of Heritage and Second Language Learners of Russian,* won a dissertation support grant from the National Federation of Modern Language Teachers Association (NFMLTA). Previously, she taught Russian language courses and developed curricula and instructional materials for the Russian Flagship Program at Portland State University.

K I L E Y M. K O S T received her PhD in Germanic studies at the University of Minnesota, where she teaches introductory language classes in German as well as courses on environmental humanities and German literature. Her dissertation, "Telling Deep Time: Geologic Narration in German Fiction after 1945," questions how literary practices are unsettled by the vast time scale of natural history in fictional, human narratives in the work of Max Frisch, Peter Handke, and Jenny Erpenbeck. Her research interests include ecocriticism, environmental humanities, critical theory, and Austrian studies.

HONG LI is director of the Emory College Language Center and professor of pedagogy in the Department of Russian and East Asian Languages and Cultures at Emory University. She is first author of *Access China: An Interactive Classroom Video Course for Chinese Learning*, volumes 1–6, and *Fun with Chinese Grammar: Thirty-Five Humorous Dialogues and Comics*. Her work has appeared in or been published by the *Journal of the Chinese Language Teachers Association*, *The Language Educator*, Tsinghua UP, and the Chinese University of Hong Kong.

CHARLOTTE ANN MELIN is professor of German studies at the University of Minnesota. Her research and teaching interests range from postwar German literature to second language acquisition and policy issues in higher education. Her publications include *Poetic Maneuvers: Hans Magnus Enzensberger and the Lyric Genre* (2003), *With or Without: Reading Postwar German Women Poets* (2013), the anthology *German Poetry in Transition, 1945–1990* (1999), and essays on German poetry and the teaching of foreign languages. She has held appointments as director of language instruction and chair in her department and served on Modern Language Association committees, including the Association of Departments of Foreign Languages (ADFL) Executive Committee.

MARC JAMES MUELLER taught German studies at Colgate University; University of Illinois, Chicago; and as associate professor at Montana State University, Bozeman. In 2015 he returned to Hamburg, Germany, where he works as professional translator, independent scholar, and teacher of both German and English language and literature at a private school, mostly for second-chance students. He has published articles on the intersection of language and identity in German intercultural writing, as well as on the interpretive aspect of poetry translation. He has published a translation volume that includes a critical introduction on José F. A. Oliver's poetry, entitled *Sandscript* (2018).

BRITTON W. NEWMAN is assistant professor of Spanish at Wofford College. His research interests include the scholarship of teaching and learning, the integration of intercultural competence into foreign language and study abroad curricula, and contemporary Cuban literature.

MARGARET ANN NOODIN is associate professor at the University of Wisconsin, Milwaukee, where she serves as director of the Electa Quinney Institute for American Indian Education. She is author of *Bawaajimo: A Dialect of Dreams in Anishinaabe Language and Literature* and *Weweni*, a collection of bilingual poems in Ojibwe and English. Her poems have been anthologized in *Sing: Poetry from the Indigenous Americas*, *Poetry Magazine*, *The Michigan Quarterly Review*, and *Yellow Medicine Review*. At www.ojibwe.net she and other students and speakers of Ojibwe have created a space for language to be shared by academics and the native community.

ANNETTE SAMPON-NICOLAS is professor of French at Hollins University. Her areas of specialization are twentieth-century French and francophone literature. Her interests include the relation between literature and the visual arts, French for international business, francophone literature, and environmental sustainability. She has developed cross-disciplinary courses on the francophone world, nature and the environment, the history of French gastronomy, Franco-Asian literature, and French children's literature. She has published articles on François Cheng, Francis Ponge, André du Bouchet, and Jean-Marie Le Clézio.

PATRICIA ANNE SIMPSON is chair of the Department of Modern Languages and Literatures at the University of Nebraska, Lincoln. She has publications on German classicism and Romanticism, visual and material culture, popular music, far-right populism in Europe, and female leadership. She is author of *The Erotics of War in German Romanticism* (2006), *Cultures of Violence in the New German Street* (2011), and *Reimagining the European Family: Cultures of Immigration* (2013). An award-winning scholar and teacher, she has received grants from the German Academic Exchange Service (DAAD), Fulbright Commission, Fulbright-Hays, German Historical Institute, and United States Department of Education. Recent work focuses on the relation between theories and practices of play and pedagogy in the long eighteenth century.

KAREN STOLLEY is professor of Spanish in the Department of Spanish and Portuguese at Emory University, where she teaches graduate and undergraduate courses in colonial and eighteenth-century Spanish American and transatlantic literary and cultural studies. Prior to Emory, she taught at Vassar College and the Middlebury Summer Spanish Language School. She is author of *Domesticating Empire: Enlightenment in Spanish America*, as well as articles in *Dieciocho, Revista de Estudios Hispánicos, Latin American Literary Review,* and the *ADE-ADFL Bulletin.* She serves on the Board of Trustees of Middlebury College and the Board of Overseers of the Middlebury Institute of International Studies at Monterey.

HAIDAN WANG is assistant professor at the University of Hawai'i, Mānoa. She played a leading role in the design and development of the course series Chinese for Business Professionals and was twice awarded the Business Language Research and Teaching grant by the United States Department of Education Centers for International Business Education and Research (CIBERs). She teaches all levels of Chinese language courses; linguistic content courses; and graduate courses on Chinese linguistics, pedagogy, and assessment. Her research interests include needs analysis, curriculum design and development, content-based instruction and project-based learning, second-language assessment, and program evaluation. She has also applied cognitive linguistic theories in Chinese to second-language learning and teaching practices.

INDEX